T0386662

EAVESDROPPING ON THE EMPEROR

PETER KORNICKI

Eavesdropping on the Emperor

Interrogators and Codebreakers in Britain's War with Japan

HURST & COMPANY, LONDON

First published in the United Kingdom in 2021 by
C. Hurst & Co. (Publishers) Ltd.,
83 Torbay Road, London NW6 7DT
Copyright © Peter Kornicki, 2021
All rights reserved.
Printed in Great Britain by Bell and Bain Ltd, Glasgow

The right of Peter Kornicki to be identified as the author of this publication
is asserted by him in accordance with the Copyright, Designs and Patents
Act, 1988.

A Cataloguing-in-Publication data record for this book
is available from the British Library.

This book is printed using paper from registered sustainable
and managed sources.

ISBN: 9781787384729

www.hurstpublishers.com

This book is dedicated to the many men and women who struggled to learn Japanese during the war, especially in Britain, India and Mauritius. They succeeded against the odds. Their efforts as codebreakers, translators, interpreters, interrogators and intelligence officers made an indispensable contribution to the war effort, but their contributions were never recognized or rewarded. Let them be remembered in this book.

CONTENTS

CONTENTS

India, Burma and Ceylon in 1940

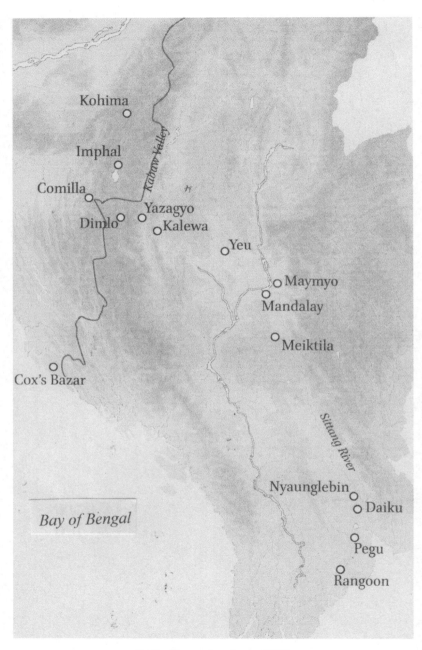

India–Burma border in 1940

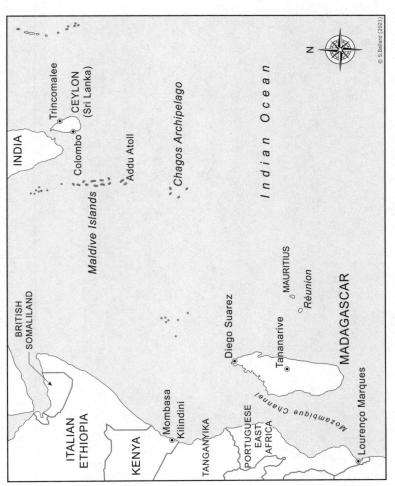

East Africa and the Indian Ocean in 1940

© S.Ballard (2021)

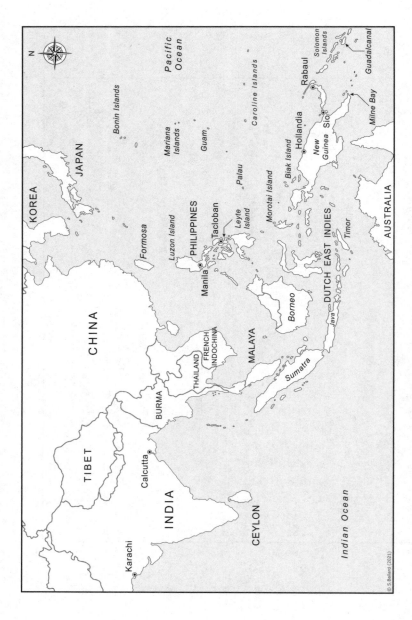

From Australia to Japan in 1940

LIST OF ABBREVIATIONS

ATIS	Allied Translator and Interpreter Section
ATS	Auxiliary Territorial Service
AWM	Australian War Memorial
BCOF	British Commonwealth Occupation Force
CACC	Churchill Archives Centre, Cambridge
CSDIC	Combined Services Detailed Interrogation Centre
CSDIC(I)	Combined Services Detailed Interrogation Centre (India)
FECB	Far East Combined Bureau
FRUMEL	Fleet Radio Unit Melbourne
GC&CS	Government Code & Cypher School
GCHQ	Government Communications Headquarters
IWM	Imperial War Museum, London
LHC	Liddell Hart Centre for Military Archives, King's College London
NAA	National Archives of Australia
NARA	National Archives and Records Administration, United States
NavTechJap	US Naval Technical Mission to Japan
NCO	Non-Commissioned Officer (i.e., corporal or sergeant)
NHB	Naval Historical Branch, HM Naval Base Portsmouth
ODNB	*Oxford Dictionary of National Biography*
RAAF	Royal Australian Air Force
RANVR	Royal Australian Naval Volunteer Reserve
RCNVR	Royal Canadian Naval Volunteer Reserve

LIST OF ABBREVIATIONS

RNVR	Royal Naval Volunteer Reserve
RNZNVR	Royal New Zealand Naval Volunteer Reserve
SACSEA	Supreme Allied Commander South East Asia
SCAP	Supreme Commander of the Allied Powers (in Japan)
SEAC	South East Asia Command
SEATIC	South East Asia Translation and Interrogation Centre
SOAS	School of Oriental and African Studies
SWPA	South West Pacific Area
TNA	The National Archives, Kew
UCBA	University of Colorado Boulder Archives
WAAF	Women's Auxiliary Airforce
WAVES	Women Accepted for Voluntary Emergency Service
WEC	Wireless Experimental Centre, Delhi
WRNS	Women's Royal Naval Service

LIST OF ILLUSTRATIONS

LIST OF ILLUSTRATIONS

LIST OF ILLUSTRATIONS

ACKNOWLEDGEMENTS

I began the research for this book about ten years ago and have often thought, while doing the research for it, that I should have begun it much earlier. Twenty years ago, many more of those who learnt Japanese during the war were alive and still retained precious memories of their wartime and post-war experiences. Now there are very few survivors left. Also, the archives of the Far East Department at the School of Oriental and African Studies, where so many were trained, were still available to be consulted; alas, they seem now to be lost.

Without the unstinting help of many people, this book would not have come into existence. The first people to thank are without doubt those few survivors who have willingly, sometimes eagerly, entrusted me with their memories and occasionally their letters, papers and photograph albums: John Cook, Sir Hugh Cortazzi,* Guy de Moubray,* Patrick Field, Elizabeth Hely-Hutchinson,* David Jones, Dr Michael Loewe, Professor Ian Nish, David Pole, Professor Donald Russell,* Revd Professor Michael Screech,* Jim Sutherland* and Ian Willison. Those marked with an asterisk have, sad to say, since died.

Secondly, the relatives or descendants of many others have kindly responded to my queries and in some cases have let me see private memoirs written for the family. They include: Martin and Tim Andrews (and other relatives of Eric Andrews), Ann and David Barclay (sister and nephew of John McEwan), Adrian Barker (son of Eileen Barker), Richard Bawden (son of Professor Charles Bawden), Professor Julia Barrow (daughter of George Barrow), John Beasley (son of Professor William Beasley), Christopher Bell (son of Alfred Bell),

ACKNOWLEDGEMENTS

Professor John Breen (son of Lawrence Breen), Martin, David and Graham Ceadel (sons of Eric Ceadel), Margaret Cribb, S. Gail Miller and Robert Naish (nieces and nephew of Mary Tate), Sir Edward Dashwood (son of Sir Francis Dashwood), Jim Eunson and the late David Partner (son and nephew of David Eunson), Nik Gowing (son of Donald Gowing), Charlotte Hall (daughter of Peter Hall), Alice Hunt (granddaughter of Elizabeth Anderson), Professor Mary Lefkowitz and Ralph Lloyd-Jones (widow and son of Sir Hugh Lloyd-Jones), His Honour Frederick Marr-Johnson (relative of Patrick Marr-Johnson), Ken Maxwell (son of Eric Maxwell/Eiichi Matsuyama), Barbara Norris (daughter of Hugh Norris), David Pulleyblank (son of Edwin Pulleyblank), Professor Robin Sellar (son of Robert Sellar), Andrew Tank (son of Rowland Tank), Rosemary Thacker (daughter of Philip Taylor), Professor William Twining (son of Baron Twining), Christian van Nieuwerburgh (son of Arthur Newington), Diana Vennis (widow of Philip Vennis), Roger Vincent-Townend (grandson of Oswald Tuck), Dominic Vlasto (the son of Alexis Vlasto), Keith Wood (son of Stanley Wood) and Barbara Wyatt (daughter of Kitty Wyatt).

I am also very much indebted to many academics, archivists and librarians who have helped me to find useful material. Among them are Professor Christopher Andrew (Corpus Christi College, Cambridge), Professor Neil Ballingal (Technical University Sydney, son of one of the SOAS students), Professor Antony Best (London School of Economics), Professor Allison B. Gilmore (South Dakota School of Mines and Technology), David M. Hays (University of Colorado Library), Dr James Hoare (SOAS), Professor Ashley Jackson (King's College London), Professor Nicola McLelland (University of Nottingham), Ōba Satsuki of Tokyo (daughter of Ōba Sadao), Julia Reacher (Christ's College, Cambridge), James Smith (Christ's College, Cambridge), Marie-Josée Martial-Craig (Royal Society of Arts and Sciences of Mauritius), Jennifer Thorp (New College, Oxford), Thomas Knollys (Trinity College, Oxford), Calista Lucy (archivist of Dulwich College), Lindsay McCormack (Lincoln College, Oxford), Professor Takeda Kayoko (Rikkyo University, Tokyo), Anna Port (Christ Church, Oxford), the staff of the research room at the Imperial War Museum in London and the staff at the Australian War Memorial

ACKNOWLEDGEMENTS

in Canberra. (Here and throughout this book, Japanese names are given in their normal order, with surname first.)

I have presented parts of this book as the John Howes Lecture at the University of British Columbia, Vancouver, and as the Meiji Jingū Lecture at the School of Oriental and African Studies, London, and I am indebted to those who invited me and to the lively audiences for their valuable and thought-provoking responses. Jozef Straczek kindly provided me with access to his excellent dissertation on signals intelligence in the Royal Australian Navy. My Cambridge colleague Richard Bowring generously produced two of the maps for me. Patrick Field and David Pole, two of the few surviving former students of the Bedford Japanese School, kindly read the whole text through and drew my attention to several errors. My wife Francesca has, as always, been my most constructive and helpful critic. The two anonymous reviewers have saved me from some mistakes and have helped me to make the book more accessible: whoever you are, I thank you both warmly. Finally, I am most grateful to Mike Dwyer of Hurst & Co. for having shown such enthusiasm for the book—it was he who came up with the title—and to Lara Weisweiller-Wu, my editor at Hurst & Co., who has eagerly shepherded me through the whole process.

The following have kindly granted permission for textual reproduction in the book:

Quotation from Geoffrey St Vincent Ballard, *On Ultra Active Service: The Story of Australia's Signals Intelligence Operations during World War II* (Richmond, Victoria: Spectrum Publications, 1991) by kind permission of Spectrum Publications, Richmond, Victoria, Australia.

Quotations from Eileen Mary Barker's memoir 'Memories of Bletchley Park' by kind permission of Adrian Barker and Val Salmond.

Quotations from Professor Charles Bawden's memoir 'Charles Roskelly Bawden: An Academic's Life' by kind permission of Richard Bawden.

Quotations for Professor William Beasley's memoir 'Traveller to Japan: Incomplete and Unreliable Recollections of my Life' by kind permission of John Beasley.

ACKNOWLEDGEMENTS

Quotations from John Chadwick's memoir 'A Relatively Peaceful War: Personal Recollections of 1939–1945' by kind permission of the Faculty of Classics, University of Cambridge.

Quotations from Professor Sir Hugh Lloyd-Jones's memoir 'Memoir of WWII Service' by kind permission of Professor Mary Lefkowitz.

Quotation from Mark Polizotti's translation of Patrick Modiano's *Suspended Sentences* by kind permission of Yale University Press.

Quotations from Leslie Phillips' 'Autobiography' by kind permission of the late Leslie Phillips.

Quotations from Edward Twining's papers by kind permission of Professor William Twining.

Quotations from Joseph Haggitt Ward's memoir 'Notes by Joseph Haggitt Ward on Army Japanese Course at Bedford, Apr 1945–Sep 1945, and Subsequent Service' by kind permission of Joseph Ward.

Quotations from John Nevile Whitehorn's 'Memoirs' by kind permission of John Whitehorn.

Quotations from documents held in the AWM, Churchill Archive Centre, the Imperial War Museum, TNA, NARA (United States), the University of Boulder Colorado Archives and SOAS Archives by kind permission of those institutions.

PROLOGUE

BRITAIN AT WAR WITH JAPAN

Elizabeth was an MP's daughter, John a shopkeeper's son. Denise was the daughter of an oil company executive, while Arthur was the son of a butcher's assistant and Francis the son of a baronet. Some were recruited straight from school, others had already been conscripted and were serving in the Army, the Royal Navy or the Royal Air Force. A few had years of experience behind them as lawyers, teachers or civil servants. But now they all suddenly found themselves back in the classroom. What was it that brought them all together? It was nothing other than their uncanny ability to learn difficult languages, for Britain's need of Japanese linguists had become desperate once Britain was at war with Japan. How did they get dragged into the war and sent back to the classroom?

In late November and early December 1941, the options for avoiding war with Japan were running out fast. Since 1937, Japan had been engaged in a full-scale invasion of China, and this had drawn the condemnation of the United States, Britain, France, Australia and the Netherlands. The United States, with the support of Britain and the Netherlands, had imposed an oil embargo and refused to lift it until and unless Japan withdrew its troops from China, a condition that was unacceptable to the Imperial Japanese Army. In the event of war, the British Isles were not directly vulnerable to Japanese attacks, but the British colonies of Hong Kong and Malaya certainly were, and so was the naval base at Singapore that was the emblem of British military power in the 'Far East', as East Asia was then termed in the West. Britain was all too aware of the vulnerability of its Asian colonies. Not long after Japan joined the Tripartite Pact with Germany and Italy on 27 September 1940, plans began to be drawn up for the defence of Malaya against a Japanese attack, and additional units arrived to strengthen the British military presence in Malaya. The Cabinet, however, had already recognized on 8 August 1940 that Singapore could not be protected in the event of a Japanese attack, because the naval and air reinforcements needed to defend Singapore were already committed to the struggle with Germany. Owing to a chance set of circumstances, the minutes of that Cabinet meeting reached Japan in December, so Japanese military planners now had proof that Singapore was vulnerable.[1]

Since the war with Germany had become a titanic struggle on land and sea and in the air, Britain was simply not in a position to protect Singapore, let alone the whole of Malaya. All that could be done, in the autumn of 1941, was to send out two capital ships, the battleship HMS *Prince of Wales* and the battlecruiser HMS *Repulse*, escorted by four destroyers, to strengthen British naval forces in East Asia. On 6 December 1941, a Royal Australian Air Force (RAAF) plane spotted two convoys of Japanese transport ships with armed escorts heading for the Malay peninsula: both Siam (Thailand) and Malaya were under threat, but because the intentions of the Japanese convoys were unknown, the British High Command in Singapore did not put its contingency plans into action. The first Japanese troops landed in Malaya just after midnight on 8 December; in Honolulu, it was 7.00 a.m. on Sunday, 7 December, and the attack on Pearl Harbor had yet to start. Within the next couple of hours, Japanese troops came ashore in southern Burma, and Singapore itself came under air attack. Farther afield, Hong Kong, Guam and American bases in the Philippines were all under attack, mostly from the air.

The British, Indian and Australian Army units based in Malaya were unable to hold back the Japanese troops as they made their way rapidly down the Malay peninsula towards Singapore. The Royal Air Force's meagre resources were no match for the Japanese fighters and bombers, and on 10 December Japanese aircraft sank the *Prince of Wales* and the *Repulse*, which had set out from Singapore in search of Japanese convoys as soon as war was declared. Singapore was now without naval protection, and the inevitable British surrender came on 15 February 1942. It was just nine weeks after the invasion had begun, and in fact thirty days sooner than Japanese planners had expected. The Hong Kong capitulated on Christmas Day 1941, and the Dutch East Indies (now Indonesia) and the Philippines, then under US control, were soon to follow.[2] The French colony of Indo-China (now Vietnam and Cambodia) had already been taken over by Japanese forces in 1940. Within a few months of the attacks on Malaya and Pearl Harbor, the British, American and Dutch presence in East Asia had been wiped out, and Japan was at war not only with the United States but also with Britain, the British Empire and the Netherlands. Disastrous and shocking though the Japanese attacks were for the Allies, Japan for its part was celebrating the end of its encirclement by foreign powers based in Hong Kong, Indo-China, the Philippines, Malaya and the Dutch East Indies. Although it was far from clear at the time, the war did in fact mark the end of the colonial era in East Asia: the Japanese colonies of Taiwan and Korea were liberated in 1945, the Philippines gained independence from the United States in 1946, Indonesia from the Netherlands in 1949, Indo-China ceased to be a French colony in 1954 and became Vietnam, and Malaya (later Malaysia) gained its independence from Britain in 1957.

The success of the Japanese military campaigns certainly put paid to racist suppositions about the poor capabilities of the Japanese armed forces, but the outbreak of war also brought another serious shortcoming into perspective. The languages of Germany and Italy were taught in schools and universities in Britain, Australia, New Zealand, Canada and the United States, so there was a pool of people who could potentially read captured documents, interrogate prisoners of war or eavesdrop on radio transmissions in German or Italian. The story of the battle with the German Enigma machines at Bletchley Park and the decryption of German wartime messages is deservedly famous, but it should not be forgotten that the decrypted messages were in German. Once decrypted, the messages could be read relatively easily in Britain and the United States, though technical vocabulary, the use of abbreviations and the clipped language characteristic of military telegrams may have created some difficulties. Nevertheless, precisely because the language of the decrypts was German, the linguistic problems are seldom mentioned in accounts of the breaking of German codes or the decryption of German messages during the war.[3] They should nevertheless be mentioned. Britain was in fact by no means well prepared linguistically even for a European war. The dominance of French in the British education system meant that knowledge of other European countries, let alone their languages, was far from adequate. As a result, it proved difficult to find military personnel able to understand German wireless transmissions even when they were *en clair* (in ordinary language, unencrypted).[4]

Japanese was another matter altogether. Although English was widely taught in Japan, Japanese was not taught in schools, and hardly at all in universities, in Britain or in any of the countries that now found themselves at war with Japan, and the lack of the requisite linguistic expertise threatened to be a major obstacle to the successful prosecution of the war with Japan. Textbooks and dictionaries were in desperately short supply, and the technical vocabulary and telegraphese used in Japanese wireless messages were hugely challenging. There was a shortage of potential teachers, too, and learning the language, if not as 'difficult' as it is often said to be, is certainly a time-consuming task for those used only to European languages.

What exactly is it that makes Japanese a challenging language to learn? The Japanese language is normally written in a mixture of Chinese characters (of which there are thousands in common use) and Japanese syllabic symbols known as *kana*, which represent either a vowel or a consonant plus vowel (thus the *kana* sign あ stands for 'a' and か for 'ka'). As there are only five vowels in modern Japanese, the language is awash with homophones—words that are pronounced identically but are written with different Chinese characters and have very different meanings. In written Japanese, these homophones pose no problems, provided that you know the characters, and in speech the context is usually sufficient to enable you to distinguish, for example, between the various words that are pronounced *kaisen* but are written with different Chinese characters. If you encounter the sentence, 'Yesterday the British and Japanese navies engaged in a *kaisen*', you assume that the word meant is 海戦 'naval battle', not 疥癬 'scabies' or 回旋 'rotation', all of which are pronounced *kaisen*. Japanese wireless messages, however, were often sent in Morse code representing Roman letters or in Japanese Morse representing *kana*, thus eliminating the clues provided by the characters. Military jargon and neologisms added to the difficulties, with the result that even educated Japanese today can often make no sense of the Japanese messages that young men and women on the Allied side had to tackle. That they managed to translate them faultlessly during the war was remarkable, and theirs is the story that this book tells.

There was, then, a huge linguistic imbalance to overcome in the Pacific War. What use were captured Japanese documents if nobody could read them? What value were prisoners of war if nobody could interrogate them? What was the point of decoding wireless messages if nobody could translate the decrypts?

There can be no doubt that Britain was ill-prepared for war with Japan. Despite many warnings from experts in universities and the diplomatic service, the War Office made no attempt to introduce training in the Japanese language until after the outbreak of war. All that it did, in June 1941, was to send out to Singapore a handful of men who already knew some Japanese, most of whom were captured and spent the rest of the war in Japanese PoW camps acting as interpreters.

Both Australia and the United States introduced Japanese-language training before the outbreak of war, so if Britain found itself with an embarrassing shortage of linguists at the outset, it only had itself to blame. Despite the immense difficulties, in this book I show that a handful of experts created what turned out to be extremely successful training programmes that turned out a constant supply of well-trained Japanese linguists until the end of the war. Governments on both sides of the Atlantic have often been airily dismissive of expertise, but without the expertise of a small number of outstanding linguists, the Allies would have been at a dangerous disadvantage in the war with Japan.

In fact, the Japanese language was seen by the Japanese and the Allies as a natural advantage for Japan, given how few people in the West had a good command of it. The Allies needed to find a way around that natural advantage if they were to gain the strategic and tactical intelligence they needed in the war with Japan. Intelligence depended, therefore, on having a pool of expert linguists to draw upon and a constant flow of freshly trained men and women as the needs grew ever greater. Until the

1990s, the language programmes that trained these men and women in Britain remained secret. What I have set out to do in this book, therefore, is to reveal what made the Japanese-language training programmes during the war so successful, who the remarkable teachers and their extraordinary students were, and what unseen contributions they made to the war effort in all the theatres of war.

Some of the men and women who learnt Japanese in a hurry were sent to Bletchley Park and joined codebreaking teams there; from there, some were sent on to India, Australia or Mauritius. Others were sent to Asia to interrogate prisoners of war, translate captured documents, interpret the conversations of Japanese pilots in real time or conduct surrender negotiations. And after the war, many of them were interrogating war crimes suspects, interviewing Japanese generals, investigating the activities of Japanese units during the war, screening surrendered Japanese military personnel before returning them to Japan and taking part in the British Commonwealth Occupation Force (BCOF) in Japan.

The vast literature on the Second World War inevitably consists mainly of the history of campaigns, of generals and their tactics, of fighting troops, and of the armaments, machines, aeroplanes and ships with which they fought. It is rare even for intelligence officers to rate much of a mention, let alone medics and nurses or those who fed the troops, transported them and kept them supplied with ammunition, clothing and letters from home. Linguists are another such group: they served on all fronts of the war with Japan—at Bletchley Park, in the Burmese jungle, on warships, on RAF stations in India and in landings on Pacific islands. Theirs was a role devoid of glamour or heroism and necessarily kept secret, but it was indispensable nonetheless in a war being fought with an enemy that had better knowledge of English than the Allies had of Japanese.

Books have already been published on the wartime linguists who were trained in Australia, Canada and the United States, but when it comes to Britain the only book that mentions them is Michael Smith's path-breaking book *The Emperor's Codes* (2000), which revealed the role of Bletchley Park in breaking Japanese military and diplomatic cyphers well before the outbreak of the war and before US codebreakers got to work. Smith's fascinating book is primarily concerned with codebreaking, both at Bletchley Park and overseas. I am much indebted to him, particularly because he managed to interview some individuals who are now no longer alive, and I have drawn upon those interviews. As Smith points out, it was only in the 1990s that many of the official records relating to the breaking of Japanese codes by British codebreakers were released and made available to the public at The National Archives in Kew. However, readers should be aware that surprising numbers of wartime records have still not been released and are retained by GCHQ, including some relating to Japanese encrypted messages and their decipherment at Bletchley Park.[5]

Although this book focuses on British linguists and their roles in the war, readers will find that there is one chapter on the United States and another on Australia. There are two reasons for this. First, a small number of British naval officers were sent to the United States to learn Japanese at the US Navy Japanese Language School, and similarly, many linguists who had been trained in Britain later served in Australia alongside American and Australian linguists. Their experiences were very different from those of the men and women who spent the war at Bletchley Park or in India. Some account of language training in the United States and Australia was therefore essential in order to contextualize the experiences of the British linguists who joined them. The second reason is that some comparison between the British, American and Australian training programmes is valuable, for they were all different, although their goals were broadly similar. Furthermore, training linguists was a task that all the nations at war with Japan faced, and it seemed to me important to underline this by giving at least an outline of how these needs were met in the United States and Australia, and in Canada, too.

Why 'Eavesdropping on the Emperor'? The choice of title is not, of course, intended to suggest that the Allies listened in to the emperor's conversations during the war. Rather, it is in part a tribute to Smith's book on the 'emperor's codes', mentioned above. What underlies both titles, however, is the fact that, between 1890 and 1947, the emperor of Japan was also the supreme commander of Japan's armed forces. So, by synecdoche, the 'emperor' stands for all of Japan's armed forces, and the Allies were certainly eavesdropping upon them.

* * *

PROLOGUE

I began the prologue with some names and the backgrounds they came from. Elizabeth Hely-Hutchinson, John Martin, Denise Newman, Arthur Munday and Francis Dashwood were five of the relatively small number of men and women who were called to wartime service and then discovered that the war with Japan would have an entirely unexpected consequence for them. They were going to have to learn a language that none of them had given a moment's thought to before. After courses lasting no more than eighteen months, and often much less, they were faced with the urgent need to produce accurate translations of captured documents or decrypted messages, to interrogate prisoners of war or to listen in to enemy radio transmissions. For all the inadequacy of their training, they needed to get it absolutely right. Lives depended upon their accuracy.

Secrecy about what they were doing was essential during wartime, but for many of them secrecy became a lifelong habit. After the war, many never told their families what they had done and took their secrets with them to the grave. I have been in touch with some of their families in the search for materials for this book, and they have been touchingly grateful for any information that I have been able to provide about the secret wartime activities of their fathers or mothers.

There is one other sense in which they and their work have remained invisible. With a handful of exceptions, none of them were ever honoured for the vital work that they did during the war, and consequently their contributions to the war effort have been forgotten. If this book sets the record straight, it will have served its purpose.

1

JAPAN MUST FIGHT BRITAIN

One summer's day early in 1942, a submarine of the Royal Australian Navy drew slowly into the naval dockyard in Melbourne. There was nothing unusual about that, but this submarine had some unusual passengers. It had arrived from the Philippines carrying several people who had escaped from Singapore on the last ship before the British garrison surrendered to the Japanese invasion forces. One of those passengers was Arthur Cooper (1916–88). Cooper was no ordinary refugee, and not only because he was accompanied all the way from Singapore to Melbourne by his pet gibbon, whose name was 'Tertius'. The arrival of Cooper and Tertius in Australia was the inspiration for *My Friend Tertius* (2017), a delightful book for children by Corinne Fenton that tells the story of his escape from Singapore and his affection for Tertius.

Cooper had a remarkable gift for languages. That had been obvious ever since he acquired fluency in Icelandic during a short holiday there as a schoolboy. Following the example of his elder brother, Josh, he joined the Government Code & Cypher School (GC&CS) (now the Government Communications Headquarters—GCHQ) and in 1939 was sent to Hong Kong to work in the Far East Combined Bureau (FECB), which was an outpost of GC&CS. GC&CS itself moved to Bletchley Park in the summer of 1939, and at about the same time FECB moved from Hong Kong to Singapore: the outbreak of war in

Europe seemed imminent and Singapore was deemed safer than Hong Kong. Much of Cooper's life is shrouded in mystery, but at some point between 1939 and late 1941 he spent some time in Japan, and he was definitely learning Japanese and Chinese in those years.[1]

Singapore, of course, turned out to be no safer than Hong Kong as a home for FECB. In January 1942, the cryptographers, together with the naval personnel whose job it was to intercept Japanese communications, were evacuated to Colombo in Ceylon (Sri Lanka), while the others were sent to India. Cooper stayed in Singapore almost to the last minute before the British surrender. With him were Lieutenant-Commander Edward Colegrave (1902–69) and Lieutenant Norman Webb, who were both Japanese-speakers and played important roles later in the war; their names will recur in this book.

Who were Colegrave and Webb? Colegrave had gone to Japan for three years as a Royal Navy Language Officer in 1927, while Webb had worked for the Rising Sun Petroleum Company in Japan, which he left to join the Army on the outbreak of war. In Singapore, the two of them, working with Cooper, monitored wireless transmissions *en clair* between Japanese bomber pilots and their controllers, in the hope of acquiring information that might be valuable for the defence of Singapore. An assessment made after the war at Bletchley Park reveals that they did indeed manage to pass critical intelligence on to the RAF controllers:

> Results were telephoned to the local RAF defence and several successful actions were fought, when after the first two or three days the RAF learnt to rely upon the accuracy of this information. ... Neither he nor Colegrave [nor Webb] had any previous experience of this sort of work. The RAF became enthusiastically appreciative.

Valuable though their interceptions were, they could only delay the inevitable surrender.[2]

Colegrave, Cooper and Webb escaped on 11 February 1942, four days before the surrender, and they were taken to Australia. Cooper spent a few months in Melbourne with Colegrave working in the Special Intelligence Bureau, but he then returned to England after donating Tertius to Melbourne Zoo. Back at GC&CS at Bletchley Park, he wrote a textbook of Japanese for wartime use and became head of the Japanese Section. He did not forget Tertius: in 1947, they were reunited at Melbourne Zoo. Colegrave left Australia too, and was later employed as a cryptographer at the GC&CS outpost in Kilindini, near Mombasa, but Webb remained in Australia and eventually became the senior British cryptographer at the Central Bureau in Brisbane, General Douglas MacArthur's intelligence organization.[3]

What exactly was the Far East Combined Bureau that Cooper was working for in Hong Kong? The bland obscurity of its name was, of course, deliberate. It was in fact a secret British intelligence-gathering operation aimed at Japan. As it turned out, it was one of the few signs that Britain, or at least GC&CS, was preparing for a possible war with Japan in the 1930s. Just thirty years earlier, however, the idea that Britain might find itself at war with Japan had seemed inconceivable to all but one or two individuals.

From allies to enemies: the trajectory of Anglo-Japanese relations

The twentieth century started out well for relations between Britain and Japan. In recognition of Japan's growing economic and military strength, Britain decided to form an alliance with Japan, for both were anxious about Russian expansion. The Anglo-Japanese Alliance was signed in London in 1902, and it put Japan for the first time on an equal footing with one of the great powers. The Japan–British Exhibition, which was held in 1910 in White City, near Shepherd's Bush in London, showcased the close relationship between Britain and Japan, and the alliance was renewed several times before it finally came to an end in 1923. By the 1920s, there was a thriving Japanese community in Britain: Japanese banks, press agencies and other organizations had all established offices in London. There were Japanese restaurants, a Japanese newspaper and all the other institutions, and amenities of an expatriate community.[4]

All the same, there were some clouds on the horizon. At the Paris Peace Conference in 1919 following the end of the First World War, Japan had proposed that the principle of racial equality be adopted for the League of Nations, which was founded in 1920. This proposal was firmly rejected by Britain, fearful for the impact on its colonies, and by the United States, concerned for the impact on immigration and on domestic race relations. When it came to a vote, a clear majority voted for the Japanese proposal, but President Woodrow Wilson, who was presiding, ruled that unanimity was required for such a controversial measure. The rejection of the proposal, despite the clear majority in favour, rankled in Japan, especially since Japan's ally, Great Britain, had opposed it.

At the same time, in Britain, Lieutenant-General Sir Ian Hamilton, who was largely blamed, somewhat unfairly, for the fiasco of the Gallipoli landings in 1915, was already in 1909 beginning to see war with Japan as inevitable once British interests in East Asia clashed with those of Japan. Hamilton was no armchair commentator. During the Russo-Japanese War of 1904–5, he had gone to Japan as a military observer of the conflict, and as soon as he had seen the discipline of the Japanese armed forces, he had concluded that Japan would win the war, though most people in Britain at the time expected Russia to win. Hamilton's prediction proved right, and within a few years he came to see Japan as Britain's future enemy in East Asia. He wrote a detailed analysis of the coming clash but for some reason never published it.[5]

In the 1920s and 1930s, Japanese writers such as Ishimaru Tōta (1881–1942) began to make similar predictions in print. Ishimaru, an officer in the Imperial Japanese Navy, wrote a number of books, all of which anticipated a future war between Japan and either the United States or Britain, with provocative titles such as *Japan Will Not Lose a War with America* (1924). Some of these were translated into English and published in Britain, including *Japan Must Fight Britain* (1936), which was translated by Guy Varley Rayment (1878–1951), a Royal Navy officer who had spent two years in Japan from 1905 to 1907 and had qualified as an interpreter. Ishimaru also translated a number of English books into Japanese, including *The Great Pacific War* (1925). *The Great Pacific War* was an astonishingly prescient book by Hector Bywater (1884–1940), a British journalist who described in great detail a war he imagined breaking out in 1931 as a result of tensions between Japan and the United States over China. In the book, the war begins when Japan launches a surprise naval attack that destroys the US Pacific Fleet near Manila and then invades the Philippines.

Bywater envisaged a war consisting primarily of naval engagements, though he also drew attention to the Imperial Japanese Navy's use of carrier-borne aircraft. Bywater realized that from the Japanese point of view, time was of the essence: 'Given sufficient time [the United States] could build up a fleet of overwhelming size, raise an army millions strong, and, above all, mobilise her matchless financial resources for an offensive that [Japan] could never hope to resist.' Japan would therefore have to make haste to secure a victory. On the other hand, he stated that in the United States '[no] fears [were] entertained for the safety of Hawaii, for it was unbelievable that Japan would send a military expedition across 3,400 miles of ocean to attack territory which served as the main Pacific base of the American fleet'. Two different Japanese translations of Bywater's book had already been published in 1925, before Ishimaru's translation appeared in 1926. Three translations in two years is some measure of the interest aroused in Japan by Bywater's book.[6]

One of those who read Bywater's book was Admiral Yamamoto Isoroku, who became naval attaché at the Japanese embassy in Washington, DC soon after it was published. In 1941, he was the architect of the plan to launch a surprise strike on Pearl Harbor and destroy the US Pacific Fleet at anchor. What Bywater had failed to anticipate when he wrote his book was that Hawai'i itself might become the target for a surprise attack. Did that sentence about Hawai'i being beyond the reach of Japan perhaps put the germ of an idea into Yamamoto's head?[7]

Yet war with Japan was by no means inevitable, and when it did break out it was by no means solely the 'fault' of Japan. From the mid-1930s up to December 1941, British policy towards Japan tended to be reactive and pragmatic in nature, responding to events rather than driven by a clear set of priorities. Relations with Japan, at a time when the Imperial Japanese Army was becoming increasingly active in China, were complicated by Britain's own economic interests in China. Further complications were the state of Anglo-American relations, for the United States was sympathetic to China, which had become the victim of imperialist interests. In addition, there were fluctuating differences of opinion between Sir Robert Craigie, who became British ambassador to Japan in 1937, the Treasury, the Foreign Office, the Board of Trade and other government departments in London. At times, there were real possibilities for rapprochement with Japan, but the nettle was never grasped, and the economic sanctions applied in conjunction with the United States in the end had the effect of precipitating action rather than preventing it.[8]

Japanese-language training

Why was Britain not properly prepared linguistically for war with Japan? Japan had been learning about Britain since the 1850s, and some members of the Japanese imperial family had spent long periods studying in Britain. On the other hand, relatively few Britons knew much about Japan. King George V and King Edward VIII had both visited Japan as young men, it is true, but only for short periods, and neither of them learnt any Japanese, unlike their Japanese counterparts, who had all made efforts to learn English. One of the consequences of the Anglo-Japanese Alliance, however, was growing interest in the Japanese language. In 1903, Japan and Britain agreed to exchange language officers: these were Army or Navy officers who would learn the language and be attached to a suitable military unit during their stay in the other country. In the same year, William Shand (1850–1909), who had worked in banking and insurance in Yokohama for twenty-seven years, opened a School of Japanese Language and Literature in London. Most of his students were military officers who then proceeded to Japan under the language officer scheme, but there were also women intending to go to Japan as missionaries and assorted commercial and private students.[9]

A similar language officer scheme came into effect between the United States and Japan in 1910, and from 1921 Australian officers were also being sent to Japan for language study.[10] In Britain, the scheme was evidently judged a success and continued even after the end of the Anglo-Japanese Alliance in 1923, but at that time there was no particular need in the British armed forces for speakers of Japanese. It was, in other words, largely an exercise in cultural and military diplomacy. Consequently, those who completed their studies in Japan before the outbreak of the First World War resumed their regular military careers afterwards, without their language skills ever being put to use. For example, among the first group who went to Japan in 1903 was Major Charles Yate (1872–1914), who spent three years in Japan but resumed his career as an infantry officer. He took part in the opening manoeuvres of the First World War but died on 20 September 1914 while in captivity and was subsequently awarded the Victoria Cross. Similarly, seven other former language officers died in combat in the First World War without ever having had a chance to put their skills to use. Even those who survived the war, like William Geoffrey Salmond (1878–1933), who flew with the Royal Flying Corps and ended his career as an air chief marshal in the RAF, did not find that their language skills were valued.[11] As yet, knowledge of Japanese was not considered particularly useful by the armed forces in Britain. Only occasionally were former language officers posted to Japan as military or naval attachés, roles in which their knowledge of the language and their contacts would obviously be valuable assets.

It was rather different in Australia. Already in 1916, some officers in the Royal Australian Navy considered that 'Japanese is undoubtedly the important Naval language in the Pacific', and that it would be more so in the future. Eventually, these considerations propelled Sub-Lieutenant Eric Nave (1899–1993) to Japan in 1921. Nave, whose name will appear often in the pages of this book, had been taking language lessons from a Japanese man living in Sydney and was evidently doing well. Professor James Murdoch (1856–1921), who had lived in Japan and was the first professor of oriental languages at the University of Sydney, wrote a very favourable report on Nave's language skills for the Royal Australian Navy. Nave, it turned out, was not only an outstandingly good linguist but also a supremely gifted cryptographer, so good in fact that the Royal Navy eventually poached him and brought him to Britain.[12]

The British armed forces may not yet have been interested in Japan, but GC&CS had already had Japan in its sights for some time. This was mainly because in the interwar years the Imperial Japanese Navy had become the third largest navy in the world after the Royal Navy and the US Navy. According to a memoir written in 1944 by Commander Alastair Denniston (1881–1961), who was the first operational head of GC&CS from 1919 to 1942, it was in 1923 that they began to take an interest in Japanese diplomatic and naval traffic. Japan therefore joined Germany, France and the Soviet Union as the main targets of British cryptographic efforts, and GC&CS was having some success in breaking Japanese codes.[13]

Commander Denniston recalled,

> For the language, which was the main difficulty, we were lucky enough
> to have recruited Hobart Hampden just retired from 30 years' service
> in the East. But for a long time he was virtually alone, but with his
> knowledge of the habits of the Japanese he soon acquired an uncanny
> skill in never missing the important.

Ernest Hobart-Hampden (1864–1952) joined GC&CS after thirty
years in the British Consular Service in East Asia, finishing his career as
British consul-general in Japan. At GC&CS, he managed to break the
Japanese diplomatic code and thus was able to ensure that Britain was
well informed about the instructions the Japanese government was
sending to its representatives at the important naval conferences held
in Washington in 1921 and London in 1930. At these conferences,
which were intended to restrict the naval arms race, Britain and the
United States sought to limit the growth of Japanese naval power while
Japan hoped to achieve a position of parity with the two largest navies
in the world. Once Britain and the United States found out from
decrypted Japanese messages exactly what the minimum terms that the
Japanese delegation was authorized to accept were, they were able to
steer the conference in the direction they wanted.[14]

Hobart-Hampden turned out to be a talented cryptographer, and
since he knew Japanese he could translate his own decrypts into
English, but he could not cope on his own. More cryptographers
with knowledge of Japanese were needed. The first to join him at
GC&CS was Lieutenant-Commander Harry Shaw, who had been a
language officer in Japan in the early 1920s and had done very well
in the final examination administered by the British embassy in
Tokyo. However, Shaw's room-mate in Japan, Nave of the Royal
Australian Navy, had done even better, getting the highest marks
ever recorded. On returning to Australia, Nave had been posted to
HMAS *Sydney*, the flagship of the Royal Australian Navy, and had
launched a programme to intercept Japanese messages. GC&CS
decided to grab him: the Royal Australian Navy agreed in 1925 to a
proposal that he proceed to Shanghai to act as an interpreter to the
commander-in-chief of the British China Squadron. At this stage, he
did not know what his real job was to be, nor did the Royal
Australian Navy. Instructions sent directly to him by GC&CS

revealed that his task was in fact to intercept Japanese naval signals and to work on them as a cryptanalyst.[15]

Japanese cryptography

One of Nave's first tasks was to train Royal Navy wireless operators to identify and record messages sent in Japanese Morse Code. Wireless operators were normally trained in the International Morse Code, which consists of thirty-six elements covering the twenty-six letters of the English alphabet and the numerals 0 to 9. The International Morse Code was used by Japanese diplomatic missions overseas, for they used Roman letters to spell out Japanese words and then encrypted them for transmission. But the encrypted naval messages that Nave was supposed to be monitoring instead used the Japanese Morse code, which was rather different. Japanese Morse represented syllables in the Japanese *kana* syllabary and therefore consisted of more than seventy different symbols. For example, the signal . _ . _ (dot-dash-dot-dash) in International Morse represents the letter 'A' (. _) twice, but in Japanese Morse this stands for the *kana* syllable 'RO'. Instead of training intercept operators to read Japanese Morse, which would take time as the operators would have to learn the Japanese *kana* syllabary, it was decided to have them record what they heard as if it were in International Morse. So when an operator heard . _ . _, he or she would write down AA or Ā, and it would be converted into RO at a later stage by someone who knew how to convert International Morse into Japanese Morse. Recording messages in Japanese Morse was thus a cumbersome two-stage process.[16]

Japanese Morse was the first barrier to overcome in order to break into Japanese naval messages, which were of course encrypted. It was not necessary to know Japanese in order to be able to record messages in Japanese Morse, but later in the war intercept operators went through a training programme to eliminate the second stage conversion mentioned above, and this involved acquiring a very basic knowledge of the Japanese written language. They could then record the encrypted Japanese messages that others would have to decrypt and then translate.

Once he had trained some intercept operators and began to get some data, Nave worked fast. He quickly made inroads into one of the

Japanese naval codes. He sent back to the Admiralty in London monthly reports containing the information he had been able to acquire and the messages he had been unable to decrypt. These, sent by secure bag rather than by wireless, provided GC&CS with ample raw material to work on in London. Nave was so successful that he was summoned to London, and in 1928 he began to work at GC&CS, which at this time was in London. He was also transferred to the Royal Navy so that he fell completely under the control of the Admiralty rather than being on loan from the Royal Australian Navy.[17]

By the end of 1928, GC&CS could read the main operational code used by the Imperial Japanese Navy without difficulty, but of course encryption systems can never stand still if they are to serve their purpose, and in the 1930s the Japanese Navy overhauled its codes. What is more, the political situation was changing rapidly in East Asia. In 1931, Japan invaded Manchuria and created the puppet state of Manchukuo; in 1933, the League of Nations ruled that Japan should withdraw from Manchuria, but the Japanese response was to walk out of the League of Nations and then to invade the neighbouring Chinese province of Jehol. Rear Admiral Gerald Charles Dickens (1879–1962), a grandson of the novelist, was director of naval intelligence at the time, and he responded to the changes in Japanese codes with a growing sense of urgency:

> The situation in the Far East has completely changed and has left our Intelligence arrangements high and dry. … Unless we can have a good grip of Japanese wireless our Intelligence will be quite inadequate. … It will be necessary to go on increasing the number of Japanese cryptographers, as it is essential now to create a strong centre on the China Station as well as in London. … Japanese cryptography must now be practically a whole time career.[18]

GC&CS was in fact making good progress with Japanese codes. In 1934, Oliver Strachey (1874–1960), who had served in the Foreign Office and then in military intelligence during the First World War, and Hugh Foss (1902–71), who was born in Kobe when his father was bishop of Osaka and therefore knew Japanese well, found a way of decrypting the messages that were produced by the cypher machines used by naval attachés in Japanese embassies. What is more, there were plenty of linguists available to translate the decrypts. Apart from

Hobart-Hampden, who was already at GC&CS, there were also some new faces, such as Harold Parlett (1869–1945), who was appointed a student interpreter in Japan in 1895 and retired in 1927 as the Japanese secretary in the British embassy, and Norman Keith Roscoe (1891–1947), who was a student interpreter in Japan from 1915 to 1920. They were both recruited by GC&CS primarily for their linguistic skills. Hobart-Hampden and Parlett had such good knowledge of the language that they produced a revised and enlarged dictionary of spoken Japanese. In addition to these three consular linguists, there were also James Weymouth Marsden (1884–1974) and Malcolm Kennedy (1895–1984), who had both spent several years as military attachés in Japan. Kennedy we will encounter again later, for he worked at Bletchley Park throughout the war and provided lectures on Japanese history for students on wartime Japanese courses. GC&CS was therefore well provided with Japanese linguists many years before the outbreak of war.[19]

It was in 1935, in response to what was perceived as the growing threat from Japan to the British Empire, that FECB was set up in Hong Kong, mainly to coordinate and enhance work on Japanese codes. That was where Cooper was sent in 1939 and that was where he acquired his pet gibbon. There was already a naval intercept station in Hong Kong on Stonecutters Island, and Nave's former room-mate, Shaw, was sent to run the so-called 'Y' Section, the term used for the interception of signals and their decryption. This was largely a Royal Navy operation, for at first there were no Army or RAF linguists or cryptographers there, and the perceived role of FECB was to give the commander-in-chief of the British Eastern Fleet ample warning of any attack by Japan. In August 1939, just before war broke out in Europe, GC&CS moved out of London to Bletchley Park, and at the same time FECB was moved to Singapore: this was a tacit recognition of the fact that, if Japan joined the war, it would be impossible to defend Hong Kong from a Japanese assault. A skeleton crew consisting of four intercept operators and Squadron-Leader Hubert Thomas 'Alf' Bennett (1910–2003), who had gone to Japan as a language officer in 1935, was left behind in Hong Kong. They kept their work going until they were taken prisoner when Hong Kong surrendered to Japanese forces on Christmas Day 1941.[20]

GC&CS cryptanalysts were certainly making good progress with Japanese codes and cyphers, but this work was necessarily being undertaken under conditions of great secrecy. Neither the British embassy in Tokyo nor the School of Oriental and African Studies (SOAS) in London had any idea of the work being done in Hong Kong and Singapore. They were both, however, getting worried about the shortage of Britons with Japanese-language expertise and the serious problems it would create in the event of war. As they well realized, war was becoming ever more likely. In 1938, the British ambassador to Japan, Sir Robert Craigie, wrote to Lord Halifax, the foreign secretary, on the subject of language expertise: 'The experience of this Embassy has led to the conclusion that three years is the minimum period during which even reasonable proficiency in the Japanese language can be attained, and then only as a result of very serious application.' This was the established view of the embassy, which had responsibility for language training and particularly for the language officer scheme. Three years was a long time to wait if there was going to be a sudden and urgent need for linguists. Surely it would be best to start training them right away? The War Office, alas, did not see it that way, and left it nearly too late.[21]

The outbreak of war

The outbreak of war in Europe in September 1939 had immediate and unexpected consequences for all sorts of people in Britain. Amateur wireless enthusiasts like Jack Mosely (1923–2018) had their transmitters confiscated for the duration of the war. He and others were eventually recognized as a valuable asset for their knowledge of the Morse Code, and some of them were put to work as voluntary interceptors listening for German signals.[22]

Censorship had already been imposed on 31 August 1939 in anticipation of the imminent outbreak of war, and censors were installed not only in post offices, newspapers and publishers but also in telephone exchanges and various cable and wireless companies. There was an obvious language problem, for many letters, telephone calls and telegrams were not in English. To some extent, the need could be met by advertising for linguists, but Dutch and the Scandinavian languages were a problem, and so too were non-European languages, especially Japanese, Chinese and Arabic. Potential censors with knowledge of these languages were scarce, so for these rarer languages neither age nor infirmity was a bar to employment as a censor. Of the four Arabic censors, one was a colonel aged over eighty and another was a gifted scholar who was totally deaf. In November 1939, the School of Oriental Studies (later renamed the School of Oriental and African Studies; hereafter it will be referred to as SOAS) made the first of several offers of help to the Postal and Telegraph Censorship Department. These offers were eventually accepted in January 1941, and from then until the end of the war SOAS staff read more than 30,000 letters in 192 languages for the Censorship Department.[23]

The outbreak of war in 1939 had created a sudden, urgent and unexpected need for people with a good knowledge of Japanese for censorship purposes. This was true not only in Britain but also in Singapore and Australia. In London, Arthur Waley, the famous scholar and translator of Japanese and Chinese literature, was recruited to run the Japanese Censorship Section. His assistant was one Captain Oswald Tuck (1876–1950), a retired Royal Navy officer, who had a much more important role to fill in the future, as we will see in the next chapter.

In December 1940, Ambassador Craigie reported to London that the British authorities in Singapore were having difficulty finding Japanese-speakers to act as interpreters and censors, and again in March 1941 he wrote that Singapore, India, Burma and Ceylon (Sri Lanka) were short of staff with knowledge of Japanese for the purpose of censorship.[24] In April, he sent a list of English and Canadian men and women in the Japanese Empire (i.e., not just Japan but also Korea, Taiwan and Manchuria) with good knowledge of Japanese. It was a painfully short list, consisting of only twenty-seven names. Most of them were long-serving missionaries, and a handful worked for the Rising Sun Petroleum Company (later Shell Petroleum), which required its British employees to learn Japanese. In fact, some of these people had already either returned home or left to work as censors in India, Singapore or Hong Kong. Craigie pointed out, further, that since Western missionary activity was no longer so easy, young missionaries would no longer be coming out to Japan. 'I regard this development as very serious', he wrote, 'both from the general point of view in times of emergency and also in connexion with the future cultural and social relations between the two countries.' By 'general point of view in times of emergency', he was probably referring to the need for linguists and people with knowledge of Japan in the event of war. In July 1941, he sent a more detailed and expanded list of forty interpreters, most of whom had been born in the nineteenth century. A few of them had experience in the Services, and a couple of them were put to use in England during the war, but most would probably have had considerable difficulty adapting to the linguistic exigencies of war.[25]

Meanwhile, even though Britain was not yet at war with Japan, the activities of Japanese citizens in Britain were now attracting the attention of Guy Liddell (1892–1958), the head of counter-espionage at MI5. In September 1939, a company called Tottenham Dust Destroyers contacted Special Branch (the security arm of the Metropolitan Police) to say that they had been asked by a Japanese contractor to burn a quantity of books and papers but not to inform the police. It turned out that the books and papers were from the Japanese embassy, and in his diary, Liddell connected this episode with a decrypt he had received of a message from the Japanese Foreign Office in Tokyo instructing Japanese embassies to burn non-essential papers. From September 1939 onwards, the activities of the military and naval attachés at the Japanese embassy in London were carefully monitored, particularly since one of them was acting as a conduit for payments to German spies in Britain. On one occasion, Special Branch had a champion cyclist at the ready when a Japanese naval attaché arranged to pay the German agent Wulf Schmidt on a bus; Schmidt was in fact a double agent working for Britain, so the point was not to expose him but to identify the source of his money.[26]

Liddell's diary reveals that he was increasingly concerned about the leakage of military information to Japan, particularly relating to aircraft, which he was becoming aware of thanks to the decrypts of Japanese diplomatic cables he was receiving. The prime suspect was William Forbes-Sempill, the 19th Lord Sempill (1893–1965), who had served in the Royal Flying Corps during the First World War and then in the Royal Air Force. In 1921, he had led an official mission to help Japan establish a naval air service using British aircraft, but after that he began passing secrets to the Japanese military. His activities became known from Japanese diplomatic cables, but he was never prosecuted. In 1941, he was still passing information to the Japanese embassy. In September, Prime Minister Winston Churchill wrote to the foreign secretary, Anthony Eden:

> At any moment we may be at war with Japan, and here are all these Englishmen, many of them respectable, two of whom I know personally, moving around collecting information and sending it to the Japanese Embassy. I cannot believe that the Master of Sempill, and Commander McGrath, have any idea of what their position would be on the morrow of a Japanese declaration of war. Immediate internment would be the least of their troubles.

This turned out to be mere bluster. Sempill was interviewed by the police and his home was searched, but he was allowed to resign. He was not dismissed, let alone prosecuted or interned, evidently because he was a member of the aristocracy.[27]

Lobbying for linguistic preparation

Meanwhile, the School of Oriental Studies in London was beginning to be concerned about the likely future need for Japanese linguists and was urging the War Office, the Admiralty and other government departments to take the linguistic challenge of war in East Asia seriously. The school had been founded in 1916, and Japanese was taught from the following year, but in the entire pre-war period only two— yes, two!—students graduated with degrees in Japanese, one in 1938 and the other in 1939. That may seem a miserable total, but before the Second World War many of the courses taught at SOAS were in fact of short duration and were intended primarily for the training of officers in the Colonial Service or the armed forces. The courses in Japanese were no different and were taken by Army and Navy officers as well as missionaries, diplomats and others who had no intention of taking a degree. For example, John Owen Lloyd (1914–82) joined the Japan Consular Service after graduating from Cambridge in 1936, but before travelling to Japan he did a six-month foundation course at SOAS to prepare for further language studies in Japan. It was only in 1939, when he had finished his language studies in Japan, that he was appointed to his first consular position. We will encounter him again in chapter 4, for he spent much of the war at Bletchley Park running Japanese courses for codebreakers.[28]

In January 1939, Sir Philip Hartog (1864–1947), a prominent educationist who was a member of the Governing Body of SOAS, wrote to Sir John Simon (1873–1954), then the Chancellor of the Exchequer. Hartog was already anticipating the possibility of war with Japan and realized that SOAS was hopelessly ill-equipped to deal with the demands that war would bring:

> At the School of Oriental Studies we have for Japanese [language teaching] only a single Englishman, aided by a Japanese assistant. In war time this would be quite insufficient. ... It is understood that in the event of war there will be special demands on the Japanese department for censorship and intelligence work as well as for instruction, and that there may be a considerable demand from India for persons knowing Japanese. The School with its present staff could not cope with those demands.[29]

He therefore appealed for more funds from the Treasury to build up the teaching resources in Japanese. But it was in vain: the government would not provide any additional funds for the new posts that would be needed in the event of war.

Shortly after the outbreak of war in Europe, the director of SOAS, Professor Sir Ralph Turner (1888–1983; director 1937–57), wrote to the War Office with a proposal that 'undergraduates and young graduates with special linguistic ability should be sent to the School to study the Oriental languages likely to be of importance in the War'.[30] Again, on 13 November 1939, Lord Harlech (1885–1964), chairman of the Board of Governors of SOAS, wrote to Admiral of the Fleet Lord Chatfield, who was minister for the coordination of defence, making the same points more forcefully and drawing attention to the time it took to acquire a good knowledge of these languages:

> Before the War we were informed by the War Office, Admiralty and Air Ministry that in the event of war we should be required to give instruction to classes of officers of all three services in certain languages, of which the most important are modern Turkish, Japanese, Arabic and Persian. ... The only students in Japanese now in training are five civilians of whom three are enemy aliens. ... Professor Turner

reports that from his contacts with the Ministry of Labour, the Postal Censorship Department and the Universities, there are not, in this country today any reserves of British subjects with a knowledge of some of these Oriental languages, particularly modern Japanese and modern Turkish. He writes—'It is now clear beyond doubt that if there is any chance of men in the fighting or Government Services being wanted in the next six months with a knowledge of these languages the instruction of a certain number as beginners should commence at once.'[31]

Chatfield's reply, when it came in January 1940, must have been bitterly disappointing. The Admiralty did not plan to send any officers to the school for training during the war, the War Office was exploring the Army's needs for officers with knowledge of Turkish, and the Air Ministry was planning to send six officers for short refresher courses in Turkish and Japanese.[32] SOAS undoubtedly made every effort at the highest possible levels to alert the government to the need to begin training in Japanese immediately, but the school's arguments fell on profoundly deaf ears in Whitehall.[33]

In the summer of 1941, a few months before the outbreak of war with Japan, SOAS made yet more representations, both to the Foreign Office and the War Office. SOAS argued that, 'in view of the threatening posture of Japan', it was necessary to pay due attention 'to the critical shortage of experts in Japanese and to the long period of training which servicemen would have to undergo to acquire a knowledge of the language'. With truly extraordinary complacency, the response of the War Office in August 1941 was, 'we feel we are at present reasonably insured in the matter of officers knowing Oriental languages'.[34] That view was suddenly to change once Britain found itself at war with Japan.

It is very difficult now to understand why the growing tensions with Japan did not encourage some in the War Office to worry about lack of expertise in Japanese. It is probable that there were a few in the War Office who were worried, and one of them was Colonel Gordon Edward Grimsdale (1893–1950), who had worked in military intelligence for six years before the outbreak of war and then went to FECB in Singapore. Writing in 1944, he claimed to have spent more than a decade before 1939 pressing for more Chinese and Japanese language officers and for them to be better treated in the Army. He used to stress that, 'owing to sickness, unsuitable temperament, or the plain fact that a number of chaps just can't "take" these languages and either take to drink or go "native" or go a bit potty, we had not enough of them for our peace time requirements and should be hopelessly short in war'. The problem was, he recalled, that the Treasury would not agree about the needs, so his arguments went nowhere.[35]

If the Treasury was partly to blame, another reason was probably the consensus in Britain that Japan was overrated as a military power. Colonel Grimsdale made strenuous efforts while in Singapore to overcome the complacency about Japanese military capabilities, again to no avail. After all, the Red Army's defeat of the Japanese 6th Army in 1939 in the Battle of Khalkhin Gol (Nomonhan), on the border between Mongolia and Manchuria, did nothing to suggest that the Imperial Japanese Army was a force to be feared. Similarly, the Royal Navy did not think much of the capabilities of the Imperial Japanese Navy, and Churchill was of the same opinion. The Foreign Office, in turn, doubted that the Japanese economy could support the strain of engaging in a war, and Japan was thought to be technologically backward by comparison with the West. The complacency, in other words, was not just about language but also stretched to the perception of the Japanese armed forces.[36]

In late July 1941, John Rupert Firth (1890–1960), who was an expert on Indian languages and taught linguistics at SOAS, attended a conference on the training of Japanese translators and interpreters. It would be interesting to know who organized this and who was present, but I have been unable to find any further information. At any rate, Firth learnt that, in the view of the scholars present, it would take five to seven years to train an interpreter in Japanese. This, he realized, was obviously totally impractical 'under the whip of a whirlwind war'. Firth began to toy with the idea of intensive courses focused solely on wartime needs, which, he thought, might greatly simplify the business of learning Japanese. As we will see in chapter 3, he went on to devise courses designed to train radio eavesdroppers who were then sent to India to interpret Japanese aircraft transmissions.[37]

Despite the arguments advanced by SOAS and by the British ambassador in Japan over the course of several years, the War Office, the Admiralty and the Foreign Office remained stubbornly oblivious to the linguistic challenges that war with Japan would pose. They took no action, and they made no plans to increase the supply of linguists. In Britain, only GC&CS was taking the language imbalance seriously and recruiting Japanese experts from the ranks of former language officers and former members of the British Consular Service in Japan. In the United States and Australia, by contrast, the linguistic imbalance was causing concern well before the outbreak of the Pacific War. The earliest to take positive action was Australia. In August 1940, the Censorship Office in Melbourne opened a Japanese School, in the first instance to train censors, and in the United States courses in Japanese began in October 1941 for the Navy and in November 1941 for the Army.[38]

In Britain, however, the need for Japanese interpreters and translators had simply not been taken seriously when war broke out. When war did break out, emergency measures had to be taken, and it was thanks to the energies, imagination and skill of a remarkable body of men and women that the lack of preparation did not prove fatal. In fact, as it turned out, Britain was astonishingly successful at meeting the urgent wartime need for Japanese linguists. But for decades an aura of secrecy hung over these Japanese courses. What made them so successful? Who studied on the courses? How did they put their skills to use for the war effort? The following chapters will answer these questions.

2

HUSH-HUSH

WHAT'S GOING ON IN BEDFORD?

It is Christmas 1941. The mood is sombre. There has been very little good news. In February, General Erwin Rommel arrived in North Africa with the Afrika Korps and then forced the British Army to retreat to Egypt. In May, the battlecruiser HMS *Hood*, the pride of the Royal Navy, was sunk by the German battleship *Bismarck* with the loss of all but three of its crew. And in June, Hitler launched Operation Barbarossa, the invasion of the Soviet Union. At home, all year long, London, Swansea, Liverpool, Coventry, Plymouth, Bristol and many other cities have been heavily bombed with huge losses of life, while at sea U-boats have plagued the Atlantic convoys, sinking many British merchant ships. As if the situation were not bleak enough, in early December, Japan launched attacks on British Malaya, Pearl Harbor, Hong Kong and the Philippines. The war has now enveloped almost the entire world. And the latest news is that the British capital ships sent out to Singapore, the *Prince of Wales* and the *Repulse*, have just been sunk off Singapore by Japanese aircraft, and Hong Kong is about to fall into Japanese hands. It is going to be a gloomy Christmas, even for those lucky families that are not yet grieving for loved ones killed in action.

Just after Christmas, buff envelopes are delivered to a few dozen households. They contain official letters instructing their sons or

21

daughters to present themselves for interview at Devonshire House, Piccadilly. Some thirty young men and a few women obediently gather there on freezing cold days in January 1942. Most of them have no idea what they are being interviewed for, and they are all astonished at the questions asked.

> Do you have any religious scruples about reading other people's correspondence?
> How quickly can you complete *The Times* crossword?
> What are your tastes in music?
> How good is your chess?
> What languages do you know?

They have absolutely no idea that they may be about to get involved in intelligence work.

What was the point of these interviews and the bizarre questions? They were in fact all being assessed to see if they would be suitable guinea pigs for an experimental course in Japanese, and afterwards for cryptographic work at GC&CS in Bletchley Park. In January, the successful candidates all received a second buff envelope, this time with orders to proceed to the Gas Industry showrooms in Bedford by 2 February. For what purpose, the letters did not say.[1]

Just who were these young men and women? Most of the men were undergraduates from Oxford or Cambridge studying classics—some of them were already graduates and in Army uniform. There were also a few with quite different backgrounds, like Alfred Bell, who had grown up in Japan and later put his skills to good use eavesdropping on Japanese bomber pilots in Burma. Mary Patricia Tate (known as Maggie at Bletchley Park; 1905–73) was the only woman chosen, but quite why she was picked is a mystery. She had taken a degree in modern languages at University College London in 1926 and had good knowledge of French and German as well as Hindi, for she had grown up in India. After graduating, she taught French at a school in London and then, from 1933, taught at an English school in Cairo for seven years; while there, she married an Army officer in the Royal Corps of Signals. She joined the Women's Royal Naval Service (WRNS) in 1940 and seems to have worked for a while at Stanmore, a Bletchley Park outpost north of London; that would have been some time after February 1941, when the first members of the WRNS were admitted to work at Bletchley Park. It is possible that, while in Cairo, she became involved with the Combined Bureau Middle East, a GC&CS outpost formed there in 1940, and was thus already connected to the intelligence services. But it is more likely that her linguistic talents were recognized while she was working at Stanmore and that she was recommended for the first course at the Bedford School.[2]

Maggie arrived a day late, but the twenty-two young men reported to the Gas Industry showrooms in Bedford on 3 February, another bitterly cold day. One of the men, Laurence Cohen, who was later to become a distinguished philosopher, did a sketch of Maggie and added a clerihew:

Mrs Tate
Is remarkably sedate
Considering that she is a Wren
Surrounded by men.

She may have been the only woman on the course, but she had indisputably been chosen for her abilities and followed the same wartime career path as many of the men. After completing the course, she was commissioned as a WRNS officer and then worked in the Naval Section at Bletchley Park.[3]

Once the whole class were assembled in Bedford, they found out what they had inadvertently got themselves into. First of all, somebody called Colonel Tiltman, whom they recognized from their interviews, impressed upon them all the need for absolute secrecy. Then each of them had to sign the Official Secrets Act. They were permitted to tell their family and friends only that they were doing clerical work for the armed forces, nothing more. Some families were irked by this explanation: why should talented young men and women be wasted on clerical work, they wondered, and pressed for more information. Loyally, their sons and daughters refused to say more. In 1978, the men and women of Bletchley Park were finally permitted to reveal what they had been doing, but that was too late for some parents: they died without ever knowing the value of the contribution made by their sons and daughters.

Japanese was a language that almost all of these young men and women had given not a moment's thought to before, but now they had to master it in a hurry. At least they were all used to learning languages, but Hugh Melinsky (1924–2018), who became a vicar after the war, recalled that the course was 'the six months' hardest work of my life'. They were guinea pigs, but they survived the experiment, and their later achievements at Bletchley Park and elsewhere demonstrated that it was possible to learn enough Japanese to be valuable cryptographers and translators in less than half a year. This chapter tells their story.[4]

Colonel Tiltman and the Bedford Japanese School

Even before the outbreak of war in Europe in September 1939, Ambassador Craigie in Tokyo and SOAS in London had been warning the government that there would be a serious deficit of linguists if Britain were to find itself at war with Japan, as we saw in the previous chapter. These warnings were totally ignored in Whitehall. The Japanese attacks on Malaya and Pearl Harbor in December 1941 demonstrated that the Japanese Army and Navy were actually formidable fighting machines, contrary to British expectations, and soon afterwards officials in the War Office belatedly realized that they needed to find a way of meeting the sudden and pressing demand for Japanese linguists, as we will see in the next chapter. Bletchley Park needed linguists immediately for codebreaking and translation, and before long linguists would be needed to interrogate prisoners of war, to translate captured documents, to intercept wireless messages and to interpret voice communications.

The War Office had picked out a few officers in the Intelligence Corps who already knew Japanese and sent them to Singapore in June 1941, as we will see in chapter 7, but it had so far resisted the idea of providing training in Japanese. The first sign of a change of heart in the War Office is a list of Japanese textbooks compiled on 1 January 1942, but it was not an impressive list. Most of the textbooks were very out of date and only some of them belonged to the War Office, the rest belonging to one Major John Chapman (1905–68). The involvement of Chapman shows that the War Office had turned for advice to an officer who knew Japanese. Chapman was at the time a General Staff officer attached to the chief of the Imperial General Staff in Whitehall and he was working for MI2c, the branch of the Directorate of Military Intelligence dealing with

East Asia. He was well qualified for this role, for he had been born in Japan, had returned to Japan as an Army language officer in 1932 and had written well-received reports on the 13th Infantry Regiment in Kumamoto, which he had been attached to for a few months, and on visits to Japanese-occupied Korea and the Japanese puppet state of Manchukuo in 1934. As the only officer at the heart of the Army who was qualified as a first-class interpreter in Japanese and who had extensive experience of Japan, he may have had a powerful voice in debates on the prospect of war with Japan, but if so any influence he brought to bear on language training has left no trace in the archives.[5]

Compiling a list of old textbooks was not much of a start. In fact, the only person in the Army who is known to have been giving urgent consideration to the question of how to meet the desperate need for Japanese linguists was Colonel John Tiltman (1894–1982) of GC&CS at Bletchley Park. Tiltman was well aware that breaking Japanese codes and translating the decrypts required far larger numbers of people with a good knowledge of Japanese than were currently available. How then could GC&CS be supplied with sufficient Japanese linguists? And how could secrecy be maintained if Japanese courses were going to be introduced to train people to work at Bletchley Park?

Tiltman was the person responsible for setting up the Japanese course at Bedford, but who was he and what qualifications did he have for the task? He has been described as a 'giant among cryptanalysts' and the 'greatest cryptanalyst of his time', and he was soon to become the chief cryptographer at GC&CS. After the war, he continued to serve GCHQ as a cryptanalyst during the Cold War, the Korean War and the Vietnam War. Unlike the War Office, Tiltman had been acutely aware of the importance of expertise in Japanese cryptography even before war had broken out in Europe. Already in the 1930s he had begun working on Japanese codes, and in 1933 he solved the Japanese military attaché code, which had been in use since 1927. This made it possible for him to read the cables that Japanese military attachés at embassies around the world sent to the Japanese Foreign Ministry and to military authorities in Japan.[6]

Although he was a brilliant cryptanalyst, Tiltman seems not to have been a gifted linguist or translator himself, and he was modest about his knowledge of Japanese:

I learned what little I know of the written form of Japanese the hard way! We had a British Army intercept station at Hongkong which from about 1935 forwarded to us considerable quantities of Japanese military intercept. ... I myself have never been able to memorise more than a very small number of the very simplest characters. I suffer from a sort of mental block which wipes out the memory of a character as soon as I take my eyes off it.

Somehow or other, he managed on his own until, in 1938, he arranged for Lieutenant Patrick Marr-Johnson (1906–93) to be admitted to the Military Section at GC&CS. Marr-Johnson had first gone to Japan as a language officer in 1933 and knew the language well; later, as we will see, he had a leading role to play in Bletchley Park's outpost in Delhi, the Wireless Experimental Centre (WEC). As we saw in the previous chapter, the Naval Section at GC&CS was well ahead of the game, for in the 1930s they had commandeered the services of Hobart-Hampden, Shaw and Nave as translators-cum-codebreakers, all of whom had learnt their Japanese in Japan. But their expertise was in naval matters, and what Tiltman needed as the head of the Military Section at GC&CS was Army experts like Marr-Johnson.[7]

In December 1941, there were ten Army officers who had already qualified as first-class Japanese interpreters, so the Army was not completely without talent to draw upon, but what Tiltman was looking for was not so much interpreters as people with a natural talent for cryptographic work. He realized that many more Japanese linguists were needed for intelligence purposes, and less than two weeks after the attacks on Malaya and Pearl Harbor he was the first to act.[8]

On 27 December 1941, a high-level meeting was held at Bletchley Park. Around the table were figures who will feature frequently in this book: the director of naval intelligence (Rear-Admiral John Henry Godfrey, 1888–1970), the head of GC&CS (Commander Alexander 'Alastair' Denniston), Denniston's successor (Commander Edward Travis, 1888–1956), Tiltman as head of the Military Section, Josh Cooper as head of the Air Section and Frank (Francis Lyall) Birch (1889–1956) as head of the Naval Section. Among other matters, the meeting addressed the Japanese-language problem and made the following proposals:

Knowledge of Japanese is so rare that all personnel with this qualification should be brought into the Y [signals interception operation] and its ancillary services and their selection should take *absolute priority*. Special efforts should be made to find more Japanese interpreters, advertisements being inserted in the Press, enquiries made from the School of Oriental Studies, travel agencies, etc.

Some anonymous comments on these proposals underlined the desperation: 'This is a very urgent requirement. It takes years to make a Japanese interpreter and many more to create a Japanese cryptographer.' But a solution was needed immediately, and it was simply not possible to wait for a couple of years. It was Tiltman who thought of a solution. He proposed to set up an experimental school to train future cryptographers in Japanese in the preposterously short span of just six months. This was the origin of the Bedford Japanese School.[9]

In June 1942, Tiltman wrote a detailed account of how the Bedford Japanese School came into being. The following lengthy extract reveals much that has hitherto remained unclear.

It was realised early in the war against Japan that the shortage of Japanese interpreters, particularly those qualified for cryptographic work, would be acute and would remain so until some attempt was made to train suitable men [and women] from scratch. At the end of December 1941 I suggested to the D.D.M.I.(O) [deputy director Military Intelligence (Organization)] that I should start a 6 months' course as an experiment using vacancies on the War Establishment of I.S.S.I.S. [Inter-Service Special Intelligence School] at Bedford. Qualified Japanese interpreters whom I consulted criticised the idea on the grounds that, owing to the extreme complexity of the language and the very large number of Chinese characters to be memorised, responsible translation could not be expected of students who had not studied the language for at least 3 years. It seemed to me, however, that an effective result might be achieved if students at the most receptive age were carefully chosen, and if the scope of the course were severely limited to our immediate requirements. After consultation with senior members of Oxford and Cambridge Universities I became convinced that the most suitable material for the experiment would be carefully selected Classical Scholars between the ages of 18 and 20. I formed the opinion that, other things being equal, the discipline of training in the Classics would be of more value for the desired purpose than modern language training, with the added advantage that the classical qualifications had no other immediate value for the war effort. This latter consideration particularly appealed to the Universities. The D.D.M.I.(O) agreed to this use of the I.S.S.I.S. War Establishment, having obtained from me an undertaking not to take anyone under the age of 17½, so as not to clash with the requirements of the War Office Dulwich scheme.[10] ... The aim originally set for the course was to train students in 6 months to translate written Japanese in the Romanised form with the aid of dictionaries and reference books, the vocabulary being restricted to words and phrases commonly used in diplomatic and service telegrams. It was realised that Romanised Japanese cannot be intelligently translated without a knowledge of Chinese characters and it was, therefore, decided to teach the use of about 400 common characters during the course together with the method of handling unmemorised characters. It was considered that the best texts for study would be intercepted plain languages telegrams. ... The apparent unexpected success of the course is entirely due to Captain Tuck's efforts, applied to a particularly keen and capable collection of students.[11]

Captain Tuck turned out to be an inspired choice and more will be said of him below. Tiltman's proposal was certainly daring and original: Would it have been accepted if he had not had some knowledge of Japanese himself and if he had not been the head of the Military Section at GC&CS? Probably not. Whether such a short course could possibly meet the needs of GC&CS was obviously another matter altogether, but the need was overwhelmingly urgent and the experiment worth trying. Since the Inter-Service Special Intelligence School was based at Bedford, that was the obvious place to run the experiment.[12]

Who exactly were the 'qualified Japanese interpreters' Tiltman says he consulted? Many have assumed that they were teachers at SOAS, and several writers have been disdainful about SOAS, although, as we will see in the next chapter, SOAS was soon running short courses itself. Most recently, John Ferris has perpetuated the myth, claiming that 'academics' insisted that three years were necessary and adding that 'Professors, focused on the fine points of poetry in foreign languages, often overrated the linguistic requirements for Sigint [signals intelligence].'[13] However, it is hardly likely that Tiltman, writing in June 1942, would have referred to SOAS staff as 'qualified Japanese interpreters': what he meant, in fact, was qualified *Army* interpreters. As mentioned earlier, there were in December 1941 ten Army interpreters with qualifications in Japanese, and it was most probably to them that Tiltman first turned. It is time to put this myth about short-sighted SOAS staff to rest, but the blame for the mistake cannot be laid on Captain Tuck, for in his history of the Bedford Japanese School he states simply that it was 'started in defiance of the opinions of experts': he made no mention of academics. In fact, the Foreign Office had long considered that Japanese training required three years, and that was the time taken by all the military language officers in Japan, including those who qualified as Army interpreters, so it is unsurprising that they would have been sceptical about Tiltman's plans.[14]

Why did Tiltman mention a preference for Oxbridge undergraduates? The simple answer is that it was the norm at Bletchley Park. When the head of GC&CS, Denniston, began the process of recruiting fresh blood for wartime work in the summer of 1939, it was to the heads of various Oxford and Cambridge colleges that he wrote, asking for the names of gifted undergraduates who could be interviewed for unspecified work, and it was mostly classicists, historians and modern linguists that he went for.[15] So Tiltman turned to Oxbridge, too. His problem, in fact, did not lie in finding promising students for a Japanese course, but rather in finding somebody capable of teaching such a course, somebody who not only knew the language well but also had security clearance and yet would not be called up for wartime service. The man he chose was a sixty-five-year-old retired captain in the Royal Navy called Oswald Tuck, who had never been to university and had not set foot in Japan since 1909. Given Tuck's age, Tiltman could have been forgiven if he had harboured doubts about his suitability, but Tuck turned out to be a brilliant choice, and his achievements, never publicly acknowledged or rewarded, were extraordinary.

Oswald Tuck in charge

At first sight, Tuck was an odd choice. He left school at fifteen, and two days later he went to work at the Royal Observatory, Greenwich. He became an enthusiastic astronomical observer and, at the age of nineteen, the youngest person ever elected as a member of the Royal Astronomical Society. In 1896, he was appointed to teach astronomy and navigation on HMS *Conway*, one of the Royal Navy's training ships, and later he became an instructor in the Navy. He served from 1900 to 1909 on the China Station, a British naval command with bases in

Singapore, Hong Kong and Weihaiwei (now Weihai) in China. It was this posting that gave him the opportunity, in 1901 and again in 1902, to visit Japan.

He hired a Japanese servant and right away began using him as a Japanese teacher: Tuck was a natural linguist and a keen learner. By early 1903, he had reached a level that impressed the Japanese consul in Hong Kong. He continued to study with two Japanese acquaintances, and in 1905, when the Navy sent him to Japan to improve his knowledge of the language as a language officer, he had already spent a total of nine months in Japan on various occasions in connection with his naval duties. Despite his low rank, but perhaps because of his unusual command of Japanese, he dined with some of the leading generals and admirals in Japan, including General Nogi Maresuke and Admiral Tōgō Heihachirō, who were idolized for their sensational victories on land and sea in the Russo-Japanese War (1904–5). In his diary, he wrote, not very respectfully, 'Got old Nogi, who was very pleased with my Japanese, to sign two postcards and a fan.'[16]

On his return to Hong Kong, Tuck began teaching Japanese to fellow naval officers, but in 1908 he was appointed interpreter and assistant to the naval attaché at the British embassy in Tokyo. He was recalled to London in 1909 to complete his translation of a secret Japanese history of naval operations during the Russo-Japanese War; this had not been published in Japan, but a copy had been made available to the Royal Navy by the Imperial Japanese Navy as a courtesy, since Britain and Japan were allies. Tuck served in naval intelligence during the First World War and then worked as an interpreter for the Admiralty in London, translating various official and secret texts into English. He was at the same time an active member of the Japan Society of London and gave lectures to the members on subjects such as Japanese drama and poetry, so he clearly had a fascination with Japan that extended beyond his naval duties. He served as head of the Admiralty Historical Section and then of the Archival Section and retired in 1937 with the rank of instructor-captain and lived in Bromley with his wife and daughter. Whatever retirement plans he may have had were rudely interrupted by the outbreak of war.[17]

In 1939, Tuck was brought out of retirement to work as assistant press censor in Japanese at the Ministry of Information, serving with

Waley, the famous scholar of Chinese and Japanese literature who had
been obliged to put his knowledge at the disposal of the war effort.
Their job was to check the dispatches that Japanese journalists based in
London were sending back to Tokyo in order to make sure that they
did not contain any secrets. But there was more to it than that. On
24 March 1941, Tuck wrote in his diary:

> A really strenuous day's work. Not only were there a lot of long cables
> from our London correspondents [for Japanese newspapers and news
> agencies] to deal with but also a number of intercepts, in particular a
> long one from Sofia to Tokyo detailing the rapturous welcome accorded
> to the German troops.

The explanation for this is that, at the beginning of the month,
Bulgaria had agreed to join the Tripartite Pact between Germany, Italy
and Japan and to permit German troops to pass through Bulgaria to
invade Greece; the message Tuck referred to was probably sent by a
Japanese diplomat in Sofia to the Foreign Ministry in Tokyo. A few
months later, Tuck wrote, 'I have been snowed under with intercepted
telegrams from Turkey (where there is an indefatigable correspondent
named Enomoto), Berlin, Moscow and Rio.' From these diary entries,
it is clear that Tuck and Waley were not only checking the dispatches
of Japanese journalists based in London but also translating Japanese
messages that had been intercepted in London, including diplomatic
communications. He was already engaged in the world of secret intelligence and the language war.[18]

But Tuck's greatest achievement was still to come. He barely
responded in his diary to the outbreak of war in December 1941,
except to note that Japanese journalists and other Japanese citizens in
Britain were rapidly interned on the Isle of Man. There was no further
need of his services as a censor, therefore, but he and Waley were still
going to the Ministry of Information to translate the Japanese intercepts that were arriving on their desk every day. Tuck offered his
services to the Admiralty, arguing that 'a new war needed an increase
of experts', but heard nothing for a long time. Finally, on 22 December,
he was invited to lunch with 'a Col. Tiltman of the Code and Cypher
School', whom he clearly did not know beforehand. That night, he
wrote in his diary: 'During lunch he told me there was an idea for
giving selected young undergraduates a six-months intensive course in

Japanese with the object of using them in the East. He thought I was the man to organize and give the course.'

Did Tiltman mislead Tuck by suggesting that the students were to be used 'in the East', or did Tuck misunderstand? At any rate, Tuck had an interview with Commander Denniston of GC&CS and was offered the job of running the experimental course in Japanese.[19]

In this way, it came about that, thirty-two years after he had last been in Japan and at the age of sixty-five, Tuck returned to active duty as a Japanese teacher. On 13 January, he went to Bletchley Park, and there Tiltman explained what he wanted him to do: 'train young undergraduates to be able to read, with a dictionary, ordinary cables in Japanese—this to be done in a six-months course'. As Tuck wrote in his diary, 'It sounds impossible, but is worth trying.' He realized that he would have to devise his own course, for existing grammars all focused on the spoken language, and he was given the next few weeks to do the necessary preparations. Waley gave him a batch of telegrams and cables that had been finished with, and he combed through these for suitable sentences to use as examples. Tuck was probably the only person available who was capable of undertaking this task: he had good knowledge of military Japanese and the right security clearance, and he was too old to serve in any other role. He turned out to be the perfect choice, for he was also an inspiring teacher.[20]

Finding the right students

The next task was to find some students. Tiltman had a preference for classicists, but why? After all, neither he nor Tuck had been to university, let alone studied classics. The simplest explanation is that there were many classicists available, for although scientists and modern linguists had already been recruited in large numbers, there was no obvious use to which classicists could be put in connection with the war effort. Secondly, they were already skilled at 'decoding' ancient languages, and, it seemed to Tiltman, they might well be suitable for Japanese cryptographic work. And thirdly, by focusing on those who had won scholarships in the Oxbridge entrance examinations, it would be relatively easy to select the best. So Tiltman turned to three classics dons: at Oxford, Alexander Lindsay (1879–1952, later Baron Lindsay of Birker), who was master of Balliol College; and at Cambridge, Martin Percival Charlesworth (1895–1950), who was president of St John's College, and Sidney William Grose (1886–1980), who was senior tutor of Christ's College. They were, according to Tiltman, well aware of the secret work the students would be required to undertake, presumably because he had told them. No other belligerent in the Second World War found such a good use for classicists, apart from Australia.[21]

Interviews were held at Devonshire House, Piccadilly, in a room used by MI8 (military intelligence). Tuck, Tiltman and an unnamed 'university don' interviewed the candidates over several days; they had not, of course, been told what they were being interviewed for. Tuck realized after the first set of interviews that since the students were 'exceptionally intelligent' he was going to have to work very hard to keep them fully occupied on the Japanese course.[22]

Perhaps not surprisingly, a couple of the students selected had been at Eton and quite a number had attended other well-known public schools. One of the Etonians was Francis Dashwood (1925–2000); after the war, he succeeded his father as the 11th Baronet of West Wycombe and the Premier Baronet of Great Britain. He left Eton with the top prizes in French and German, but when he tried to join the Grenadier Guards he was rejected on the grounds of poor eyesight, and the same happened when he tried to join the Oxfordshire and Buckinghamshire Light Infantry. Bedford seemed the obvious answer, but he hankered after a more active military life. While still on his Japanese course, he managed to get accepted by a Special Air Service (SAS) team active in Yugoslavia, but he was then told that he knew too many secrets to be allowed to risk capture. According to a fellow student, Dashwood left Bedford most weekends to go to The 400 Club in Leicester Square and other night spots in London. All the same, he did well at Bedford: he graduated third in his class of twelve and was posted to the Government Communications Bureau in Berkeley Street, London, which was an offshoot of GC&CS focusing on diplomatic and commercial communications.[23]

Dashwood was still keen to serve overseas and finally managed to be selected as one of the three Bedford graduates to be sent to join the intercept operation on Mauritius. On his way out by air, he stopped in

Cairo, and at the British embassy he handed in a letter from his father; he had hardly settled down in his hotel when a Rolls-Royce with motorcycle escort came to take him to the embassy to stay with the ambassador. It was only much later that he discovered that this was partly due to the fact that his father was also involved in secret work, in his case trying to identify the Axis spy known as 'Cicero', who turned out to be the valet of the British ambassador in Ankara. Dashwood will reappear later in this book, in the chapter on Mauritius.

Dashwood's selection might give the impression that the Bedford School was dominated by people from wealthy and privileged backgrounds. In fact, there was quite a social mix, for the only criterion for entry was linguistic ability of a high order. George Hunter (1920–2008), for example, was the son of a journeyman electrician and grew up in a tenement in Glasgow. In 1941, he graduated from Glasgow University with an MA in English, joined the Royal Navy and taught himself Russian, which drew attention to his linguistic abilities and resulted in his selection for Bedford. Like many other Bedford graduates, he had a distinguished academic career after the war, in his case becoming the Emily Sanford Professor of English at Yale University. Similarly, John Martin was the son of a shopkeeper, Charles Mayou the son of a builder and Arthur Munday the son of a butcher's assistant— what they all had in common was their exceptional talent for learning languages, and most of them were brilliant enough to have won entrance scholarships to Oxford or Cambridge colleges.[24]

Facing the students

On 3 February 1942, with thick snow all around, Tuck faced his first class in the demonstration room of the Gas Industry showrooms in Bedford, which had been taken over by the Inter-Service Special Intelligence School. There were no textbooks or dictionaries to give the students, for none were available apart from the ones that Tuck himself owned. Tuck had no choice: he dictated his grammar lessons, he dictated the sample sentences and he even dictated the texts the students had to wrestle with. As he put it in the account of the Bedford School he wrote in 1945:

> The first lesson was on case-endings and the primary verbs and inflections; and the day ended with the men [the only woman, Maggie Tate,

arrived a day late] making up sentences which were then read out and criticized by the whole class. This created a healthy rivalry for producing the longest and most original sentences and had the good effect of fixing at least the words learned that day firmly in the memory.

That was a pretty tall order for the first day: Is it credible? By the end of the second day, according to Tuck, 'One man, who the previous morning did not know a word of the language produced in flawless Japanese the sentence "Mr. Churchill made a long speech in Parliament on the subject of the bad relations between Japan and the United States of America."' You do not have to know Japanese to realize that to translate such a complex sentence into any language after just two days of instruction is a remarkable achievement. That was just the beginning: a week later, the students began learning Chinese characters, which added another layer of complexity and difficulty. They did not learn the characters for 'cherry', 'blossom' or 'beautiful' but instead learnt the characters for 'kill', 'combat' and 'shoot'.[25]

By the end of February, the students were in sore need of dictionaries. One of the more able students, Lance-Corporal Eric Ceadel, who already had a degree in classics from Cambridge, took a day off to go down to London and scour the second-hand bookshops. He managed to come back with a dozen dictionaries to share out. The lack of dictionaries was a problem in Australia and the United States, too: the supply of dictionaries from Japan had naturally dried up on the outbreak of war, and the number of copies available was hopelessly inadequate. Since it was wartime, however, flouting copyright rules was not a problem. Early in 1942, Harvard University published photolithographic editions of the best English–Japanese and Japanese–English dictionaries and of *Ueda's Daijiten*, a huge dictionary of Chinese characters more than 2,500 pages long. In the middle of May, copies of these dictionaries finally arrived at Bedford, sufficient for all the students to have their own. These dictionaries were all large and heavy, and they added substantially to the weight of the kitbags of those who later found themselves in the Burmese jungle or on the beaches in the Philippines. One man was saved by his dictionaries when they stopped the bullets in their tracks, as we will see in a later chapter.

Britain did not lag behind the United States in flouting the normal copyright rules. The London publishers Lund Humphries published photolithographic editions of several dictionaries too, including the *Japanese–English Dictionary of Nautical Terms* in 1943. Later in the war, some new dictionaries and textbooks were produced on both sides of the Atlantic. For example, in 1943 a guide to military Japanese was published in California that included sections on how to question Japanese prisoners and what to say if you were captured by Japanese troops. One of the most widely used textbooks later in the war was Joseph Yamagiwa's *Modern Conversational Japanese*, which was first published in November 1942. In the same year, Joseph Yamagiwa (1906–68), who was born in Seattle, became the director of the Army Military Intelligence Japanese School at the University of Michigan, and his textbook was based on his own courses. However, the focus was on everyday spoken Japanese, and there was no attempt to introduce military vocabulary.[26]

At the Bedford School, on the other hand, the objective of the course was to teach, in as short a time as possible, the essentials of the language for military purposes. Therefore, Tuck did not waste time on the vocabulary needed for everyday conversation. At first, he used some of the reports sent by Japanese journalists in London to their head offices in Kyoto, which he had got hold of through his work as a censor. These provided authentic material on a variety of topics but were not the kind of text that the students would find themselves working on at Bletchley Park. Ideally, they should have been using the decrypts of real diplomatic and military cables. However, although all the students had read the Official Secrets Act and had signed declarations to that effect, the cables were considered highly confidential, and the authorities at Bletchley Park refused to release any of them.[27]

Tuck, however, was no pushover. He made repeated protests and eventually these bore fruit:

> [A] certain number of messages which had been broadcast in plain Japanese by radio were sent to the Bedford School, and formed a welcome body of the right kind of material. Many of the messages had suffered mutilation or omissions, and dealing with these exercised the knowledge and ingenuity of the students, and added an interest to the routine work of mastering the complicated grammar and vast vocabulary of the official Japanese language.

By this time, it must have dawned on the students what they were learning Japanese for. Any doubts would have disappeared when the

Bedford School was visited by Colonel Tiltman and Josh (Joshua) Cooper (1901–81), the head of the Air Section at Bletchley Park, for they gave the students a coded message to break. On 4 June 1942, Tuck sent Ceadel, Hugh Lloyd-Jones, Robin Gibson, Christopher Wiles and Maurice Wiles to a Bletchley Park outpost to translate a recently captured Japanese Air Force codebook; this gave them their first taste of the secret war and they were 'immensely bucked about it', Tuck wrote.[28]

In later life, the students remembered the hard work, the difficulty of the language and Tuck's kindly instruction. It was not all hard work, though. During their lunch breaks, they went to the nearby 'British Restaurant' (the communal kitchens where cheap, nourishing meals could be had), and then played table-tennis or chess. What was there to do in Bedford in the evenings? The BBC Symphony Orchestra was based in Bedford until the end of the war, and men and women in uniform could attend the rehearsals for free. Sir Adrian Boult, the director of music for the BBC, conducted some of the concerts himself, and he even went to the Bedford Japanese School to talk about music on one occasion.[29]

The Bedford School had started as an experiment and, according to Tuck, Tiltman had expected it to produce only half a dozen linguists who could be of use to Bletchley Park. Was the experiment a success? After less than six weeks, Tiltman was convinced that the experiment was working well, so he put plans in place for a second course. Tuck, too, was delighted, and he reported in May that 'The progress made has far exceeded my most sanguine expectations.' Finally, when the students had completed four months of study, Tuck requested an independent assessment of the standards being reached by his students. Three passages for translation were provided by members of Bletchley Park's Japanese Section, and they were favourably impressed by the progress that Tuck's students had made, given that they had known nothing of the language until 3 February.[30]

It was now June 1942. Early in the month, the Imperial Japanese Navy suffered a decisive defeat in the Battle of Midway, losing four of its six large aircraft carriers to American carrier-borne aircraft. At around the same time, Rear-Admiral Godfrey, the director of naval intelligence in the Admiralty, visited the Bedford Japanese School in person and told the assembled students that they and their knowledge were urgently needed by the Navy. A few weeks later, on 27 June 1942, the first course came to an end, after less than five full months. Tuck wrote in his diary: 'As I quite honestly told them I think my work with them has been the happiest time in my life.'[31]

The experiment had been a triumph. True, the students would have been completely lost if they had been asked to order a cup of coffee, buy a train ticket or make polite conversation in Japanese. But they had a good command of military vocabulary and of the terse language used in encrypted wireless messages, and this made them much sought after. To complete their training, they were given a short course in crypt-analysis to prepare them for their future work. Most were then sent to Bletchley Park, but a few were sent to the Government Communications Bureau in Berkeley Street, London. Three were sent to India to help expand the operation of the WEC in Delhi, an organization similar to Bletchley Park. One of them was Lloyd-Jones, who later became Regius Professor of Greek at Oxford. Another was Wilfrid Noyce, who, as an accomplished mountaineer, had been asked to run a mountain warfare course before he left for India. After the war, he took part in the successful 1953 Everest expedition, but he died in a mountaineering accident in the Pamirs in 1962. We will encounter both of them again in later chapters.

The success of the experimental course at Bedford suggested that similar courses elsewhere could provide an additional supply of translators in Japanese, and so on 16 July a conference was held in London to explore the possibilities. It was attended by representatives of the Intelligence Departments of the War Office and the Air Ministry and by five members of staff from SOAS. Two of the first graduates from the Bedford School were also present, Gibson and Ceadel, who had come first and fourth respectively in Tuck's final examination. Those around the table expressed some incredulity about the level reached by Tuck's students, so the two who were present were put to the test:

> One of the London staff happened to have with him the script of a Dōmei report, similar to a Reuter's bulletin, written in Chinese characters. This was handed to the two Bedford men as a test of their progress and they retired to another room with dictionaries to study it. In a quarter of an hour they returned, having finished the first page; and

when they proceeded to read it out and translate it, and further to translate another page at sight, there was no longer any doubt that they had really a workable knowledge of the language.

Tuck's methods had proved their worth.[32]

After the end of the first course, it was decided that Ceadel, as one of the most able students, would be retained as Tuck's assistant. However, it was also thought important that the instructors be commissioned officers, so Ceadel was dispatched to an Officer Command Training Unit and returned to Bedford later as a lieutenant in the Intelligence Corps. From then on, there were at least two teachers available. This made it possible to run two courses simultaneously.

There was a gap of three months between the second and third courses, and during this time Ceadel spent nearly two months in the various sections of Bletchley Park to which the Bedford graduates were sent. This was so he could get a feel for the kind of texts they would be working on, but he also spent some of the time reorganizing the course materials and the texts for the students to work on back at Bedford. Ceadel has been described as an 'organizational genius' or 'rather a disciplinarian': he put together a grammar of formal Japanese military language and from then on, he did much of the teaching, dictating his grammar for the students to write down. This left Captain Tuck free to concentrate on the written language and the overall running of the courses.[33]

Neither Ceadel's grammar nor Tuck's teaching materials have survived. Fortunately, however, one of the students, Patrick Field, kept all his notes and the decrypted telegrams he was given to translate. Field was on the eighth course, which began in October 1944, and he worked at GCHQ after the war. His notes, which were based on Ceadel's grammar lectures, include the sentences used to illustrate points of grammar. For example, to show how relative clauses work in Japanese, he was told to write down the following two sentences:

Eigun wa Biruma ni sakusen shi teki o gekihatchū nari.
The British Army is operating in Burma and is smashing the enemy.
Biruma ni sakusen suru eigun wa teki o gekihatchū nari.
The British Army which is operating in Burma is smashing the enemy.

Since there is no word for 'who' or 'which' in Japanese, relative clauses introduced by these words in English are in Japanese simply placed before the noun they apply to. The first sentence is a straight-forward statement, but in the second, the noun 'eigun' (British Army) is preceded by the relative clause 'which is operating in Burma'. It was in late 1944 that Field wrote these sentences down, and the Burma Campaign was indeed going well for the Allies by then. But these are not the sorts of sentences normally used for teaching Japanese.[34]

For the next four years, Tuck kept the school going with Ceadel and several other assistants. In the end, eleven courses were run alto-gether, producing in all over 220 graduates, nine of whom were women. Those who were not already in uniform subsequently joined the Army or the RAF. They did not join the Royal Navy, for naval officers were expected to have gone through 'lower deck' (i.e., ser-vice as naval ratings or ordinary seamen) or the training depot HMS *King Alfred* beforehand. Consequently, Bedford graduates needed by the Navy at Bletchley Park or overseas tended to remain as civilians, unless, like Charles Bawden (1924–2016), they were already in the Navy when selected for the Bedford School—we will see later what Bawden did with his Japanese. After graduating, most of the students, including Bawden, went first to Bletchley Park. For many of them, that was only a stepping-stone: once they had acquired some crypto-graphic know-how and experience, they were sent to other places where they could be useful, including Delhi, Kilindini in Kenya, Colombo, Mauritius and Australia.[35]

The last six courses at Bedford were designated as either military or naval courses. The naval ones were taken by RNVR (Royal Naval Volunteer Reserve) officers or ratings who had already gone through their naval training and had shown some linguistic ability. One of the naval students was Geoffrey Barrow (1924–2013), who later became a professor of Scottish history at the University of Edinburgh. In September 1943, after completing two years of study at St Andrew's University, he joined the Royal Navy and was sent to HMS *Royal Arthur* for training. This was not a ship, and it did not even look like a ship. It was in fact the first Butlin's Holiday Camp, which had opened in 1936 at Skegness. The whole camp was taken over by the Admiralty for training purposes, though Barrow noticed that the staff had failed to take down Butlin's famous welcome message above the gates, 'Our true intent is all for your delight', which probably did not reflect the atmosphere under Admiralty orders. After basic training, Barrow was sent to the Royal Navy Signals School near Petersfield in Hampshire, but he was then offered the chance to go on a Japanese course. He passed an interview in the Admiralty and joined the seventh course at the Bedford Japanese School in March 1944 as a sub-lieutenant in the RNVR. The teaching materials that Barrow and the others cut their teeth on included decrypts from the Japanese naval codes known to the Allies as JN25 and JN40. The decrypts had been supplied by the Naval Section at Bletchley, but only after Tuck had made repeated requests for material that was suitable for naval students.[36]

By the time of the tenth course, which ran from April to September 1945, there was no longer any secret about the existence of the Bedford School, though its connection with Bletchley Park was still a secret. When Joseph Ward reached the age of eighteen, his head teacher suggested he sign up for the Army Japanese course at Bedford. After some initial Army training and then further training with the Intelligence Corps, he was sent to Bedford a month before the course began. During that time, he and others in the same position were given some training in cryptography by specialists from Bletchley Park. When he finished his course in October 1945, the war was already over, so he was sent to India to study colloquial Japanese in Karachi and then to Burma to work in a war crimes court, until he was demobilized in 1948. We will come across him again in Karachi.[37]

Very little is now left of the Bedford Japanese School. Some of the teaching materials and Tuck's mark sheets for the regular tests he set for his students are preserved in Cambridge and Bletchley Park. Tuck evidently sent Bletchley Park regular reports on the students' progress, but only a handful of these have survived:

Olive Ferguson: 'A reliable translator and hard worker. Her translations of difficult material are commendably accurate and reflect a careful and systematic study of the language and its construction, although not unnaturally, she possesses a smaller knowledge of technical military matters than do the others.'

Elizabeth Anderson: 'Started the course under many disadvantages compared with the remainder, and was at first unable to make much progress. Steady work has brought about a good improvement, and in text containing few difficulties her translations are now fairly accurate.

41

It would, however, seem useless to ask her to translate material of above average difficulty for which her knowledge of vocabulary and structure and insight into idiom and usage are insufficient.'

This report was signed by Tuck and his assistant, Ceadel, who was not enthusiastic about the participation of women in the courses. Ferguson spent the rest of the war in the Japanese Military Records Section at Bletchley Park, while Anderson, who had been working at Bletchley Park since 1939, was sent out to Mauritius, where we will encounter her again.[38]

Bedford graduates were active all over the world during the war. And even after the war was over and the school had closed down, many of them continued to haul their weighty dictionaries around and to serve where their skills were still required. We will encounter many of them in later chapters as they dealt with the aftermath of the war in Singapore and South East Asia, interrogated war crimes suspects and policed the Occupation of Japan.

The end of the Bedford School

On 17 July 1945, a meeting was held at Bletchley Park to discuss the future of the Japanese courses. Tuck was there with his chief assistant, now Captain Ceadel. On the other side were Tiltman, Josh Cooper and a few others. Although none of them realized that the end of the war was only a few weeks away, they evidently considered that the school was coming to the end of its life. The current course, for Army linguists, was due to end in October, and that would be the last one for the Army. The RAF had no more need of Bedford graduates either. It was agreed, though, that one more course for the Navy would commence in November or December. Tuck thought that the war with Japan might go on longer than expected, and it was agreed that, by continuing courses, the Navy 'was holding the door open so that the other Services might restart courses if their judgment had been wrong'. Four weeks later, they found that their judgement had been right, and the last naval course was cancelled. So ended the operations of the Bedford Japanese School, the activities of which were kept secret for decades.[39]

Tuck had succeeded magnificently. How had he done it, and what did his students think of him? Leaving his personal qualities aside for a moment, his decision to teach the language of military communications, and only that, was clearly the right one. Joseph Axelrod, who studied at the US Navy Language School in Colorado, wrote in 1945 that his course had included polite conversation and stories, and the vocabulary had included flowers, seasons and objects in the classroom. Tuck ruthlessly excluded all such irrelevant vocabulary. He also realized that his students were used to working on their own, so the classroom hours of instruction and dictation were balanced by hours in which his students worked in groups or on their own, and he fostered a sense of rivalry and competition among them. In addition, he recognized that despite their dedication to their studies of the language, his students needed some further stimulation, so he organized weekly lectures on various topics relating to Japan. Some of the lecturers came from Bletchley Park, such as Captain Malcolm Kennedy (1895–1984), who had been a language officer in Japan from 1917 to 1920 and had subsequently worked for GC&CS; he was the author of *The Military Side of Japanese Life* (1924) and other books, and he gave lectures on Japanese history and politics. John Pilcher, who was a diplomat working in the Ministry of Information and who later became British ambassador to Japan, lectured on Japanese culture, and others spoke on geography and other topics. Despite the war, there can be no doubt that Tuck retained a lot of sympathy and respect for Japan and made sure that his students had all-round knowledge of the country. He never made derogatory comments about Japan during the classes, his students claim.[40]

Even while at Bedford, Tuck received numerous letters and visits from his former students, who wrote to tell him what they were doing with the skills he had taught them. Dashwood, one of the three who were sent out to Mauritius, sent him some tea and sugar, which were available in abundance there but rationed in Britain, and in 1945 Denise Newman, who in 1988 was to sail single-handed across the Atlantic at the age of sixty-four, sent him a piece of her wedding cake. Tuck was not forgotten after the end of the war either. In 1946, several former students dropped in to see him at the Royal Naval College, Greenwich, where he was supervising a translation party working on captured Japanese documents.

Tuck had never in his life had anything to do with Oxford or Cambridge, or indeed any university, but in May 1946 he visited

Cambridge as the guest of Ceadel, who was by then a postgraduate studying Chinese and Japanese and was later to become a lecturer in Japanese and finally the head of Cambridge University Library. Later that month, Tuck went to Oxford as the guest of Cohen, who had resumed his classical studies at Balliol College. Many of his former students came to see him there on that occasion, including Lloyd-Jones and Donald Russell, who were both to become professors of classics at Oxford. Tuck was clearly held in great affection by his former students. Perhaps most of them felt as Peter Soskice did, who wrote to Tuck from the WEC in Delhi, 'I thought you might like to hear once again from an old (& devoted) pupil of yours, over the vast spaces.' Soskice worked after the war for the United Nations in Prague and learnt Russian. Another tribute to Tuck came from David Goldberg, one of the many Jews at Bedford and Bletchley Park: 'I should like you to accept the little book enclosed herewith as a token of my thanks to you for the past six months so pleasantly spent in Bedford, and especially for helping me to keep our Jewish religious observances throughout the period.'[41]

Many years after Tuck's death in 1950, his students retained affection and admiration for their wartime teacher, no matter how eminent they later became as teachers themselves. Donald Russell, who became senior translator in the Japanese Military Attaché Section at Bletchley Park during the war and spent the rest of his career as fellow and tutor in classics at St John's College, Oxford, wrote that 'Tuck was a wonderful teacher—perhaps the best I have ever known.' John Cook, who spent the rest of the war in the Naval Section at Bletchley Park and ended his career as director of education in Edinburgh, described Tuck as humble and modest, and added that he rarely wore his uniform with captain's stripes. For Lloyd-Jones, he was 'not only a highly intelligent but also a charming person, and he proved to be an excellent instructor'. Michael Loewe, too, who spent his career teaching Chinese at Cambridge and is the last survivor of the first course, never saw Tuck in uniform and described him as having a fine commanding presence and being very clear, rigorous and demanding but friendly. Tuck, it seems, wore his uniform only when he had visitors to impress, when he was interviewing candidates for his courses or when a class photograph was to be taken.[42]

* * *

Although it operated mostly in secret, the Bedford School produced the goods, justifying Tiltman's faith both in Tuck and the students. In June 1942, an American intelligence officer visited the school from Bletchley Park, and when Tiltman visited the Bedford School on 25 August 1942 he mentioned that 'the school for teaching Japanese in America had heard of the results obtained'. He did not say which of the several schools in America he was referring to, but how could they have heard if he had not told them? At any rate, since the American authorities did not believe that a great deal could be achieved in six months, he said, they wanted full information about the Bedford School and copies of all the material used. At Tuck's suggestion, a couple of the graduates from the first course were asked to write a detailed account: as he put it, 'coming from them it would show the practical results, whereas if produced by the teacher it might be regarded rather as his ideals which may or may not have been realised in actual fact'.[43]

The two students chosen were Robert Robins and Maurice Alabaster, who were both now working in the Air Section at Bletchley, and they sent in a short grammar reinforced by examples. As they modestly put it in the preface, 'The contents of this grammar embody notes taken during a six months course in Japanese; they represent points observed and difficulties experienced while reading contemporary texts', and as examples of the texts they included a number of decrypted telegrams reporting on events during the war, such as the British surrender of Singapore. In Tuck's estimation, 'it was astonishingly complete and accurate, and was altogether a remarkable achievement for two young men who seven months before did not know a word of Japanese'. Their grammar was duplicated by the War Office and used at Bletchley Park; the one surviving copy contains the signature of the Welsh composer Daniel Jenkyn Jones (1912–93), who as a captain in the Intelligence Corps worked in the Japanese Forces Section. The following year, Tuck was himself asked to send to America a full report on the methods of teaching used with such success in the Bedford School, but of this I have not been able to find a copy.[44]

Why did the Bedford School attract American interest? Because once the war with Japan had started, all the Allies became painfully aware of their acute need to train linguists as quickly as possible. Tuck had instinctively prioritized speed rather than breadth of knowledge, and he seems to have got the balance right. As we will see in a later chapter, in the summer of 1942 a Japanese course for cryptographers began at Arlington Hall in Virginia along the same lines as Tuck's first course: given the timing, it is possible that information about the Bedford School method had reached Arlington Hall and inspired the courses there.

The ultimate accolade for the Bedford School came in a message sent by Lieutenant-Colonel Alastair Sandford of the Australian Corps of Signals at the Central Bureau in Brisbane. The Central Bureau was General MacArthur's cryptographic and intelligence operation in Australia and, as we will see in a later chapter, quite a few Bedford graduates ended up working there during the war. In a message sent to the War Office on 23 July 1945, when the war was about to end, Sandford asked for more: 'Your Bedford trained translators most highly esteemed here and would like as many as we may have. Could you indicate possible figure and I shall initiate official request. We can never have enough.' This reached Tuck five days later, and he proudly copied it into his diary. There was no time to act on it, for within three weeks the war was over. When Sandford sent his request, he had been expecting the war to continue into 1946, when the Japanese mainland was to be invaded. There was now no longer any need for Bedford graduates.[45]

Shortly after the end of the war, Tuck was asked to write a history of the Bedford Japanese School. He duly sent it in, and the deputy director of GC&CS, Frank Birch, wrote to thank him:

> What you haven't said in your history (but, thank goodness, it sticks out a mile) is your tremendous triumph over wrongheaded experts, red tape, neglect and almost impossible conditions. The tremendous value of your contribution and its great significance in the total British effort in the Japanese war—that, I hope, will be recognised in the G.C.C.S. histories (it certainly will in the Naval history) now being written.

It was indeed cited by Birch and by others, but there is now no copy of Tuck's history to be found in GC&CS papers in The National Archives or in GCHQ. Tuck received no public recognition for his contribution to the war effort, until in 2020 he was recognized in the form of a biography in the *Oxford National Dictionary of Biography*.[46]

3

THE DULWICH BOYS AND THEIR SUCCESSORS

The Bedford Japanese School functioned primarily as a provider of linguists for cryptographic work at Bletchley Park and its outposts abroad. The Bedford students learnt a peculiar form of written Japanese that is far removed from the spoken language, so who was going to do the interrogating when Japanese prisoners were taken? Who was going to listen in to radio conversations in Japanese and understand what was being said? In Britain as well as in Australia and the United States, linguists were required for these important wartime purposes, too, so there was a need for other courses that paid more attention to the spoken language. And that is why young Guy de Moubray (1925–2015) started learning spoken Japanese in London in the summer of 1942.

Guy was a schoolboy when, early in 1942, he applied for a scholarship to do a wartime course in oriental languages at SOAS. After finishing his course, he was sent out to India and Burma as an Army intelligence officer, where he followed the front-line troops and intercepted Japanese radio messages. At SOAS, he had chosen to do Japanese rather than one of the other languages on offer, and he had good reasons for his choice.

It was all because of what had happened to his parents. In 1940, his father, Major George de Moubray (1888–1975), had become British advisor to the sultan of Terengganu. Terengganu is now one of the federated states of Malaysia, but it was then a British Protectorate, and the 'advice' offered by the British advisor was not supposed to be disregarded. George and his wife, Katherine, had been living in British Malaya for many years while he pursued a career in the British Colonial Service. As was the common practice at the time, they sent their son Guy to a boarding school in Scotland from the age of five and only saw him during brief periods of home leave every three years.[1]

On 8 December 1941, Japanese troops invaded the north-east coast of the Malay Peninsula, not far from Terengganu. The de Moubrays suddenly found themselves in great peril. They were forced to hurry south on foot along jungle paths to Singapore, where they naturally assumed that they would be safe. They were not. The Japanese troops 'scissored through terrain the British had considered impassable' and overwhelmed the British, Australian and Indian troops opposing them. In February 1942, the British had no choice but to surrender Singapore, and the de Moubrays became two of the many civilian and military prisoners who spent the war in Japanese PoW camps.[2] At the end of the war, they were both in the Sime Road Camp in Singapore, where civilians were interned. Food supplies were inadequate, and by 1945 they were probably as undernourished and emaciated as their fellow prisoners. Would they ever see their son again?

Guy was one of the so-called 'Dulwich Boys', a group of schoolboys who studied on wartime courses at SOAS while living at Dulwich College, a leading public school to the south of London. Before the war, SOAS had done all in its power to draw attention to the language deficit that Britain would suffer from if war broke out with Japan, but to no avail. The War Office was not interested in exotic languages. But everything changed once Britain found itself at war with Japan, and the War Office turned to SOAS for help. While the Bedford School trained future cryptographers, SOAS made a valuable contribution to the war effort by training hundreds of young men and women for work as translators, interrogators, eavesdroppers and cryptographers. Guy was one of them.

SOAS lobbies the War Office again

A month after war had broken out with Japan, SOAS made yet another determined attempt to expand its teaching of languages useful for the war effort. Sir Philip Hartog (1864–1947), a prominent member of the governing body of SOAS, wrote to the president of the Board of Education (from 1944 known as the Ministry of Education), renewing the arguments he had first made in 1939:

> There is now a great paucity of Japanese, Chinese, Thai and Turkish linguists for the Intelligence and Interpretership Services of the War Office and we have had demands not only from the War Office but also from the Air Ministry for linguists in some or all of these languages. ... Professor Turner, the Director of the School of Oriental Studies and I foresaw more than two years ago that such needs would arise and we made representations asking various Government Departments to take the necessary steps to meet them. We were unsuccessful but I need not go into that.

This time Hartog and Turner were more determined than ever. As well as writing to the Board of Education, they also took the bit between their teeth and confronted Brigadier William A. M. Stawell (1895–1987), the deputy director of military intelligence in the War Office. After two meetings with Hartog and Turner, Stawell was convinced. The War Office immediately drew up a scheme that would 'extend the recent War Bursary scheme for science students to boys ... who are willing to take courses at the School of Oriental Studies in the following languages needed for War purposes; Japanese, Chinese, Thai and Turkish'. From this, it is clear that, unsurprisingly, the War Office was now interested in 'exotic languages' and was no longer pretending to have enough linguists on hand.[3]

Three days later, the War Office sent its proposal to the Board of Education. The War Office now acknowledged that the Army's need of people with knowledge of Turkish, Persian (which had for some reason replaced Thai), Chinese or Japanese for purposes of interpretation, interrogation and liaison far exceeded the available supply. The nub of the War Office's proposal was this:

> The right policy seems to be to catch them young and teach them before the age for military service. Our idea is to pick, say, fifty boys at Public or other secondary schools, aged 17–18 and with a marked aptitude for languages, and give them special facilities to study one of these languages at the School of Oriental Studies ... while continuing their general education.[4]

At last the War Office had responded to the challenge! The proposal suggested that fifty scholarships be made available, and that the courses for Chinese and Japanese might last as long as two years, though it was hoped that eighteen months would prove sufficient. When they had completed their courses, the boys—for only boys were eligible—would proceed to undergo normal military training. A remarkable feature of the scheme was the proposal that the students would be housed at Dulwich College and would commute to SOAS for their lessons. What lay behind that part of the proposal?

SOAS had in fact already taken steps to find solutions to the practical problems of housing students in wartime by approaching the master (head teacher) of Dulwich College, Christopher Herman Gilkes (1898–1953). He had agreed to make two of the school's boarding houses available, one for the students of Chinese and Japanese and one for the students of Turkish and Persian. This solved the problem of accommodation, but it was also good news for Dulwich College. The college had been in financial difficulties for several years, but by charging the Board of Education £131 per student the college finances were by 1943 restored to a healthy state. The scheme was, therefore, very much in the college's interests.[5]

In just a month—unusual haste, but then it was wartime—all the details had been worked out. In mid-February 1942, a printed 'Memorandum to Headmasters' was sent out to solicit applications for the scholarships: there were to be twenty for Turkish, five for Persian, fifteen for Japanese and ten for Chinese, numbers that suggest that the overwhelming need for Japanese linguists had not yet been fully grasped. The applicants were 'required to give an undertaking to be at the disposal of the Government for a period of not more than five years after the termination of their scholarship'. There were no advertisements in the press, but word of the scheme seems to have leaked out and a few local newspapers reported on it.[6]

The response was extraordinary, and most likely way beyond the expectations of the War Office and the Board of Education. A total of 660 applications were sent in, a huge number given that the applicants knew next to nothing about these languages or the countries in which they were spoken. For the ninety-nine Scottish applicants, interviews were held in Edinburgh in late January 1942 and there was a rigorous examination, including written and oral language-aptitude tests. In the end, sixteen scholarships were offered in Chinese, eight in Persian, twenty in Turkish and thirty in Japanese. The increased number of scholarships for Japanese indicates that it had at last been recognized that the need for Japanese was the most pressing. And yet, even thirty is not such a large number. Hundreds were going to be needed, but at this stage nobody seems to have realized that.[7]

The boys selected were allowed to express a choice of language, but their choices were often disregarded. Only two or three of them had expressed a preference for Japanese, but the Japanese course started with thirty students. Patrick O'Neill, a future professor of Japanese at SOAS, expressed a preference for Chinese or Turkish but was assigned to study Japanese. One of the few who deliberately chose Japanese was de Moubray, but that was for family reasons: he knew that his parents were prisoners of the Japanese Army.[8]

It was in such circumstances, then, that SOAS launched the first of a series of eighteen-month Japanese courses on 1 May 1942, three months after the Bedford School opened. There can be no doubt that SOAS was fully behind the war effort and committed to providing the language training needed, but there was a shortage of qualified teachers. How was that going to be made good?

Finding the teachers

There had never been much demand for Japanese at SOAS, and in January 1941 there were only two teachers of Japanese available. One was Yoshitake Saburō (1889–1942), who had already been teaching at SOAS for many years and was an expert on ancient Japanese; for some reason, he was not interned on the outbreak of war, so he remained on the staff. The other was Commander Noel Isemonger (1883–1951), who had qualified as an interpreter of Japanese in 1909 and had been teaching at SOAS since 1921. Although they both contributed to the wartime teaching at first, neither of them was a young man: Yoshitake died in 1942 and Isemonger retired in 1943. Some new blood was needed, and in 1939 Frank Daniels (1899–1983), who was living in Japan, was appointed as a new lecturer. Owing to the outbreak of war, it was not until early in 1941 that he and his Japanese wife were able to reach England via the United States. Daniels had gone to Japan in 1928 and was teaching English in Otaru, Hokkaido, when war broke out in 1939. He found when he eventually reached London that there were only three students to teach: two were doing a special course for the Air Ministry, while a certain Miss A. F. Stephen was learning Japanese to work in the Censorship Office of the Ministry of Information. 'This life of ease', he recalled, 'ended in May of the following year when the teaching of Japanese began in earnest for the purposes of the war against Japan.' All of a sudden, the task of finding the staff and organizing the curriculum to teach thirty eager young men fell on his shoulders. After the war, he became the first professor of Japanese at SOAS.[9]

Unlike the Bedford School, most of the SOAS courses were supposed to develop oral and aural skills, and for this purpose native speakers were essential. But with just one Japanese man on the staff, who was already in his fifties and had been living in London for years, it was clear that SOAS was hopelessly ill-equipped to handle the influx. The first addition was Daniels' Japanese wife, Otome (1903–79). In March 1942, before the start of the first wartime course, she was appointed a temporary lecturer.

Frank and Otome married in Japan in 1932. There, she was what was known as a 'modern girl', more used to skirts than a kimono and often with a cigarette-holder in her hand. She had been disowned by her parents for some reason, so there is a bit of a mystery about her. Whatever her past, she always wore a kimono in London. As the wife of a British citizen, she had British citizenship and therefore was not interned, but life in wartime London was by no means easy for her. On one occasion, a woman in the street recognized her as a Japanese and slapped her. Her students were 'deeply upset' to hear what had happened, recalled one of them. 'She was extraordinarily distressed because this had brought to the surface something she must have felt all her time teaching there—a Japanese helping her country's enemies.' It was a poignant and difficult role for her to play. At a party at the end of the first course, her natural affection for the country of her birth got the better of her and she pleaded with her young students, who were about to go off to war with Japan, 'Please look kindly on my people.'[10]

Otome was much admired and appreciated as a teacher. But there is no denying that the Japanese spoken by women is very different from that spoken by men, especially military men. That is still true today, but it was even more so back in the 1940s. It was essential, therefore, to recruit some Japanese men as well, but where were they to be found in wartime Britain? In the United States or Canada, that would not have been a problem, as there were thousands of US or Canadian citizens of Japanese descent, the sons and daughters of people who had migrated in large numbers earlier in the twentieth century. As we will see in chapter 8, those in the United States who had good knowledge of Japanese were drafted in as teachers at military language schools in the United States, while many others were recruited as students. But in Britain there were virtually none. Who, then, could be found to serve as native speakers to teach spoken Japanese?

The answer came from Canada, which was now a self-governing dominion in the British Empire. In July 1942, just after the start of the first SOAS course, three new teachers arrived in London, all of them warrant officers in the Canadian Army—James Tsubota, Fumi Yamamoto and Eiichi Matsuyama. A fourth man joined them in January 1943, Peter Shoji Yamauchi. As their names show, all four of them were of Japanese origin. Why, it seems reasonable to ask, were they not needed in Canada?

Although many Japanese Canadians had fought with distinction for Canada during the First World War, they were not full citizens for they were ineligible to vote. Discrimination became more vicious in the interwar years, and as the prospect of war grew closer, Japanese Canadians were required to register as persons of Japanese origin, and Prime Minister Mackenzie King excluded them from military service. After the attack on Pearl Harbor, almost all Japanese Canadians in British Columbia were rounded up, deprived of their property and sent to internment camps, including soldiers who had fought for Canada during the First World War. Until January 1945, no person of Japanese descent in British Columbia was permitted to serve with the armed forces. Elsewhere in Canada, there was no such ban, and many Japanese Canadians did in fact serve with the Canadian armed forces. However, the Canadian Army made no effort to train Japanese linguists until August 1943, when the Japanese Language School in Vancouver opened its doors. Canada's contribution to the training of Japanese linguists for the war thus came very late in the day. Furthermore, although the US Army had turned to Japanese Americans as teachers and students from the outset, in Canada negative attitudes towards Japanese Canadians persisted. As a result, it was only in 1945 that the Japanese Language School admitted Japanese Canadians as teachers. In these circumstances, it is clear that in 1942 there was no demand in Canada for the language skills of Japanese Canadians, so these four men were free to cross the Atlantic and teach at SOAS.[11]

Who were these four men and what contribution did they make? James Tsubota had been in action with the Canadian Expeditionary Force in the First World War. In 1917, he had been wounded in the decisive Battle of Vimy Ridge near Arras on the border between France and Belgium, in which the Canadians defeated the German 6th Army. Undaunted, he volunteered for the Army again when the Second World War broke out and was sent to England as a teacher. Less is known about Fumi Yamamoto, who enlisted in 1940, but Eiichi Matsuyama (1915–2004) had been born in England to a British mother and went to Emanuel School in Clapham. He travelled to Japan in 1935 and in 1938 was working as a clerk in the Imperial Hotel in Tokyo. Worried by the growing militarism in Japan, he left in 1941 to return to England; he travelled via Canada where he changed his mind and joined the Canadian Army. Peter Shoji Yamauchi (1917–2006), whose parents had migrated to Alberta in 1905, was called up in 1941 and posted to the Service Corps in England, but once he learnt that Japanese-language teachers were wanted in Britain, he volunteered his services. Like many second-generation Japanese Canadians, he could not read or write Japanese, but he could speak it well, so at SOAS he taught conversation and pronunciation.[12]

The arrival of these four men was a godsend for SOAS, for male speakers of Japanese were in short supply, but there was one snag: not one of them spoke standard Japanese. O'Neill recalled that one of them 'spoke Japanese in ... a weird provincial accent and had a unique teaching method in which he would bring a big Japanese–English dictionary into the classroom, open it at random and read out any words and examples that caught his eye'. Although he may not have been an ideal language teacher, teaching was not the profession of any of the

Japanese Canadians or of Matsuyama, and in wartime SOAS had to be grateful for what it could get.[13]

In the summer of 1942, more Japanese courses were launched at SOAS, so Daniels, as the youngest and most active of the three permanent teachers, had to hunt for more temporary staff. He turned to those members of the Japanese community in London who had been interned on the Isle of Man at the outbreak of war but had declined the offer of repatriation to Japan. Despite having the uncomfortable status of 'enemy aliens', they proved willing and even eager to teach their language to British men and women in uniform. One of them was Yanada Senji (1906–72), who had come to Britain in 1933 after graduating from Tokyo Imperial University, partly because he was worried about the increasingly strident militarism in Japan. From 1935 to 1941, he was the London correspondent of the *Yomiuri Shimbun* newspaper, and when war broke out he said the Japanese government was like 'mad dogs' and was determined not to go back to Japan. He was interned on the Isle of Man until he was released to begin teaching at SOAS in September 1942. In 1943, he was joined by Matsukawa Baiken, who came to London in 1915 and worked as a correspondent in London for the Dōmei Press. His English translation of one of Ishimaru Tōta's works on the future conflict between Japan and the Western powers was published in Britain in 1937 as *The Next World War*. Although he was married to an English woman, he was interned on the Isle of Man until he was released for teaching duties. Both of them remained in Britain after the war, perhaps because they were worried about how their wartime teaching activities would be perceived in Japan. They were, after all, teaching the 'enemy'.[14]

Daniels also found a Japanese merchant seaman in a PoW camp near Argyll and a Taiwanese theologian who had been educated in Japan, graduating from Tokyo Imperial University in 1937. In this way, he managed to gather enough native speakers to be able to offer the intensive training in spoken Japanese that the services wanted. All the same, he also needed more staff who were able to provide grammatical instruction and train the students in translation. Some of the students, as we will see, were later sent to India and Burma where they were required to translate captured Japanese documents in the field, most of them handwritten.

For the grammar teaching, Daniels was fortunate to find an expert on military Japanese who had also written a book about Japanese hand-written documents. Major-General Francis Piggott (1883–1966) was available to help and was too old to serve his country in any other capacity. He had spent some of his early years in Japan when his father was a legal advisor to the government in the late nineteenth century, and from 1904, when he was a young Army officer, he had spent two years in Japan as one of the first language officers. Later, he served as military attaché in Tokyo from 1922 to 1926, and again from 1936 to 1939. He had an outstandingly thorough knowledge of written and spoken Japanese, as well as a deep sympathy for Japan. In the years and months before December 1941, he made strenuous efforts to avoid the outbreak of war between Britain and Japan by incessantly meeting Japanese diplomats and influential British politicians in an attempt to bridge the gaps. He was unfailingly optimistic about the prospects, but he was distrusted in official circles in London. He was indeed strongly pro-Japanese, but once war broke out, he devoted his energies to the SOAS courses.[15]

In addition to Piggott, Daniels recruited several female missionaries who had spent years in Japan and then been repatriated home, a former consular official who had served in Japan, and some serving officers who had somehow or other acquired knowledge of Japanese. One of the officers was Flight-Lieutenant Edmund Barry Cahusac (1895–1968), who had been born in Yokohama and awarded the Military Cross during the First World War as a member of the Royal Flying Corps. Another who had lived in Japan was Edwin McClellan (1925–2009): he had been born in Kobe and was repatriated to Britain in 1942; he taught at SOAS until he joined the RAF in 1944. In this way, Daniels successfully press-ganged an extraordinary range of people to teach on the SOAS courses, and when he needed still more he persuaded some of the better students from the early courses to stay on as teachers. Altogether, they were undoubtedly a motley crew, but they were the only ones available and they rose to the challenge, to judge by the wartime accomplishments of their students.[16]

The Dulwich Boys

On 1 May 1942, some seventy schoolboys made their way to Dulwich College from all parts of the United Kingdom. One of them, Peter

Parker (1924–2002), would later become the chairman of British Rail and receive a knighthood, while de Moubray would later rise to become a senior member of the Bank of England. But all that lay in the future. For the moment, they had to put their skills to the service of their country: they were all good linguists, chosen to learn languages needed for the war effort. Parker was assigned to learn Japanese and de Moubray chose to do so, while others were assigned to learn Chinese, Persian or Turkish.[17] Unlike their counterparts at Bedford or later generations of wartime students at SOAS, they were all male and thus became known as 'the Dulwich Boys'. They lived in Dulwich College and commuted by train to SOAS just off Russell Square in central London. Since they were not destined for work at Bletchley Park, they were not bound by secrecy. In this way, SOAS began to make its contribution to the war effort, training young men (and later women, too) for work as interpreters, interrogators, translators of captured documents and eavesdroppers on Japanese voice communications *en clair*, especially air-to-air and air-to-ground radio communications.

They had their instruction at SOAS in the mornings, with further work in Dulwich in the afternoons and evenings, including some general education. Most of the students were distinctly unimpressed that they were subject to school discipline even though they were undertaking courses of university standard taught by university teachers. What is more, they were all expected, whether they liked it or not (and some did not), to take part in the military training that was provided for pupils at Dulwich. In their free time, they could participate in various sporting activities, and Alexander 'Sandy' Wilson (1924–2014), a lyricist and composer who later had great success with the musical *The Boy Friend* (1953), put together a satirical review entitled 'A Matter of Course' based on the course of study that he was himself pursuing. It was clear that his talents lay elsewhere, and he was one of the few to leave the course, in 1943.[18]

The Dulwich Boys doing Japanese were, of course, younger than the Bedford students, being just out of school, and their course was to last much longer than the Bedford courses. On the other hand, they had a much wider range of material to cover, from spoken Japanese to the language of military dispatches. One advantage they had over the first course at Bedford was that by the middle of 1942 British and American publishers had published reproductions of Japanese dictionaries and other teaching material, so they were not short of textbooks or teachers. At the end of the first year, they were tested on their knowledge in two written examinations and an oral, and at that point were divided up between the three services: six of the Japanese students were destined for the Royal Navy, two for the Royal Air Force and the remainder for the Army.[19]

By the end of their course in December 1943, most of the students had attained remarkable proficiency. The Governing Body of SOAS agreed:

> This result was largely due to the fact that for a considerable part of their course they dispensed entirely with English in talking to their Japanese instructors. A number of students acquired a remarkable competence in writing essays and letters in Japanese script. ... Both the School and the students owe an incalculable debt to Mrs. [Otome] Daniels for her devoted and brilliant work in the teaching and training of these young students.

However, as far as Japanese was concerned, there were to be no more Dulwich Boys, for students on future courses, it was decided, would be men and women already in the services, and they would not be housed at Dulwich College.[20]

Courses for the services at SOAS

Once the Dulwich Boys had started learning their languages, SOAS began running courses for men and women who were already in the services, and the courses were tailored to their needs. Airmen did not need to know Japanese naval terms, whereas sailors did, so most of the courses were run for one branch of the services at a time. The records of these courses were still in SOAS when Ōba Osamu wrote his book on what he called the 'secret' London school of Japanese (though it was not secret), but these appear, sadly, to have been lost. However, some records were passed on to GC&CS and survive in The National Archives, so this account is based on those records and on personal reminiscences by those who attended the courses.

The Dulwich Boys had been recruited by public advertisement, but from now on the focus would be on serving members of the armed forces. Sometimes, however, promising students were identified and then enrolled in one of the armed forces. This is what happened to Stanley Radcliffe (1922–2015), who was evidently a talented linguist. In October 1941, he had entered Liverpool University to study French, German and Spanish but was approached by the professor of German, who had been asked by the War Office to identify suitable recruits for Japanese courses. Radcliffe found this an intriguing prospect so he was called up and made to undergo infantry training, and then, in October 1943, he joined a class at SOAS along with Louis Allen, whose activities as a translator in India and Burma will feature later in this book. Another in the class was Ronald James Beverton, who was studying German at Bristol University when, in a similar way, he was directed to the Japanese courses by his professor of German.[21]

In order to identify suitable candidates in the armed forces, an Inter-Services Committee for Language Training was set up, showing that the Air Force, the Navy and the Army all now recognized the need for linguists. The committee worked closely with Professor Turner, the director of SOAS, and Josh Cooper of GC&CS. We have encountered Josh Cooper before, and his involvement shows that GC&CS was also planning to recruit linguists from SOAS. Later in the war, the Royal Navy began to operate its own selection board: naval conscripts did some language aptitude tests in the Admiralty, and in their interviews they were asked about puzzles and crosswords—a sure sign that they were being assessed as possible cryptographers.[22]

All those selected for the later SOAS courses were already in uniform and therefore were subject to usual service discipline. George Aspden (1925–2015), for example, who was an aircraftman (the lowest rank in the RAF) and was housed in barracks run by the Air Ministry, remembered the details clearly when he wrote his memoirs. He and his fellow student-airmen were checked in and out of the building, they had to attend a morning parade every day and on Friday evenings they were not allowed out until they had cleaned and polished their quarters well enough to pass an inspection. Even in the 1940s, this was somewhat different from normal student life. At the weekends, they were free to enjoy a 'cup o'char 'n' a wad' (cup of tea and a sandwich) or even go out to a restaurant or a cinema, but in the evenings some of them had to take their turns at fire-watching during air-raids.[23]

The chosen students began their courses in July 1942, just a couple of months after the Dulwich Boys had started work on their course. At the insistence of the services, and against the explicit advice of SOAS, separate year-long courses were run, one for interrogators, with emphasis on the spoken language, and one for translators, with emphasis on the written language. In 1943, it became clear that the strict division between interpreters and translators was artificial and counterproductive, so in 1944 it was abandoned altogether, and students were taught together. In both cases, the key to success was 'economical teaching', concentrating on what was essential and ruthlessly discarding what was not, a technique that had been pioneered by Captain Tuck at the Bedford School.[24]

Many of the SOAS graduates were destined to be sent to India or Burma to translate documents gathered on the field of battle. These documents were for the most part handwritten, sometimes scrawled, and they were a real challenge for translators who had not been studying the language for long. To help them get to grips with handwritten Japanese before they headed out to India, in 1944 SOAS published a dictionary of the handwritten forms of the characters that Otome Daniels had compiled. Many of her students, including Allen, whom we will meet again in later chapters, found this knowledge indispensable as they laboured in their tents in Burma trying to make sense of documents rapidly written by hand that were brought in for their attention. Fortunately, Otome Daniels probably never knew that some of the documents they were to read came from the bodies of her countrymen who had died in combat.[25]

By July 1943, SOAS was also running special Japanese courses for RAF personnel who were destined for signals intelligence work at home and abroad, like Aspden mentioned above. The focus was on written Japanese, with an emphasis on the language of telegraph communications and on official language. The courses were taught by John Kennedy Rideout (1912–50), who had learnt Japanese at SOAS before the war and had also worked on cryptography at GC&CS, and they were modelled on those pioneered by Captain Tuck at Bedford, which had become something of a gold standard. Like Tuck, Rideout used telegrams sent by newspaper correspondents, and perhaps also some decrypted telegrams, for the students to cut their teeth on.[26]

THE DULWICH BOYS AND THEIR SUCCESSORS

The courses mentioned so far were all the responsibility of the Far East Department at SOAS, where Chinese and Japanese were normally taught. Quite separately, the Phonetics Department at SOAS was also running courses for RAF personnel, even though the members of staff were mostly experts in Indian languages and not one of them knew Japanese. But that was not a problem, for they were experts in training students to recognize and make sense of the sounds they heard irrespective of the language, and they placed their valuable skills at the service of the war effort. The key figure among them was Firth, who, as we saw in chapter 1, began to get interested in the problem of how to train Japanese interpreters in the shortest possible time in the summer of 1941. He was an expert on the phonetics of two Indian languages, Gujarati and Telugu, but he foresaw at the outset of the war that there would soon be a big demand for people trained to eavesdrop on Japanese radio communications. He set about studying the problems of hearing and recording that this kind of training posed, and by the summer of 1942 he had worked out a system that would enable people to be trained in a short period to eavesdrop on Japanese conversations and interpret what they heard.

On 12 October 1942, some RAF personnel arrived to take the first of a series of courses taught by Firth. He used captured Japanese code books and other secret materials to build up an essential vocabulary list that the airmen had to master, and he persuaded Yanada, one of the internees from the Isle of Man who had become a teacher, and Warrant Officer Yamamoto of the Canadian Army to make recordings on gramophone records. Sitting in front of record-players, students heard the kinds of expressions that RAF eavesdroppers in India or Burma heard on their earphones, such as:

Bakugeki junbi taikei tsukure!
Take up formation preparatory to bombing!
Hojo mokuhyō Parenbangu tsūka. Ijō nashi.
Have passed Palembang [in Sumatra], the secondary target. Nothing to report.

These courses were taught in the Phonetics Laboratories at SOAS, which were specially fitted out with additional equipment for recording and reproducing Japanese speech. Yanada and Yamamoto were not

61

permitted to have any direct contact with the RAF personnel taking the course, presumably because they were not completely trusted.[27]

Bletchley Park also took an interest in the training of the RAF personnel, probably because many of them were destined for intelligence work. Firth sent detailed reports on the performance of each student, and some of these can now be seen at The National Archives in Kew. The RAF personnel who completed courses at SOAS were not sent straight out to India; rather, they first went to RAF Newbold Revel, an eighteenth-century country house near Rugby in Warwickshire that was used for intelligence training. Nobody there knew anything about Japanese, but what they could provide was training in wireless telegraphy and how to draw useful intelligence from the messages intercepted. Only after this specialized training were the trainees ready to be posted to India or to Central Bureau in Brisbane.[28]

In July 1942, the director of SOAS informed the Admiralty about the course for RAF personnel and suggested that the Admiralty might like a similar programme of training to be laid on for naval personnel. The Admiralty was not remotely interested. However, less than a year later it changed its mind when the director of naval intelligence realized that the Royal Navy, too, needed training in Japanese for intelligence purposes and wrote to say that there was an urgent need for fifty naval ratings destined for the Eastern Fleet to be given a course in Japanese phonetics. In 1943, now that the tide of war was turning, the Eastern Fleet was operating in the Indian Ocean and needed both translators and men and women who could monitor wireless and radio traffic either on shore or at sea. The first course began on 30 August 1943.[29]

SOAS also ran longer courses for personnel in the Royal Navy. In his memoirs, Hugh Norris explained how he came to join one of these courses. In 1943, at the end of his first year studying history at Trinity College, Cambridge, he registered for conscription and was offered the choice of going down the mines or joining the Royal Navy. Having sensibly opted for the Navy, he was trained as a naval coder and one day was doing some repainting chores when, as he recalled, 'someone from the ship's office put his head round the door and called out, "No one 'ere wants to learn Japanese, do they?" and promptly disappeared'. Norris chased after him and learnt that the Admiralty was indeed looking for volunteers to learn Japanese. After passing an interview at the

Admiralty, he joined the second Royal Navy translators course at
SOAS along with Denis Twitchett, who later became professor of
Chinese at Cambridge, and Richard Rutt (1925–2011), who spent
many years as a missionary in Korea after the war and eventually
became bishop of Leicester.

'We were told at the outset that the course would be extremely
demanding and take up every moment of our waking lives', Norris
recalled, but they were not told what they were being trained to do.
Unlike the airmen, normal naval discipline was set aside for the duration
of the course, but they all found the going tough, as Norris explained:

> During our first fortnight we studied phonetics, listening and re-listen-
> ing to Japanese speech as it had been recorded on specially produced
> gramophone discs; anonymous, obviously foreign tight-lipped voices
> could be heard rattling off strings of incomprehensible syllables which
> apparently meant terse announcements like 'Attention! Enemy cruiser
> bearing 256 degrees!', or 'Three hostile aircraft!' There was nothing
> remotely relaxed or personal about any of the language we heard: we
> did not pick up any hints about how to make elegant love under the
> cherry blossom.

For these introductory lessons, they were under the charge of what
Norris called a 'severe spinster': Hester Marjorie Lambert knew no
more Japanese than the other phoneticians at SOAS, but she was an
expert in her field and wrote books on several Indian languages. Once
she had finished training them to distinguish the sounds of Japanese,
they started on the written language under Rideout. After completing
the course, they were told to report to an obscure village north of
London called Bletchley, and thus they found themselves thrown into
the world of decryption and intelligence and translating messages in
the Imperial Japanese Navy codes JN25 and JN40.[30]

Security was such an important consideration for this course that,
with the agreement of the director of SOAS, a 'barred zone' was created on the third floor of the SOAS building with guards on duty to
ensure that no unauthorized persons entered the zone. This was
because of anxiety that the presence of code books and other captured
materials might leak out and undermine intelligence operations.
Service personnel could only study such secret documents in the barred
zone, far from inquisitive eyes. What is more, the teachers allowed

access to the zone were strictly limited to Firth and the other SOAS phoneticians teaching the course. To all other SOAS teachers and students, the zone was out of bounds.[31]

Firth was deeply involved in both the planning and execution of Japanese courses from the beginning. In an address he gave to the annual meeting of the Modern Language Association in 1945, just before the end of the war, he explained how he became involved:

> Some months before Pearl Harbour, I attended a conference on the training of linguists which had to face the problem of producing a certain number of interpreters. ... I was not at all surprised to hear our oriental scholars say that it would take an Englishman from five to seven years to learn Japanese. ... I had some difficulty in bracing myself for a further conference *after* Pearl Harbour. In face of a universe of exotic culture, and sentence of from five to seven years' hard labour, a drastic review of the language-learning business had to be made, not by balancing circumstances, tradition, and educational theory, but under the whip of a whirlwind war.

The two conferences that he refers to were probably meetings of the Committee of Linguists, which advised the Ministry of Labour and National Service, but no records of these or other meetings seem to have survived. Hartog chaired this committee, and as we have seen, he had been well aware of the likely language deficit if Britain found itself at war with Japan. It is clear, therefore, that some official consideration was being given to this issue before the outbreak of war, but it is frustrating that no further details are available.[32]

Firth understood right away that the best results would be achieved by intensive courses in which only war-related vocabulary would be taught: 'The progressive nipponification of the young service man [and woman!] is a systematic process in which he is not encouraged to saunter through the groves browsing and picking up tasty little bits of culture. He is put through an intensive course of discipline in every sense of the word.' Firth ran innumerable Japanese phonetics courses throughout the war based on these principles, and the work his students did after leaving SOAS is proof of his effectiveness as a teacher of a language he did not himself know.[33]

One of the courses run at SOAS was mainly for women in the Women's Auxiliary Air Force (WAAF). They were taught the combined course covering both phonetics and the written language, and they referred to themselves as the 'Jappy WAAF'. The best of the class was Denise Gifford-Hull (later Moller): like some of the others, she had already been working in the Air Section at Bletchley Park and returned there after the course. Bletchley Park was now, it is evident, not only sourcing linguists from the Bedford School but also turning to SOAS, for at no point did they ever feel they had enough Japanese linguists. Another in the class was Eileen Clark (later Barker, 1918–2013), who had joined the WAAF early in 1943 and wrote down her recollections after the war:

> In 1943 after completing a meteorological course I was due to be sent to Scotland to a posting but just before going, I fell ill with diphtheria and so missed the posting. When I was in hospital my mother met an old friend of mine who was a WAAF Admin Officer who told her that there was a course in Japanese for graduates at the SOAS in London. I had a Classics degree from University College London and was very interested. After I had recovered, I applied and following two interviews in London I was accepted for the course. There were seven of us WAAFs and some Naval and Army personnel. The course was very intensive and we had tests every two weeks when we had to get 75% correct. Failure meant that we would have to leave the course. On completion of the course we were sent to BP, although we had been told that our destination was probably the Far East. Our 'Jappy Waaf' group were billeted in BP in hut 133. ... We enjoyed concerts in the big house and I particularly remember the opera *Dido and Aeneas* being performed. We seven formed a very close friendship and had many happy reunions subsequently.

Eileen Barker worked for the rest of the war in the Air Section, at first compiling a dictionary of Japanese Air Force terms and then translating messages relating to Japanese air forces. She and Arthur Cooper compiled a guide to the use of Chinese characters in military Japanese, *Characters in Service Japanese*, and when she got married she was given a congratulations card in Japanese signed by Cooper and two of the women Bedford graduates working in the Military Wing at Bletchley Park.[34]

The wartime courses continued up to 1946, and one of the last entrants was Leslie Phillips (1927–), who began his Army life in January 1945, when he was seventeen. He had already been accepted for a course at SOAS, but first he had to endure six weeks in the General Service Corps in Glasgow undergoing basic training. His memoirs show that life for new recruits was tough—for all the restrictions, life as a service student at SOAS was much easier:

> It was diabolically cold [in Glasgow], and impossible to wash our greasy mess tins in the outdoor (near-frozen) water troughs. There was no warm water for washing/shaving for the first 2/3 weeks, and showering was out of the question. Time was spent with drill, kit inspection, kit inspection, drill, and so on, weather permitting.

After basic training, he went on a four-month course with the Intelligence Corps for officer training, and only in June 1945 did he begin his course at SOAS, commuting from Nissen huts erected in Finsbury Park. Most of the initial teaching was done by Otome Daniels. He described her as 'apparently subservient, softly and gently spoken', but 'a better tutor would have been hard to find'. After eighteen months, at the end of 1946, he and his fellow students were shipped out to Japan via Singapore to take part in the British Commonwealth Occupation of Japan.[35]

The SOAS graduates

The Bedford School trained altogether around 220 men and women during the war, so what was the contribution of SOAS? Did it make a difference to the language deficit? Owing to the loss of the wartime SOAS records, it is not easy to put a figure on the numbers of men and women who were trained there in Japanese during the war. Putting together surviving statistics and lists of names, it can safely be said that at least 500 underwent some kind of training in Japanese at SOAS, either in the Far East Department or the Phonetics Department. The true number may well be higher. What is more, while Tuck kept careful records of where his students served after leaving Bedford, no such records survive for the SOAS students. I have managed to track some of them down, and we will encounter them in later chapters. But they amount to fewer than 100. Most of the rest probably ended up in India or Australia, but since there are no surviving personnel records of the WEC in Delhi or the Central Bureau in Brisbane, we shall probably never know where they served during the war or what their roles were.[36]

Sometimes, by sheer chance, a name in a list comes to life. That is the case with AC2 (Aircraftman 2nd class) G. Aspden, who came top of his Japanese phonetics class at SOAS in 1944. I knew no more than that until, in March 2020, I managed to get in touch with the son of another wartime RAF translator. He passed on to me a memoir that he had received from a friend of his father's. This turned out to have been written by George Aspden, whose experiences in the Air Ministry barracks I have already mentioned. Thanks to the memoir, we can now follow his later movements. From SOAS, he went to RAF Chicksands, an intercept station near Bedford, where he was trained in the procedures for turning Japanese Morse intercepts into normal Japanese ready for decryption and translation. His reward for completing this course was promotion to sergeant. He then spent a short time at Bletchley Park, where he and his colleagues did practice translations under the supervision of both Arthur and Josh Cooper, and then, a week before Christmas 1944, he flew out to Brisbane. There he worked at Central Bureau, the Australian equivalent of Bletchley Park, doing translations of Japanese Army messages that had already been decrypted. Finally, after the end of the war in Europe, he and many others from Central Bureau were transferred to San Miguel outside Manila in the Philippines, where they lived in tents and continued with their translations of Japanese decrypts until the war ended. He was not the only one from SOAS to follow this kind of trajectory, and he names some of the others who were with him. We will come back to him in later chapters, for he provides many fascinating details in his memoir.[37]

Aspden was one of the many success stories: he passed his course at SOAS and spent the rest of the war making a contribution to the war effort as a translator. What about the failures? According to Frank Daniels, a total of fifty-one students did not complete their courses in the Far East Department. Two were killed in German bombing raids on London and sixteen withdrew for reasons of ill health, but as many as thirty-three were 'rejected as unlikely to reach a satisfactory standard'. That is nearly 10 per cent of those who began courses in the Far East Department, which is a much higher failure rate than the Bedford School. That may be some indication of the rigorous standards that SOAS maintained on these wartime courses, but the Bletchley Park view was different. There, they considered that the SOAS students were less intellectually able than the Bedford students, were older and had spent some time in circumstances where, as they rather snobbishly put it, 'a lower premium is put on intellectual activities', and consequently were more likely to fail. Whatever the truth, lives depended on translators producing accurate translations and on interpreters understanding what prisoners of war told them, and there is no indication that the SOAS graduates were any less capable in the field than those trained at Bedford. In some cases, as we will see, they were considerably more capable.[38]

* * *

The credit for the wartime Japanese courses at SOAS belongs to Frank Daniels and Firth, but the efficient administration of all the wartime language courses in the Far East Department at SOAS was due to Professor Evangeline (Eve) Edwards (1888–1957), who worked tirelessly throughout the war to keep the courses running smoothly. She had gone out to China as a missionary in 1913 and had learnt Chinese there before returning to Britain in 1919. In 1931, she completed a doctorate in Chinese literature at SOAS and in 1939 was appointed professor of Chinese and head of the Department of the Far East, a rather uncommon position for a woman in British universities before the war. During the war, she oversaw a huge expansion of staff and students and, as the director put it at her memorial service in 1957, she had 'a strong, practical grasp of affairs' and 'was magnificently successful in organizing war-time courses for young men [and women!] from the Services, always winning their respect and affection and opening to them new worlds, new opportunities'.[39]

Is it possible now to make any assessment of how good the SOAS courses actually were? It seems that, in the opinion of their superior officers, the Army men who learnt their Japanese at SOAS and then worked in India were 'exceedingly good', even in the case of those who had not done particularly well at SOAS. At Bletchley Park, it was considered that one of the strong points of the teaching at SOAS was the focus on technical and military language, and it helped having a number of people in uniform among the teachers. By contrast, as R. T. Barrett at Bletchley Park pointed out, the staff who taught at the US Navy Language School in Colorado were all civilians. Barrett went on:

> Two ex-students of the School of Oriental and African Studies posted to Washington were of [the] opinion that the U.S. schools failed to get commensurate results from their intensive cramming. It was a test of endurance rather than intelligence and the weekly examinations defeated their own ends. Their best men were those who knew the language before the war.

That was the view of Bletchley Park at the end of the war. As we will see later, many of those trained in the United States also did more than was expected of them once they were in action, including a group of Royal Navy officers who were sent out to be trained in Colorado. After all, the courses run in the United States, Australia and Britain were all necessarily of limited duration, and the graduates found that when they were in the field they had much more to learn.[40]

After finishing your course at SOAS, where were you likely to be sent? If you had done one of the courses for interpreters or translators, you could only be of use where prisoners were being captured and documents found. That meant that you were likely to be sent out to India in the first instance to take part in the Burma Campaign. Some SOAS wartime graduates were sent to Bletchley Park, it is true, but most went overseas, to India, Australia and Ceylon, and a small number served in shipborne units, as we will see. In a few cases, however, their skills were not put to good use. According to Professor Turner of SOAS, 'Some were employed on duties in which their knowledge of Japanese was not used, and others were held in this country and also allowed to get rusty.' This was particularly true of Army and RAF graduates, while the Navy, he pointed out, made better use of them. This was probably because linguists in the Navy were invariably commissioned as RNVR officers after completing the course, and the Navy therefore sought to make good use of its investment in linguistic talent. Corporal Radcliffe, who had been recruited from Liverpool University, was one of those who felt that his training was being wasted. After completing an SOAS course, he and two others were sent to Belgium to work for MI6. It was only when he questioned the suitability of this posting that he was ordered back to Britain and commissioned. By the time he got to Singapore, the war was over, but he was put to work there investigating war crimes and interrogating Japanese intelligence officers.[41]

Once the war was over, SOAS gradually returned to its peacetime role, and the partitions used to create the 'barred zone' were removed. The decrypts and the other secret material used in teaching were either returned to Bletchley Park or destroyed, and the gramophone records were handed over to Arthur Cooper at Bletchley Park. The wartime records of the Far East and Phonetics Departments have unfortunately long since been thrown away, but we will encounter some of the graduates in later chapters, thanks to their memoirs and other sources.[42]

Finally, what happened to de Moubray and his parents, whose story I told at the beginning of this chapter? Once the war had ended, Guy asked to be part of the group that went to liberate Singapore from the Japanese occupying forces. Landing on 5 September 1945 as a lieutenant interpreter attached to a battalion of the 5th Indian Division, he was the first British soldier to go ashore in Singapore. Two days later, he met his parents again for the first time in six years, and their encounter featured in a local newspaper.[43]

4

HMS *PEMBROKE V*, ALIAS STATION X,
ALIAS BLETCHLEY PARK

In March 1938, Hitler moved his armies across the border and annexed Austria, the first step in his campaign to create what he called the 'Greater Germanic Reich of the German Nation'. Two months later, Admiral Sir Hugh Sinclair (1873–1939), the head of the Secret Intelligence Service (MI6) bought a large English country house, apparently with his own money. The house, which was conveniently close to a railway station, was called Bletchley Park. This purchase made it possible for GC&CS to move out of London in August 1939 into a more secure setting. At first, the main house was all there was, and the proliferating huts and the thousands of people working in them lay in the future. So did its aliases—one of the codenames for Bletchley Park was Station X, while naval personnel who got a posting to HMS *Pembroke V* later in the war were sometimes disappointed to discover that it was not a ship but a country house in Bletchley.

One of the original members of the small group that started working in the main house in the summer of 1939 was Elizabeth Anderson (1906–93, later Ramsay). After taking a degree in classics at Bedford College, London, she taught for a few years in a school in South London but did not take to teaching. Her cousin 'Madge' was already working for the Foreign Office and may well really have been working for MI6, for in 1939 she married Frederick Winterbotham, an RAF officer who definitely was working for MI6. At any rate, Madge came to the rescue and recommended her for a job. In this way, Elizabeth joined the Foreign Office in 1935 and quickly became involved in secret intelligence work. She was breaking codes and translating from Italian under the supervision of Tiltman, who, as we know from chapter 2, had something of a weakness for classicists.[1]

In 1939, Anderson's section was one of the first to move to Bletchley Park. She worked in the main house under Josh Cooper, Arthur Cooper's brother, who had become head of the Air Section at GC&CS in 1936. As more and more staff arrived and priority shifted to German signals, she was moved out to Hut 5 and then Hut 10, still decoding and translating Italian signals. Following the Armistice of 3 September 1943 that led to the Italian surrender, all the personnel working on Italian codes suddenly became surplus to requirements, but for security reasons they could not be released from service at Bletchley Park. We will learn what happened to Anderson's colleagues later. Unusually, perhaps because she was a classicist, she was asked to go to the Bedford Japanese School where she joined the fourth course under Captain Tuck. After that, again unusually, she did not return to Bletchley Park. Instead, with years of cryptographic experience behind her and with knowledge of Japanese to boot, she spent a short while in the Government Communications Bureau in Berkeley Street (a GC&CS outpost for diplomatic and commercial communications) and was then sent out to Mauritius to work on Japanese signals. There, as we will see in the next chapter, she had valuable contributions to make as a teacher of Japanese.

In this chapter, I will be approaching Bletchley Park from an unfamiliar angle. My focus will not be on the Enigma machine or even the Japanese 'Purple' machine, and codebreaking will barely be mentioned. Instead, we will explore the linguistic side of the wartime work at Bletchley Park and discover how those dealing with Japanese decrypts solved their language problems.

Keeping the secret

Security was tight at Bletchley Park. And what went on there remained a closely guarded secret long after the war. There were several probable reasons for that. One was the desire not to undermine the military defeat of the Axis powers by drawing attention to the role played by the interception and decryption of Axis signals during the war. Another was related to the Cold War: after all, Britain, Australia and the United States had (for the most part) shared intelligence with each other, but little of that intelligence had been passed on to the Soviet Union, their supposed ally. And a third reason was to avoid drawing attention to the successes of Allied codebreakers and so alerting other countries, China and the Soviet Union in particular, to the danger that their signals might be vulnerable.

As a result, up to the early 1970s, there was not a whisper in public about the wartime codebreaking at Bletchley Park. Then Sir John Cecil Masterman (1891–1977), who had had a senior role in intelligence operations during the war and later became vice-chancellor of Oxford University, wrote a book on his experiences entitled *The Double Cross System in the War of 1939–45* (1972). In the pre-publication version, he made some references to Ultra, the codename for intelligence derived from intercepted and decrypted messages, but these passages were suppressed and removed from the text before it was published in 1972. In 1974, however, Group-Captain Winterbotham, who had been responsible for distributing Ultra intelligence during the war, was evidently permitted to publish *The Ultra Secret*, which finally laid bare the secrets. Four years later, in 1978, the foreign secretary, Dr David Owen, eased the restrictions and issued a statement to the effect that Bletchley Park veterans could now reveal what they had done during the war without fear of prosecution. By then, of course, it was too late for some to tell their families.[2]

There were obviously good reasons for keeping the security tight, but nevertheless there were some serious security breaches during the war. In 1942, for example, there were two serious cases of information leakage. In one, a nineteen-year-old mathematician at Bletchley Park foolishly told his former tutor and other dons in his college common room what was going on there. The director of public prosecutions was in favour of prosecuting him under the Official Secrets Act, but the director-general of GC&CS considered that prosecution would make things worse, for even if the trial were held in camera a lot of people would get to know what was going on at Bletchley Park.

However, all those who had been present in the common room on that day were discreetly interviewed in their homes and presumably intimidated and sworn to silence.[3]

The potential for security breaches was ever present. Vast quantities of paper were being processed every day, and some pieces escaped the net. You might use the back of a secret document you had finished with to write down a telephone number. That was not a problem, but what if you took it outside Bletchley Park and accidentally left it in a telephone kiosk? Again, reusing envelopes in wartime was a natural economy, but what if you forgot that you had left some of the original, secret, contents inside? These are not hypothetical cases: they actually happened. For these reasons, security was constantly monitored, and anything out of the ordinary prompted anxious enquiries.[4]

It goes without saying that people coming in and out of Bletchley Park were closely monitored, too. One day in August 1943, a certain C. J. Morris came to Bletchley Park to give a lecture. While there, Morris asked if Bletchley Park staff could supply by telephone the correct Japanese equivalents of various English terms that cropped up in the news. The reason, he explained, was that neither Mrs Aiko Clarke, who read the BBC radio news in Japanese, nor Mr Frank Hawley of SOAS who translated the news into Japanese, were familiar with military terminology in Japanese. This prompted an alarmed response from somebody responsible for security: 'Who gave leave for Mr Morris to come? Did he enter the Park? To whom did he think he was lecturing? What was he told? ... I don't like it a bit and will decide when I know more of Morris.' The response was reassuring: 'He is Director of [the] Japanese Section of Overseas Broadcasting. He was told nothing, except that he would be lecturing to some people about to take a course in Japanese.'[5]

There was, after all, no security breach in this case. All the same, the visit of Morris throws light on some aspects of what was going on at Bletchley Park that have so far been hidden in the shadows. Brilliant though much of the cryptographic analysis undoubtedly was, it was accurate translation that produced the intelligence coming out of the decrypts, and that is where the linguists, working behind the scenes, made their contributions. It may be hard to believe, but even translators working with European languages in Bletchley Park had difficulty getting access to the technical dictionaries and reference material that they needed to produce reliable translations. Although there was no shortage of linguists who knew French, German or Italian in Britain in 1939, relatively few had knowledge of the military or technical vocabulary that they needed to translate decrypted messages. For example, when some translators who were working on decrypts of Spanish naval messages asked the Admiralty for a Spanish naval manual, the Admiralty, not understanding the needs of translators, bridled, 'Are you suggesting that the Spanish Navy has anything to teach us in seamanship and gunnery?'[6] In the case of Japanese, there were never enough translators, and even the graduates of the Bedford Japanese School had only limited knowledge of the requisite military and technical vocabulary. So Japanese-language training remained a concern of Bletchley Park throughout the war. The decrypts produced by the codebreakers needed to be translated accurately, but that was no easy task. One can be forgiven for wondering why exactly they were so difficult to translate, so an explanation is in order.

Handling Japanese decrypts

Japanese diplomatic messages, including those sent by the military and naval attachés who worked alongside the diplomatic staff at Japanese embassies, posed extraordinary difficulties. This was because, when decrypted, they consisted simply of Japanese sentences written out in Roman letters. Let us take a simple example:

> *Shookankonpan kichoosu kokoni atuku zaioochuuno gokonjooshasi setuni gokenshoo inorusakakibara.*

This was a diplomatic message sent in December 1942 by a Japanese diplomat in Sofia, Bulgaria, to a colleague in Budapest. Before being sent, it was encrypted using the machine cypher used for communications between Japanese diplomatic missions overseas and the Japanese Foreign Ministry in Tokyo. When decrypted, it simply consisted of a string of Roman letters, so word breaks had to be inserted to make sense of it. This particular decrypt, with a few (but inadequate) word breaks but without any punctuation, was used as part of a test given to the eighth class at the Bedford Japanese School. One of the students,

Field, translated this as follows: 'I am just returning home. I hereby warmly thank you for your kindness to me (while I have been) in Europe. I earnestly hope you are (will be) well. *Sakakibara.*' The words in parenthesis were added in red ink by his teacher at Bedford but, after less than six months' study, he got it more or less right. This was no mean achievement, for the text he was given to translate contains several words that are not in any dictionary and others that have several completely different meanings depending on the Chinese characters they are written with.[7]

To appreciate Field's achievement, first I shall give the test sentence as it would appear in Japanese and then how it would nowadays be transcribed in Roman letters, with punctuation.

小官今般帰朝す。ここに篤く在欧中のご懇情謝し切にご健勝祈る。榊原

Shōkan konpan kichō su. Koko ni atsuku zaiōchū no gokonjō shashi, setsuni gokenshō inoru. Sakakibara.

To begin with the very first word, there are many words pronounced 'shōkan' in Japanese, but Field correctly deduced that this was the humble word for 'I' used by government officials. He recognized that the last word 'inorusakakibara' should be separated into two words, the first, 'inoru', meaning 'pray for', 'hope for', and the second, Sakakibara, being a surname. He was unfazed by the omission of some grammatical particles that were left out to reduce the number of letters in the message and he coped with 'gokonjooshasi', which consists of the word 'konjō' with the honorific prefix 'go-', thus meaning 'your kindness', and the verb 'shasu' in its suspensive form 'shashi', meaning 'I thank you and [earnestly hope]'.

It will, I hope, be obvious even to readers who know no Japanese that to have made sense of this simple diplomatic message—to say nothing of the far more complicated ones that were included in the test—was a remarkable feat. It reveals not only Field's own familiarity with the language of such messages but also the effectiveness of the highly concentrated courses that Captain Tuck had devised in great haste. This particular message was of no diplomatic or military significance, and that is why it was released by Bletchley Park to the Bedford School for training purposes. But many messages turned out to be of great importance, and people's lives depended on the translations being accurate.

Japanese diplomatic messages were generally sent encrypted in Roman letters, but many military and naval messages were sent using Japanese Morse, and they posed difficulties of a different kind. As explained in chapter 1, Japanese Morse represents Japanese syllables and therefore consists of more than seventy different symbols, far more than are used in International Morse. Intercept operators were trained in receiving and recording International Morse, so one way of dealing with the problem was having them simply write down what they heard as if it were International Morse, leaving it to somebody else to work out what this meant in Japanese Morse and then to write down the Japanese in *katakana*, one of the Japanese syllabaries. This was not ideal, but it worked. This was what Aspden learnt to do at RAF Chicksands after finishing his course at SOAS and before being sent to Australia. There were, however, alternative solutions.

In 1924, Captain Laurance Frye Safford (1893–1973), a US Navy officer and cryptographer, devised a way of adapting a typewriter so as to type in the Japanese *katakana* syllabary, and he arranged for the American Underwood Typewriter Company to produce what eventually became known as model RIP-5. These came into production in 1929. The keyboard remained in the familiar QWERTY arrangement, but when you depressed the keys what was printed on the paper was *katakana*, so operators had to learn which key to press to produce the desired *katakana* syllable. When a key was pressed without using the shift, as for producing lower-case letters on a normal typewriter, it produced the *katakana* letter that had the same sequence of dots and dashes in Japanese Morse as the QWERTY letter had in International Morse. For example, the sequence _._. (dash-dot-dash-dot) represents both C in International Morse and the syllable *ni* in Japanese Morse, so by pressing the C key you printed *ni* in *katakana* on the paper. When the keys were pressed using the shift, the various *katakana* syllables that did not have direct equivalents in International Morse were printed.[8]

When the Underwood *katakana* typewriters first reached Bletchley Park, a decision was taken to continue with current practice, so the intercept operators would continue to work with paper and pencil, recording what they heard as if it were International Morse. Their written records were then sent to transposers, whose job it was to use the Underwood typewriter to convert what the operators had written down into encrypted Japanese written in *katakana*. The committee responsible for this decision considered that the keyboard design could be improved and recommended that a British typewriter manufacturer be approached with a view to producing an improved version. As a result, the Imperial Typewriter Company began producing *katakana* typewriters in 1943 with a different layout. Another recommendation was that the General Post Office be asked to see if Japanese *katakana* teleprinters could be produced for transmitting intercepted messages in Japanese Morse from interception stations to Bletchley Park: this, it was thought, would eliminate the errors that inevitably occurred when transposing messages from *katakana* to alphabet and vice versa, but nothing seems to have come of this suggestion.[9]

Learning to use the Underwood or Imperial *katakana* typewriters was not easy, even for those who were already familiar with the QWERTY keyboard. It required a fortnight of intensive training before intercept operators could take Japanese Morse down from headphones. Since operating the typewriter required two hands, it was impossible for the operator to make minor adjustments by hand to the frequency of the signal on their receiver, but this was a shortcoming they had to live with. Those who underwent the first course of training were then sent out to Singapore or sent to the RAF intercept station at Flowerdown in Hampshire, where Cecilia Juliet MccGwire (1923–2018) and seven other Wrens worked with *katakana* typewriters, typing out in *katakana* what the Navy men took down by hand.[10]

Captain Tuck's students go to Bletchley Park

In June 1942, Colonel Tiltman set up a new section under the Military Wing at Bletchley Park devoted to the encrypted dispatches of military attachés at Japanese embassies. It was no coincidence that the first course at the Bedford Japanese School had just finished, for several of the graduates immediately joined the Japanese Military Attaché Section. Among them was Christopher Wiles (1919–2014), who eventually became the chief translator in the section, and his younger brother, Maurice (1923–2005).

In 1943, Maurice Wiles moved on to join a small group whose job it was to handle messages encrypted in the Japanese Army Air Force

General Purpose Code. These messages related to the flying branch of the Imperial Japanese Army: Japan did not have a separate air force like the RAF or the Luftwaffe, so both the Japanese Army and Navy had their own air forces. The General Purpose Code was based on a code book, in which a word was assigned to each four-figure group of numerals. Later in the war, a copy of the code book that had been buried by a Japanese officer was found and this revealed what word each four-figure group stood for, but by that time Wiles and his colleagues had already worked out what most of them stood for. His colleagues included several other Bedford graduates, but also Elsie Hart, a sergeant in the Auxiliary Territorial Service (ATS) who had not been on any of the courses but, as she recalled, 'gradually I picked up what I needed to know'. As Wiles explained: 'The key figure was Elsie Hart, whose combination of high intelligence, dedication to the task, and unfailing good humour, made "Elsie's index" the hub around which the activity of the section as a whole revolved.' It was her job to create an index of all the code-groups and the words they denoted so that it became a reference dictionary for all of them.[11]

The leader of the group was Alexis Vlasto (1915–2000), a remarkable and brilliant man who had been born in England to a family of Greek shipping agents. He had an elite education at Eton and then King's College, Cambridge, and in 1939 he was recruited for Bletchley Park. In late 1942 or early 1943, he was sent on one of the Japanese courses for RAF personnel at SOAS, but, most unusually, he was withdrawn from the course early and returned to GC&CS. Professor Thomas Boase (1898–1974), an art historian at Oxford who had been recruited to Bletchley Park in 1939, wrote to SOAS to thank them for their teaching and explained that, since Vlasto had evidently 'acquired a remarkable knowledge of one sort of Japanese in the course of his time' there, he was needed immediately. His cryptographic and linguistic talents must have been extraordinary, for on returning to Bletchley Park he was put in charge of this group. According to Maurice Wiles, he 'presided over the operation with quiet humour and with unfailing grace and wisdom', but after the war he never wrote or spoke about his wartime experiences.[12]

Another section that absorbed some of Captain Tuck's students was the Japanese Military Intelligence Section. This is one of the few parts

of the Bletchley Park operation for which a complete staff list has survived, from the head, Charles Parkin (1910–84), down to the typists,
who were mostly in the ATS. The linguists included William Skillend,
who was later to become professor of Korean at SOAS, several other
Bedford graduates, and Daphne Seamark (later Allan; c1920–2015),
who subsequently became the librarian at the Tavistock Clinic. She
joined Bletchley Park in 1942 straight from school, having excelled at
French and German. Since she was later decrypting and translating
Japanese signals, she must have done one of the courses at SOAS or in
the Naval Section.[13]

The Naval Section

The Military Wing at Bletchley Park mostly concerned itself with
German and Italian codes, and the only Japanese codes it dealt with
were those used by military attachés and the Army Air Force. Most of
the work done on Japanese Army codes was done in Delhi, for the
messages could be picked up and intercepted more easily in India, and
that is why so many Bedford graduates were sent out there.

By contrast, the Naval Section at GC&CS, which had been founded
in 1924, had long been dealing with various Japanese codes.
Furthermore, it was well served with linguists even before the outbreak of war with Japan, most notably by Nave and his former room-
mate in Japan, Shaw. In early 1941, there were two of them working
in the Naval Section at any one time, with another six serving at FECB
in Singapore. But the Naval Section had an insatiable demand for linguists and eventually devised its own solution to the problem.

After the outbreak of war with Japan, more and more Japanese
linguists were recruited, at first relying upon the small pool of people
who already had some knowledge of the language. In October 1942,
Lieutenant-Commander James Penton McIntyre (1906–2003) joined
the Naval Section as chief linguist: he had gone out to Japan in 1933 as
a language officer and after three years had acquired a good knowledge
of the language and qualified as an interpreter. Under him in 1942
were eight Japanese linguists: six of them were graduates of the first
course at the Bedford Japanese School, and the other two were Major
H. E. Martin, who had for three years been the superintendent of the

HMS *PEMBROKE V*, ALIAS BLETCHLEY PARK

Blue Funnel shipping company in Japan and had been recruited by Tiltman himself, and Lieutenant-Commander Philip Leslie Nicol (1905–87), an ex-naval engineer officer who had qualified as a first-class interpreter in Japanese. Nicol had not been a language officer in Japan, so how he acquired his knowledge of the language is a mystery. By the end of 1942, the numbers of linguists had risen again: the Foreign Office lent the Naval Section three young consuls who had been student-interpreters in Japan, Ronald Watts (1914–93), Henry Norman Brain (1907–2002) and John Owen Lloyd, and in addition Commander Arthur Richard 'Dick' Thatcher (1898–1967), another former language officer, also joined; some of them we will encounter again later. So far, then, the needs for linguists were satisfactorily met by recruiting people who had already acquired a good knowledge of Japanese before the war through training in Japan, either as consular officers or as Royal Navy language officers.[14]

In the summer of 1942, the first batch of graduates from Bedford arrived, but the Naval Section had to compete with the Military and Diplomatic Sections of Bletchley Park as well as with Delhi, Colombo, Kilindini and Mauritius for the graduates of the Bedford School, and the demand was greater than the supply. Once the SOAS courses were up and running, the Naval Section began to recruit from that source as well. Special courses were run for ratings and junior officers, as we saw in the previous chapter. Most of them were recruited to the Naval Section and remained there until the end of the war, but eight were sent out to HMS *Anderson*, the Royal Navy's cryptography centre in Colombo.[15]

There was also one woman recruited from SOAS, Carmen Blacker (1924–2009). She had started learning Japanese out of personal interest well before 1941, but in 1942 she started studying Japanese formally at SOAS. In 1943, she joined the Naval Section at Bletchley Park, where her task was to make a vocabulary of Japanese words from captured documents. She found this work singularly unappealing and felt that she had been left with the unimportant work. Nora Malvin (1922–2016, later Nora MacLaren), one of the Bedford graduates, had a similar experience: she was required to make a gazetteer of place-names in the Pacific Ocean area and found the work not only 'unbelievably boring' but a waste of her training. At her request, she was eventually transferred to a group doing translations of older messages and

81

some decryption; she left Bletchley Park at the end of 1944 when she discovered, shortly after her marriage to a fellow Bedford graduate, that she was pregnant. That was one of the few legitimate ways of getting out of Bletchley Park and returning to normal life. Blacker, on the other hand, was most unusually permitted to leave Bletchley Park and move back to SOAS as a teacher on some of the wartime courses. Needless to say, she was still bound by the Official Secrets Act.[16]

Unappealing the work may have been, and it is certainly possible that Blacker and Malvin were given uninteresting tasks simply because they were women, but indexing was in fact important, and Blacker's knowledge was sorely needed, as one of the official historians pointed out in 1945:

> If the Japanese Index staff had consisted of a team of fluent Japanese linguists working on the original Japanese text, it is probable that the system could have been applied equally successfully [as the German] to the Japanese Index. This, however, was by no means the case. The linguistic knowledge of the girls originally allocated to the task of marking the translated Japanese text [i.e., picking out the words that needed to be indexed] was confined to English and did not even include an adequate knowledge of English naval terminology. The results were disastrously inaccurate.

The index, consisting of Japanese words found in messages with their English translations, was needed to standardize the translation of Japanese technical terms. But since the indexing staff did not know any Japanese, they could not pick out the important words and had no idea how they should be translated. As a result, translations varied widely and lacked consistency.[17]

Another veteran of the SOAS courses and the Naval Section was Peter Laslett (1915–2001), who graduated from Cambridge in 1938. He joined the Fleet Air Arm in 1940 but in 1942 was sent to learn Japanese: 'They ... told us that if we couldn't read Japanese within a year we would be sent back to our ships. I had been on the Murmansk route, which was extremely dangerous, so I learned Japanese under sentence of being drowned.' He passed the course and was then sent to the Naval Section at Bletchley Park in 1943. This meant that he did not have to return to the Arctic convoys that were taking essential supplies for the Soviet Union to Murmansk.[18]

Although graduates from the courses at the Bedford School and SOAS continued to pour in, the demand was so great that the section decided in 1943 to start running its own courses in Bletchley Park itself rather than having to rely on Bedford and SOAS. These courses would have the obvious advantage of being able to concentrate exclusively on naval vocabulary, unlike the generic vocabulary of the Bedford graduates. Another consideration was the imminent Italian surrender, which freed up its Italian cryptographers for other work. The Naval Section therefore ran a series of four 'long' courses lasting six months each. The object, in their words, was 'to produce, in the shortest possible time, men and women who would have a sufficient knowledge of written Japanese navalese to enable them to cope with the linguistics of cryptography, bookbuilding [i.e., building up an index of terms] and translation'.[19]

In August 1943, before the first of the courses began, a series of lectures were provided for the chosen students, many of whom had been working on Italian cryptography and knew nothing about Japan. What they needed was a condensed introduction to the recent history of Japan so that they could retrain themselves as Japanese cryptographers. This was why Mr C. J. Morris of the BBC turned up at Bletchley Park and alarmed the security personnel. His lecture at Bletchley Park was entitled 'Japan after Pearl Harbor', and he was one of the few Britons who could speak on this subject from personal experience. John Morris (1895–1980) had gone out to Japan in 1938 at the invitation of the Japanese government to work for the Foreign Ministry as an advisor, and while doing this job he also taught English, mostly at Keiō University, one of the leading private universities in Japan. After the outbreak of war, unlike other Britons and Americans, he was not interned, possibly because he was still technically employed by the Foreign Ministry, and he was even allowed to do some teaching. He was finally repatriated in July 1942, but by that time he had had an unrivalled opportunity to observe Japanese society in the midst of war. Apart from Morris, the other lectures included Captain Tuck on his reminiscences of Japan, Arthur Cooper on the Japanese language and Paul Grice (1913–88) on the Japanese Navy. Grice, who was later to become an eminent philosopher, joined the Royal Navy on the outbreak of war and at first served on destroyers in Atlantic convoys, but from 1940 until the end of the war he worked in naval intelligence in the Admiralty.[20]

When the language courses began, the students found that they would have access to the kinds of Japanese texts they would have to work on, for they were of course freely available in the Naval Section. This was the advantage of running the courses within Bletchley Park, for GC&CS was generally reluctant to make decrypts available for teaching purposes either to the Bedford School or to SOAS. Another reason for running courses 'in house' was the conviction in the Naval Section that only naval translators could be trusted to produce useful translations based on a complete understanding of Japanese naval vocabulary and jargon. Perhaps they were right: all those working on Italian naval codes would already have some grasp of naval vocabulary and would only need to learn the Japanese equivalents.[21]

There was no problem with finding a teacher for these courses, for there was just the right person available. John Lloyd (1914–82) had joined the Consular Service and gone to Japan in 1937 as a student interpreter; as such, his first task was to learn Japanese. He had then been appointed vice-consul in Hankow (now part of Wuhan), which had been invaded and occupied by the Japanese Army in 1938. In 1942, along with other British diplomats and citizens stranded in Japan, he was repatriated to Lourenço Marques (now Maputo in Mozambique), where they were exchanged with Japanese diplomats from Britain and the United States. He was subsequently sent to Melbourne to work at Central Bureau, General MacArthur's codebreaking organization, and then was ordered back to England by the Foreign Office to work at GC&CS, where his knowledge of Japanese could be of use.[22]

The students who took Lloyd's courses were mostly civilians working in the Naval Section, but there were also a couple of naval officers and some members of WRNS. In addition to these long courses, fourteen short courses were put on. Lloyd explained why it was worthwhile running short courses: 'It was considered at the outset of the Japanese language course scheme that a period of one month spent in learning the essentials of Japanese would be of some help to cryptographers in their approach to their cryptographic problems.' Lloyd taught the short courses too, along with a couple of those who had done one of his long courses.[23]

Lloyd was under no illusions about the difficulty of the task facing the students, who were expected to learn a lot in just one month. After one of the short courses, Lloyd wrote, in October 1943:

> I would like to commend in particular the work of Messrs. [David] Foxon, [Harry] Middleton, [Anthony] Phelps and [Hugh] Thurston, who have shown an unbounded enthusiasm for what is perhaps the most soul-destroying and unrewarding of all languages, and who put their enthusiasm to very good effect. While singling out the above 4 persons for special mention, however, I would also like to pay a tribute to the way in which all the members of the short course applied themselves to the language, the back of which they may all be said to have successfully broken.

By the time the Naval Section courses were under way, there was a much better range of textbooks available, some of them produced 'in house'. Arthur Cooper, who had escaped from Singapore with his pet gibbon Tertius, produced the basic textbook used in the courses, *The Elements of Written Japanese*, while somebody else produced an intermediate textbook, which consisted of the kinds of sentences that appeared in Japanese telegrams with added notes and grammatical explanations. Also available was the latest American textbook, *Grammar of Modern Written Japanese*, which had been published by the War Department in Washington, DC in August 1944.[24]

What was unusual about the Naval Section courses is the preponderance of women among the students. This was partly because many Wrens worked in the Naval Section once it had become clear to the males in charge that they were perfectly competent to do the work. In January 1943, there were just two WRNS officers and five ratings in the Naval Section, but by August 1945 there were 570 officers and ratings in the section. Those who were working on Italian codes needed to retrain after the Italian armistice, but many Wrens who had not worked on Italian codes were recruited to learn Japanese. It was in this way that Kitty Wyatt unexpectedly found herself learning Japanese. She had been called up in 1942, and after attending the WRNS training centre at Mill Hill for two weeks, she had hoped to be sent to sea. She was at first excited to learn that she had been posted to HMS *Pembroke V*, and then was disappointed to discover that it was not a ship and not even near the sea: it was the Navy codename for Bletchley Park. Her mother had refused to allow her to consider going to university when she finished school, so she had done a secretarial course. Predictably enough, at Bletchley Park she was employed initially for her typing skills. At some point, her talents must have been recognized, for she was sent on one of the long courses. 'This', she recalled, 'was when my interest and enthusiasm really took off.' When she finished the course, she was put to work translating captured Japanese documents, mostly naval.[25]

No records survive for those who did the short courses. Some of the women who did Japanese translation in the Naval Section learnt their Japanese initially on one of the short courses. Elizabeth Hely-Hutchinson was one of them. Through her father, Maurice Hely-Hutchinson MP, she had landed a job at the Government Communications Bureau in Berkeley Street, and then was transferred to Bletchley Park. After learning some Japanese, she was translating whatever came in—commercial, diplomatic or military messages. Sometimes she was working up to midnight, she recalled, but when not working she was out dancing. Later in the war, she was sent out to Mauritius with Anderson, whose story began this chapter.[26]

Another who entered Bletchley Park and ended up working with Japanese was Rozanne Medhurst. Her father was Air-Vice-Marshal Charles Medhurst (1896–1954), head of intelligence at the Air Ministry, so she had known about Bletchley Park before she ever set foot there. It was undoubtedly nepotism that got her and Elizabeth Hely-Hutchinson their jobs, but it was probably a better idea for family members like Rozanne Medhurst to be on the inside and constrained by the Official Secrets Act rather than possibly talking on the outside. Rozanne's father drove her down to Bletchley, and he teased her saying that she would be shot if she ever mentioned to anybody what she was doing there. She had spent some time living in Rome, and her knowledge of Italian proved useful. One night in 1941 at 1.30 a.m., she decoded a message saying that a number of Italian bombers were due to leave Tripoli in Libya for a raid on Malta at 4.00 a.m. It passed rapidly up the hierarchy at Bletchley Park and was then sent to RAF units in North Africa, with the result that all the bombers were shot down. She was much congratulated: 'It was my moment of glory in three years of slog.' She later moved to the Japanese Air Forces Section and worked on Japanese codes. Most likely, she, too, took a short course in Japanese to prepare herself.[27]

There were also men who shifted to Japanese after working on Italian codes and messages for several years. One of them must have been Edwin Pulleyblank (1922–2013), who later became professor of Chinese at the University of British Columbia. When he was still a student at the University of Toronto studying classics, one of his professors asked him if he would be interested in doing 'secret war work'. He was, and he became one of a small number of Canadians at Bletchley Park, where he became proficient in reading Japanese. Since he did not go to the Bedford School and did not do one of Lloyd's long courses, he must have started off on one of the short courses.[28]

One who certainly did learn his Japanese this way was John Chadwick (1920–98), who was perhaps the only person to put the cryptographic skills he acquired during the war to use in his scholarly work after the war. Together with Michael Ventris (1922–56), he applied his knowledge to the undeciphered Mycenaean script known as Linear B, and they made the dramatic discovery that the script was used to write a form of ancient Greek. For this, he became famous, but he also left a memoir that provides details of his wartime work.[29]

Chadwick volunteered for the Royal Navy in 1940 after completing the first year of his classics course at Oxford. At first, he served in the Mediterranean as an able seaman aboard the light cruiser HMS *Coventry*, which had a harrowing time being torpedoed by an Italian submarine and attacked by Stuka dive-bombers, but in 1942 he was sent ashore in Egypt for a mysterious interview. He was surprised to find that this was with no less a person than a Royal Navy captain who was the chief of the Intelligence Staff in the Middle East and quite at the other end of the naval hierarchy from Able Seaman Chadwick. After the interview, without any explanation, Chadwick was immediately posted to Egypt for intelligence duties and was promoted to temporary sub-lieutenant. It was assumed that, since he knew Latin, he would be able to handle Italian, and he was told that he would be trying to decipher Italian naval signals. He worked on Italian codes in Egypt until the Italian surrender and even managed to beat the Bletchley Park Naval Section to the solution of the 'Giove Delfo' Italian naval code. This feat enabled him to warn the Admiralty that the Italian Navy was trying to raise a British submarine that had been sunk near Taranto in order to obtain its codebooks.

In September 1943, when his Italian expertise was no longer needed since Italy was no longer in the war, he was given two options: do a Japanese course or remain in Egypt on general intelligence duties. Chadwick found the choice an easy one and flew back to England. As he wrote later:

> After the almost peacetime atmosphere of Alexandria, it was odd to be back in a shabby and battered London, with its black-out and severe shortages. I managed to phone my parents, who were surprised to learn that I was back in England, and even more astonished to learn I had come in an aeroplane.

Yet learning Japanese at Bletchley Park was, he found, far from being an easy option:[30]

> Once the Japanese language course began we had to work extremely hard. Studying intensively for eight hours a day is something it is almost impossible to maintain for long, and we all suffered from the strain. ... After initial stages we graduated to the use of a text-book specially chosen to teach the kind of Japanese we should need. It was a photostat reproduction of a captured document, the hand-written log-book of a destroyer squadron. In addition to the [language] problems ... this gave us the problem of coping with handwriting, and of course hastily written with a fountain pen, not carefully calligraphed with a brush.

The two who did best in the final exam were those with previous careers as students of classics, Chadwick and a student from Northern Ireland. 'In my own case', he wrote, 'the result of doing so well on the exam led to a major disappointment. I had anticipated returning to the absorbing business of cryptography; instead I found myself assigned to a group of expert translators.' This group was led by Lieutenant-Commander Nicol, the engineering officer mentioned earlier who had not been a language officer but had somehow acquired an excellent command of the language, and under him were two consuls who had served in Japan.[31]

Chadwick wrote his memoir in 1989 but was under the impression that the work he did during the war was still covered by the Official Secrets Act. Nevertheless, he gave some tantalizing details of the work he actually did as a translator.

The translations we had to handle were deciphered messages passing between the Admiralty in Tokyo and the Japanese Naval Attachés round the world. There was for instance a man in Stockholm, whose information was largely derived from British newspapers and periodicals, but all his signals had to be translated, if only to see what subjects Tokyo thought worth having reported. I did a lot of this work. But our prize pieces, and these of course were given to the more expert translators, were from the Naval Attaché in Berlin. He was given a great deal of technical information by his German Naval colleagues, which he painstakingly translated into Japanese and transmitted back to Tokyo.

According to Chadwick, many of the messages were on highly technical subjects, and the vocabulary posed enormous difficulties, because the naval attaché code used Roman letters and as a result interpretation was a nightmare:

> I well remember one of the problems which one of my Foreign Office colleagues took a lot of time and research to solve. He was translating a report from Berlin which dealt with night-vision among fighter pilots, and would have been interesting to the medical experts. Among the key terms he found the word *suikan*, which was not in any of our dictionaries. We kept notebooks for all the difficult terms we had encountered and solved, but no one had found this before. It had therefore to be tackled by trying to guess the characters. Now *sui* is a rare syllable as a reading of a character, except for a very common one which has the meaning 'water'; but there is one alternative, the geometric figure 'a cone'. *Kan*, however, is the reading of dozens of characters ('warship' and 'boiler' ... are only two). But after studying books on the anatomy of the eye, my colleague noticed that the structure of the retina consisted of what were called 'rods and cones'—and 'rod' was one of the many meanings that could be extracted from *kan*. So he concluded that *suikan* was the Japanese technical term for this structure. ...

Despite the difficulties, he and his colleagues produced a lot of valuable technical information:

> [I]n developing acoustic mines which would be detonated by the noise of ships' propellers, the Germans had to conduct lengthy experiments to determine what noise levels could be expected. They therefore laid a series of microphones on the sea-bed and recorded the sound levels as a variety of ships passed over them at different speeds. The Admiralty experts were delighted to get all this technical information on the

results of these trials. ... Even more important was a series of messages giving full details of the new class of submarines the Germans were still developing in 1945. It was the first submarine designed for high under-water speeds, and had a revolutionary kind of engine, which used liquid hydrogen peroxide as a fuel. If the war had lasted much longer, these boats would have been a severe threat. But at least knowing their capability gave us an advantage in planning to defeat them.

In October 1945, Chadwick, who was by now a full lieutenant in the RNVR, was demobbed and he went back to Corpus Christi College, Cambridge, to complete his degree in classics:

The change was summed up for me on arrival at Corpus, where the Porter instantly recognised me; I asked, in the fashion natural to an officer and gentleman, if my luggage could be sent up to my room. 'Oh no, sir,' he said, 'you'll have to do that yourself now.'

Chadwick was just one of many in the Naval Section who were forced by circumstances to switch from Italian to Japanese. It is thanks to his memoir that we can follow his career in such detail and get a glimpse of the satisfactions and frustrations of working on Japanese decrypts.

The Air Section

Bletchley Park had been investigating Luftwaffe communications since the outbreak of war, but much of the actual work was done in the intercept stations that were the first to pick up the signals. Britain was, of course, too far away from East Asia to pick up oral communications between Japanese pilots and their bases or wireless messages sent from one base to another. Any encrypted telegraphic communications intercepted in India and Ceylon that could not be decrypted on the spot were relayed to Bletchley Park, and to deal with them the Japanese Air Intelligence Section was created in October 1943. At its peak in July 1945, it had a huge staff consisting of forty civilians, twenty-four RAF officers, nine RAF other ranks, thirteen WAAF officers, thirty-eight WAAF other ranks, one British Army officer and one US Women's Army Corps officer. One of the civilians was Pamela Margaret Beryl Draughn, who was told to learn Japanese from a book: she did so for a few days and then, as she recalled, she picked it up as she went along. Her job was to monitor translated messages sent in from Colombo and to make index cards for the contents to make cross-referencing possible.[32]

Like the Naval Section, the Air Section had also identified some special needs that could not be met by generic courses like those at the Bedford School or SOAS. To meet these needs, it took the obvious step of instituting its own language courses. This is another example of a creative local response to the need for more linguists, and we will come across more of them later in this book.

The Air Section was throughout the war headed by Josh Cooper, the elder brother of Arthur, and it seems that a 'Japanese from scratch' course was run there, probably in late 1942 or early 1943—a surviving roster of the students gives the names and ranks of fifteen RAF personnel. It is possible that the course was actually run at SOAS rather than Bletchley Park itself, but no other records survive to decide the matter. In late 1944, however, Arthur Cooper was definitely teaching Japanese in the Air Section to a mixed group of full-time and part-time students. They included several RAF officers, an American sergeant and two WAAF officers. One of the WAAF officers was Diana Newcombe (1921–2009), who later served as a Conservative MP and was ennobled as Baroness Elles.[33]

Another roster gives the names and ranks of eleven RAF students studying Japanese phonetics, one of whom was Acting Pilot Officer Louis van Praag (1926–93), a prominent industrial designer after the war. No other records of these courses seem to survive, but Tiltman referred to them after the war:

> My opposite number J. E. S. Cooper, who was head of the Air Section at GCHQ [i.e., GC&CS] throughout the war, tried a rather more tricky experiment. What the Royal Air Force needed was interpreters who could read RT [radio transmission] air-to-ground and air-to-air conversations and for this purpose he started an intensive 11 weeks' course at which the students were bombarded incessantly with Japanese phonograph records ringing the changes on a very limited vocabulary. The course was directed, not by a Japanese linguist, but by a phonetics expert. I remember taking a U.S. Army Japanese interpreter, Col. Svensson, round the course. Stunned by the volume of sound in every room, Svensson mildly asked the Director whether all the students made the grade and the reply he received was: 'After the fifth week

they're either carried away screaming or they're nipponified [i.e., turned into Japanese linguists].'[34]

It is not entirely clear from Tiltman's account if these courses were run at Bletchley Park or at SOAS. However, the names in the 'Japanese phonetics' list match with those in a report sent to Bletchley Park in March 1943 by Firth at SOAS concerning the results of a course for RAF personnel. In December 1942, Firth submitted a report on the first course for RAF personnel, which included three men who had completed the first course at the Bedford Japanese School and who, according to Tuck, had been sent to SOAS to do a course on Japanese phonetics. It can only be concluded, therefore, that these courses, at least, were run in the phonetics laboratories at SOAS. As mentioned in the previous chapter, some of the gramophone records used on the course certainly contained the kinds of Japanese sentences that might have been uttered by bombing pilots on a mission.[35]

The students who completed Firth's course were not sent back to Bletchley Park but to RAF Newbold Revel, a country manor house near Rugby, to do a wireless telegraphy intelligence course. What subsequently became of most of them is unknown, but since it was only in India and Burma that it was possible to eavesdrop on Japanese pilots' conversations and thus only there that their newly acquired skills could be of use, the likelihood is that they all went to India at first, some perhaps following the Army into Burma when the Japanese Army was in retreat.[36]

Unlike the courses instituted by the Naval Section, which were designed to train people working at Bletchley Park, the courses devised by the Air Section had very different aims. They were designed to produce RAF personnel who could eavesdrop on Japanese wireless conversations, skills that were of no use at all at Bletchley Park. That kind of training could only be done at SOAS, but Bletchley Park was closely involved, probably for reasons of secrecy: if the Japanese Army Air Force in Burma became aware that RAF personnel were being trained to eavesdrop, then it might have instructed pilots to give away less information over the radio.

Reading the dispatches of Japanese diplomats and attachés

Some of the most valuable intelligence derived from Japanese signals at Bletchley Park came from close to home. It came in fact from the dispatches sent to Japan by Japanese diplomats and naval and military attachés who were based in Europe, particularly those based in Berlin. The extraction of this intelligence, it goes without saying, depended not only on superb cryptanalysis but also on accurate translation of the Japanese decrypts.

The key figure was without a doubt General Ōshima Hiroshi (1886–1975), who was for most of the Second World War the Japanese ambassador in Berlin. His father, who was also a general, had studied in Prussia and perhaps for that reason was keen for his son to learn German, a decision that was to have consequences he could not have foretold. In his childhood, Ōshima took lessons in German with a German family in Tokyo and subsequently served in Japanese embassies in Austria and Germany. Thanks to all this exposure to German, he had a remarkable command of the language, sufficient to be able to converse for hours alone with Hitler or von Ribbentrop (the foreign minister) without any interpreters present.

According to Fujiyama Naraichi (1915–94), who finished his career as Japanese ambassador to Britain (1979–82) but who joined the embassy in Berlin in 1942, Ōshima's mastery of German was such that he could give witty impromptu speeches. Also, Ōshima was so successful at gaining the confidence of the Nazis that Germans used to joke that he was number three in the Nazi hierarchy after Hitler and Deputy Führer Martin Bormann. Nonetheless, it should be noted that the Gestapo did not trust the Japanese diplomats: Japanese-speaking Gestapo officers listened in to their international telephone conversations and cut them off when, for example, they mentioned Allied air raids on Berlin. When the embassy needed to communicate by telephone with the Foreign Ministry in Tokyo, therefore, both ends employed speakers of the Kagoshima dialect of Japanese, which defeated even the Gestapo's efforts to eavesdrop since it differs markedly from standard Japanese in vocabulary and especially pronunciation.[37]

Ōshima's lengthy dispatches, often reporting in detail on his conversations with Hitler, were encrypted using the diplomatic encryption machine that was known to the Allies as 'Purple' and had been introduced in 1939. British and American cryptographers began working on it straight away, but the US Signal Intelligence Service devoted all of its efforts to solving it at the expense of all other Japanese codes. According to Foss, who had been born in Kobe and was fluent in Japanese, his team at Bletchley Park had 'got some way with it', but the

> Americans had been luckier or more clever or both and found a verbatim crib in English [i.e., hint to the right solution of a code: in this case, a document in English that was translated and then encrypted by the Japanese embassy using Purple], an American State Department document officially handed to the Japanese Ambassador in Washington … from this crib they had reconstructed the internal wiring of the machine and built some models for themselves.

All that remained was to identify the daily sequence of the plugs so as to be able to read the messages. The US Army built eight replica Purple machines, and when a small delegation from the United States visited Bletchley Park in 1941, they exchanged information about the Purple machines for information about the encryption systems used in Italy, Germany, the Soviet Union and Latin America. They reported to Washington that the 'material furnished … will result in a saving of several years of labor', so they were evidently satisfied with the exchange. By October 1941, four of the Purple machines were in Washington (two each for the Army and the Navy), three in London and one at the US base on Corregidor in the Philippines.[38]

The originals of Ōshima's dispatches sent from Berlin were either destroyed by him in the United States, where he was taken after his capture, or had already been destroyed before he left Berlin. These messages must have been received and decrypted in Tokyo, but the Japanese decrypts do not survive: they seem to have been destroyed in a convenient fire on 15 August 1945, the day of the Japanese surrender. As a result, all that survives now are the translated decrypts to be found in The National Archives in Kew and in the US National Archives in Maryland. These show that his dispatches were of incomparable value for their insights into Hitler's intentions and plans. They reveal, among many other things, the planning for Operation Barbarossa (the invasion of the Soviet Union in 1941) and Hitler's conviction that D-Day would be launched in the Pas-de-Calais rather than Normandy.[39]

Towards the end of the war, Ōshima remained convinced of Germany's ability to continue to wage war effectively. However, in a memo dated 31 August 1944, the War Office in London noted that there were doubts in Tokyo about the credibility of his dispatches:

We have ascertained through a reliable, but delicate, channel, that a Japanese Military Attaché in a neutral country told a friend the following in mid-August:

(i) The Japanese Government is very dissatisfied with its Ambassador in Berlin, General Oshima, because his appreciation of Germany's strength, both military and political, has proved incorrect.

(ii) Tokyo does not, however, wish to recall him at present, because the Germans regard him as a friend and it is felt that his recall would therefore make a bad impression in Berlin.

Perhaps he was referring to the unreliability of these dispatches when, after the war, Ōshima expressed regret for having deceived the Japanese public.[40]

On the other hand, it has been suggested by a Japanese writer that Ōshima's upbeat messages about the prospects for Germany in 1945 were sent in full knowledge that his messages were being read by the Allies. According to this argument, Ōshima was cunningly trying to dishearten the Allies by trying to demonstrate that Germany was in a stronger position than it really was.[41]

Intriguing though this suggestion is, it is in fact belied by the interviews conducted by Major-General Kubo Muneharu and other officers with Ōshima in 1959, well before the successes of Allied cryptography became common knowledge in the 1970s. In the autumn of 1941, Ōshima stated, he had received a warning from Heinrich Stahmer (1892–1978), who in 1943 was to become German ambassador to Japan. Stahmer warned Ōshima that there were signs that the Japanese diplomatic codes had been broken by the Americans. Ōshima told his interviewers that, upon investigation, it became clear that messages that were encrypted simply using the Foreign Ministry code were indeed being read. He was confident, however, that this did not apply to the messages sent from Berlin to Tokyo because he re-enciphered them after they had been encrypted using the Foreign Ministry code. These interviews took place four years after he had been released from prison on parole in 1955, when the Occupation of Japan was long over. It is difficult to suppose that at that time he would have been so bullish about the security of his messages had he not in fact been confident that his messages were not being read. Furthermore, these were private interviews conducted by military men in which he revealed other surprising information, such as that he had been unaware of the result of the Battle of Midway in 1942 until he returned to Japan after the end of the war. The likelihood is, then, that Ōshima never knew that his dispatches were being read.[42]

The more likely explanation for his upbeat despatches in 1945 lies in his credulity in the face of what Hitler and his other Nazi contacts told him. Ōshima and his wife were captured by the US 7th Army on 11 May 1945 and were held in the United States until he was repatriated to Japan in December 1945. According to the US authorities responsible for him: 'His views were so notoriously pro-Nazi and his political judgment so warped as to cause doubt in the minds of even some of the Japanese statesmen. He has remained arrogantly and fanatically fascist in his views, even since surrender.'[43] In fact, Ōshima's sympathies had already raised doubts at Bletchley Park about his reliability. However, the Japanese naval attaché in Berlin was also sending dispatches, and these proved to be a valuable counterweight.[44]

The dispatches of Japanese naval attachés at various European embassies provided valuable information about German technical and scientific developments. Most of the despatches were machine-encrypted using the JNA20 code, but this had the drawback for codebreakers and translators that the messages were in Roman letters. That was true of the Purple machine too, but the use of Roman letters was much more of a problem in the case of the dispatches sent by attachés, for many technical terms in Japanese are pronounced exactly the same and are only distinguished by the Chinese characters used to write them, as was the case with the word *suikan* that Chadwick's colleagues puzzled over. For the Allied cryptographers, unravelling the ambiguity was a serious problem. Watts, a former consul who later wrote the official history of the Naval Section, explained the value of the work later:

> The task before us was not only full of difficulty, it was also of very great importance. The Berlin–Tokyo series of telegrams contained the most important part of the traffic. The Head of the Japanese Naval Mission in Germany, Vice-Admiral Abe [Katsuo], the Attaché Rear-Admiral Kojima [Hideo], and the members of their staff in Berlin, supplied Japan after her entry into the war with extremely detailed information about the latest scientific, technical and industrial developments in Germany, which Japan then adopted as her own. Other messages

were concerned with questions of join[t] Axis strategy, the operations of blockade-runners, U-Boats proceeding to or from Far Eastern waters and German military dispositions and plans in Europe.

The JNA20 cypher was solved in April 1944, but translating the decrypts was by no means easy, for, as one of the translators declared, 'the Japanese language is in itself a most secure code'. Nevertheless, translating it was satisfying: Donald Russell (1920–2020), a Bedford graduate, wrote, 'The only period when I felt I was being really useful was in the spring of 1944, when there was a lot of good stuff from Berlin about the defences of the French coast.'[45]

A translation party was set up to concentrate on these decrypts, led by Lieutenant-Commander Nicol. He was the only one in the party with knowledge of technical vocabulary. The others included several former consuls who had worked in Japan and a few Bedford graduates. The only woman was Patricia Margaret Norman (1920–2013), who had read French and Italian at Somerville College, Oxford. On joining the Naval Section in 1942, she had at first worked on Italian messages but, after the Italian armistice, had done one of the long Japanese courses in the Naval Section. Watts commented that 'on the whole the experiment of giving classical scholars and others [like Patricia Norman] a rapid course in Japanese, and then plunging them into the difficult task of interpreting the tortuous and technical phraseology of Japanese Naval Attachés has been a great success'. Norman was one of those who followed this trajectory, and the same was probably true of nameless others in the Naval Section.[46]

The translators were, unusually, allowed to consult technical experts outside Bletchley Park in order to ensure that their translations made scientific sense in British English. As Watts pointed out, 'there are great differences between British and American terminology in technical as well as in naval and military matters'. Consequently, although the British and American sides exchanged copies of all translations, there was little other cooperation, and no attempts were made to develop a standard vocabulary.[47]

What difference did their work make? Watts provided a provisional assessment of the work they had done in his report:

the details of the defences of the Channel coast before D-Day, the positions of blockade-runners in the Atlantic and Indian Oceans, the manufacturing processes of jet-propulsion fuels and the secrets of rocket missiles before these were launched, the revolutionary designs for submarines with high underwater speed, the details of the A/A [anti-aircraft] defences of Berlin, the development of the acoustic torpedo, and so forth, would seem to have counted not a little in the successful prosecution of the war.

A large number of translations produced by this small translation party survive as Ultra decrypts, including, for example, reports from Berlin on the performance of the Henschel fuel injection pump (for aircraft and land vehicles), on experiments in radar-controlled shore fire against ships and on Admiral Doenitz's decision in February 1945 to send some U-boats to Japan.[48]

* * *

Translation was the key to the extraction of usable intelligence from the Japanese messages and despatches decrypted at Bletchley Park. The challenges faced by the translators were at their most extreme in the scientific and technical despatches sent by the Japanese naval attachés, but despite the brief periods most of them had spent studying the language they coped. Watts at least appreciated the magnitude of their achievement.

Fig 1: Arthur Cooper with his pet gibbon Tertius. He is wearing winter clothing, so this photograph was probably taken in the Australian winter of 1942, not long after he had escaped from Singapore. (Courtesy of Gabrielle Cooper)

Fig 2: Eric Nave on board an unidentified warship of the Royal Australian Navy (RAN). The wide band on his sleeve indicates that at the time he was a Lieutenant in the Supply and Secretariat Branch of the RAN, which also covered intelligence work. He was promoted to Lieutenant on 1 September 1921 and served on the light cruiser HMAS *Brisbane* in 1923: there is insufficient detail to be sure, but it is possible that the photograph was taken on the *Brisbane*. (Courtesy of the Sea Power Centre—Australia)

Fig. 3: Mary (Maggie) Tate in WRNS uniform during the war. She had a degree in French and German and had lived in Cairo for seven years before she joined the first course at the Bedford Japanese School (Courtesy of Margaret Cribb)

Fig. 4: Colonel John Tiltman in civilian clothes, probably after the war in the United States. (Courtesy of National Security Agency, USA)

Fig. 5: A passport photograph of Captain Oswald Tuck as he was at the time when he was running the Bedford Japanese School. (Courtesy of Churchill Archives Centre, Cambridge; The Papers of Oswald Tuck, TUCK 6/2)

Fig. 6: Some of the members of Class IV at the Bedford Japanese School. No photographs of any of the earlier classes are known to survive. From left to right (the names of those mentioned in this book are in bold): **George Hunter**, Douglas Petrie, **Elizabeth Anderson**, Ernest Taylor, **Olive Ferguson**, Stanley Wilkinson, **Marie-Rose Egan**, Peter Soskice, Oliver Knox, Frederick Lindars, **Charles Bawden**. (Courtesy of Richard Bawden)

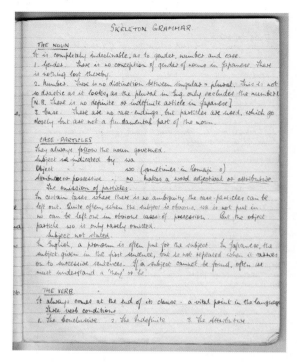

Fig. 7: Patrick Field's grammar notes from the first day of his Japanese course at Bedford. (Courtesy of Patrick Field)

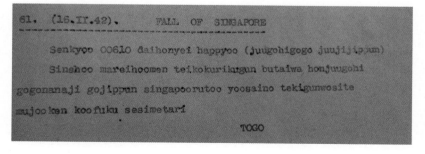

Fig. 8: One of the Japanese 'war situation' communiqués issued by the Imperial General Headquarters in Tokyo that the students at the Bedford Japanese School were given in order to familiarize them with formal military Japanese. This communiqué reports that the Imperial Japanese Army had, on the evening of 15 February 1942, forced the enemy to surrender Singapore unconditionally. (Courtesy of Bletchley Park Trust; Bletchley Park Archives D1315-001(7))

Fig. 9: The members of Class IX at the Bedford Japanese School. In this photograph Dorothy de Turville, who was a member of Class IX, is missing. Back row from left to right (those mentioned in this book are in bold): Stanley Reeder, David Bentliffe, Peter Hudson, Robert Staton, Hugh Wilkinson; middle row: Deryk Draughn, Alan Barrett, Ralph Baxter, J. W. Statham, **John Cook**, David Brazell; front row: **Ian Willison, David Stockton**, Frederick Winston (former student turned teacher), **Captain Tuck**, Sergeant Hatch (Administrative Assistant), Kenneth Howkins, Cyril Dumbleton. (Courtesy of John Cook)

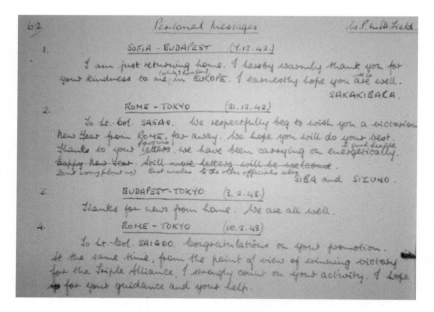

Fig. 10: Patrick Field's translations of some personal messages decrypted at Bletchley Park and made available to the Bedford School for teaching. The corrections were made by one of his teachers. (Courtesy of Patrick Field)

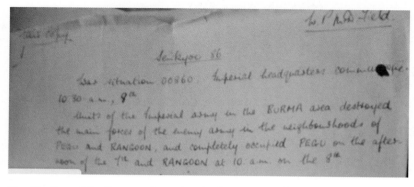

Fig. 11: One of the Japanese 'war situation' communiqués as translated by Patrick Field. (Courtesy of Patrick Field)

Fig. 12: The members of Class XI at the Bedford Japanese School. Unfortunately, this photograph lacks any indication of the names. (Courtesy of Churchill Archives Centre, Cambridge; The Papers of Oswald Tuck, TUCK 5/3)

Fig. 13: A photograph taken by the Czech photographer Erich Auerbach (1911–77) to accompany an article on wartime training at SOAS, which appeared in the magazine *The Illustrated* on 13 October 1945, pp. 10–11. In the picture are shown, left to right, Pilot Officer M. J. Fawcett, Naval Coder P. R. Collins and Lieutenant Robert Sinclair Chadwick Aytoun (1920–2002) listening to records with headphones to improve their pronunciation and their aural recognition of Japanese. The photograph was probably taken in 1944, for all three of them were on SOAS courses which finished in that year.

Fig. 14: Peter Yamauchi (1917–2006), one of three Japanese-Canadians in the Canadian Army who joined the staff at SOAS during the war. (Private collection)

Fig. 15: Eileen Clark (1918–2013), after her marriage known as Eileen Barker, in her uniform as a sergeant in the Women's Auxiliary Air Force. (Courtesy of the family of Eileen Barker)

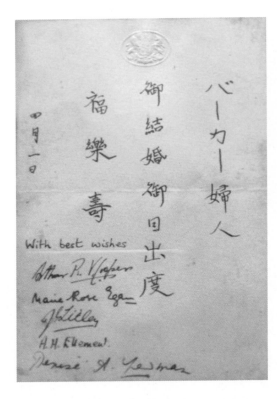

Fig. 16: A congratulatory card written in elegant Japanese by Arthur Cooper to mark Eileen Clark's marriage on 1 April 1944. It is signed by a few of her Bletchley Park colleagues (those mentioned in this book are in bold): **Cooper** himself, **Marie-Rose Egan** (a Foreign Office civilian who had been on the 4th course at the Bedford School), Lilley (possibly N. G. Lilley, a WRNS officer), Audrey Helen Ellement (a WAAF intelligence officer) and **Denise Newman** (a Foreign Office civilian who had been on the 5th course at the Bedford School).

Fig. 17: Professor Evangeline (Eve) Edwards (1888–1957), the head of the Far East Department at SOAS throughout the war (*Bulletin of the School of Oriental and African Studies* 21 [1958], p. 220. Reprinted with permission)

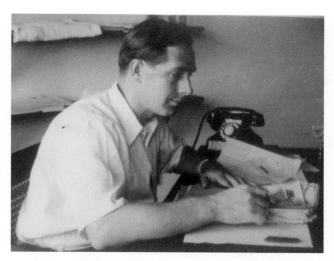

Fig. 18: John Owen Lloyd (1914–82) in Singapore on Christmas Day 1947. He had been in the British Consular Service in Japan before the war but once back in Britain he ran Japanese courses for the Naval Section at Bletchley Park. At the time of this photograph, he was working for Lord Killearn's mission to South-East Asia in connection with post-war food shortages. (Courtesy of David Lloyd)

Fig. 19: Patrick Field in Army uniform about 1944. After completing the 8th course at the Bedford School, he spent the rest of the war in the Japanese Forces Section at Bletchley Park. (Courtesy of Patrick Field)

Fig. 20: Maurice Wiles (1923–2005) in 1941. Wiles was one of the top group of students in the 1st course at the Bedford School, and he spent the rest of the war at Bletchley Park, ending up as chief translator in the Japanese Forces Section. (Courtesy of the Wiles family)

Fig. 21: Christopher Wiles (1919–2014) in Army uniform in 1940. After completing the 1st course at the Bedford School, he spent the rest of the war at Bletchley Park, like his brother Maurice. He ended the war as chief translator in the Japanese Military Attaché Section. (Courtesy of the Wiles family)

Fig. 22: Photograph taken by Christopher Wiles at Bletchley Park. The upper half of the bespectacled face of his brother, Maurice, is in the middle, with mouth and nose hidden by the head of the man in front of him. The others must have been the people he worked with at Bletchley Park, but none of them can now be identified. (Courtesy of the Wiles family)

Fig. 23: John Chadwick (1920–98) in later years when he was teaching in the Faculty of Classics at Cambridge. After several years as an able seaman in the Navy, he worked on Italian codes in Cairo and then did one of the Japanese courses in the Naval Section at Bletchley Park. (Courtesy of the Faculty of Classics, University of Cambridge)

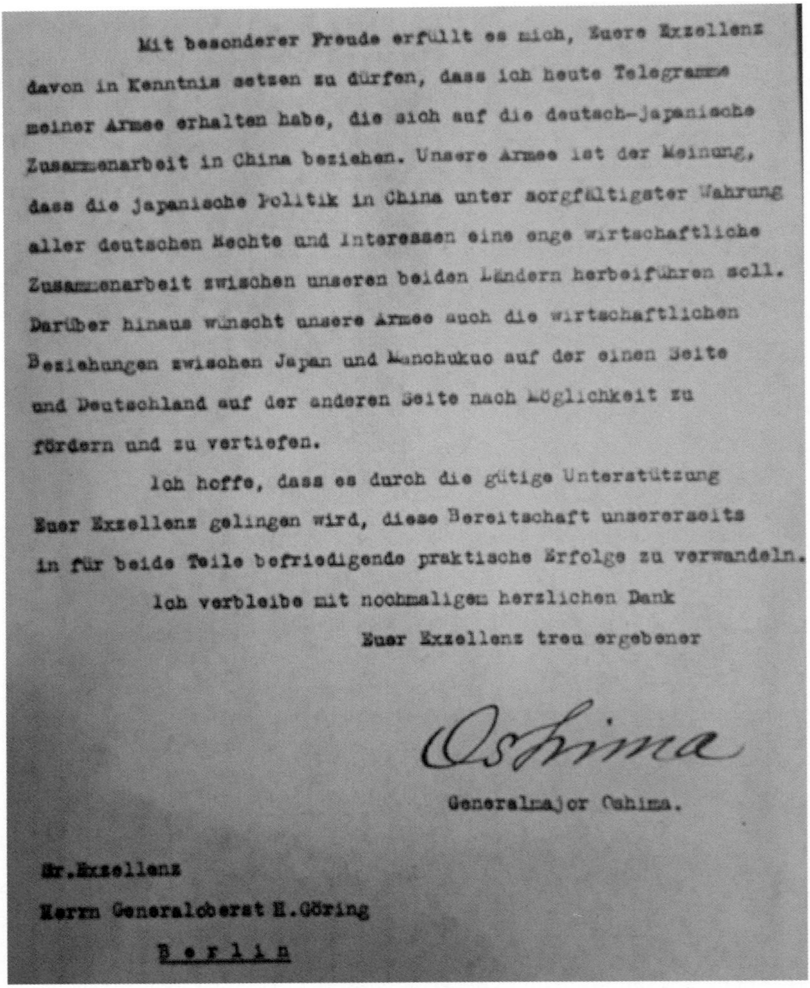

Mit besonderer Freude erfüllt es mich, Euere Exzellenz
davon in Kenntnis setzen zu dürfen, dass ich heute Telegramme
meiner Armee erhalten habe, die sich auf die deutsch-japanische
Zusammenarbeit in China beziehen. Unsere Armee ist der Meinung,
dass die japanische Politik in China unter sorgfältigster Wahrung
aller deutschen Rechte und Interessen eine enge wirtschaftliche
Zusammenarbeit zwischen unseren beiden Ländern herbeiführen soll.
Darüber hinaus wünscht unsere Armee auch die wirtschaftlichen
Beziehungen zwischen Japan und Manchukuo auf der einen Seite
und Deutschland auf der anderen Seite nach Möglichkeit zu
fördern und zu vertiefen.

 Ich hoffe, dass es durch die gütige Unterstützung
Euer Exzellenz gelingen wird, diese Bereitschaft unsererseits
in für beide Teile befriedigende praktische Erfolge zu verwandeln.

 Ich verbleibe mit nochmaligem herzlichen Dank

   Euer Exzellenz treu ergebener

Oshima

  Generalmajor Oshima.

Mr.Exzellenz

Herrn Generaloberst H.Göring

  B e r l i n

Fig. 24: Latter part of a letter sent by Major-General Ōshima Hiroshi to Hermann Göring on 21 October 1937 in faultless formal German. At this time Ōshima was Military Attaché at the Japanese Embassy in Berlin. In the letter he thanks Göring for undertaking to send 30 new Heinkel He 111 medium bombers to Japan by February 1938. In the event, this arrangement was for some reason cancelled. Later in the letter, Ōshima confirms that the Japanese Army will respect German interests in China and expresses the hope that economic relations between Japan and Germany will prosper. The image comes from the microfilms of German war documents which were made for the British Foreign Office and the US State Department in 1952. (Courtesy of The National Archives; GFM 33/3118/8133)

Fig. 25: Ambassador Ōshima Hiroshi and his wife, Toyoko, with Herbert von Dirksen (1882–1955) in Berlin (after 1939 and before 1943); the identity of the Japanese man on the right is unknown. Herbert von Dirksen had been German ambassador in Tokyo from 1933 to 1938; in 1938 he became ambassador in London, a post he held until the outbreak of war. This illustration comes from Edmund Fürholzer, *Freundesland in Osten: ein Nipponbuch in Bilder* [Friendly country in the East: a Japan book in pictures] (Berlin: W. Limpert, 1943), p. 187. (Courtesy of Quelle & Meyer Verlag, Wiebelsheim)

Fig. 26: A Japanese decrypt in the form in which it was passed to the translators. Word divisions and some explanatory notes have been added, either by the translators or by students using this decrypt as a text. This message reports that although the German Army in Tunisia had ordered the French General Georges Barré (1886–1970) either to withdraw from Tunisia or to cooperate with the Axis armies, he had refused in accordance with orders received from Admiral François Darlan (1881–1942). These events took place in November 1942, when the Allies invaded Morocco and Algeria, which were then both French territories, as was Tunisia. (Courtesy of Bletchley Park Trust; Bletchley Park Archives D1315-001(1))

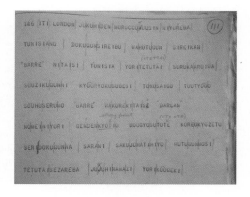

Fig. 27: Evelyn DuBuisson (1895–1983). She led a quiet and uneventful life except for her years in Mauritius, when she was Twining's first assistant and proved to be an accomplished codebreaker. (Courtesy of Professor William Twining)

Fig. 28: Edward Francis 'Peter' Twining (1899–1967) while in Mauritius during the war. He was officially Chief Censor, but behind the scenes he ran a successful intercept station. (Courtesy of Professor William Twining)

5

MAURITIUS IN DANGER

Long before the outbreak of war, GC&CS was already well experienced in the covert arts of intercepting foreign telegraph and wireless messages and trying to break foreign codes. After September 1939, of course, the intensity and the rising pressure led to a huge expansion in the numbers of staff working at Bletchley Park. But not only at Bletchley Park. As the war progressed, the 'Y' organization (i.e., 'wi', standing for wireless intelligence), which was responsible for the interception of enemy signals, also needed to grow, and some of its intercept stations began to undertake codebreaking and decryption on the spot. That naturally required having translators and intelligence officers at the ready. One of those outposts was on Mauritius. It is true that Mauritius does not immediately spring to mind as a suitable site for a 'Y' operation, but it was in fact an ideal place from which to intercept hostile communications on account of its mountainous terrain and the lack of any landmass nearer than Java. Its location enabled it to intercept a remarkable range of enemy communications that could not be picked up elsewhere, and the intelligence provided by Mauritius was highly appreciated by the Royal Navy and Bletchley Park and even came to the attention of President Roosevelt.

An unexpected stay in Mauritius

Evelyn DuBuisson (1895–1983) was an improbable intelligence officer. Not only was she a woman, at a time when military intelligence was an almost exclusively male domain, but she was also already past her forty-fifth birthday when Britain declared war on Japan. War and circumstances, however, gave her the chance to fulfil a role that would otherwise never have come her way.

Evelyn and her first cousin and close friend, Helen 'May' DuBuisson (1896–1975), were no strangers to warfare. When the First World War broke out, they were in their late teens, and in 1915 they volunteered to serve as Voluntary Aid Detachment (VAD) nurses at Clandon Park near Guildford, a country house that had been converted into a hospital for wounded troops brought straight from the front. There they got used to the terrible sight of severely wounded soldiers, most of them infested with lice and many lacking a limb.

When the war was over, Evelyn found work as a school secretary and for many years lived an unremarkable life. May, on the other hand, took a degree in medicine at King's College, London, and then embarked on an adventurous career, going out to Northern Rhodesia (now Zambia), which was then a British colony, to work as a medical officer. In 1928, May married Edward Francis 'Peter' Twining (1899–1967). Twining was connected with the Twining tea family, but at the time he was an Army officer serving in Uganda in the King's African Rifles. In 1928, probably because May did not want to be an Army officer's wife, he transferred to the Colonial Service. This was a move that was to transform their lives and take them, in 1938, to the British island colony of Mauritius. There they both discovered where their real talents lay.[1]

In 1939, Evelyn DuBuisson, who was not married, decided to visit the Twinings for a long summer holiday. Mauritius did not yet have an airport, so Evelyn had to make the long journey to join them by sea. She arrived in May 1939 and planned to return home after a few months. But she found herself trapped on Mauritius when Britain declared war on Germany and the Second World War began. Why should she have been trapped? Surely there was time to get away by ship? Perhaps so, but there were good reasons to fear that German raider ships might target Allied shipping in the Indian Ocean, just as they had done during the First World War. And, sure enough, in November 1939 the German pocket battleship, *Admiral Graf Spee*, came into the Indian Ocean and sank a tanker, so the danger was real.[2]

MAURITIUS IN DANGER

It was obvious that it would be hazardous for Evelyn to attempt to return home by sea, so she decided to stay where she was. What started out as a holiday became a job that ultimately lasted for five years. May was working as a medical officer and as assistant director of the Red Cross in Mauritius, work for which she was awarded the OBE in June 1944, but what was there for Evelyn to do? She may have had no formal qualifications, but she was soon busily working for a clandestine organization set up by Twining, her brother-in-law. Her work was vital, but too secret for her to receive any recognition. At her funeral in 1983, the Twinings' son, William, gave the address, but at the time even he had no clear understanding of the work she had been doing. It was only later, he told me, that he came to appreciate all that she had done on Mauritius. Like so many others who did clandestine work during the war, she took many of her secrets with her to the grave.[3]

Mauritius at war

Mauritius lies over 500 miles east of Madagascar in the Indian Ocean. It is now an island republic that has been independent since 1968, but it was a French colony until 1810, when a British fleet took possession of the island in a distant episode of the Napoleonic Wars. It was agreed at the time that the French settlers could continue to use French and that French law would remain in force, but from that point onwards Mauritius was a part of the British Empire. Following the abolition of slavery on the island in 1835, large numbers of indentured labourers were brought from India to work on the sugar cane plantations, and their plight prompted Mahatma Gandhi to spend two weeks on the island in 1901. During the First World War, the British garrison on the island was withdrawn, and many Mauritians departed to play their part in the war, some on the Western Front and others in a labour battalion in Mesopotamia.[4]

When Evelyn DuBuisson arrived in 1939, more than half the population was of Indian origin, descended from workers on the sugar plantations. The remainder consisted of a Creole community descended from African and Malagasy slaves from Madagascar, a community of French origin, and a smaller British community, which mostly consisted of administrators and military personnel and their families.

Racial tensions were high and distrust was rife: Twining wrote to his mother in 1942 that 'the French, Coloured, Hindoo, Mahomedan and Chinese communities all hate us and each other ... and [the French] detest us and are pro-Vichy'.[5] Of course, it was not in fact true that all French Mauritians sympathized with the Vichy French regime of Marshal Pétain that collaborated with Nazi Germany, and Twining knew that: in fact, he went on to employ some of them in his secret organization, and they became trusted members of his staff.

On 3 September 1939, the British governor of Mauritius announced on local radio that the British Empire, Mauritius included, was now at war with Germany. Once again, Mauritians were sent away to war, serving mostly in the Middle East and mainly as members of the Royal Pioneer Corps supporting the front-line troops. As in the First World War, race was never very far away, for the officers came almost exclusively from the British and French populations on the island.

Since Mauritius was far from the major conflict zones, it seemed obvious to correspondents and family members in England that the Twinings would have a peaceful and uneventful war. Twining wrote to his mother several times to correct the impression:

> Although we are remote we feel the war far more that you would imagine. ... I am very much amused at the general impression I gather from all our letters from home that we live a peaceful, comfortable life, remote from the war and its worries, untouched in fact by world events, on a romantic island populated by naked savages. ... Actually we have, despite our remoteness, been very closely concerned with the war since 3rd Sept 1939 (I since 21st August 1939). It is true that we have not yet been bombarded from the sea or air or invaded. That may be a treat to come. ... We are in the Indian Ocean and danger is nearer. I do not believe that we will be overrun here but we may be bombarded and bombed by a raider.

The war did indeed come to Mauritius. Instead of being a remote island paradise, Mauritius was situated on the shipping routes to Australia and India. If it had fallen into enemy hands, then British naval command of the Indian Ocean would have been imperilled, and so too would maritime communications with India, Australia and New Zealand.[6]

From 1940, German raiders began patrolling the Indian Ocean and sinking Allied shipping, and from 1942 German, Italian and Vichy

French submarines were hunting for Allied shipping in the Indian Ocean. Many ships heading to or from Port Louis, the capital of Mauritius, were sunk in nearby waters. And the risk of invasion was far from negligible. These dangers were real and they were taken seriously. The governor of Mauritius began to make preparations for the defence of the island even before the war broke out. A Naval Wireless Station had been established during the First World War at Rose Belle, in an elevated part of eastern Mauritius with a good command of the Indian Ocean. It had been closed down in the 1930s but now in 1939 it was reopened. In 1942, a Royal Naval Air Station (now the international airport) and an RAF flying-boat base were constructed to raise the island's defence systems. In the end, Mauritius was not directly attacked; instead, later in the war, it became the base for a number of operations that were carried out to intercept enemy shipping. One of these actions was Operation Covered in March 1944, which resulted in the sinking of a German tanker that was refuelling U-boats to the south of Mauritius.[7]

As soon as Japan went to war, Japanese forces gained control of South East Asia alarmingly quickly and Singapore fell into their hands in February 1942. From that time on, the Imperial Japanese Navy began to roam freely and widely in the Indian Ocean. In March and April 1942, for example, a Japanese fleet consisting of five aircraft-carriers and four battleships attacked British shipping in and around Ceylon but failed to find the British Eastern Fleet, which had a secret anchorage in the Maldive Islands to the south. The Chiefs of Staff in London had foreseen the dangers threatening Mauritius and, in February 1942, approved a plan for the defence of the island to protect it from aerial or naval bombardment. These measures were only partly reassuring, for Mauritians began to feel that an attack was inevitable.[8]

Meanwhile, in Berlin, Vice-Admiral Kurt Fricke, the Chief of Staff of the German Maritime Warfare Command, was having a series of meetings with Vice-Admiral Nomura Naokuni, the Japanese naval attaché, about the division of labour between their two navies so as best to ensure Axis domination in the Indian Ocean. In April 1942, the Japanese side agreed to commit four or five submarines and some surface vessels with the task of controlling the sea lanes between Aden at the tip of the Arabian Peninsula and the Cape of Good Hope in South

Africa. However, the Japanese refused to tell the Germans what their intentions were in Madagascar, which was administered by officials loyal to the Vichy government. To underline their commitment, on 5 June 1942 Japanese submarines carried out a concerted attack on Allied shipping in the Mozambique Channel between Madagascar and Mozambique. Mauritius was now more exposed than ever.[9]

The Allies were already worried that the Imperial Japanese Navy might seek to establish a base on Madagascar with Vichy approval, and they feared that Japanese submarines operating from there might wreak havoc on Allied shipping in the Indian Ocean. A report written by Ōshima, the Japanese ambassador in Berlin, made it clear to his government in Tokyo that the Germans hoped the Japanese would occupy Madagascar. His report, like all his dispatches, was intercepted and then decrypted and translated in Bletchley Park, and finally presented to a meeting of the Chiefs of Staff planning committee in London on 20 March 1942. What gave credibility to the anxiety about Madagascar was the precedent of French Indo-China: there the French authorities had allowed Japanese forces a free hand, so might they not do the same in Madagascar? *The Times* commented: 'The fate of Madagascar may also be involved in the general situation. If the island should fall into Japanese hands "by agreement" with the [Vichy] French the Cape route to Australia would be imperilled, and there has been natural anxiety in South Africa.' Churchill therefore gave his approval to a pre-emptive operation to invade and take control of Madagascar.[10]

The Battle of Madagascar is now a forgotten byway in the history of the Second World War. The amphibious landings, which began at the northern tip of Madagascar on 5 May 1942, encountered no serious opposition. Despite continuing low-level resistance and notwithstanding the interference of several Japanese submarines, the whole island was under British control by November, and in the same month British and Free French forces took control of the island of Réunion (close to Mauritius), which was also under the control of Vichy loyalists. The size of the Allied fleet committed to the Battle of Madagascar—two battleships, two aircraft-carriers, six cruisers (one Dutch), more than twenty destroyers (four Australian, two Dutch) and innumerable other ships, to say nothing of the ground troops and carrier-based aircraft—testifies not only to the importance of the operation but also to the

Allies' determination to wrest control of the Indian Ocean from the Axis powers, including the Vichy regime, and to prevent the Japanese Navy from gaining a foothold.[11]

Twining takes the bit between his teeth

There was another dimension to the strategic importance of Mauritius, but it was known to very few during the war and has largely been forgotten since. That was Mauritius' contribution to the secret war. It was Twining himself who initiated intelligence operations on Mauritius, and he was no inexperienced amateur.

Earlier in his military career, Twining had served in Dublin as an intelligence officer and was already known to the War Office for his intelligence work in Ireland before he joined the Colonial Service. In February 1939, when he reached Mauritius, he took up the position of director of labour, but even before war broke out his responsibilities changed significantly. On 1 September 1939, postal, telegraphic and wireless censorship was imposed in Mauritius, and Twining was appointed chief censor and information officer as well. During the period of the so-called 'Phoney War', from September 1939 to April 1940, there were twenty full-time staff working in the Censorship Office. They were quite sufficient to deal with the volume of post and telegrams coming into and going out of Mauritius, and the work was largely routine. That all changed after the fall of France.[12]

In June 1940, as the German armies closed in, the French government abandoned Paris, and in July the Vichy regime was established under Marshal Pétain in Vichy, a town to the west of Lyon. These developments dramatically altered the importance of Mauritius, for close by were the French colonies of Madagascar and Réunion, and since they both now backed the Vichy government, they posed a potential threat to Britain. Their telegraphic links with Paris were for some reason no longer functioning, so all private and official messages sent from Madagascar and Réunion and intended for French recipients were routed through Mauritius on the British Cable and Wireless network. Under the Official Secrets Act, Cable and Wireless were obliged to make all messages sent on their cables available for official inspection, so Twining had unfettered access to all this French traffic.

Postal and Telegraph Censorship headquarters in London instructed Twining to retransmit these messages to London unbeknownst to the senders or recipients.

There was, however, nothing to stop those messages being read on Mauritius before being retransmitted to London. Evelyn recalled:

> It struck EFT [Twining] that interesting information might be gathered in this way so he had operators trained in Morse and the results were handed to two or three of us to see what we could find. We managed to get a good deal of information about cargoes from commercial cables and we also started recording the names of private persons. In this way we learnt of departures from Madagascar and Réunion and from Indonesia. For instance, the captain of a sloop of some kind had a 'chère amie' in Tananarive [now Antananarivo, the capital of Madagascar] and every time he went on a voyage he sent her cables from the ports he touched at. ... At the beginning our organization reported to the Ministry of Economic Warfare and EFT had the greatest difficulty in financing his various activities.

Evelyn was already by this time working for what she called 'our organization' and making use of her knowledge of French, but she was considering returning home in the summer of 1940. 'She is very loath to give up her naval decoding job', May rather indiscreetly wrote in April 1940, 'and would willingly stay for the duration but she feels her duty lies with her parents.' For some reason, Evelyn changed her mind and decided to stay. Perhaps it was not such a difficult decision to make, for travelling by ship was risky—Axis submarines were by then regularly sinking ships in the vicinity of Mauritius.[13]

The signals intelligence operation on Mauritius was entirely Twining's brain-child. On his own initiative and without any instructions, he began intercepting messages and combing them for intelligence about Vichy shipping and cargoes. At this stage, it was all entirely informal: he was relying on Evelyn and a few others for unpaid help. He sent weekly intelligence reports to London using the codename Chesor, a contraction of 'Chief Censor', and copies also went to the commander-in-chief of the Eastern fleet in Trincomalee, Ceylon.[14]

In October 1940, however, when the Vichy authorities switched from cable to wireless transmission, the flow of telegraph messages from Madagascar dried up. In response, Twining now set up a Wireless

Interception Service, using the Censorship Office as cover, in order to expand the range of signals he could intercept. He purchased what wireless equipment he could find on Mauritius, had some more sent from South Africa, and recruited wireless operators, clerks, typists and translators from the local population. His reports began to circulate more widely, and in the United States they were retyped and circulated to US agencies, providing them mostly with economic and commercial intelligence taken from French and German messages, and later Japanese messages, too. At the same time, Twining's staff gradually expanded in number: by 1943, he was employing more than 300 people. Almost all the staff were recruited locally, and they included Mauritians, teachers and scientists working for the government of Mauritius, and the wives of British military and civil officials. Finding money for the salaries and equipment was Twining's biggest headache until the Treasury stepped in, and that only happened once the value of Twining's intelligence had been recognized in Bletchley Park.[15]

What actually was the value of Twining's intelligence so far? One stream of wireless messages that he and his team intercepted provided the Eastern Fleet with information about the movements of Vichy merchantmen between Dakar in French West Africa and Madagascar and Saigon in French Indo-China. Some of these ships carried troops or German citizens, and they needed to be intercepted and checked, for Vichy merchant ships were seen as potentially hostile by the Allies. Twining's reports also carried information about Vichy naval vessels, such as the sloop *D'Iberville*, which was based at Madagascar, the submarine *Vengeur*, which took to escorting Vichy merchantmen around the Cape of Good Hope, and other submarines based at Diego Suarez (now Antsiranana) in northern Madagascar. On one occasion, he was able to report that the *Vengeur* was at sea, for a private message addressed to a member of the crew was returned to sender marked 'addressee absent'. How the Royal Navy responded to this information he was not told—all that he needed to know was that it was seen as valuable and he was asked to keep providing it.[16]

In July and November 1941, Twining visited Ceylon to make personal contact with the Eastern Fleet. Fleet intelligence officers were already highly appreciative of the intelligence he was passing on and helped him by pressing the Admiralty to let him have the cypher tables that would enable him to deal with encrypted French maritime messages and to provide him with enough money to hire more operators. The information he provided enabled the Navy to act on numerous occasions: the Vichy merchantman *Surcouf*, for example, was taken into Aden for inspection and then confiscated and registered as British.[17]

Twining's operation was clearly doing well in its interception of French signals. A greater challenge was yet to come, and that was posed by the interception of messages in Japanese. As we will see, even those did not prove to be an insuperable difficulty on Mauritius.

The intelligence that Twining and his growing team gathered from wireless interception was encrypted and transmitted to Bletchley Park, where it provided, along with similar intelligence from Kilindini near Mombasa and from Colombo, up-to-date information about the movements of German armed merchantmen and cargo vessels in the Indian Ocean. Any coded messages that they intercepted were relayed to Bletchley Park for decryption there. As the official history of the Postal and Telegraph Censorship Department noted with incredulity, it was remarkable that Twining's intercept operation remained secret on Mauritius until the end of the war: only the governor, the colonial secretary and the security officer were kept informed of what was going on, and nobody else on the island knew about it, except for those who worked for him. Of course, people did notice that the numbers of people on his staff were growing, but it was assumed that he was employing an unnecessary number of people engaged in simply 'censoring letters and fixing the prices of cabbages', as a local critic put it, and their real activities were not suspected.[18]

Mauritius in the war with Japan

In 1941, FECB in Singapore asked Twining to intercept Japanese diplomatic messages being sent by wireless from Tokyo to Germany and to Siam and to forward them to Singapore. This was the beginning of Mauritius' involvement in the war against Japan, but there was much more to come. Evelyn recalled many years later:

> When Japan entered the war our little organization became much more important. The situation of Mauritius and reception conditions made

the island particularly suited to intercepting wireless messages and the operators were able to pick up code messages in large numbers which were retransmitted to England.

Messages in European languages were one thing, but how were they going to cope with messages in Japanese? As Twining himself explained when he reported to London on his work with Japanese signals, he turned for advice to the *Encyclopaedia Britannica*, where he learnt that 'The difficulties that confront an Occidental who attempts to learn Japanese are enormous.'

> This is not very encouraging if we are to be left to our own resources to deal with the mass of telegrams in pure Japanese transmitted in the Japanese Morse Code. We shall certainly make an attempt. ... I appreciate the shortage of interpreters but a visit here by one to give an intensified course to selected staff would be better than no inter-preter at all.

Even in Mauritius, then, the exigencies of wartime made Japanese language-learning imperative, and Twining was determined to meet the challenge. It is a testament to his resourcefulness and ingenuity that he managed to give his team the knowledge of Japanese that they needed.[19]

By this time, Twining's organization had grown. He evidently had a talent for picking the right people to work for him. In January 1940, Dr Reginald Edward Vaughan (1895–1987), a biologist working for the Agriculture Department who had arrived on Mauritius in 1923 and had been appointed assistant censor under Twining, became involved in the wireless interception operation. He stayed on Mauritius for the rest of his very long life and became the first curator of the Mauritius Herbarium after the war.[20]

Another addition was Captain Arthur Stamberg (1904–2001), who had met Twining in Cape Town in 1941 when Twining was looking for wireless equipment. He was a Jerseyman who had joined the Army and served in India before joining the Royal Household at Buckingham Palace in 1935. On the outbreak of war, he had become involved in intelligence work, and he arrived on Mauritius a few weeks before December 1941 with his wife, Evette, who had been working in the Censorship Department in London. By then, Twining's staff were keeping a twenty-four watch on the wireless transmissions coming out of Madagascar and Réunion, and there was a desperate need for more clerical staff. Stamberg wrote about this in his memoirs:

> In order to evaluate all the mass of information … we had to have an organised sorting office, a typing section, a cypher section and a number of girls to do the filing. To obtain the necessary staff we had to call on completely untrained volunteers and I had to interview a series of young Mauritian girls, few of whom had ever done a hand's turn of work in their lives. As often as not Papa came along too to decide whether I was a suitable employer! When it became known that I was a married man and my wife would be working in the office, their apprehensions largely disappeared.

Stamberg later became military secretary to the governor and had no further part to play in Twining's organization, but he had brought some professional military expertise to the organization. Nevertheless, Twining remained in overall control until he left Mauritius in 1944 and continued to be responsible for procuring funds, staff and equipment as well for policy decisions and for communicating with Bletchley Park.[21]

The Mauritius 'Y' station, or Wireless Interception Service, was based in Curepipe, an inland town that had an elevation of more than 500 metres above sea level and was thus certainly 'well situated from a technical point of view'. What exactly were Twining and his colleagues up to there? Since he omitted this part of his life from his autobiography, it is not easy to say. However, in the spring of 1942, an Army intelligence officer came from India to make an assessment of the Curepipe Wireless Interception Service's capabilities and his report gives us some details.[22]

According to this report, there were already nineteen receivers at Curepipe that were being monitored twenty-four hours a day, and the operators were intercepting several thousand plain-language or coded messages coming from territories occupied by Vichy French or Japanese forces every day. The coded messages were being passed on to London, while the plain-language messages in French presented no problem on Mauritius. To deal with the plain-language messages in Japanese, Twining had, the intelligence officer reported, already secured the services of a Japanese interpreter. 'Interpreter' may have been a rather grand term to use in the circumstances, as we will see.

Evelyn DuBuisson recalled that some of the plain-language messages in Japanese were sent in *rōmaji*, that is to say Japanese written using the Roman alphabet, but since not a single person on Mauritius had the slightest knowledge of Japanese, it made no difference that the Roman alphabet was used rather than Japanese script. Eventually, Evelyn explained, 'one of my colleagues, a little Welsh biologist, retired to bed for three weeks with a stomach ailment' and a dictionary. With the knowledge he acquired in this rough-and-ready way, he started instructing Evelyn and three of her colleagues, and so 'we did pick up enough to collect a certain amount of information regarding rice shipments from Burma'. What made this task particularly difficult was the fact that the messages were sent in batches of sixteen letters, so Evelyn and her colleagues had to work out where the breaks between the words were: tough and frustrating work even if you know the language well, but for them, with their necessarily limited knowledge, it is nothing short of miraculous that their perseverance or obstinacy sufficed to get some results.

Evelyn's explanation, which was written years after the war, seems implausible, but in fact her memory was not at fault. The 'little Welsh biologist' who became the first Japanese instructor on Mauritius was Dr Harry Evans (*c.*1907–83), who worked at the Sugar Research Institute. He had been working for Twining's organization since early 1942, and Twining had a high opinion of him: 'He [Evans] has taught himself Japanese and has achieved a high standard of accuracy; he has gained a good knowledge of the economic situation in the Far East, particularly in Indo-China and Siam [Thailand].'[23] Another linguist similarly forced by circumstances to learn some Japanese was Arthur Pollard (1922–2002), who after the war became professor of English at the University of Hull: as an intelligence officer in the Army, he was sent to Mauritius in 1943 and, according to his obituary, was 'presented with a Japanese dictionary and told "to get on with it"'.[24]

In September 1942, the governor of Mauritius sent Twining to Madagascar to deal with intelligence and propaganda activities there now that it was under the Allies' control. By this time, both the governor and Twining himself were beginning to think that he could be more useful in Kilindini (the port of Mombasa), where the British Eastern Fleet was now based, than in Mauritius, for much of the intelligence he was gathering was of greatest interest to the Eastern Fleet. If he were based there he could pass the intelligence directly to the fleet's intelligence officers. A meeting was therefore held in Nairobi on 11 November 1942 for Twining to explore the possibilities with the top intelligence staff in the East Africa Command, and a cable was sent to London pointing out that the monitoring of French traffic had been overtaken in urgency by the Japanese traffic, that the need for the Mauritius organization would cease if the traffic picked up there could be or was being picked up elsewhere, and that 'This excellent organisation has been developed by Twining on an amateur basis but lacks personnel with "Y" and technical experience.' What was more, Twining's outfit had no official status in the 'Y' organization and would need to be regularized by having a 'Y' administrative expert sent out to take charge.[25]

Commander Denniston at Bletchley Park, the deputy head of GC&CS, was far from convinced by any of this. His view was that Mauritius was a better location because it was on a direct cable route to Britain, and thus intelligence could be passed immediately and securely to Bletchley Park. Denniston also feared that, if Twining moved to Kilindini, he might be asked to tackle naval interception, which would deprive Bletchley Park of the diplomatic intelligence he was providing from Mauritius. 'Both the Japanese and the French sections [at Bletchley Park]', he added, 'have obtained important material from Mauritius.' He appended a table showing that in August and September Mauritius had intercepted many communications between Tokyo and Hanoi, Saigon or Bangkok: except for a handful that had been picked up at the Abbottabad listening station in India, most of them had been intercepted on Mauritius and nowhere else. Again, most of the Vichy French, German and Italian diplomatic and colonial communications intercepted on Mauritius had been picked up nowhere else. These were important considerations and Denniston got his way. A cable was sent from London to the commander-in-chief in East Africa insisting that 'Material received here from MAURITIUS Listening Service of great value and continuance is essential.' Consequently, Twining's operation remained on Mauritius until the end of the war.[26]

On 1 April 1943, responsibility for Twining's operation was transferred from the Censorship Department to the Foreign Office. This regularized Twining's participation in signals intelligence, and in August Twining made a brief visit to England to attend a number of meetings that were intended to improve the efficiency of intelligence gathering on Mauritius. He presented Bletchley Park with a detailed report on the value of plain-language intercepts, which were in Japanese (either in *rōmaji* or in the Japanese *katakana* syllabary), English, French, Italian, German, Spanish and Portuguese. 'We are in a position to translate all these', he wrote, but Japanese in *katakana* could 'only be dealt with laboriously':

> We have five so-called Intelligence Officers, each dealing with particular subjects, areas or firms. Three have sufficient knowledge of Romaji [Japanese written in Roman letters] to translate almost any telegram which confronts them. The other two are learning Romaji and making fair progress. Two of them can tackle Japanese (Kana), though somewhat laboriously. Another lady with linguistic qualifications (but not Romaji or Japanese) is on route to us but held up at Durban. Another lady does the spade work of the financial intelligence.

There can be no doubt that Twining's operation was successfully meeting the linguistic challenges posed by Japanese: with minimal resources, he had ensured that some of his staff could deal with messages in a language that none of them had ever thought of learning before. How had he done this?[27]

Twining clearly had administrative abilities of a high order: he was later to be governor of Tanganyika (now part of Tanzania), knighted and finally rewarded with a life peerage as Baron Twining. 'His assets', wrote Evelyn, 'are a quick mind, a willingness to take responsibility and a gift for getting on with other people and getting work out of his subordinates.' He had developed a carefully worked out system for the translation, assessment, collation and distribution of all the intelligence derived from the intercepts. His intelligence officers added commentary to the raw translations and gave high priority to certain types of message, such as those that gave information about naval and merchant shipping movements, those that suggested suitable bombing targets and those that revealed the activities of German firms in East Asia.[28]

How, we may wonder, was it possible for Twining's staff to derive useful intelligence from messages sent in plain language? For one thing, he said, the 'French are noticeably slack in their security ... on several occasions we have intercepted messages in plain language on the following lines:- "Censorship will not accept your message unless the following words are deleted—'am sailing from Saigon on S.S. Compiegne tomorrow afternoon'"! The same was true of Japanese messages: 'We have gained the impression that the Japanese consider their language to be so difficult to a Westerner that they take liberties which shock our sense of security. Certainly they permit in plain language telegrams a lot of information that we would not allow.'[29] Both for these reasons, and because seemingly innocuous messages often turned out to have unexpected value, the hard work put in by Twining's staff was yielding valuable intelligence.

This intelligence needed to reach those who could make good use of it, of course. Twining and his staff therefore put together weekly intelligence reports that were sent to London, Colombo, New Delhi, Canberra and the chief of the intelligence staff of the Royal Navy's Eastern Fleet, based in Kilindini near Mombasa. These reports included appendices that contained translations of selected messages with commentary. From late 1943 onwards, most of the messages translated had been sent in Japanese, either in Roman letters or in *katakana* (Japanese Morse). Some of the intercepts were communications about insurance, which revealed details of ship cargoes, about the losses of ships as a result of enemy action or other causes, or about Japanese and French ship movements in East Asian waters. Occasionally, intercepted communications between Japan and Germany revealed that German machine tools and other supplies were to be sent to Japan, or that supplies of tea or other goods were to be sent to Germany. One concrete example is the report of 15 April 1943, which includes information about French ships in Indo-China requisitioned by Japanese naval authorities, details of French naval vessels in Saigon, the movements of Italian ships in East Asia, and the names, routes and destinations of Japanese merchant ships, based on data from Japanese, Chinese, Thai and Indo-Chinese ports.[30]

Twining ended his report to Bletchley Park with some questions: Should he and his team continue their work and were the results valuable? Perhaps Twining had not received enough reassurance about the intelligence he was providing, but it must soon have become clear to him that the Mauritius intelligence-gathering operation was valuable:

not only was he urged to continue his work but the Treasury even agreed to foot the bill for enhanced equipment and increased staffing levels. He was to be sent more staff, new and better wireless equipment and six of the *katakana* typewriters made in America, as described in the previous chapter.[31]

Twining's staff get to grips with Japanese

Some of Twining's staff had already been given some training in Japanese Morse by an Admiralty civilian, and in August 1943 they began to conduct a sweep of all intercepted signals to identify those that were in Japanese Morse. This work was entrusted to a group of twenty women, whose job it was to transcribe the messages from Japanese Morse to Japanese written in *katakana*. This was not easy, and they found it difficult to keep pace with the volume, for messages from more than 100 stations transmitting in Japanese Morse were being intercepted on Mauritius. The six *katakana* typewriters would help, Twining thought, but the operators needed to be trained how to use them. To deal with these problems, Twining set up a school to give seventy local operators the training in Japanese Morse Code that would make them useful. That was by no means the limit to his resourcefulness, for he also, somehow or other, managed to get hold of some Japanese textbooks, which he gave to his intelligence officers so that they could acquire some basic knowledge of the language.[32]

In addition to the machines, Twining was also promised a technical officer, an intelligence officer and eight Japanese linguists. These would put the efficiency of his operation on a much higher level. When it came to the linguists, Twining made it quite clear what he needed: 'We do not want Japanese scholars or people who have been taught what the Japanese think about cherry blossom. We require people who can apply themselves to the specialised work of translating messages in clipped telegraphese and in government or commercial jargon.' In other words, he wanted the kind of people who were being produced by the Bedford School, but it is unlikely that he had ever heard of it. Ideally, he wanted linguists who could provide his staff with instruction in Japanese. Until such a person was provided, he had to make do with a schoolmaster who had lived and worked in Japan but now lived on

Mauritius and was a member of his staff. For the time being, Twining thought that he would suffice. Twining also put in a request for multiple copies of *Kenkyusha's Japanese–English Dictionary* (1918), Arthur Rose-Innes's *Beginners Dictionary of Chinese–Japanese Characters and Compounds* (1900) and Basil Hall Chamberlain's *Grammar of Written Japanese* (1886). Twining did not know a word of Japanese, but he had done some homework and knew which dictionaries to ask for.[33]

By the end of 1943, Twining's operation was running at full steam, with new equipment and a large staff. They were listening to messages going in both directions between Tokyo and Paris, Geneva, Hanoi, Saigon, Thailand, Shanghai, South America and the Japanese puppet state of Manchukuo in north China, and a growing proportion of these were in Japanese Morse, either coded or in plain language. In a memorandum he sent to Bletchley Park, he explained what he was doing with encrypted messages:

> We have never attempted to break down any high grade cipher messages ... because we considered it to be improper unless we were directed to do so. We are in possession of the standard international commercial codes and several French commercial codes which are in occasional use. We have broken down to a large extent the Melchers code used by German firms. We have broken down the two [Vichy] French Government low grade codes, and can undo any messages sent in them.

In the same memorandum, he explained that they were also processing a lot of messages sent *en clair*, for they found that there was a great deal of intelligence that could be derived from them.[34]

By 1943, the volume of work was immense, and the pressure to produce accurate transcriptions intense. Nevertheless, the men and women who were producing the results never received any recognition. Not even a full record of their names has survived, only a farewell card given to Evelyn DuBuisson, which preserves many of their names.

Twining's three main intelligence officers were said, in a secret memorandum written after the war, to have been a local official of Mauritian nationality (unidentified), a botanist in the Agricultural Department (obviously Evans) and 'an ex-lady Secretary to a Headmaster who had "a crossword puzzle mind" and had been mainly responsible for breaking down the French Code Defence'. The last named must be Evelyn DuBuisson, and from this it is clear that she was engaged in cryptographic work in addition to French and Japanese translation work and intelligence assessments. The cypher staff were all the wives of British officials, while the subordinate staff were, according to the secret memorandum, recruited from 'good Mauritian families who, if their standard of intelligence is not high, are keen, hardworking, sound and adequate'. In the memorandum, these condescending words are placed in inverted commas and are evidently a quotation: they were presumably taken from a report sent by Twining or by his successor.[35]

In December 1943, the first of the promised linguists arrived, by air owing to the urgency. Robert Milne Sellar (1923–96) had won a scholarship to St John's College, Cambridge, to study classics, but in the middle of his course he was whisked away and soon found himself attending the first course at the Bedford Japanese School. He was one of two students on the course who were so linguistically talented that they were able to write passable poetry in Japanese after just three months of study. The second to arrive, by ship in the spring of 1944, was Elizabeth Anderson, who had been working with Colonel Tiltman in the Foreign Office before the war and subsequently at Bletchley Park and who had then done a course at the Bedford School—she arrived in time to sign Evelyn DuBuisson's farewell card. The last to arrive was Dashwood, who had been on the seventh course at Bedford after leaving Eton and who thoughtfully sent Captain Tuck some tea and sugar, which were easily available on Mauritius but rationed in Britain.[36]

After finishing their courses at Bedford, but before being sent out to Mauritius, the three of them—Sellar, Anderson and Dashwood—had been sent to the Government Communications Bureau at Berkeley Street. There they were put to work translating Japanese diplomatic decrypts and in the process getting training in intelligence work. A fourth Japanese translator, Elizabeth Hely-Hutchinson (1921–2020), travelled out to Mauritius with Elizabeth Anderson: she had not attended any of the Bedford courses but instead learnt her Japanese on one of the Naval Section courses at Bletchley Park.[37]

Mauritius must have been a surprising and exotic destination for all of them. Sellar, at least, took full advantage of the opportunities. In his letters to his brother back in Scotland, he wrote mostly of his leisure activities. 'Life here is not too bad—when not working it consists chiefly of walking, climbing, swimming, talking French, playing bridge and eating fruit.' 'I have out here a very good time having many friends of both sexes, and getting much bathing, sailing, fishing, climbing, walking etc.' And then there were the palm trees, coral reefs, coconuts, pineapples and octopuses; it was tropical in appearance but was often raining, and 'at night there is a hell of a racket from frogs and crickets'.[38]

Dashwood, too, made the most of the opportunities, as he explained in his autobiography:

> The work in Mauritius was interesting, and became doubly so when my boss [Twining?] fell ill and I was deputed to take over his work of editing the weekly report to London and Washington. During my spare time I decided to start a Mauritian dance band. ... The band consisted of Robert Mui on the piano, Bill Gray, clarinet, and Arthur Wilkinson, double bass, with me on the drums. We played at the Bastille Ball at Government House and were due to broadcast on Radio Mauritius, but on our big night the King's African Rifles were embarked at Port Louis for East Africa and the band folded up.

Not long afterwards, a fierce cyclone hit the island, and before long the house he was sharing with three Army intelligence officers and three women from the Foreign Office began to shake violently. Dashwood picked up his trumpet and played Glenn Miller's 1939 hit 'In the Mood', with his tin hat perched on his head.[39]

The post-Twining era

Twining left Mauritius for good in August 1944, having been appointed administrator of St Lucia in the Caribbean. Evelyn, together with his wife and younger son, went with him by ship to Durban, braving the risk of submarine attack. The Treasury, in tacit recognition of the work she had done over the previous five years, generously offered Evelyn a substantial contribution to her travelling costs, simultaneously pointing out that her salary would no longer be paid after her return to Britain! Thus, her remarkable years as a salaried intelligence officer were over. Their departure brought an end to her role in the clandestine organization Twining had set up. On Mauritius, she had discovered a hidden talent for codebreaking that she used to the full as her contribution to the war effort, a talent that ever after lay dormant.[40]

The Wireless Interception Service continued its work until the end of the war, now under the direction of Charles Anthony Langdon Richards (1911–96). Richards had been serving in the Colonial Service in Uganda when he first met Twining. On the outbreak of war, he had joined the King's African Rifles, but in 1941 he was seconded to Mauritius to assist Twining's intelligence work. By August 1943, he was presiding over the daily conferences and vetting all the intelligence telegrams before they were despatched. 'For [the] past 13 months', Twining wrote to London, 'he has been almost solely engaged on the work of this organization, has had my complete confidence and is familiar with every aspect of our work.' Twining considered him the only possible successor.[41]

Soon after taking over, Richards wrote a series of reports for Denniston at Bletchley Park that demonstrated his determination to get the most out of the Japanese traffic they were intercepting. He abandoned use of the *katakana* typewriters and concentrated on 'teaching our girl-clerks more and more about Kana procedure until the material which they handle becomes a living correspondence which they can follow'. The object was not only to transcribe accurately but also to sort out the dross from the gold, and for that the clerical staff needed to know enough Japanese to be able to distinguish between the important and the trivial. Now that was no longer a difficulty: as he reported to Commander Denniston, 'Sellar (whose services have proved invaluable) has been teaching Japanese to a class of eleven (assistant intelligence officers, army officers, and clerks).' He continued:

I am trying to keep Sellar outside the fixed sorting–translating–intelligence lay-out, so that he can work as a kind of referee on all translations which appear in the weekly report and also be available for any code-reading which we undertake. I have little doubt that he will, with his unbounded enthusiasm, be fully occupied!

To help Sellar, there were of course the two new linguists who had just arrived by ship, Anderson and Hely-Hutchinson.[42]

Evans, Evelyn DuBuisson and the other self-taught staff working for Twining had done remarkable work on plain-language messages in Japanese, but the three Bedford graduates brought with them much deeper knowledge of the language and familiarity with some Japanese codes. In July 1944, Anderson wrote to Denniston with her impressions of her working life in Mauritius:

> There is a happy and friendly atmosphere in the office and I find it very pleasant and easy to work for Captain Richards. Much of the work is dull and rather depressing, as I feel it is valueless; Sellar and I are having a crusade for more ruthless discarding, and I am now taking a second batch of people through a speedy Japanese course to give us more 'translator-discarders'.

Richards wrote in 1945 that he regarded her as one of the better linguists, and it is clear from her letter above that she was confident enough to be running Japanese courses for the staff and to be writing letters to Denniston himself, whom she had probably known since her arrival in Bletchley Park in 1939. Her honest comments on the nature of the work are borne out by the recollections of others at Bletchley Park, as we have seen, but Shaw, a veteran cryptographer at Bletchley Park, added this comment to her letter: 'though the hand is that of Elizabeth I think I recognise the voice of Sellar. Sellar has always preferred cryptography to translating; he has homed in on the TOA KAIUN (East Asia Maritime Transport) code, and has just sent us suggestions about another new code.'[43]

The new arrivals made it possible to expand the work even further. In January 1944, soon after he arrived, Sellar was communicating directly with Shaw at Bletchley Park about the decryption of coded Japanese messages, and Twining was impressed: 'Sellar is proving invaluable on the linguistic side and in general has been able to put his finger on several minor blemishes in the organization.' As a result of the increased capacity, and because it had been realized that coverage of some frequencies was better in Mauritius than in Colombo or Calcutta, in April 1944 Mauritius began to monitor encrypted Imperial Japanese Navy traffic for the British Eastern Fleet, which had by this time returned to its base at Colombo. This was an important addition to their portfolio of interceptions, and it was probably due both to the excellent reception on Mauritius and to the calibre of the staff Twining had working for him.[44]

By the end of 1944, there were twenty-five Japanese linguists at work on Mauritius, an amazing figure for a small island. Some of them had been sent out from England, some were self-taught and some had done courses on the island. Sellar was considered the best, and he was the ultimate arbiter when it came to Japanese translation: he corrected the mistakes of others and coached the beginners, and he was the only one who could handle colloquial Japanese messages. After Sellar, in Richards' judgment, came Evans; Victor Lemprière (1899–1948), a schoolmaster from Jersey who had taught English in Japan for three years in the 1920s and who was loaned by the Mauritian government; and Anderson.[45]

Richards found tasks for all of them that were suited to their level of abilities. Hely-Hutchinson could only handle simple translations, but she quickly mastered Japanese Morse, and owing to her fluent French she was put in charge of the '30 Mauritian girls' who were doing transcription from *katakana* into Roman letters. Barbara Dainton and Dorothy McConochie had been trained at SOAS and arrived in the summer of 1944 to add to the roster of linguists; they had a good knowledge of grammar but were initially unfamiliar with telegraphese and commercial vocabulary. Lieutenants Pollard and Cecil William Chilton, seconded from the East Africa Command of the British Army, and Donald Taylor, a school-leaver from an English Mauritian family, all did Sellar's course and were proving useful. The names of those at a lower level, like Marguerite Adam, Laurence Pitot, Anne-Marie Desvaux de Marigny, Françoise Raffray and Miss Fayd'Herbe, show that they were almost all Mauritians of French descent—they all took Anderson's course and then did valuable work as sorters whose job it was to assess which messages were trivial and which needed translation.[46]

When it came to decryption work, however, Sellar was in a class of his own:

> We have also had a couple of successes on the crypto side in unpicking *kana* codes used by the Yokohama Specie Bank and the Southern Area Development Bank—the latter has 30 recypherment tables and involves the building of a book in Japanese [i.e., building up a list of the Japanese words represented by code-groups], so I am full of admiration for what has been achieved by our one expert, Sellar (even he is only a 21 year-old with just over two years' experience).

The unofficial operation begun by Twining on a shoestring was now operating at a very high level and providing a constant stream of commercial, maritime and other intelligence.[47]

The aftermath

As the war came to an end, work inevitably diminished and the staff had more time on their hands. In late July 1945, when the end was near, Sellar went away on holiday to Réunion, just 100 miles south-west of Mauritius, and did some mountain climbing. On 15 August, the day of the Japanese surrender, Sir Edward Travis, the operational head of Bletchley Park, wrote to Richards in Mauritius:

> I wish to express the appreciation of myself and all at GC&CS for all the help and co-operation you have shown throughout the Japanese war. We have admired your efforts in dealing with the toughest of problems under the most difficult conditions, and rejoice in the success which you have achieved.

A couple of days earlier, Anderson and Hely-Hutchinson had left Mauritius by ship, to be followed by Sellar and the others, and the whole operation was wound down, to remain shrouded in secrecy for more than sixty years.[48]

Sellar returned to Cambridge but switched to Russian and French for his degree and later worked in southern India for J. & P. Coats Ltd, the cotton thread manufacturer. Anderson married Captain George Norman Ramsay (1905–86) of Nairobi on 5 December 1945 and then raised a family in Kenya. Evans left Mauritius with Anderson and Hely-Hutchinson and resumed his pre-war work on sugarcane technology, this time in Trinidad and Guyana, for which he was eventually awarded an OBE. Lieutenant Chilton, who had graduated from Oxford in 1936, became an academic, teaching classics at the University of Hull from 1947 onwards. Stamberg, who was recalled to Buckingham Palace in early 1945, returned to his royal duties and accompanied the queen and Prince Philip on several royal tours. Finally, Dashwood, who had suffered a serious illness while on Mauritius, went up to Oxford and later made an unsuccessful attempt to become a Conservative Member of Parliament. The Franco-Mauritians who had worked for Twining's organization resumed their pre-war life, but Mauritius was changing. The new Constitution of 1947, by extending suffrage to all literate adult males, increased the representation of Indo-Mauritians and reduced that of Franco-Mauritians.

How had this motley band come together and managed to achieve so much? Memoirs are sadly lacking, but Sellar's son has reflected on what his father had told him:

> I think one of the great gifts that Twining had was his ability to communicate with all of his team. He hugely impressed my father (and maybe ruined him for life) but his ethos of work hard/play hard engendered a great esprit de corps. He would meet my father once every three days for lunch to see how things were going on decryption. A bottle of gin was placed on the table and it always had to be finished by pudding. They had a lot of fun and that must have helped them all to get through so much grinding, boring message-reading. The only secret that my father did let out was that they had intercepted a message relating to 'Cicero' and that the Germans had a copy of the D-Day plans.[49]

'Cicero' was the codename used by Elyesa Bazna, who was the valet to the British ambassador to Turkey and who passed on to the Germans numerous documents including some relating to Operation Overlord (the invasion of Normandy in June 1944). Presumably Sellar intercepted some German message relating to 'Cicero', but I have not so far been able to find any documents relating to this in The National Archives. Like Evelyn and the others, Sellar was highly conscious of his obligations under the Official Secrets Act, so his letters and photographs give a misleading impression of a life full of pleasures. There can be no doubt, though, that the work they all did was demanding and required concentration, judgement and a high level of linguistic skill.

What was the value of all their efforts? They were certainly appreciated, as Sir Edward Travis's remarks show. Much earlier, on 12 July 1943, Captain Tufnell, the chief of the Intelligence Staff of the Eastern Fleet, wrote to Twining: 'The value of your information is undoubtedly great. Yours is the only source we have from Indo-China.' There must have been some truth to this, for Tufnell even offered to provide a Japanese interpreter if Twining needed more help to keep the shipping intelligence flowing. And Richards and his entire team were delighted when informed that President Roosevelt and Admiral Mountbatten both wanted to see some of the intelligence from Mauritius.[50]

What Twining, Richards and their staff never did know, and what is not evident from the archives, is how exactly the intelligence they supplied was used. That is, of course, in the nature of intelligence gathering: the weekly reports from Mauritius were cogs in a vast machine. Before Japan came into the war, the reports focused on Vichy French merchant shipping and convoys travelling to and from Indo-China and seem likely to have prompted Royal Navy interceptions.[51]

Later, the weekly reports contributed to the constantly changing assessment of the economic basis of the Japanese Empire, and the information about cargoes and shipping movements may well have prompted naval action against ships carrying materiel to warzones in East Asia. For example, in October 1944 a Japanese marine products company sent a message *en clair* to its branch office in Saigon saying that the *Kinsei-maru*, one of the ships used by the company, had sunk off Amami Ōshima island to the south of Kyushu but the crew were safe. This was picked up in Mauritius, translated, forwarded to Bletchley Park and included in the collections of raw communications that were then passed on to intelligence analysts. If the ship had been sunk by a submarine, then this message would have provided confirmation of a claimed sinking as well as providing another statistic in the gradual destruction of Japanese commercial shipping. But for those in Mauritius, like those who worked at Bletchley Park, it was rare to find out how the intelligence was used. When Mavis Batey and her colleagues at Bletchley Park were informed that their work had enabled Admiral Andrew Cunningham at the head of an Anglo-Australian fleet to defeat the Italian Navy in the Battle of Cape Matapan in 1941, they were elated, but elation was a rare commodity in intelligence work, and one that the personnel in Mauritius had to do without.[52]

Intelligence in the war with Japan absolutely depended upon knowledge of Japanese, and the difficulties that posed were immense. The multinational staff in Mauritius easily coped with the linguistic challenge—and then after the war promptly put their linguistic competence and their intelligence work completely out of mind. Evelyn DuBuisson, that improbable intelligence officer, resumed her previous life in Surrey. She cared for her parents in their old age, helped Twining with his retirement research on the crown jewels of the European monarchies and tended her garden. She never did paid work again, but she did revisit Mauritius in 1977. She was the only one, in her later years, to put some of her recollections on paper, but she discreetly avoided mentioning her own contributions.

6

THE BACKROOM BOYS—AND GIRLS

By the end of May 1942, the students on the first course at the Bedford Japanese School had already made astounding progress and their services were much in demand. Many were quickly sucked up by Bletchley Park once their course was over, and most of them stayed there for the remainder of the war. This was not surprising, for the Bedford School was, after all, Tiltman's brainchild, and it was designed to provide Bletchley Park with the linguist-codebreakers it needed. But there were other potential customers looking for linguists, too, and Captain Tuck had in fact already received a request from the British Army in India for some of his students to go out there to work for an organization similar to Bletchley Park. The three chosen were Walter Robinson (1920–81), Lloyd-Jones and Noyce. Why them? They were not the best in the class, for in a class of twenty-three they had come seventh, fifteenth and eighteenth respectively. Was Bletchley Park simply keeping the best for itself, or did these three have some personal attributes that particularly suited them to this posting? We will probably never know the answer to that question.

The three of them went from Bedford first of all to the Government Communications Bureau in Berkeley Street to familiarize themselves with the kind of work expected of them, and then they received their marching orders for India. They had a shocking reminder of the harsh realities of war when they returned to Bedford to collect their belongings before their departure, as Lloyd-Jones recalled:

We telephoned our landlady in Bedford, and asked when we could come and collect our things. At first we were to come in two days' time, but then our landlady said that it would be more convenient if we came the next day. So we did this; and on the following night a German plane flying back from a raid dropped the only bomb that fell on Bedford during the war. It fell on what had been our room, killing our landlady's two children who were now sleeping there.

Lloyd-Jones was writing many years later, and any grief he felt at the time for the death of the children had been pushed into the background by all the terrible sights he saw in Burma.[1]

Since time was of the essence, they flew to Sierra Leone, and then across Africa to India, stopping in Palestine, Bahrain, Karachi and Gwalior. They made the last part of the journey by train to Delhi. Unlike Robinson and Noyce, who were already lieutenants in the Army when they went to Bedford, Lloyd-Jones was still a civilian, so he was hastily called up into the Army as a private, a lowly rank for a future Regius Professor of Greek at Oxford. Since codebreakers at the new facility in Delhi were supposed to be officers, Lloyd-Jones had to kick his heels in India for three months waiting for his commission to come through. He spent the time as a sergeant in the Wireless Experimental Depot, an intercept station at Abbottabad in the Northwest Frontier Province (now Pakistan). Eventually he was summoned for an interview:

After many weeks I was summoned to the district headquarters at Rawalpindi to be interviewed by the major-general who commanded there. ... The general asked me what I had been doing before I joined the army, and I replied that I had been studying at Oxford. 'What college?', said the general, and I replied 'Christ Church'. 'Ah!', said the general, 'my father was there! Well, what regiment do you want to go into?', and that was all.

Lloyd-Jones certainly had an easy interview thanks to his college affiliation. He was now ready to begin work at an organization with a deliberately misleadingly name, the Wireless Experimental Centre in Delhi. We will return to Lloyd-Jones and the WEC later in this chapter.

The WEC was not, of course, the first British codebreaking centre in Asia. FECB, which we met in chapter 1, was the first, but by 1942 it had been disbanded. What had happened to it?

THE BACKROOM BOYS—AND GIRLS

The Far East Combined Bureau

FECB had been established in Hong Kong in 1935 to work on Japanese codes and cyphers. Captain Shaw, a naval officer who had been a language officer in Japan from 1920 to 1923 and who had been trained in Japanese cryptography at GC&CS, was sent out to run the bureau. The bureau, which was a small-scale operation at first, was based in Hong Kong dockyard. On Stonecutters Island, about an hour away by launch, a dozen junior telegraphists from the Navy and the Air Force intercepted Japanese consular, naval and military wireless traffic, with occasional interruptions: whenever there was a typhoon threatening, they had to take down the huge aerials to prevent damage. The intelligence produced by FECB was recognized to be valuable, so there were soon twenty cryptographers working in the bureau thanks to Shaw's continuous agitation for more staff.[2]

On 25 August 1939, in anticipation of the outbreak of war, the staff and all the records were shipped out from Hong Kong to Singapore, which then seemed much less vulnerable to a Japanese attack. Copies of the current codes were left behind with Squadron-Leader Hubert Thomas 'Alf' Bennett, who had orders to destroy them immediately if hostilities broke out with Japan. He and four intercept operators continued to work there for two more years, sending on to Singapore the intelligence they got from Japanese signals they picked up. From July 1941, they were intercepting Japanese air-to-ground communications and providing the military authorities in Hong Kong with real-time information about Japanese movements. Bennett and his intercept operators were all captured when Hong Kong surrendered on Christmas Day, 1941, but not before they had destroyed anything suggestive of what they had been doing there. Bennett survived his years of captivity, but the fate of the others is unknown.[3]

FECB was, of course, no safer in Singapore, which was forced to surrender in February 1942. Nobody yet foresaw that, however, and by 1941 the bureau had become a much larger operation, with representatives from all three of the armed services. In April 1941, a party of twenty chief petty officers in the WRNS arrived in Singapore by sea under the command of 2nd Officer (i.e., Lieutenant) Helen Elizabeth 'Betty' Archdale (1907–2000). They had all been trained in wireless

127

telegraphy and Japanese Morse, and they had all indicated on recruit-ment that they were willing to serve abroad. To mark their departure from England, there was a farewell party at WRNS headquarters in the Admiralty, hosted by Princess Marina, the Duchess of Kent, as the patron of the WRNS, along with Albert Alexander, who was the First Lord of the Admiralty, and Admiral Sir Charles Little, the Second Sea Lord. Their presence is some indication of the significance of the occa-sion: Archdale's Wrens were in fact the first British servicewomen to be sent overseas during the Second World War.[4]

Although their commander, Betty Archdale, knew where they were bound, the other Wrens did not. They had, however, been issued with tropical uniforms before they left and that must have given them a clue. On arrival in Singapore, they were sent to work in shifts at the Kranji intercept station on the northern part of Singapore island, where they were accommodated in bungalows. Their arrival predictably caused a sensation:

> Men from both the Army and the Navy, plus some civilians kept watch at Kranji, and they were wildly excited over our arrival. They organ-ised a dance for the Saturday night, and, looking upon us as *theirs*, they intended to hog us for themselves. They therefore did not send any invitations to the other establishments.

Before long, another ten Wrens arrived. They had originally been intended for Alexandria, but since Rommel was now posing a serious threat to British forces in Egypt, they were sent to Singapore instead. They must have received training in Japanese Morse on arrival.[5]

Archdale, the Wrens' commanding officer, was by any standards a remarkable woman. Her godmother was Emmeline Pankhurst and her mother had been imprisoned as a suffragette for smashing windows in Whitehall. Betty herself graduated from McGill University in Montreal and then captained the victorious English women's cricket team when it made a tour of Australia in 1934–5 in the first Women's Test series. She subsequently trained as a lawyer and had just been called to the bar when the war broke out, so she volunteered for the WRNS. She underwent officer training and volunteered for service overseas. She was rather disappointed to be posted to Singapore, for at the time it seemed far removed from the war, and she had no reason to think that that would change.[6]

The Wrens at Kranji worked in shifts, monitoring the airwaves for Japanese wireless signals and recording what they heard. It was for others to decode and translate. The conditions were tough: their equipment generated so much heat in the intercept office that the temperature never dropped below 36°C even at night. After Japanese troops landed on the coast of Malaya in December 1941, their work 'increased ten-fold and there was never a moment's relaxation'. In January 1942, it was time to leave. Elizabeth Miller, who had served in the WRNS as a signaller during the First World War, was Archdale's second-in-command. She was tasked with taking their luggage and equipment down to the docks:

> We had just arrived at Keppel Harbour when a wave of Jap planes came swooping down dropping bombs and machine-gunning everything in sight. ... They were so low that we could see their faces quite plainly and I must confess that I was very frightened to find myself looking into the eyes of the enemy at such close range.

She and the other Wrens marched on board MV *Devonshire*, a purpose-built troopship, and as she looked back all she could see was the 'thick pall of smoke which hung over the city'. Once they were underway, they all slept for fourteen hours, for over the previous five weeks at Kranji they had never had more than two hours of unbroken rest at a time.[7]

Singapore was already doomed as a British naval base, and when the Wrens left on 5 January 1942 they were accompanied by the naval cryptographers, interpreters, intelligence officers and wireless intercept personnel who were working at FECB. This time they moved to Colombo in Ceylon (Sri Lanka). The Army and RAF personnel stayed behind in Singapore for a while but then moved to India, where they were eventually absorbed into the WEC in Delhi. In effect, FECB now ceased to exist. Personnel from the three services were no longer 'combined', and it was no longer based in the 'Far East'. Britain no longer even had a toehold in East Asia.[8]

From Colombo to Mombasa and back

Colombo, in turn, proved to be no safer than Singapore for the naval refugees from FECB. Japanese carrier-based aircraft attacked the city on 5 April 1942, and a few days later they attacked the British naval base at Trincomalee on the east coast of Ceylon. The British Eastern Fleet had prior warning of this raid from a Japanese radio transmission that had been intercepted, decrypted and translated in Colombo, so the fleet promptly left Trincomalee for Addu Atoll in the Maldives archipelago to the south. Had the fleet not done so, the losses might have been catastrophic. As it was, the light aircraft-carrier HMS *Hermes* and the Australian destroyer HMAS *Vampire* were sunk, and the heavy cruisers *Cornwall* and *Dorsetshire* were caught and sunk as they tried to escape to Addu Atoll. For fear of losing more ships, the fleet, now consisting of the large carriers *Indomitable* and *Formidable*, five battleships, seven cruisers (one from the Royal Netherlands Navy), sixteen destroyers and seven submarines, abandoned Trincomalee and retreated to Kilindini, the port of Mombasa in Kenya. The naval elements of FECB went with them, including all the Wrens, who were seeing rather more of the world than they had expected.[9]

The Wrens left Colombo before the male intercept operators, who were kept there until the last moment. They travelled on HMS *Alaunia*, a Cunard liner converted into an armed merchantman. For the Wrens, the significance of this was that it was now a ship of the Royal Navy, but they were probably unaware that Wrens counted as 'boys' on naval ships. They lined up with the men for their ration of rum, but all that the Wrens were entitled to was lime juice. Once they had reached Kilindini, the Wrens now had sole responsibility for intercept operations until their male counterparts arrived. Their abilities and usefulness were now clearly recognized by the Navy, even if it denied them their rum. The commander-in-chief of the Eastern Fleet, Admiral Sir James Somerville, had himself been a wireless officer during the First World War and perhaps for that reason was in a better position to appreciate the importance of their work. At any rate, he went several times to see the Wrens at work.[10]

The move to Kilindini did not at first, however, bode well for naval intercept operations or cryptography. There was a shortage of equipment and a shortage of intercept operators, not to mention bats and flying insects to cope with. Worst of all, unlike the intercept station on Mauritius, Kilindini was at sea level and was therefore less well placed physically to intercept Japanese wireless messages. The unpublished history of naval intelligence written at the Admiralty after the war recognized the problems at Kilindini: 'The East Africa period was the unit's lowest ebb. Reception was poor, more members of the Singapore team fell out [perhaps due to illness?], and the unit was again housed several miles from Naval Headquarters. There was no liaison with the other services.' The prospects were not good, and this was one of the reasons for the continued importance of the intercept operation on Mauritius.[11]

The naval team that had come from FECB in Singapore via Colombo settled into the Allidina Visram School for Boys, which had been taken over for the duration of the war. In the usual naval fashion for shore bases, this one was named HMS *Allidina*. At first, HMS *Allidina* was under the command of Captain Shaw, Nave's old room-mate, but by the end of 1942 he had returned to London, exhausted and unwell, and Commander William Bruce Keith (1898–1974) came out from Bletchley Park to take over. Keith, who had been sent out to Japan as an Army language officer in 1922, found the situation unsatisfactory: Kilindini was intrinsically unsuitable for radio interception on account of its location and he had insufficient staff; he estimated that only 600 out of a possible total of 3,000 transmissions were being intercepted each day. It was worrying that such large numbers were not being picked up at all.[12]

By December 1942, a few new people had joined the cryptographic staff, including Lieutenant-Commander Leo Brouwer of the Royal Netherlands Navy, who had been working on Japanese cyphers in the Netherlands East Indies up to 1941, and Lieutenant-Commander Colegrave, who had been a language officer in Japan and who had escaped from Singapore in 1942 with Arthur Cooper. They both now had years of experience behind them as well as a good command of Japanese. They and their colleagues were mainly working on the Japanese naval cyphers JN25D, JN40 and JN4, but they were mostly reliant upon assistance and data from Washington. Why was that?

By the summer of 1942, Admiral Somerville had become concerned that there was no liaison between signals intelligence in Kilindini and Washington. The signals intelligence centres in Honolulu and Melbourne were linked directly to Washington, but Kilindini had to wait for GC&CS to forward material sent from Washington, using the secure Typex encryption machine. This was inefficient and slower, so

Somerville was right to be worried about Kilindini being out of the loop. Accordingly, he dispatched Lieutenant-Commander Malcolm Burnett (1904–84) to London to make representations in the hope of improving the situation. To Burnett's surprise, the director of naval intelligence in London refused to see him and told him instead to go to Bletchley Park for what turned out to be an unsatisfactory meeting. Burnett now understood that 'Washington is now and can never be other than the main Japanese cryptographic centre, by virtue of volume of traffic and unlimited availability of staff.' It was, after all, in Washington that American cryptographers had broken open the secrets of the Purple encryption machine, enabling them to build replicas, which were made available to Bletchley Park and Central Bureau in Brisbane. It was therefore a real disadvantage for Kilindini not to be directly connected with Washington. Burnett concluded his report in April 1943 with a bleak assessment: 'I cannot but look upon the B.P. [Bletchley Park] effort as anything but a primary brake on our primary objective, which is the supply with the least possible delay to C. in C. E. F. [commander-in-chief of the Eastern Fleet] of all information from Japanese special intelligence sources.' Burnett, wrongly, did not consider that Bletchley Park was in much of a position to make progress on Japanese cyphers. On the other hand, his arguments for Kilindini to have a direct connection with Washington would have been much reinforced if he had known that, between his departure and the submission of his report, the Kilindini cryptographers had finally made a real breakthrough, justifying their efforts and their very existence.[13]

The breakthrough came with JN40, the cypher used by Japanese merchant shipping. Brian Townend (1917–2005) and John MacInnes, both Foreign Office cryptographers working at Kilindini, were the first to find a solution to this in November 1942, thanks to a mistake made by a Japanese operator. This enabled them to read all previous messages in this cypher and to decrypt each new message as it came in. Thanks to this breakthrough, Kilindini was able to monitor, for example, the movements of a Japanese merchant ship called *Kasuga-maru* that was taking a cargo of stores from Singapore to Port Blair in the Andaman Islands, which Japan had taken and occupied, but as a result of Townend and MacInnes' interception, a submarine went after the *Kasuga-maru* and sank it.[14]

Success breeds success: Kilindini obviously needed more code-breaker linguists. To meet the need, on 4 March 1943 three Bedford graduates boarded ship at Liverpool headed for Lagos in Nigeria, and from there they were flown across Africa. The dispatch of three of the precious Bedford School graduates to Kilindini was an investment of talent that indicates confidence in the intelligence that was being produced there and was then being circulated to London, Washington and Melbourne.

One of the three chosen, Hugh Denham, described the routine as follows:

> The 'front line' of the unit was the wireless operators [many of whom were Wrens], who intercepted the enemy messages; then the analysts and their staff stripped off the additive key [the encrypting element]; the linguists established the meaning of the code-groups and translated the texts, for prompt reporting to COIS [chief of Intelligence Staff] at Naval Headquarters. At the end of each day we went to the back of the building and supervised the incineration of the secret waste.

Denham was very appreciative of the contribution made by the steadily growing number of Wrens. At first, there had been just a couple of dozen, Archdale's group from Singapore, but now there were well over 100. Who they were we do not know.

> The Wrens, almost without exception, did a superb job. They were young, usually well educated, away from home probably for the first time, living under tight discipline on low pay in austere accommodation, and engaged on routine work of an opaque nature. They did it all accurately, conscientiously, and cheerfully.

One evening, he recalled, two Wrens who had just arrived and were on their first spell of duty were asked to fetch a file from the next room but took rather a long time about it. 'Then, five minutes later, with iron self-control, one of the girls asked, "By the way, what do you do when there's a snake in the filing cabinet?"'[15]

Men and women, they all 'worked long hours, usually seven days a week, with a half day off when convenient', Denham reported. In August, he got leave to cross the border into Tanganyika and climb Mt Kilimanjaro with a companion. When they got back to Kilindini, they were horrified to find the place deserted. During their absence, the Eastern Fleet and the cryptographic teams at HMS *Allidina* had moved back to Colombo, so they had to follow in a warship. What could have happened to persuade the fleet to return to Colombo?[16]

The Eastern Fleet moved back to Ceylon because, by September 1943, Japan had already suffered several serious naval reverses. In April 1943, Admiral Yamamoto Isoroku had been shot down and killed by American fighters responding to intelligence from a decrypted message that gave his itinerary for a tour of inspection. Moreover, the ability of the Imperial Japanese Navy to reach across the Indian Ocean had been seriously diminished by losses inflicted by the US Navy. As a result, Colombo was now deemed safe again for the Eastern Fleet. The naval and other staff from Kilindini travelled on troopships crossing the Indian Ocean in convoys accompanied by warships, for the danger of torpedo attacks by Japanese submarines was ever present.

One of the troopships was the SS *Khedive Ismail*, an Egyptian ocean liner that had been requisitioned as a troopship by the British administration in Egypt. The *Khedive Ismail* sailed from Kilindini to Colombo taking large numbers of East African and Indian troops, a Royal Navy contingent and eighty-three women in uniform, including Wrens and nursing sisters. Some of Archdale's group were among them, but six of her Wrens had already returned to Britain—their ship travelled around the Cape and was sailing off the west coast of Africa when it was torpedoed and sunk. They and the others who were saved had the grim ordeal of clinging to a raft for a night and a day, but then they were rescued and taken to Freetown in Sierra Leone.[17]

On the afternoon of 12 February 1944, the SS *Khedive Ismail* was sighted by a Japanese submarine that had penetrated the defensive perimeter of the convoy it was travelling in. The ship was hit by two torpedoes and disappeared beneath the waves in less than two minutes after the first torpedo struck. In all, 1,220 men and seventy-seven women lost their lives, including fifty-one members of the East African Military Nursing Service, eight members of the Women's Territorial Service (East Africa) and seventeen Wrens, eight of whom had been operating British Typex cypher machines at HMS *Allidina* in Kilindini. One of those on board was Beryl Crace (1919–44), who had gone out to Singapore in the second batch of Wrens to work under Betty Archdale. She worked successively at Singapore, Colombo and Kilindini, where she married Surgeon Lieutenant-Commander Leslie

Merrill; she, her husband and their baby Anthony were among the many who perished. Only six women survived—three nursing sisters, one member of the Women's Territorial Service (East Africa) and two Wrens. In terms of loss of life, it was the third most costly merchant shipping disaster in the war, the largest single loss of Allied service-women in the war and the largest single loss of African troops (676). The exciting overseas career that most of the Wrens had signed up for ended in a terrifying death.[18]

The intercept operators, linguists and cryptographers who reached Ceylon safely were given a new location for their work in Colombo, the Anderson Golf Course, which was about 6 miles from the head-quarters of the Eastern Fleet. It was naturally called HMS *Anderson*, and from September 1943 onwards this was the British naval cryptography centre in Asia. However, as the director, Keith, noted: 'Interception in Anderson was of poor quality, owing mainly to the proximity of an over-head electric high tension line, a motor-bus terminus, and various electrically operated machines essential to the functioning of other sections of Anderson.' Once again, the lessons that should have been learnt from the advantages that Mauritius enjoyed as a result of the high location of its intercept operation were ignored. As a result, HMS *Anderson* was hampered in its work until, in late 1944, two new aerials dramatically improved the reception. On the other hand, in September 1944, twenty-six Underwood *katakana* typewriters that had been sup-plied by the United States earlier in the war were brought into use, and these enabled the operators to record directly all the messages they received in Japanese Morse.[19]

HMS *Anderson* was intended to be primarily an 'exploiting centre', rather than to engage in cryptographic research. In other words, its function was, as quickly as possible, to provide the commander-in-chief of the Eastern Fleet with intelligence derived from translations of Japanese naval traffic which had been intercepted locally. Research and strategic intelligence, on the other hand, were supposed to be the domain of the Naval Section at Bletchley Park, which handled Japanese naval messages forwarded from a variety of intercept stations. It was also the Naval Section at Bletchley Park that was responsible for train-ing and selecting personnel to send to *Anderson*. The main criterion was competence as a translator: 'No "duds" are sent overseas.' This is some indication of the importance of the translators in the naval intelligence operation at HMS *Anderson*.[20]

More and more Bedford graduates and other linguists were sent out to augment the teams working on cryptography, radio direction finding, radio finger-printing, translation and all the other tasks being carried out at HMS *Anderson*, and by late 1944 it had become a huge organization. Captain Keith sent a monthly report to Commander Travis at Bletchley Park, and in October 1944 he attached a breakdown of the staff and how they were employed. There were 876 men and women working at HMS *Anderson* by then, including a total of eighteen WRNS officers and 397 other Wrens, who were employed in every department including the Intelligence Section. The one exception, in 1944, was the Translation Section, which consisted solely of five naval officers and eight Foreign Office officials. By July 1945, however, there were six Wrens in the Translation Section, including Shirley Brereton-Smith who been operating the Bombe at Bletchley Park earlier in the war. If they were employed as translators, then they probably did one of the short courses in the Naval Section at Bletchley Park, for the records of the short courses are incomplete, but they may have been employed in a clerical capacity.[21]

Dorothy Smith was one of the WRNS petty officers at HMS *Anderson*, and she recalled that all 400 of them lived in a 'Wrennery', a large house in Colombo that served as their mess; they lived in the grounds in huts with palm-leaf rooves. The daily journey to HMS *Anderson* was made by bus or lorry, and she recalled the driver taking a swig from a bottle of *arak* (distilled spirit) before setting off. 'The favourite evening spot', she recalled, 'was the little nightclub, the Silver Fawn, where we'd be taken for a really glamorous evening's dinner-dancing, the live band playing favourite dance tunes, the lights low, flowers for one's dress, gorgeous food. It was incredibly heady stuff for girls of our age', particularly since few of them had ever been abroad before.[22]

The range of different skills required at HMS *Anderson* was vast, and many acquired additional skills on the spot that led to further opportunities. One man who did just this was Edmund James Edworthy Stowers (1924–2015), who had joined the Navy in 1942 and was trained as a telegraphist. In 1944, he was serving on the frigate HMS *Bann* when he was deposited at HMS *Anderson*. There he worked as a high-frequency direction finder, but then spent five weeks learning *katakana* and Japanese Morse. With those skills under his belt, he was asked to volunteer for wireless intelligence duties in a mobile team working with intelligence officers who decoded and translated intercepts then and there. After the end of the war, he was flown to Saigon to take over the Japanese radio station from the Japanese staff.[23]

At the end of October 1944, Keith sent Travis a table showing how the thirty-three individuals who had done one or other of the courses at SOAS were employed. Perhaps there had been a query he needed to respond to. More than half of the SOAS graduates had done the phonetics course, but very few of them were in fact employed in roles that made any use of the knowledge they had acquired. Four, it is true, were assistants to the air intelligence officer, but others were engaged in traffic analysis, research or even security. It should have been obvious to Travis from this that the skills being painstakingly imparted at SOAS were not always being put to the best use. This, as we saw in chapter 3, seemed to Professor Turner, the director of SOAS, a waste of their specialist training.[24]

On the other hand, the Bedford graduates were not being wasted. One of the naval translators at HMS *Anderson* was Charles Bawden, who had been by far the best student on the fourth course at Bedford. After leaving Bedford, he had spent some months in the Naval Section at Bletchley Park getting some experience working on decoded Japanese messages. Then he and two others were sent out to Colombo, arriving by ship in the summer of 1944. Many years later, when he was professor of Mongolian at SOAS, he wrote of his experiences:

> It was not for us a violent period, but the experience of working on current enemy messages, always incomplete and requiring emendation, the experience, that is, of applying text-critical techniques, learned on the spot, to practical warfare, was something never to be forgotten. It was, too, a period when lifelong friendships were formed. We were a compact and harmonious group of civilians, naval officers and Wrens, and the unique association we formed then has lasted, for some of us, ever since. ... Until the end of the war we spent our working time trying to make sense of Japanese naval messages, taken down by hand by naval ratings, decrypted and decoded as far as was possible by Wrens, and presented to us in sometimes a very incomplete form.

It was, he thought, the most formative part of his life. It is clear from this that translating the messages called for much more than knowledge of the language: he needed intuition, inspiration and depth of experience with naval messages to be able to make sense of the incomplete ones. It is also clear from his account that some of the Wrens were employed in decryption work.[25]

Although work on Japanese codes and cyphers was mainly being done in the United States and Bletchley Park, the operation at HMS *Anderson* had its own rationale. Apart from lingering mistrust and/or rivalry between British and American codebreakers, there was also a material difference. The British Eastern Fleet and South East Asia Command (SEAC) were, for obvious reasons, more interested in naval intelligence relating to the Indian Ocean and South East Asia, while the US Navy was more interested in intelligence relating to the Pacific. Their operational needs were thus very different.[26]

The Wireless Experimental Centre in New Delhi

At the beginning of this chapter, we left the three Bedford graduates, Robinson, Lloyd-Jones and Noyce, just after they had arrived in India. All three of them joined the WEC, but what kind of an operation was it and what kind of work did they do there?

In January 1942, an Intelligence School was set up in Calcutta, for it was obvious that India and the British Indian Army would soon become much more involved in the war now that Japan was moving into Burma. Included in the new Intelligence School was a section for training cryptographers, which was led by Lieutenant-Colonel Marr-Johnson, who knew Japanese as he had been living in Japan in the 1930s and who had been working in the Army Section of the FECB before he left Singapore. This was just a start, of course, for the scale of the intelligence problem of dealing with Japanese messages was yet to be fully grasped.[27]

In March 1942, shortly after the surrender of Singapore, the 'Y' Committee in London took up a proposal made by the commander-in-chief, India, Field Marshal Sir Archibald Wavell, for the reorganization of intelligence work directed against Japan. Wavell was keen to avoid unnecessary duplication of effort 'in view of the paucity of Japanese speaking personnel and Intelligence resources applicable to Japan'. The 'Y' Committee agreed that in future British work on Japanese Army cyphers would be done in India, with the proviso that long-term research would continue to be handled at Bletchley Park and that raw material (i.e., undecrypted messages) would continue to be transmitted to Bletchley Park.[28]

It was in these circumstances that the Wireless Experimental Centre in New Delhi was formed on 1 June 1942, housed in Ramjas College in Anand Parbat. It was, in effect, an outpost of Bletchley Park, and there was a flow of personnel between the two organizations. Unlike Bletchley Park, the WEC was not a fully inter-service operation, for, as we have seen, there was a separate organization for handling naval messages in the Indian Ocean and East Asia. Accordingly, the personnel of the WEC came either from the Army or the RAF. Some of the initial members came from Singapore when the FECB was dismantled, but there were at first too few who knew any Japanese. Just as at Bletchley Park, security here too was supposed to be tight, but there were lapses. The man supposed to destroy confidential waste instead passed it on to a fruit-seller to wrap his fruit in.[29]

What kind of a life awaited Robinson, Noyce and Lloyd-Jones (once he had got his commission) when they joined the WEC in 1942? 'Hello Chaps! This is Delhi', announced the booklet given to new military arrivals. Among the tips and tourist information, there were suggestions for 'collecting a few souvenirs of India for your wife or girl friend' and 'meeting girls who will be willing to do a movie with you, to go to a hop or possibly to have you meet their home folks'. Despite the American feel to the language, this booklet was aimed at British arrivals, and although it could have been taken for granted, when it was first produced, that all new service arrivals would be men, that did not remain the case. A company of the Women's Auxiliary Corps (India) had been formed as early as June 1942 to work at the WEC. Sergeant D. Singh joined against the wishes of her family, and she objected to being wolf-whistled (presumably by the British personnel there), but she said in 1945 that life in the corps 'makes one bold, courageous, and independent, and moulds one's personality'. In Britain, however, there were objections to the posting of British women in the ATS or the WAAF to India, and it was only when these objections had been overcome by an act of Parliament that a contingent of ATS and WAAF women were posted to the WEC. There were supposed to be 300 of each, but only some WAAF officers had arrived before the war ended, to be followed a few weeks later by a party of ATS recruits, who featured on the cover of the September 1945 issue of the WEC magazine in a photograph showing them being guided around by two Indian members of the Women's Auxiliary Corps (India).[30]

Robinson, Noyce and Lloyd-Jones joined Section C in the WEC once they had settled in. This was the key section, for it was responsible for codebreaking. There were already a dozen cryptographers working on Japanese messages by the time they arrived.[31]

They did not get off to a particularly good start, owing to the fact that they rather prematurely considered themselves to be experts in Japanese, as Lloyd-Jones recalled:

> The most powerful personality of the centre was the commander of 'C' section, Lieutenant-Colonel Patrick Marr-Johnson, whom I had heard spoken of with high regard by Colonel Tiltman. He was a regular soldier, who had been at school at Wellington; he had been stationed in Japan and had a good knowledge of its language. Highly intelligent and with great personal charm when he liked to use it, he was not without a streak of ruthlessness. ... Robinson and I made a somewhat awkward start by not concealing our feelings about some of the officers who were there because they had been businessmen in Japan but had only a rudimentary knowledge of the spoken language, which was useless for our purposes. But after a time, we got on excellently with Colonel Marr-Johnson and his wife and with Major [Reginald] Divers, the only one of the businessmen who had a serious knowledge of Japanese.

Marr-Johnson certainly had better knowledge of the language than either Lloyd-Jones or Robinson. He had been a language officer in Japan for several years from 1933, and in 1938 he had been appointed as the first Japanese interpreter in the Military Section at GC&CS. He is said to have spoken Japanese so well that he could pass as a native speaker. Nevertheless, he was extremely grateful to Colonel Tiltman for the Bedford graduates who had been sent to him. 'They have reached a standard', he wrote, 'that I frankly never thought possible', and he expected them to develop into first-class cryptographers.[32]

At first, Lloyd-Jones, Noyce and Robinson commuted to Army HQ in Delhi and worked on Japanese documents that had been found on the battlefield or recovered from aircraft that had been shot down. There were two Army linguists already working there, and they had much to teach the newcomers, whose knowledge of military language was still rudimentary. Later, the three Bedford graduates worked alongside the others at the WEC, which was constantly expanding.

Thanks to the fact that Noyce's father was Sir Frank Noyce, who had been a member of the viceroy of India's executive council before the war, the three of them enjoyed an interesting social life. Lloyd-Jones recalled: 'as his [Wilfrid Noyce's] friends, Robinson and I were entertained by a number of prominent persons. Some of these were British and others Indian, and as Sir Frank had been decidedly sympathetic to the movement towards Indian independence, we met persons on both sides of Indian politics.' Noyce described the work at the WEC as continuous, and wrote to Ian Grimble, a fellow Bedford graduate who also came out to Delhi, that he had not had a day off for a month, partly because he was having to supervise the work of two other Bedford graduates, who had both done the phonetics course at SOAS after leaving Bedford but had less experience. Since he was also an expert mountaineer, Noyce was subsequently sent to the Aircrew Recreational Centre at Srinagar where he gave instruction in mountain climbing.[33]

The WEC did not normally interrogate POWs, for that was the job of units in the field, as we will see. An exception was made, however, when a POW had specialized knowledge of use to the WEC. One such case was Sergeant-Major Hirose Yutaka, who had been chief code clerk at the 114th Infantry Regiment HQ. He was captured at Myitkyina in Burma on 3 August 1944 and was interrogated from 13 to 20 August, cooperatively providing his interrogators with extensive information on Japanese wireless procedures and coding practices.[34]

There are no surviving rosters of the staff at the WEC, but what is certain is that there were many other linguists working there apart from the three Bedford graduates, and more were joining all the time. A photograph of Section C taken in August 1944 shows Marr-Johnson sitting in the middle and forty-eight men around him. The owner of the photograph, Philip Telford Taylor (1911–71), whom we will return to shortly, thoughtfully added the names of his colleagues on the back: some were later graduates of Bedford, others had done courses at SOAS, while other names I have not encountered before.

Some of them may have done courses at Simla, as we will see in the next chapter.

One of the fresh young faces in the photograph is that of a new-comer, Pilot Officer Michael Kerry (1923–2012). He had done a Japanese course at SOAS and worked with both Lloyd-Jones and Noyce in Section C. He recalled that Lloyd-Jones was 'a great character' and that Noyce had 'a very battered face' from falling off mountains. At first, they were all working mainly on Army messages, which consisted mostly of daily reports on weapons, rations and sickness. That might not seem very important, but the struggle between the Allies and the Japanese in north-eastern India had reached a critical stage and the fighting was desperate. The Imperial Japanese Army surrounded the British garrison at Imphal in the Indian state of Manipur but in July was finally forced to acknowledge that it had been defeated and retreat back into Burma. In the process, the Japanese Army lost at least 50,000 men, and double that number were wounded. In August, when the WEC photograph was taken, the British 14th Army was pursuing the Japanese eastwards, and the information derived from decrypts told the Allies much about the exhaustion, disease and malnutrition that were also taking their toll on the enemy.[35]

Kerry was later working on messages in a code used by the Japanese Army Air Force, which had already been broken at Bletchley Park. Since messages in that code could now be decrypted and read without difficulty, he and four others were sent to 355 Wireless Unit at Comilla (now Cumilla, in Bangladesh), where their intercepts could be put to immediate use. They picked up the signals of Japanese bombers that used to operate from Mingaladon air base in Rangoon, which is now the international airport. On one occasion, he recalled, RAF night-fighters shot down all of them, so 'all night we could hear Mingaladon air base calling for its lost children'. Rapid responses like this depended, of course, not only upon Kerry's cryptographic skills but also upon his ability to translate the decoded messages and make meaningful intel-ligence out of them. As a secret post-war history put it, 'Subsequent interrogation of P.O.W. [prisoners of war] has shown that in the final stages of the Burma Campaign, our knowledge of the disposition of J.A.A.F. [Japanese Army Air Force] units was more complete than that of the Japanese commanders themselves.'[36]

Taylor, who wrote the names on the back of the photograph, also worked in Section C at the WEC and became good friends with Noyce. He was older than most and already married with a daughter when he was called up; he joined the RAF and was sent to India as a clerk. He was in Dohaguri near Darjeeling in 1943 when a circular came around from Delhi asking any graduates of Oxford or Cambridge with first-class degrees in languages or mathematics to volunteer for special duties. He fitted the bill as a classicist from Cambridge, so he volunteered. Never again, he realized, would he have to take cover under his desk every time a Japanese bombing raid took place. He was first sent to do some training in Havelian, near Abbottabad (now Pakistan), but the details are obscure. Abbottabad was the location of the Wireless Experimental Depot, an intercept station, and they may well have run some courses there. Whatever the truth, it is certain that he was given a commission as a pilot officer and then began work as a cryptographer, and also certain that he had acquired some knowledge of Japanese. After spending some time at the WEC, he was sent out to 368 Wireless Unit, which in March 1945 moved to Cox's Bazar (now Bangladesh), not far from the Burmese border, and therefore much closer to the action. Here he would have needed to know some Japanese.[37]

Both Kerry and Taylor worked for wireless units: What was their function and why did they need to know Japanese? At a basic level, they were the RAF's answer to the Mobile Sections that served with the Army, as we will see in the next chapter, and they made it possible for RAF squadrons to have the latest intelligence about Japanese movements in the air, just as Arthur Cooper had done in the dark days of February 1942 in Singapore. Another who worked in the wireless units was Alfred Bell (1923–87): after completing the first course at the Bedford Japanese School, he had been sent to the Air Section at Bletchley Park as an RAF officer. He had then done a course in Japanese phonetics at SOAS before being posted out to India. He, Kerry, Taylor and many others were tracking Japanese air movements by intercepting air-to-ground communications and thus enabling RAF fighter squadrons to engage Japanese aircraft and strafe Japanese positions on the ground during the dark days when Kohima and Imphal were in danger of being overrun by the Japanese Army. After the Allies had gained air supremacy in the middle of 1944, British and American bomber crews were flying Liberators to destroy Japanese bases, camps and communications in Burma, as celebrated in a contemporary newsreel titled 'Inside Burma with the RAF'. It was the wireless units that provided the pilots and their controllers with up-to-the-minute information about Japanese activity in the air, either from decrypted wireless messages or from voice messages.[38]

On a quite different level, these wireless units worked together to locate Japanese transmitters using 'direction finding'. If three or more receivers tracked where enemy signals were coming from, then by plotting the lines on a map the location of the transmitter could be pinned down—and destroyed if it was on the ground or tracked if it was in the air.[39]

As the tide turned, the 14th Army went forward into Burma following the retreating Japanese armies. It was supported by its Mobile Sections and protected by RAF and USAAF aircraft, which in turn were supported by their Wireless Units. Towards the end of the war, even some of the desk-bound men at the WEC found themselves having to get used to a more uncomfortable life nearer the front lines. Lloyd-Jones, for example, was sent out into the Burmese jungle, where there were new hazards:

Early in 1945 I was concerned in one piece of work which had a definite, though a very limited, military effect. Mainly owing to the work of Robinson, we were in a position to read messages in a code used by the enemy at corps level [a corps contains two or more divisions], and it was necessary to dispatch a party to the north of Burma so that messages should be handed without delay to those in action. About seven officers and fifteen other ranks were flown to the headquarters of 33rd Corps, then encamped at Yazagyo, just east of the native [Indian] state of Manipur. Our camp was in the jungle. Not long before we arrived, a soldier had gone out to relieve himself, and while doing so noticed an enormous tiger casually strolling down a path that led in his direction. Luckily, he was too scared to move, and the tiger slowly walked past him, casting him a glance of unutterable contempt.

Lloyd-Jones seems to have relished being in the thick of things, partly perhaps because he and his colleagues were able to make a real contribution to the war effort through their skills:

The enemy seemed to have no idea that their signals might be being read; from time to time a cipher clerk would forget his duty and send a message *en clair*. On one occasion a message indicated that a force whose number it conveniently gave was to move down a particular road at a particular time; the day after we had dealt with this, the Director of Intelligence came in person to thank us for having made possible a successful ambush by Gurkhas hiding in the bushes. The troops at corps headquarters, who called us 'the backroom boys', were friendly and grateful, and we were given 33rd Corps flashes.

Lloyd-Jones' attachment to units in the field brought him into much closer contact with warfare and its terrible human cost:

At one stage the corps headquarters moved south from Yazagyo to Kalewa. Our forces were pursuing the Japanese down the road going southwards level with the coast; since the enemy had no aircraft left, their retreat down the road had been conducted under unremitting fire. We moved at night, and each vehicle had an officer with a rifle sitting next to the driver. The jungle came right up to the road, close to which lay numerous wrecked enemy vehicles and innumerable corpses of enemy soldiers. Since the flesh of their faces had been eaten by the vultures, their bones shone brightly in the moonlight. At the end of the month the code changed, and almost all of our party returned to Delhi [because they could no longer decrypt the messages]. But as there was always a possibility that uncoded messages might be intercepted, I was left behind together with one sergeant, and we stayed on for a short time, until another officer who knew Japanese could come from Delhi to relieve me.

With the war approaching its end, the tactical value of intelligence was in decline and Lloyd-Jones' wartime career was coming to an end.

In April 1945, the war in Europe was in its final phase, but nobody guessed that it was soon to come to an end in Asia, too. Allied armies were approaching Rangoon, and it was obvious that the Burma Campaign at least was nearing an end. In that same month, the Wireless Experimental Centre Players produced *A Midsummer's Night's Dream* in Lodi Gardens in Delhi: perhaps there was a sense that the dream was coming to an end and they would all be returning to their normal lives. In August, the war came to a sudden end when the Japanese government took the decision to surrender. The September issue of the WEC journal carried a picture of the VJ (Victory over Japan) parade on its cover and a history of the WEC inside, without, however, saying exactly what the WEC had been doing all that time. The WEC was finally disbanded on 1 April 1946.[40]

Interception at sea

While the WEC and the Wireless Units had been working with the Allied armies and air forces to defeat Japanese forces in Burma, the Royal Navy was beginning to take the war to the remnants of the Imperial Japanese Navy, too. In June 1943, as the tide was beginning to turn, the Eastern Fleet realized that it needed Japanese linguists for operations at sea. The fleet was soon to take the offensive.

The problem of training linguists for shipboard operations was taken up by the Naval Section at Bletchley Park. What was necessary was some knowledge of Japanese as well as training in Japanese naval and air radio transmissions, air wireless telegraphy and high frequency direction finding. Somehow, the section managed to find twenty-two civilians who already had some knowledge of spoken Japanese; who they were and how they had learnt Japanese we will perhaps never know. At any rate, they were sent to train in destroyers cruising up and down the east coast of Britain in what were called 'Headache Operations'—after all, you spent long hours with headphones on your ears getting used to Japanese Morse. In addition to these twenty-two civilians, some fifty naval ratings were also targeted for training. Some of them attended a course at SOAS and then went to RAF Newbold Revel for general training in air communications; after that, they went out to India for further training on the spot. By April 1944, these trainees were fully fledged and were being employed on ocean-going warships, and they were doing well enough working on low-grade naval traffic and air-to-ground communications to be judged a success.[41]

Before these newly trained men came on line, RAF personnel were detached from 357 Wireless Unit in India and lent to the Navy as a ship-borne intercept party. That was for Operation Cockpit in April 1944. Operation Cockpit was a joint British and American attack on Japanese port and oil facilities on the island of Sabang, off the northern tip of Sumatra (now in Indonesia). To support the operation by supplying intelligence in real time, Flying-Officer A. Frankish boarded the battlecruiser HMS *Renown* with a corporal and several airmen, while an RAF corporal boarded the battleship HMS *Queen Elizabeth* with two airmen. As Frankish put it in his subsequent report, 'This was the first

blow that is to carry us back along the road to Singapore and Tokio.'
When they set out, the destination was unknown to most of the crew,
but once they neared their target, Admiral Somerville, the commander-in-chief of the Eastern Fleet, made a general announcement:
'The target for our aircraft will be Sabang. We do not appear to have
been spotted. The Japs have regular habits, and therefore we expect to
catch them with their kimonos up, and heads well down.' This was,
Frankish noted, 'the first time a "Y" [communications interception and
decryption] Party had accompanied the Fleet on operations in Asian
waters. The enemy reaction was slight, but the party justified itself,
and in addition useful lessons were learnt for future operations.'
Although they had very limited space in which to work, and the temperature there during action stations was 46°C they managed to pick
up enemy sightings of the attacking aircraft, so they could inform the
pilots when they had been spotted. What they learnt from this operation was that, as a result of the interference of the ship's own communication systems, interception worked best when the ship was close
to the target.[42]

Where Frankish had learnt his Japanese is unknown, but he must
have had a good command of spoken Japanese to be able to understand
Japanese spoken under the pressure of attack. We do not know where
Flying-Officer C. W. Sugden learnt his Japanese either. He led the
intercept party on HMS *Renown* in June 1944 in Operation Pedal,
which was an attack on Japanese facilities at Port Blair in the Andaman
Islands between India and Burma. Here, too, his party kept close watch
on Japanese frequencies despite the cramped conditions, the high tem-
peratures and the very rough seas, but owing to the lack of enemy
reaction to the attack, they did not manage to furnish any useful information, as they admitted in their report.[43]

RAF personnel continued to participate in shipboard operations for
some time, probably because they already had a lot of experience on
land. During Operation Light, an attack on the port of Belawan on the
island of Medan (Indonesia) on 18 September 1944, the intercept
party on board the battleship HMS *Howe* managed to intercept
Japanese alerts and sighting reports, which they passed straight to the
bridge. Again, in late April and early May 1945, Flying Officer
W. S. Grace led a party on board HMS *Queen Elizabeth* in Operation

Bishop around the Nicobar Islands in the Indian Ocean, and later in May in Operation Dukedom in the Malacca Strait. During Operation Dukedom, he was able to report to the admiral's bridge on 16 May that the Japanese authorities on Medan had instructed the base at Lhokseumawe on Sumatra that their 'fighters are to seek out and attack enemy aircraft carriers with all strength; first priority is to be given to repelling enemy air strength'. This message was probably spoken and therefore *en clair*, and Grace's intervention showed the value of being able to understand orders and pass on warnings to the pilots taking off from the aircraft-carriers.[44]

Although the RAF personnel were good at intercepting messages *en clair*, once naval personnel began to conduct shipboard intercept operations, they also undertook some decryption. One example comes from Operation Adoption, off the coast of Burma, in June 1945. Sub-Lieutenant M. P. Donald on the cruiser HMS *Ceylon* wrote in his report that he had been able to decipher some messages in the codes JN166 and ABC10, adding, 'of those which could be deciphered only the weather reports were of use, though the party was able to pass information regarding enemy reaction to the carrier force operating in the Malacca Straits'. By this time, the intercept teams included both RAF and Navy personnel, and included specialists in traffic analysis, cryptography and interception.[45]

In all of these operations, at least one member of the intercept party must have been able to understand Japanese. Both Flying-Officer Grace and Sub-Lieutenant Donald, as well as some of the others mentioned in reports on other operations, had completed courses at SOAS. Frankish and Sugden had probably done so as well, but the surviving records are incomplete. What they had succeeded in doing was showing that shipboard interception could provide valuable real-time intelligence provided that at least one member of the party had a reasonable command of Japanese. Their teams did for the Navy what the Mobile Sections were doing for the Army and the Wireless Units for the RAF.[46]

* * *

It is of course true that the main burden of the conduct of the war against Japan fell on the US Army under General MacArthur and on the US Navy under Admiral Chester Nimitz. But there was another side to the war against Japan, and that was the Burma Campaign, which ended in the rout of an entire Japanese Army. In that campaign, the British and Indian armies bore the brunt of the fighting. In the air and at sea, it was units of the RAF and the Indian Air Force, together with some US Air Force units, and at sea the Eastern Fleet, that carried the war to Japan. In this chapter, we have followed the components of those forces that constituted the 'backroom boys and girls', from the intercept operators to the codebreakers. This massive intelligence operation, so rarely acknowledged, was based on skills honed at the Bedford Japanese School and at SOAS, and at the heart of it was mastery of Japanese.

7

ON THE FRONT LINE IN BURMA

The population of Mauritius was anxious about the threat from the sea, justifiably so since ships were being sunk in nearby waters, but the island itself was never attacked during the war. India, by contrast, soon found itself in very real danger. It all started in Burma (Myanmar) in January 1942, when the Imperial Japanese Army mounted a rapid and successful invasion.

How does Burma fit into the picture? In the early nineteenth century, when the British East India Company controlled the greater part of the Indian subcontinent, the company fought the kingdom of Burma over jurisdiction in the border areas. In 1852, the company provoked further conflict, which resulted in the annexation of a substantial area of Burmese territory. In 1885, the British government, which had taken over control of India after the uprising of 1857, declared war on Burma and the following year seized the entire country. Once Britain had, quite unjustifiably, crushed Burmese independence and sovereignty, Burma became a province of British India. As a result, Rangoon (Yangon) became a city of Indian merchants, administrators and soldiers with a much smaller British colonial presence.

Resistance to British rule in Burma continued for some time and was brutally suppressed. In the twentieth century, Burmese nationalist movements came to the fore and opposition to British rule took the form of hunger strikes and rebellions. Eventually, in 1937, the British government detached Burma from India and gave Burma a new constitution, but that did not stop the protests, which in 1938 developed into a general strike. British mounted police turned their guns on an angry crowd and killed seventeen protesters. In the light of all this, it is not at all surprising that some Burmese were so viscerally opposed to British rule that they welcomed the Japanese as liberators. In 1941, the Burma Independence Army was formed to facilitate the Japanese invasion and, it was hoped, thus put an end to British rule, rather as the Indian National Army was seeking to do in India.

As elsewhere, the Japanese Army moved with lightning speed and overwhelmed the British and Indian forces trying to defend their positions in Burma. By March 1942, the Japanese Army had taken Rangoon and its victory was complete. There was no other option for the British and Indian armies: lacking popular support and faced with the overwhelming might of Japanese forces on land and in the air, they were compelled to move northwards and westwards to India, in yet another Allied retreat from the Japanese military machine. In the process, they lost most of their equipment and transport, but they did manage to reach Imphal, the capital of the state of Manipur in north-east India, before the monsoon broke in May 1942.

What was the Japanese goal in this campaign? In the first instance, it was simply to capture Rangoon and prevent Allied supplies from reaching China along the Burma Road, which leads from northern Burma to south-west China. The invasion of Burma was thus linked first and foremost to Japan's invasion of China, which had begun in 1937. By 1941, the invasion had run into difficulties as a result of stiffer resistance from Chinese troops, who were being supplied by the Soviet Union and by the United States. By taking control of Burma, Japan hoped to be in a position to put a halt at least to the flow of military supplies being sent by the Allies along the Burma Road to support the Chinese armies.

That was not the only reason, however. One of Japan's war aims was to put an end to the European colonial empires in Asia. Japan certainly succeeded at the outset, supplanting European colonial administration in Hong Kong, French Indo-China, the Dutch East Indies, British Malaya and Burma, and all that remained were the British colonies of India and Ceylon. In March 1942, Japanese forces made their first move against India, invading the Andaman and Nicobar islands in the Bay of Bengal. Japanese planes bombed Calcutta several times beginning in December 1942 and other cities on the east coast of India, including Madras (Chennai), were also bombed occasionally. Madras was evacuated in 1942 for fear of a Japanese invasion that never happened. At the same time, Japan sought to encourage Indian opponents of British rule in India to overthrow the British. To that end, Japanese officers encouraged and supported the Indian National Army, an anti-colonial force led by Subhas Chandra Bose, and Japanese aircraft dropped propaganda posters. These posters, with texts in Hindi, Bengali, Urdu and occasionally English ('God bid Nippon to help India drive out the British devil'), used colourful imagery to suggest that Britain was responsible for India's woes, especially the Great Bengal Famine of 1943, and that Indians would be better off linking hands with other Asians, including Japanese.[1]

In 1943, a new and ambitious Japanese commander was appointed in Burma, Lieutenant-General Mutaguchi Ren'ya (1888–1966). He had taken part in the invasion of Malaya in December 1941 and had been wounded in the battle for Singapore in February 1942. Mutaguchi was convinced that an attack on Assam in north-east India might well be followed by the complete collapse of British rule in India and the end of the British Empire in Asia. Early in 1944, therefore, he led his armies, including a contingent from the Indian National Army, into north-east India and surrounded the city of Imphal, where Allied forces were concentrated. But Mutaguchi's supply lines were long and uncertain, and the defenders of Imphal doggedly kept up their resistance. It was at this point that the tide turned and the 14th Army, mostly consisting of British and Indian troops under the command of Lieutenant-General Sir William Slim, counter-attacked. Finally, in July 1944, Mutaguchi had no choice but to acknowledge that he had suffered a major defeat and his troops began their long retreat eastwards through Burma.[2]

For the British and Indian armies on the ground and in the air, the grim months of their retreat at the beginning of 1942 marked the start of what was to be a long and desperate campaign. Eventually, they succeeded in repulsing the Japanese invasion of India, turning the tables on the Imperial Japanese Army and ultimately retaking Burma in the summer of 1945, but it was a brutal campaign that lasted right until the end of the war. Throughout the campaign, battlefield intelligence proved to be crucial, and it was provided by a corps of translators and interpreters who operated in the most arduous jungle conditions in high humidity and often incessant rain: they were interrogating prisoners, poring over captured documents and then typing up translations and reports in their tents. Who were they, and how well prepared were they for their work as translators and interpreters in the field?

Two translators in the Burma Campaign

In August 1945, two translators in the British Army met for the first time in Rangoon. Both had been in the thick of the action as intelligence officers, and they were to remain friends for the rest of their lives. One of them was Richard Storry (1913–82), who spent the rest of his career teaching Japanese history at Oxford. The other was Louis Levy (1922–91), who later adopted his mother's original surname and changed his name to Louis Allen. After the war, Allen taught French at Durham University, but he also wrote extensively on Japan and the Burma Campaign. Their lives were profoundly shaped by their wartime experiences, but how had they ended up in wartime Burma?

Storry first went to Japan before the war. In 1937, after graduating from Oxford with a degree in history, he made an adventurous career choice, deciding to become a teacher of English at Otaru Higher Commercial School (now Otaru University of Commerce) in Hokkaido, northern Japan. He enjoyed the experience, apart from the increasingly intrusive attentions of the Kenpeitai, the military police. I attended his lectures on modern Japanese history at Oxford in 1969–70, and they had an immediacy and a sense of lived history that were unique, for he could talk about the pervasive influence of the Kenpeitai from personal experience and had himself seen some of the key players in the murky politics of the late 1930s.

The outbreak of war in Europe and the worsening situation in Japan propelled Storry back from Japan to Britain in 1940. For a while, he served in the Home Guard, but at the end of December 1941, when the War Office was at last picking out those with some knowledge of Japanese, he was commissioned into the Intelligence Corps and posted to Singapore. His ship survived an attack by a Japanese bomber just before he reached Singapore on 28 January 1942. He was, of course, unaware that very soon he would be leaving again in hurry. As instructed, he joined a Japanese course for ten people who, like him, already knew some Japanese.

It was a shocking and harrowing time for everybody in Singapore in January 1942. There were constant air-raids, and every day Storry saw with his own eyes the destruction in the streets. He had been there barely a fortnight when, on 13 February 1942, he and the other students were given half an hour to get down to the docks and get away. Japanese speakers like him were too rare a resource to be wasted, and they had to be got out of Singapore, which was now doomed. Storry admitted in his diary, 'To pretend I was not glad to leave would be ridiculous humbug. I was damn glad.' He got on board the SS *Kuala*, which was carrying large numbers of women and children out of danger. The ship managed to get away with several other vessels, and the convoy took shelter at Pom Pong Island, to the south of Singapore and close to Sumatra. Storry and some others disembarked to explore the island, but while he was on shore Japanese bombers attacked and sank his ship and several others. Storry heard 'terrible cries from those on board and in the sea', but there was nothing he or anybody else could do. Eventually, some motorboats came and took the survivors to Sumatra. From there, some were taken to Australia, but Storry made his way to India.[3]

After the surrender of the British garrison in Singapore on 15 February, Storry's parents were informed that he was missing. As far as they knew, he might have been taken prisoner or even killed.

Soon after he arrived in Delhi, Storry managed to telephone his parents to let them know he was safe. Now, how could he make himself useful in Delhi? In view of his knowledge of Japanese, he was posted to the Combined Services Detailed Interrogation Centre (India), or CSDIC(I), an organization set up in Delhi to deal with Japanese prisoners of war. This was one of a bewildering number of organizations that were set up during the war to process Japanese intelligence. In the previous chapter, we encountered the WEC, but later in this chapter we shall encounter the South East Asia Translation and Interrogation Centre (SEATIC) and in later chapters the Allied

Translator and Interpreter Section (ATIS). The main reason for the profusion of names is the reorganization of the Allied forces conducting the war with Japan. Both the WEC and CSDIC(I) were British entities that were staffed mainly by personnel from the British and Indian armed forces. In 1943, however, SEAC was created as the Allied body overseeing the war against Japan on land and sea and in the air over the vast area between India and what is now Vietnam. It was the counterpart to the South West Pacific Area (SWPA) command, which was based in Australia and consisted overwhelmingly of American and Australian personnel. To coordinate intelligence, SEAC created SEATIC and SWPA the Allied Translator and Interpreter Section, so these two bodies operated in different theatres of the war against Japan.

In January 1943, after Storry had spent some time in Delhi, probably learning the art of successful interrogation, he was sent out to the front as an interrogator in No. 1 Mobile Section, a small, self-sufficient unit that could handle both interrogations and the translation of captured documents. From March to July 1944, he was in Imphal during the ferocious battle for control of the city, and in October 1944, as the Japanese forces retreated, he took No. 1 Mobile Section across the Chindwin River to the township of Yeu in northern Burma, a distance of 1,065 miles. There he joined the advance on Rangoon, which he reached in early June 1945. Storry was very close to the action throughout much of this period.[4]

What did Storry accomplish in Burma? In his diary, he is modest about his command of written Japanese but recalls that 'in November 1943 at Dimlo, Chin Hills, a Gurkha battalion captured a marked map from a dead Japanese officer; and by working on it for hours with a dictionary I was able to make good sense of it; and this map was of immediate importance'. On some days during the Battle of Imphal, heaps of Japanese documents were brought in for him to examine; they were 'often bloodstained and odorous', for they had usually been recovered from corpses. There were two Americans of Japanese descent (Nisei) attached to his Mobile Section, and they undertook many of the translations. Sometimes maps or operation orders were found, for Japanese officers often carried sensitive documents with them into battle. Although British translators were often surprised by such carelessness and poor security awareness, this was not in fact a peculiarly Japanese failing. In 1942, Rommel's intelligence personnel reported that British officers in the 8th Army were routinely doing the same. At any rate, when such documents were found, Storry worked with the Nisei to produce a translation, and he provided headquarters with a constant flow of intelligence.[5]

Although many Japanese soldiers chose to kill themselves rather than be captured, some prisoners were in fact taken. In a couple of months in late 1944, for example, as the 5th Indian Division made its way down the Tiddim Road south of Imphal, fifty-three prisoners were taken. Each of them had to be interrogated in the hope that they might have useful information to provide. In general, Storry said, the atmosphere during interrogation was invariably friendly, which he did not find difficult to explain: most of the interrogators had lived in Japan, and although they had no illusions about Japanese society or the Imperial Japanese Army, 'the Japanese race did not seem to them—as it did, inevitably, to so many—to be made up of an antlike horde of sub-human-fanatics'. Perhaps partly for that reason, Storry found the prisoners extremely cooperative, largely, he thought, because they had no security consciousness and had not been told what to say if captured. The assumption in the Imperial Japanese Army was that all ranks would prefer death to capture. All the same, interrogating a prisoner so as to get the best possible intelligence is not an easy matter. Storry had a bilingual interrogation manual to rely upon, which he kept for the rest of his life. By following the guidance it contained, he managed to find out the enemy's strength, strategic intentions, levels of morale and the locations of ammunition dumps and lines of communication.[6]

On one occasion, Storry had to conduct an interrogation in front of the news cameras. Vice-Admiral Lord Louis Mountbatten, as Supreme Allied Commander South East Asia Command, visited Storry's unit and wanted to witness an interrogation. A rare Japanese deserter had been captured, and Mountbatten asked some questions that Storry had to interpret. By this time, of course, Storry was a seasoned interrogator. When he returned to England in 1945, the commander of CSDIC(I) summed up his career as follows: 'An intelligence officer of exceptional ability and knowledge. Has 3½ years active service in Burma.' To put it another way, Storry had put his knowledge of the Japanese language to the ultimate test, providing hot battlefield intelligence over several taxing and demanding years.[7]

Storry finally reached Rangoon in early June 1945, a month after the Allied armies first entered the city on 6 May. He saw the victory parade there on 15 June and kept the printed programme, too, for the rest of his life. It was there, too, in August that he met his lifelong friend Louis Allen for the first time. How had Allen got to Rangoon?[8]

Unlike Storry, Allen had never been to Japan. He was an eager student of languages at Manchester University when he was picked out by his French professor as a likely prospect for one of the SOAS courses in Japanese due to begin in February 1943. He was a physically large man, and he struck his fellow students as a natural leader. His reaction to his first encounter with Japanese people was similar to that of many who took wartime language courses: 'every Japanese who had taught us, and every Englishman too, had filled us with liking for the Japanese at a time when it was fashionable to regard them with hatred, distrust or contempt'. In 1944, after finishing his course, he was sent out to Delhi, where he had his first encounters with Japanese documents and prisoners of war.[9]

Allen was then posted to CSDIC(I), not to the headquarters in Delhi but to the Mobile Sections base in Pegu, Burma. After a while, he was assigned to No. 2 Mobile Section, a similar outfit to the one commanded by Storry. This turned out to be a lucky posting, for it gave Allen the opportunity to make a real contribution to battlefield intelligence, through a combination of luck and talent. How did this come about?

No. 2 Mobile Section was attached to the 17th Division, which in July 1945 had a key part to play in the final battle of the Burma Campaign. The situation was this: the remnants of the Japanese Army were trapped on the west side of the Pegu Range of mountains and planned to break through to the east, cross the Mandalay Road and then make their way across the Sittang River in order to escape capture. Allen was in the thick of it:

> I saw the battle from start to finish. ... Before the battle began, I translated the Shimbu [Shinbu] Force Operation order ... and together with a Nisei sergeant from Hawaii and another Japanese-speaking British officer, interrogated every prisoner who fell into the British net along the front ... from Pyu in the North to Nyaunglebin and Daiku in the South.[10]

The Shinbu Force referred to by Allen was the name of the Japanese Army that was supposed to lead the breakout. The rough details of the plan were already known from captured documents that had given the numbers of troops involved, their state of health and their ammunition levels but had not specified the date. On 2 July 1945, a platoon of Gurkhas overwhelmed a Japanese patrol and brought back to 17th Division headquarters an assortment of photographs and paybooks together with a despatch bag found on the bodies of those they had killed. Allen sifted through the documents in the bag and suddenly realized that he was looking at an operation order for the breakout on 20 July, which was signed by Major-General Nakazawa Kan'ichi. He pulled over his typewriter and began to type out a translation. 'It was a peach of document from the intelligence point of view', he realized, and he managed to put together a more detailed account of the Japanese plans from the other documents in the despatch bag.

By 7 July, Allen's translations had been distributed to 17th Division. On 10 July, a new and more accurate translation was made at IV Corps headquarters in Pegu, and on 16 July the operational order was retranslated in New Delhi. But Allen's translation, rough and ready though it may have been, was in the right hands on 7 July, a good fortnight before the break-out began on 20 July. The result was the destruction of a large part of the Japanese Army in Burma, which was already much depleted by sickness: 8,500 Japanese troops died during the break-out, but only ninety-five Allied troops lost their lives. In recognition of the value of his contribution to this final action in the Burma Campaign, Allen was subsequently mentioned in despatches for his 'gallant and distinguished services in Burma'.[11]

As Allen himself emphasized, the campaign to retake Burma was certainly approaching a conclusion by July 1945, but neither he nor anybody else had any inkling that the end of the war was less than a month away, so the pressure to pursue and defeat the Japanese Army in battle had not let up. Even Mountbatten, who had been informed beforehand by Churchill of the plan to use atomic bombs against Japan, was still expecting to be involved in operations against Japan in the spring of 1946. The end came suddenly and unexpectedly. Once Japan had announced its intention to surrender, Allen found another use for his knowledge of Japanese as he shepherded Japanese personnel into holding camps, so it was a little later that he reached Rangoon, where he met Storry.[12]

Linguists sent to Singapore

Storry's diaries and other papers are now in the Imperial War Museum. According to his diary for 1942, in early February he was in a class of ten people taking lessons in Singapore to improve their Japanese. Storry did not name his teacher, but it was most probably Revd Eric Leicester Andrews (1886–1951), who was sent out to Singapore to teach Japanese in the middle of 1941. Andrews probably taught his first classes not long after his arrival, well before the Japanese invasion of Malaya, and if so that means that these classes actually represent the first British attempt to train Japanese linguists. It is frustrating that no further details have come to light, but perhaps it is inevitable since any records that were kept might not have survived the surrender. But who was Revd Andrews, and how did he come to know Japanese well enough to teach it?[13]

Andrews was one of a group of intelligence officers who reached Singapore in June 1941. They had responded to a notice placed in *The Times* by the War Office, 'Linguists wanted for military service.' Applicants were required to be 'really fluent in at least one language, preferably learnt in the country of origin'. Andrews seemed a perfect fit: he had been born in Japan and grew up there, and he spent the years 1921–35 as a missionary in Japan. By 1940, he was back in England and was the rector of St Andrew's Church in the village of Sandon in Essex. He was already in his fifties, but he nevertheless answered the appeal from the War Office and joined the Army in May 1941. More than a year had passed since the notice appeared in *The Times*, but that may have been because the War Office in 1940 had been thinking of European languages and changed its mind in 1941 as relations with Japan deteriorated. At any rate, Andrews was commissioned as a captain in the Intelligence Corps and went out to Singapore.[14]

By the time of the Japanese attack on Malaya on 8 December, there must have been quite a number of intelligence officers in Singapore who had knowledge of Japanese, but no details have come to light. On 18 December, General Sir Archibald Wavell, the commander-in-chief of British forces in India, was so worried about the threat to Singapore that he sent an urgent telegram to the War Office. In it, he recommended the immediate transfer to India of all technical equipment and personnel that was 'practically irreplaceable', including 'personnel employed on Japanese counter propaganda and as many Japanese speaking intelligence officers as can be spared'. Wavell clearly knew that the Japanese-speaking intelligence officers in Singapore were a precious resource that needed to be extracted, and that was why Storry and his colleagues were ordered to leave.[15]

Unlike Storry, Andrews did not leave Singapore before the surrender. Although he was in the Army as a captain in the Intelligence Corps rather than as a clergyman, it may be that he chose to stay behind to minister to his fellow POWs in captivity, or it may simply be that he was caught before he could escape. What is certain is that he spent the rest of the war as a prisoner in Adam Park POW camp in Singapore. There he built a chapel, recruited a choir and conducted services, and at the same time acted as interpreter for his fellow prisoners in their dealings with the Japanese camp commandant. For the final months of the war, he was in the notorious Changi Gaol and, according to his obituary, never recovered from the malnutrition and deprivations he suffered there.[16]

Andrews was not the only Japanese speaker who spent the war interpreting in POW camps. The most well known is perhaps Cyril Wild, who will feature in chapter 11; Wild had arrived in Singapore in November 1940, and although he had grown up in Japan, he was not at first employed by the Army for his language skills. However, Andrews had not arrived in Singapore alone, for he was one of a group of linguists sent out together. One of those who travelled with him was William Mortimer Drower (1915–2007), who stated in his autobiography that they had been despatched to Singapore in order to interrogate POWs in the event of war. If this is right, it shows that the War Office was not only beginning to appreciate the value of Japanese-speakers but was also expecting Singapore to be attacked by Japanese forces. Drower described one of his companions as a former missionary who had good knowledge of the language, and that was probably Andrews; the others, he wrote, had been commercial representatives in Japan, but they cannot now be identified.[17]

After graduating from Oxford in 1936, Drower had worked for the Japanese embassy in London until Japan leaned decisively towards Nazi Germany and Fascist Italy. After the outbreak of war in 1939, he left the Territorial Army to become an intelligence officer and was sent to Singapore on the strength of the Japanese he had acquired while working for the embassy. Drower worked as an interpreter at the Malaya Command in Singapore until captured and then spent several years as a POW and an interpreter for the Australian POWs working on the Burma–Siam Railway. He experienced severe maltreatment and was unconscious when released from captivity.

Another in the group was Oswald Morris Wynd (1913–98), who had grown up in Tokyo as the son of Scottish missionaries and after the war wrote a number of successful novels set in Japan. He was at Edinburgh University when the war broke out in 1939; he joined up, was commissioned into the Intelligence Corps and then sent out to Singapore. After the Japanese invasion of Malaya, he was attached to the 9th Indian Division and was in the jungle of southern Malaya when he was captured, which explains why he was unable to escape as Storry had done. As a prisoner of war, Wynd, like Andrews and Drower, made use of his Japanese to help his fellow prisoners, initially at a camp in Malaya and later in a POW camp in Hokkaido. At least twenty-six other British intelligence officers were captured in Malaya or Singapore at this time. Andrews and Wynd knew Japanese, and to a lesser extent so did Drower, but it is not known how many linguists were captured and how many escaped. The capture of these three, and possibly others, was a serious loss, given the small number of linguists available to the War Office. On the other hand, there can be no doubt that in captivity they, and perhaps others too, were of inestimable service to their fellow captives, sometimes at great risk to their own lives. Even in captivity, the linguists thus found a use for their knowledge of Japanese as they endeavoured to stand up for their fellow prisoners in front of their captors.[18]

Linguists in the Burma Campaign

Both Storry and Allen worked as members of Mobile Sections that made operational intelligence available to commanders in the field, as

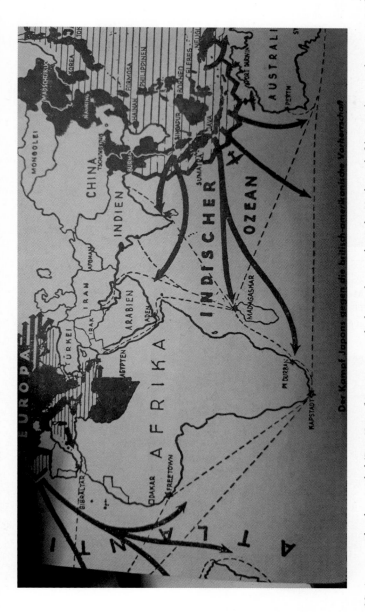

Der Kampf Japans gegen die britisch-amerikanische Vorherrschaft

Fig. 29: A map, said to be entitled 'Der Kampf Japans gegen die britisch-amerikanische Vorherrschaft' ('Japan's struggle against Anglo-American domination) and to have been produced in Germany. This map appeared on the cover and as the frontispiece of a book published in South Africa in 1944, *Japan's Bid for Africa*, written by the historian Eric Rosenthal (1905–1983). It shows the expected expansion of Japanese control to cover the whole of the Indian Ocean.

Fig. 30: Robert Sellar (1923–96), in jacket and tie, with some of his colleagues in Mauritius. Back row (those mentioned in this book are in bold): **Lt. Chilton, Dorothy McConochie, Elizabeth Anderson, Sellar**, unknown, **Barbara Dainton**. The racial hierarchy on the island is mirrored in the placing of the British personnel on a higher level. (Courtesy of Professor Robin Sellar)

Fig. 31: Sellar off duty with Elizabeth Anderson (1906–93), October 1944. Anderson had been working at the Government Code and Cypher School since before the war. (Courtesy of Professor Robin Sellar; an identical photo in Churchill Archive Centre, Tuck 5/3, identifies the figures and gives a date)

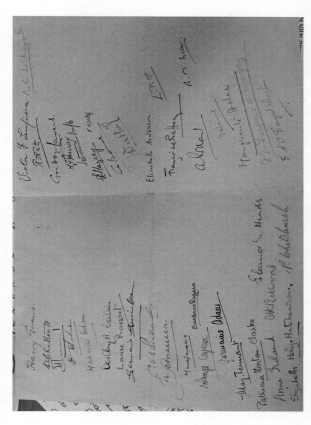

Fig. 32: The signatures on the farewell card for Evelyn DuBuisson. They include, on the left (those mentioned in this book are in bold), **Harry Evans**, **Lt. Cecil William Chilton**, Dorothy A. Collins, Louise Rousset, **Charles Anthony Richards**, Germaine Adam, May Tennant, Patricia Morton-Clarke, Anne Ireland, Eleanor M. Hinds, **Elizabeth Hely-Hutchinson**, P. Whitchurch, and, on the right, **Victor Lemprière**, Gordon Lavers, **Elizabeth Anderson**, Laurence Pitot, Françoise Raffray, **Robert Sellar**, **Arthur Pollard**, Marguerite Adam, Anne-Marie Desvaux de Marigny and E. d'V. Fayd'Herbe. Patricia Morton-Clarke was the wife of Major James Morton-Clarke, a British Army officer based in Mauritius. The identities of the other English and Mauritian signatories cannot now be ascertained, but this card proves that they worked for Twining's organization. (Copyright of Surrey History Centre; reproduced by permission of Surrey History Centre)

Fig. 33: This photograph from Elizabeth Hely-Hutchinson's album shows some of the British staff working for Twining in Mauritius during the war. It is titled 'I. O. (Information Office) Hostel inmates' and the figures are named, from left to right, as Sellar, Dorothy McConochie, Elizabeth Hely-Hutchinson, Lt. Chilton, Elizabeth Anderson and Barbara Dainton. There is an identical photograph in Sellar's album. (Courtesy of the late Elizabeth Hely-Hutchinson)

Fig. 34: Betty Archdale in WRNS officer uniform. This photograph was probably taken in 1941 before her departure for Singapore, for she is not wearing the WRNS tropical uniform. (Courtesy of the Mitchell Library, State Library of New South Wales, Betty Archdale papers Box 5/1).

Figs. 35a and 35b The guardhouse and entrance to HMS *Anderson*, Colombo. Both British sailors and Ceylonese (Sri Lankan) employees can be seen. These photographs come from the album of Stanley Wood (1923–78), who joined the Royal Navy in 1942. After being trained in wireless procedures and Japanese Morse he was sent out to Colombo and worked at HMS *Anderson* for two years from December 1943. He was a member of the Anderson Players and the Anderson Dance Band, which provided some of the social life in the camp. On 14 August 1945 he ran a dance class in a cinema in Colombo: buses were provided for the Wrens. After the war he married Pearl Hood and they ran a successful school of dancing in Worthing. See the website http://pearlhoodstanleywood.org.uk/ (Courtesy of Keith Wood)

Fig. 36: Off-duty Wrens of 'C' Watch at HMS *Anderson*. (Courtesy of Keith Wood)

Fig. 37: A damaged photograph of Charles Bawden (1924–2016) which he sent home from HMS *Anderson* in 1945. He is wearing tropical uniform of a junior RNVR officer. (Courtesy of Richard Bawden)

Fig. 38: A group photograph of the staff of C section at the Wireless Experimental Centre, Delhi. Shown are the white male expatriates only; Indian support staff and female clerical staff were not included. On the back the individuals are identified. From left to right, they are as follows (those mentioned in this book are in bold). Front row: Mackickan, Owen, **Noyce**, Keale, Dominy, Byas, **Marr-Johnson** (the head of the WEC), Gloag, **Steed** (the head of C Section), Hutchinson, **Robinson**, Ashby; middle row: **Kerry**, Rickenburg, **Taylor**, Smith, Fancey, Miller, Singer, Gibson, Marston Green, Scott-Kabert, Martin, **Lloyd-Jones**, Geary, Meihardt, Bradbury, Stobie; back row: Morgan, Johnson, Culbert, Thomas, Powell, Parker, Neames, **Bownas**, **Grimble**, Fricker, Prescott, Brown, Howrie, Roberts, Embleton, Rose, Copson, Harvey, George. (Courtesy of Rosy Thacker)

Fig. 39: (George) Walter Robinson (1920–81) as a young man, perhaps taken in 1940. He was one of the first three Bedford graduates sent out to join the Wireless Experimental Centre, Delhi. By the end of the war, he was a Major. (Courtesy of William Robinson)

Fig. 40: Alfred Edwin Bell (1923–87) in tropical evening dress after the war. He was in the first course at the Bedford School, recruited not because he had been studying classics at Oxford or Cambridge, but because he had grown up in Japan. As an RAF officer he worked on Japanese air-to-ground communications in India and Burma, and after the war he was in the Secret Intelligence Service but ostensibly a diplomat. This photograph may have been taken when he was serving in Rangoon in the early 1950s. (Courtesy of Christopher Bell)

L. to R.: sitting, Cpl. Margaret Shaw (Nottingham); Sgt. Nesta Hawgood, W.A.C. (I); L/Cpl. Morfudd Lewis (Wales); Sgt. Rachel Verghese, W.A.C. (I); Cpl. Pamela Bowker (Burnley); Cpl. T. George, W.A.C. (I); Cpl. Anne Stephenson (Leeds); L/Cpl. Lorna Gridley (Harpenden); L/Cpl. Patricia Myott (Newcastle-under-Lyme); Sgt. Hermione Hastings (London).

Fig. 41: The first contingent of Auxiliary Territorial Service women in Delhi being shown around by three members of the Women's Auxiliary Corps (India). This photograph appeared on the cover of issue 21 (October 1945) of *Saint Christopher's Review*, the magazine issued by the Church of England padre at the Wireless Experimental Centre. (Courtesy of the late James Sutherland)

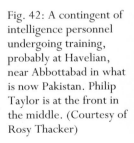
Fig. 42: A contingent of intelligence personnel undergoing training, probably at Havelian, near Abbottabad in what is now Pakistan. Philip Taylor is at the front in the middle. (Courtesy of Rosy Thacker)

Figs. 43a and 43b: On the left, Hugh Cortazzi in RAF uniform in 1941, prior to being sent out to India; on the right, as British ambassador to Japan. (Courtesy of the Cortazzi family)

Fig. 44: The School of Japanese Instruction in Karachi, July 1946. On the back of this photograph all are identified. They are, from left to right (those mentioned in this book are in bold): Front row: Lt Low, Mr Kao, **Major Dicker**, **Lt-Col. Steed**, **Mr Goh**, **Miss Goh**, **Mr Kitaoka**; middle row: Clifford*, Healy*, Thompson*, **Whitehorn**, Thomson*, Tyson, Gnr Ings, Phillips, Lt Greenwood+, Lt Williams+; back row: Sgt Cartwright, McKenzie, **Ward***, Gnr Bennett, **Pte Nish**, **Lt Leslie Phillips**, Pte Navin. The symbols are explained thus: * = ex Bedford course, + = ex London course. (Courtesy of John Whitehorn)

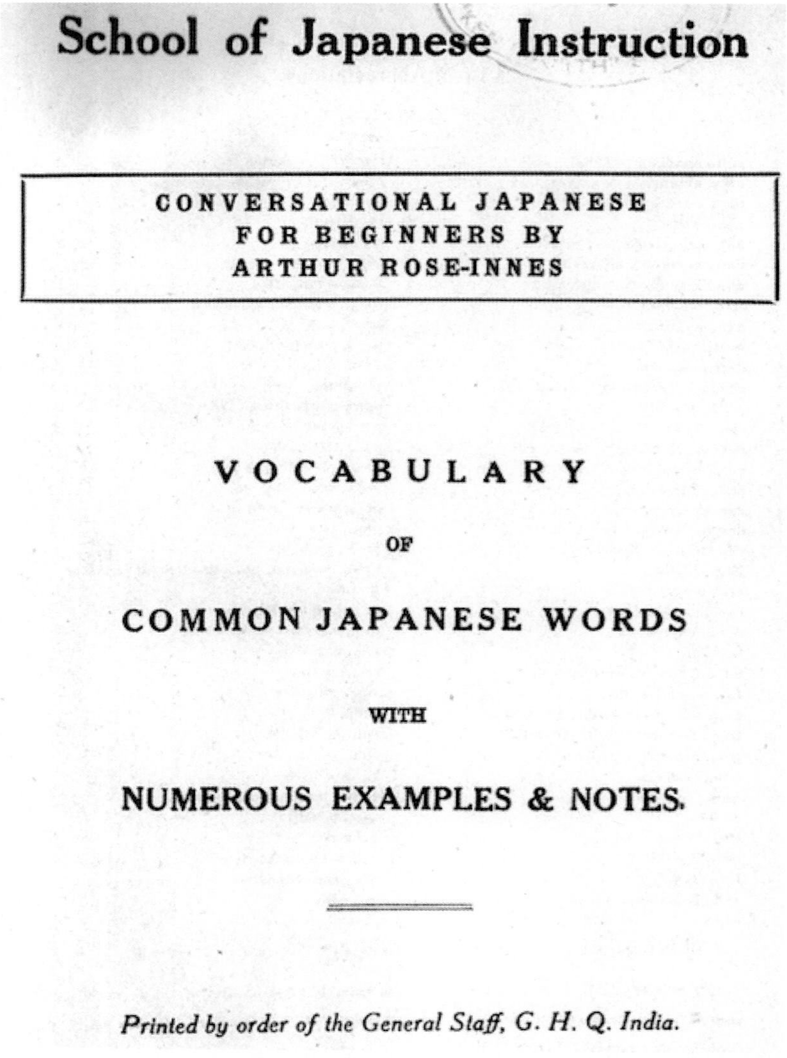

School of Japanese Instruction

CONVERSATIONAL JAPANESE
FOR BEGINNERS BY
ARTHUR ROSE-INNES

VOCABULARY

OF

COMMON JAPANESE WORDS

WITH

NUMEROUS EXAMPLES & NOTES.

Printed by order of the General Staff, G. H. Q. India.

Fig. 45: Cover of a volume containing a vocabulary of common Japanese words extracted from Arthur Rose-Innes' *Conversational Japanese for Beginners* and printed by the Government of India Press in Simla in 1944.

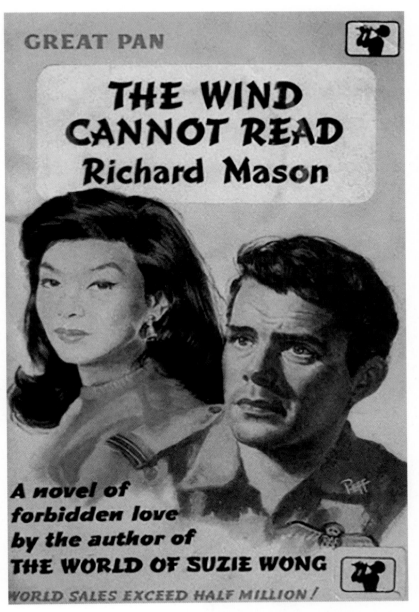

Fig. 46: Cover of the 1959 Pan Books paperback edition of Richard Mason's novel *The Wind Cannot Read*, originally published in 1946. (Courtesy of Pan Macmillan; reproduced with permission of the Licensor through PLSclear)

Fig. 47:Four young RNVR officers at Boulder. From left to right: Gowing, Beasley, Birrell and Kennedy. (Roger Pineau collection, Box 3, Folder 4, Item 1, Special Collections & Archives, University of Colorado Boulder Libraries)

Fig. 48: Joseph K. Yamagiwa (1906–68) after the war. He was already teaching at the University of Michigan when America joined the war. (Courtesy of Bentley Historical Library, University of Michigan: HS7290, News and Information Services Faculty and Staff Files)

Fig. 49: The Japanese exchange ship *Tatsuta-maru* as seen from the periscope of US submarine *Kingfish* in October 1942. She reached Lourenço Marques (now Maputo in Mozambique) on 27 August 1942, so when this photograph was taken she was on her way home with Japanese diplomats and other Japanese citizens from Europe and the United States. She was still marked as an exchange ship and therefore not to be attacked. Subsequently the *Tatsuta-maru* was used as a troopship and was sunk by another American submarine in February 1943 with the loss of all her crew and the troops aboard. (Official US Navy photograph)

Representatives of Nine Services at Central Bureau
(Left to Right) Top Row: Sgt David Eunson, RAF; Cpl William Sanders, AMF; T/5
Bud Curtner, USA; Sgt Dennis Olmstad, Royal Canadian Air Force, W/O Richard
Bellingham, British Army; Cpl Ross Rampling. RAAF. Front row: T/5 Stella Kurkul,
WAC, USA; Cpl Cynthia Hickey, WAAAF; Cpl Dorothy Hilliard, AWAS (1944/45).
From "SIS Record".

Fig. 50: Representatives of nine different military services working at Central
Bureau. This photograph can be found online and in Geoffrey St Vincent Ballard's
book, *On Ultra Active Service: The Story of Australia's Signals Intelligence Operations during
World War II*. In each case, it is attributed to 'SIS Record'. This may refer to *Signal
Intelligence Service in the Far East 1942–1946: an historical and pictorial record* (SIS
Record Association, 1946), but I have not been able to consult a copy.

we have seen. The staff of the WEC in Delhi worked behind the scenes on encrypted messages, but early in 1942 CSDIC(I) was formed at the Red Fort in Delhi; it was modelled on the Combined Services Detailed Interrogation Centres in the European theatre of the war, and it focused on the interrogation of prisoners and the exploitation of document finds. The problem in India, as ever, was the chronic shortage of linguists able to fill either of these roles. At first, this was not a serious problem since there were few prisoners to interrogate: many Japanese troops preferred to kill themselves with a hand-grenade rather than be taken prisoner, and those who were captured made persistent attempts to kill themselves in captivity. What is more, most prisoners who did not kill themselves turned out to be too junior in rank to have any valuable information to offer. It was for this reason that the first report CSDIC(I) produced, in January 1943, was based on interrogations not of Japanese prisoners of war but rather of Burmese people who had crossed into India and of a small number of British and Indian prisoners of war who had managed to escape captivity and make their way to India. These interrogations provided only thin intelligence about what was going on in Burma, and that was not what CSDIC(I) had been set up to provide.[19]

The spearhead of CSDIC(I) was the Mobile Sections, which were capable of moving independently wherever they were needed. They had at their disposal several lorries, motorbikes and other vehicles, Indian Army drivers, orderlies and cooks and British Army non-commissioned officers, not to mention the linguists. On the language side, No. 1 Mobile Section, for example, had two Nisei from the US Army and five captains in the British Army—four of them had been in business in Japan and had attended the School of Japanese Instruction in Simla in India (see below) and one had done a course at SOAS. Similarly, the No. 4 Mobile Section consisted of six British officers and two Nisei NCOs. One of the officers was Peter Bates (1924–2005), who had been a Dulwich Boy at SOAS and had then been sent out to India. From September 1944, he was operating with No. 4 Mobile Section in Arakan (now Rakhine State) in Burma. He and the others were mostly dealing with captured Japanese documents such as diaries, manuals, instructions and orders and trying to establish the enemy order of battle. The Nisei, he recalled, could read cursive handwritten Japanese better than he could, but they were not good at putting it into 'proper English'—by that, he probably meant the formal language of the British Army, for most Nisei had a better knowledge of English than of Japanese. At any rate, by the end of the year the number of Japanese prisoners was increasing, and this meant that Bates and his colleagues needed to spend more time conducting interrogations before the captives were sent on to Allied prison camps.[20]

The Mobile Sections produced translations and interrogation reports, but very few of these seem to survive in the archives. One exception is a set of interrogation reports sent in by No. 2 Mobile Section between December 1943 and March 1944, which is preserved in The National Archives. This file was to be withheld from public view until 2029, on the grounds that some of the people named might still be alive. Since many other documents in The National Archives name people who are still alive, I challenged this; my challenge was rejected, but my appeal was partially upheld, and I was informed that a partially redacted version would be made available, but at the time of writing it has still not been made available.[21]

Each Mobile Section was supposed to send captured documents back to Delhi for translation. This would obviously cause delays and defeat the purpose of the Mobile Sections, which was to provide immediate battlefield intelligence, so the linguists checked the documents they captured before sending them on. Documents were being handed in to the Mobile Sections in a constant flow; they were usually recovered from corpses, as Storry and Allen found, and sometimes they were of immediate tactical value. For example, in March 1944, Corporal Charles Frederick George of the Border Regiment was leading a patrol in the Kabaw Valley in northern Burma on the border with the Indian state of Manipur when his patrol came upon a stationary Japanese staff car. They attacked, killed the occupants, gathered all the papers that the officers had been carrying and hastily withdrew. What he had got hold of turned out, astonishingly, to be the plan of operations for the Japanese attack up the Kabaw Valley towards the British lines.[22]

For the valuable intelligence that his attack yielded, Corporal George was awarded the Distinguished Conduct Medal, but appreciation of the work of translators or even intelligence officers is rare. It is rarer still in battle histories. Important though the work of the Mobile

Sections undoubtedly was in the war against Japan, it is usually taken for granted by historians. Geoffrey Evans, however, who was the brigadier in command of 123rd Indian Brigade at Imphal, certainly did not take it for granted. In 1962, he and Antony Brett-James published a history of the Battle of Imphal, and in the preface they acknowledged the contributions made by all those who are normally forgotten:

> Here too is some account of those who sifted the information, translated the captured documents and interrogated the prisoners, thereby helping to complete the final Intelligence jigsaw puzzle; of the Staffs and of those responsible for providing the food and ammunition, of the American Field Service, the doctors and nurses and members of the Women's Services, all of whom played such an important part in keeping 4th Corps fit to fight.

Evans explained that the job of the fighting patrols like that led by Corporal George was to obtain identifications, valuable documents and marked-up maps by killing or capturing the enemy. But, he added, 'While the capture of documents was one thing, the translation of them was quite another matter.' The tasks of the CSDIC(I) officers were, he wrote, 'varied, intricate, sometimes very arduous and not infrequently odorous when they had to handle bloodstained and evil-smelling papers'. He was deeply appreciative of the work they did:

> The contribution made by these interrogators and translators was of immense value, for without them, a detailed knowledge of the Japanese and their intentions could never have been built up. Moreover, all the physical hardships and dangers undergone by the forward troops in collecting documents and other items of Intelligence would have been to no purpose. In consequence, they were indirectly responsible for saving the lives of many British, Indian and Gurkha soldiers by providing commanders and staff with vital and urgent information on which to base plans to defeat the enemy with the least number of casualties.

On many occasions, documents found on the battlefield had a material effect on operations, but, as he was careful to emphasize, that depended on having knowledgeable translators on hand.[23]

The fact was, however, that there were never enough linguists available to satisfy the urgent need for translators who could serve as intelligence officers. It is remarkable but true that in 1944, when Major-General David Tennant Cowan launched his attack on Meiktila to the north of Rangoon, an attack that resulted in a decisive victory and marked the beginning of the end for Japanese forces in Burma, there were only two men among the 11,000 under his command who could read and speak Japanese. These were the two linguists attached to No. 2 Mobile Section who were Allen's predecessors. Since Cowan was desperate to know what forces he was facing, they simply had to pull out all the stops in order to keep him well informed. Allen explained that they did so by 'tireless interrogation of prisoners and endless scouring of the battlefield for identifications from corpses—paybooks, photographs, identity discs, diaries, maps. A single document taken at Meiktila, for instance, gave a complete breakdown of the order of battle of [the Japanese] 15 Army.'[24]

The Mobile Sections performed exceptionally well in exacting conditions, but that role was coming to an end in the summer of 1945. One of the last to join them was Hugh Cortazzi, who was sent out to India after finishing his SOAS course and reached the Delhi headquarters of CSDIC(I) just as the war was ending. He was attached to No. 5 Mobile Section, which was commanded by Major Eric Crane. Crane had been raised in Japan and had a Japanese mother and therefore had a better command of Japanese than a wartime SOAS course could possibly impart. Early on the morning of 15 August, No. 5 Mobile Section left Delhi for Secunderabad, near Hyderabad in central India, but they had only reached Agra when they heard the news of the Japanese surrender. This was the beginning of the end of the Mobile Sections, but it was certainly not the end of Cortazzi's war. He soon found himself on a ship to Singapore as the personal interpreter to General Miles Dempsey, the commander of the 14th Army, and we will encounter him again in chapter 10.[25]

On 1 August 1945, the Mobile Sections were brought under the control of SEATIC, which we will turn to below. The commandant of SEATIC summed up their contribution as follows:

> The task confronting these translators was an unenviable one; for every document of immediate operational intelligence retrieved, at least a thousand were carefully scrutinised and burned—or, alternatively, classified as being of secondary importance only, and shipped to DELHI for more careful translation in HQ SEATIC. It may be truthfully said that SEATIC Translators, working in the field with CSDIC(I) Mob[ile]

Sec[tion]s, acquitted themselves excellently, a fact fully appreciated by superior formations.

How much was it appreciated? The history of SEATIC refers to 'the intense personal interest displayed by Gen[eral] Gracey (20 Div), Gen[eral] Evans (7 Div) and Gen[eral] Rees (19 Div) in the work and activities of its Mobile Sections'. This suggests that the commanders did indeed appreciate the intelligence that came out of the work of the Mobile Sections, but there are sadly no further details.[26]

One final word on the Mobile Sections comes from Lieutenant-General Slim, the commander of the 14th Army. In a book published in 1956, he complained that he had not had the depth of intelligence that other commanders enjoyed, such as detailed information about the characters of the Japanese commanders opposing him. At the time his book was published, however, it was not yet possible to write in public about secret intelligence such as that produced by Bletchley Park or the WEC in Delhi. Much later, he turned to the subject again and revealed that the secret intelligence he received had indeed informed him about the desperate supply situation facing the Japanese forces in Burma and about the weakness of the Japanese air forces, but he also acknowledged that he had in fact derived much of this information from translations of captured documents, which were of course supplied by the Mobile Sections in the first instance.[27]

Allen and Storry were both Army officers, and the Mobile Sections focused on the needs of the Army, but there were also RAF translators doing similar work. In their case, however, the documents and diaries were recovered from crashed Japanese aircraft, so they were often fragmentary or partially burnt. One example is the diary of an NCO pilot whose plane crashed at Feni in India (now in Bangladesh) on 1 April 1943, presumably shot down while attacking the Allied airfield there. The surviving parts of his diary relate to the latter half of 1942 and are strikingly personal:

Java seems to me very like Japan. I was reminded of my parents, brothers, but all this merely turned my thoughts to my own country. How sad are memories of the past! ... We got up at 0730 this morning for floating target practice. As I am not fully trained in gunnery, I had numerous stoppages and felt extremely humiliated. ... How stupid we are to be passing our days, which will nevermore return, so aimlessly. Henceforth should we not consult our own interests more?

He was optimistic about the prospects for Japan and ended one entry with the words, 'On to Australia', expressing confidence that Japan would be victorious there, too. He obviously did not know that, at the highest level, tentative plans for the invasion of Australia had already been shelved.[28]

All of the RAF translations I have found so far were signed by Squadron-Leader Alexander Rodney Boyce (1898–1961) on behalf of the chief intelligence officer of the Air Headquarters in India, and they were widely distributed to intelligence and RAF units in India as well as to the US Air Force. It is not clear, however, if Boyce did the translations himself or was simply the responsible officer for a team of translators. He had, at any rate, probably more knowledge than anybody else about Japanese air force terminology. Although born in Queensland, he had served in the First World War as a junior officer in the Royal Engineers and then went to Japan in 1924 as a language officer. After his three years, he was sent back to Britain, but he then left the Army and returned to Japan in 1929 as a civilian: at first, he worked for a Canadian company in Tokyo, but in 1931 he became a teacher of English at the Tokyo Higher School, a post he retained until he went back to Britain in 1938. In 1941, he joined the RAF and was sent to India, probably in 1942. What he was subsequently doing is unclear, but his expertise is apparent from the fact that he produced a dictionary of Japanese air terms, which was published in Calcutta, and later he acted as an interpreter at the Japanese surrender of Singapore.[29]

The South East Asia Translation and Interrogation Centre

SEATIC came into being in Delhi in May 1944 under the command of Vice-Admiral Mountbatten, now enjoying the title of Supreme Allied Commander South East Asia (SACSEA). SEATIC acquired its personnel by absorbing some Nisei from the US Army, some RAF officers who had served with the Mobile Sections in Burma, some Royal Navy translators who had been trained at SOAS, and some other SOAS trainees. Canadian Nisei were also recruited, but this proved more difficult to arrange, as the Australian government had discovered in March

1944 when it asked the Canadian government to send 200 Japanese Canadians. As mentioned earlier, Japanese Canadians were regarded with suspicion by the Canadian government and were not used as language teachers or linguists until 1945, with the exception of a handful who became teachers at SOAS in London. SEATIC needed more linguists, however, so in May 1944 Captain Donald Mollison (1916–87) of the British Indian Army was sent to Ontario to get some. He had been raised in Yokohama where his father was born and had been running Japanese propaganda broadcasts from India using Japanese-speaking Koreans, but they had not proved to be a success, as he discovered when Japanese POWs under interrogation gave their opinions of the broadcasts. In Canada, Mollison managed to find some suitable recruits, but the Canadian War Cabinet, giving way to anti-Japanese political pressure from British Columbia, refused to allow them to serve as Canadian soldiers and would not guarantee that, if enlisted in the British Army, they would be permitted to return to Canada. Early in 1945, the Cabinet reversed its position. This may have been because Churchill had brought pressure to bear on the Canadian government, but in the view of the Special Operations Executive based in the United States the main reason for the change was a request for some Canadian Japanese personnel from the Australian chiefs of staff. Be that as it may, Mollison's recruits headed to Britain and were sent on to India to join SEATIC, while others were sent to Australia.[30]

Another source of personnel for SEATIC was the British Army Central Translation Section in Delhi, but it is now surprisingly difficult to find out what this unit was doing. It was probably formed in Delhi in 1942, and it came under the director of military intelligence at General Headquarters (India). Until the end of 1943, it consisted of just a handful of staff officers who were responsible for the translation of captured documents. In some cases, they were probably checking or revising translations done in the field. In December 1943, the first group of linguists trained at SOAS arrived in Delhi, and some of them went to the Army Central Translation Section, but other than that little is known about its activities. In short, it was a unit of the Indian Army that only features in the archives when it was absorbed by SEATIC.[31]

SEATIC produced regular bulletins that contained translations and the results of interrogations, and these were distributed to intelligence staff in Delhi, London and Washington. At the end of the war, the American personnel were withdrawn so that they could go and work for MacArthur in occupied Japan, but SEATIC now had many more tasks to undertake. There was an urgent need for interpreters and translators in all parts of SEAC, and SEATIC detachments were sent to Bangkok, Saigon, Hong Kong, Batavia (now Jakarta), Palembang, Medan and North Borneo to screen hundreds of thousands of surrendered Japanese personnel before their return to Japan, to interrogate war crimes suspects and to interrogate senior Japanese officers for intelligence purposes. In October 1945, SEATIC moved to Singapore, close to SACSEA headquarters, and in June 1946 it acquired a new home in Johore Bahru (now Johor), just across the strait separating the Malay Peninsula from Singapore. It also acquired a new role, as we will see in chapter 11, and it was in fact in its post-war role that it made the greatest impact.[32]

Training linguists in India

Since there was a constant demand for Japanese linguists in British India, it is hardly surprising that the military authorities turned their minds to a local solution. After all, there were never going to be enough Bedford and SOAS graduates to spare. At some time in 1942 or 1943, the British Army established a School of Japanese Instruction at Kenilworth House in Simla, the hill station in northern India that was the summer resort of British officers and administrators and was therefore normally off-limits to 'other ranks'. Now there was to be an exception to the rule, for by no means all the students at the School of Japanese Instruction were officers.

In its time, the School of Japanese Instruction must have produced a lot of paperwork—syllabi, rosters of staff and students, examination results and so on. Unfortunately, none of this seems to have survived, and I have found very little to go on apart from memoirs and reminiscences. What I can be sure about is that, in addition to courses for beginners, by the summer of 1943 the school was also offering six-week refresher courses for CSDIC(I) officers in need of a break from service in the front lines, and one of those who attended was Major Storry.[33]

One of the first students at the School of Japanese Instruction was Horace Phillips (1917–2004), and his memoirs provide a glimpse of the school in its early days. He had grown up in Glasgow, the son of Jewish immigrants from Eastern Europe, and was working as a clerical officer in the Inland Revenue when war broke out. He joined the Army, and it was only after he was posted to India that his linguistic talents were recognized. In January 1943, he was commissioned and underwent training in the Intelligence Corps Training Centre in Karachi. In later life, he had a distinguished career, for he became the first Jew to rise to the upper ranks of the diplomatic service when he was appointed British ambassador to Indonesia in 1966. According to his memoirs, after his training in Karachi he was sent to Simla for a six-month course in Japanese. He was one of a dozen students from all three services, and they had to endure what he called 'punishing day-long study' in order to reach a sufficient standard: they were required to reach a level that would enable them to understand captured documents or radio messages *en clair*. He recalled that the teachers were Koreans released from internment (because Japan had annexed Korea in 1910, Koreans were Japanese citizens and were educated in Japanese) and some Japanese residents in India, including the Japanese wives of British Army officers. Who these teachers or the other students were is as yet unknown.[34]

To meet the need for textbooks, the Government of India Press in Simla quickly produced a local reprint of Rose-Innes' *Conversational Japanese for Beginners*. They also published a volume entitled *Documents*, which contained handwritten Japanese military orders and correspondence for students to familiarize themselves with handwritten Japanese and exercise their skills upon before having to deal with handwritten documents in the field. This is the only glimpse we now have of the school in Simla.[35]

In September 1945, the War Office was planning to send forty trainees to Simla and expected to have sixty-five translators available for work in Japan, so it is clear that the training of linguists was to continue in India even though the war had come to an end. Shortly after this, the Japanese school was moved to Karachi, in what became Pakistan after the Partition of India in 1947. From this point onwards, there are rather more memoirs and reminiscences to draw upon. The move to

Karachi was made because it made more sense for the School of Japanese Instruction to be based in the Intelligence Corps Training Centre, which happened to be in Karachi. Although a long way from the front line, the training centre was well focused on the war with Japan. It was under the command of Colonel George Thexton Wards (1897–1991), who had been a language officer, then assistant military attaché and finally military attaché at the British embassy in Tokyo (1923–8, 1937–41). Here, then, was a former language officer who necessarily had good command of the language but also had extensive knowledge of the Japanese Army.[36]

After the school had moved to Karachi, five students on the tenth course at Bedford were given tropical kit and sent out by aeroplane. They were given no explanation, except that they were to learn spoken Japanese, but Ward, who was one of them, supposed that there was now a greater need for Japanese speakers to process prisoners of war than for cryptographers. He was quite right, for some of them were later sent to Kuala Lumpur to work as interpreters at a series of war-crimes trials that began there in January 1946. One of the five wrote to Captain Tuck to say that there were forty to fifty students in the Karachi school and that the focus of the course, which lasted for a year, was spoken Japanese, although the students were also required to learn 1,000 Chinese characters and to familiarize themselves with military vocabulary.[37]

According to Ward, they settled down into their new quarters near Karachi with charpoys (Indian rope-beds) in bare Nissen huts in the middle of a sandy desert. 'Some of our group', he recalled,

> were less than happy about spending another 9 months as Privates in a hot sandy environment trying to learn a difficult foreign language. ... In Karachi, [we] were allowed to use a magnificent building not far from the barracks, known as the Contact Club. I remember the sumptuous chairs, refreshments (including cold drinks—generally beer or Vimto [a soft drink]), tennis courts (racquets and balls provided), piano recitals, etc.

Karachi may have been hot and dusty, but with access to the Contact Club the privates had more privileges than they would have had in Simla, where it was certainly cooler but where most such places were out of bounds for them.[38]

John Whitehorn joined the course in September 1945, when the war was already over and the school had moved to Karachi. He had been working as an Army administrative clerk when he had seen a circular saying that the Army wanted volunteers to learn Japanese. 'I could see that it would be two years before I would be demobilised', he recalled, 'and learning a language sounded more interesting than sitting around polishing guns.' After a long train journey across India, he was surprised to discover that the school was run on military lines: 'we were marched to the school, studied for about seven hours, and then were marched back again'. In July 1946, the school was closed down.[39] Although the war was now over, there was still plenty of work for Japanese linguists, so most of the graduates were sent to Kuala Lumpur to work on the war-crimes trials there, to Singapore to work at SEATIC or to Japan to take part in BCOF.

Among Whitehorn's possessions is a photograph of the school that was taken when the last class graduated in July 1946. On the back of his copy, all present are identified, and from this it is obvious that the teachers were rather different from those who had been teaching in Simla. When Phillips was studying there, they had been either Koreans, Japanese residents in India or the Japanese wives of British officers. In the centre of Whitehorn's photograph sits Lieutenant-Colonel Frederick Charles William Steed (1899–1975), who had gone to Japan as a language officer in 1929 and was the commandant of the school. Another former language officer on the teaching staff was Major Bertie Percival Dicker (1898–1970), who had been in Japan from 1923 to 1926. He had been working as a translator for SEATIC but in December 1944 was sent with five other British Army officers to work as a translator at the Pacific Military Intelligence Research Service at Camp Ritchie, Maryland. Why British linguists were needed there is unknown, but he must later have returned to India. Rather more mysterious are the figures identified as Mr Kao, Mr Goh, Miss Goh and Mr Kitaoka. Kao was probably a Taiwanese and therefore, since Taiwan was a Japanese colony, a Japanese speaker. Mr Goh's real name was Kondō, and he had been practising as an osteopath in Burma when the war started; he and his two daughters retreated to India with the British Army and were living in Karachi; he had presumably adopted a Chinese name to avoid anti-

Japanese prejudice in British India. Of Mr Kitaoka I have been able to discover nothing, but he must have been a Japanese resident in Burma or India who preferred teaching to internment.[40]

At the back of the photograph stands the young Ian Nish (1926–). He had tried to apply for the SOAS courses while still at school in Edinburgh but had been rejected since he was too young. Several years later, now in India as a trained infantryman, he recalled in a memoir, he applied for a course at Simla and this time was accepted:

> I carried all my baggage and my rifle to Simla, where the School of Japanese Studies had been reopened in an old mansion. We stayed at the Simla YMCA, and were the only British Other Ranks in the hill station. The school moved to Karachi. We had strong courses in the language, but nothing in Japanese history or the nature of Japanese society. When we graduated in 1946, the school was wound up and the library divided among the avaricious students. My share was a wartime edition of Kenkyusha [Japanese–English dictionary], Arthur Rose-Innes' character dictionary and Creswell's dictionary of military and naval terms.

Armed with these dictionaries, Nish was then posted to Japan to take part in BCOF, and we will encounter him again in chapter 11. He kept the dictionaries and the other books he got from the School of Japanese Instruction throughout his long career as a historian of Japan at the London School of Economics.[41]

Few documents have survived to tell the history of the school at Simla/Karachi, but one is preserved in records from the very pinnacle of the British armed forces. On 17 August 1945, when the war with Japan had just ended, a meeting of the Chiefs of Staff Committee in London approved a recommendation that the School of Japanese Instruction at Simla be enlarged to meet the demands for Japanese linguists. The recommendation is dated 9 August 1945, before the Japanese decision to surrender, and it addresses a need for sixty-five translators rather than interpreters. Since the Chiefs of Staff were at this stage already considering how the Occupation of Japan was to be carried out, it is probable that they were thinking of the need for linguists in the British contingent of the Occupation forces, but that is not made fully clear in this document. Be that as it may, what is clear is that by this stage of the war even the Chiefs of Staff were aware of military linguistic requirements and of the institutions that existed to provide the necessary training.[42]

The wind cannot read

More than a decade after the end of the war, Richard Mason (1919–97) found success with his novel *The World of Suzie Wong* (1957), which tells the story of an artist's romance with a prostitute in Hong Kong. It was later put on the stage on Broadway and in the West End, and in 1960 it was made into a film. *The World of Suzie Wong* was by a long shot Mason's most successful novel, but in an earlier novel he wrote of a romance between an RAF officer learning Japanese in India and the Japanese woman who was teaching him. This was based on Mason's own experiences, for he, too, had been a wartime translator of Japanese.

Mason joined the RAF at the outbreak of war, and as a sergeant did the first course for RAF personnel at SOAS in 1942–3. He was sent to India and joined the 14th Army as an intelligence officer, but by this time he had already published a murder mystery set during the war, *The Body Fell on Berlin* (1943). He was sent on a three-month Japanese refresher course at Simla and then in 1944 worked alongside Storry in No. 1 Mobile Section during the Battle of Imphal. These were harrowing and dangerous times, but somehow he managed to find the time and space to write his second novel, *The Wind Cannot Read*, which was published in 1946. His inspiration for the title came from a Japanese poem, which appears in Mason's own translation on the fly-leaf: 'Though on the sign it is written: "Don't pluck these blossoms"—it is useless against the wind, which cannot read.' This poem also appears on Mason's gravestone in Rome.[43]

The connections between the novel and Mason's own experiences are obvious from the outset. The main character in the novel is Flying-Officer Michael Quinn, who is sent to learn Japanese in Bombay. 'Only the best brains can learn Japanese', he is told. 'It requires a reorientation of the mind. You think backwards and write upside down.' In Mason's fictional school of Japanese, the chief instructor is a retired brigadier who has spent most of his sixty-five years in Japan and who 'made his classes amusing and coloured them with anecdotes of Japan'. Here there are reflections of Mason's time at SOAS, for the brigadier is clearly modelled on Major-General Piggott, whom we have already met as a teacher at SOAS and who indeed spent many years in Japan as a language officer and then as a military attaché. On the other hand, in the novel the Japanese teachers are said to be men who had been in India when the war broke out and who preferred teaching to internment, rather like those who taught at the Simla/Karachi School of Japanese Instruction.

At any rate, once the course is under way in Bombay, a new teacher arrives from Britain, the attractive Miss Wei. It turns out that she is in fact Japanese but uses a Chinese name because she is concerned about anti-Japanese prejudice in India. Quinn falls in love with her, but instead of using her real name, Hanako, calls her 'Sabby', short for the Japanese word *sabishii*, 'lonely, sad'. Quinn's Japanese improves by leaps and bounds, naturally. When he finishes his course, Sabby leaves her teaching job and goes to Delhi, where she is employed to read the news in Japanese for broadcasts aimed at Japanese forces in Burma. Quinn, on the other hand, starts using his Japanese to interrogate prisoners in a prisoner of war camp before being sent to Imphal. So far, his experiences more or less match Mason's, except that in the novel the school is located in Bombay. Before Quinn can reach Imphal, he is captured by Japanese soldiers. He escapes but is wounded as he gets away; he is then evacuated from Imphal and finally reaches Delhi. There he finds that Sabby is dying of what seems to be a brain tumour.[44]

Mason later admitted that *The Wind Cannot Read* was partly based on his own wartime experiences. If Mason was the original for Michael Quinn, who then was Sabby? It has been suggested that she was Aiko Clarke (née Itō Aiko, 1912–75), who divorced her British diplomat husband after coming to Britain in 1941. She taught at SOAS from November 1942 to July 1943, and then worked in the Japanese broadcasting service of the BBC. But Sabby may also owe something to the daughter of Mr Goh, who taught at Simla along with her father. Be that as it may, in 1958 *The Wind Cannot Read* was made into a film, with screenplay written by Mason himself and with Dirk Bogarde in the lead role and Tani Yōko as Sabby. It remains the only film to include scenes of military personnel buckling down to learning Japanese in wartime, and some trouble was taken to make these scenes authentic. In one scene, Quinn and his colleagues are sitting at their desks with copies of the red wartime edition of *Kenkyusha's New English–Japanese Dictionary* printed in California in front of them, and they even make brave attempts to produce sentences in Japanese, Bogarde included. The film inevitably departs from the book, including the change of setting from Bombay to the Red Fort in Delhi, but the most significant departure is the change of the heroine's name from Hanako to Aiko, in what was clearly a belated tribute to Aiko Clarke, Mason's wartime teacher at SOAS.[45]

* * *

In the last two chapters, I have told the story of a handful of the people who worked as Japanese linguists during the Burma Campaign. The names of many of the others will probably now never be known, but whether they were working on Japanese codes at the WEC in Delhi, in the Mobile Sections in north-east India and the Burmese jungle, or later in SEATIC, they depended upon the knowledge of the Japanese language that they had acquired in unseemly haste and upon the weighty dictionaries that they all carried around with them. In the next two chapters, I shift my gaze to the Pacific Campaign. This was dominated by the US Navy and Army, but there were many others involved too, including British and Australian codebreakers and linguists. In the following chapter, I will use the experiences of some RNVR officers in the United States to trace the American commitment to training men and women in Japanese during the war.

8

THE WAVY NAVY IN THE UNITED STATES

In October 1943, five junior officers in the 'Wavy Navy' responded one by one to an Admiralty circular calling for volunteers to learn Japanese. 'Wavy Navy', because most men who became naval officers in wartime Britain joined the RNVR, and their ranks were indicated in wavy gold braid on their sleeves, while career officers of the Royal Navy wore straight gold braid. By 1945, there were more than 43,000 RNVR officers, and they served in all theatres of the war alongside regular Navy officers. Among those who served as RNVR officers were: Ian Fleming, the author of the James Bond books, who was personal assistant to Admiral Godfrey, the director of naval intelligence; actor Alec Guinness, who commanded a landing craft in the Allied invasion of Sicily in 1943; and naturalist Peter Scott, who commanded a gun boat in the English Channel.

When those five RNVR officers volunteered in 1943, they probably did not know that they would not be going to SOAS or the Bedford School but would instead have to make their way to the United States. Following orders, they went to Liverpool and boarded the *Mauretania*, a Cunard White Star passenger liner that had been requisitioned for war service. The ship was full of British naval personnel, most of whom were crossing the Atlantic to collect warships that had been built in American shipyards for the Royal Navy.

Several shocks awaited them on board. The first was that junior officers like them were expected to sleep six to a cabin in bunks, and the second was that, because the *Mauretania* regularly carried American troops, it was a dry ship and the bars served only soft drinks. When they reached New York, their first port of call, one of them recalled, was naturally the bar in their hotel. Once their thirst was quenched, they travelled to Washington to meet the naval officers who were going to be in charge of them, both at the Naval Intelligence Section of the British embassy and at the US Navy Department. Then they made their way by train across the plains to Denver and from there to Boulder, Colorado. Boulder was a former gold-rush town with a spectacular setting at the edge of the Rocky Mountains, but in 1941 it had a population of only around 13,000 (now around 100,000).

Why Boulder? Boulder was the location of the University of Colorado. But the real reason for their journey was that in 1942 the university became the home of the US Navy Japanese Language School, and that is where they were going to learn Japanese. In 1943, Boulder could still be reached by train from Denver, and when they stepped on to the platform at Boulder there was another surprise in store for them: as one disgruntled recruit put it, 'Boulder is as dry as a bone; about all one can get is nauseating 3.2 [per cent] beer.' That was indeed true, but there was a legal solution, for just outside the city limits there were liquor stores that sold wares that were of more appeal to thirsty RNVR officers. But why had they been sent to Boulder in the first place, and how, for that matter, had the US Navy Language School ended up in such a remote location?[1]

Only a small number of British personnel went to America for their training in Japanese, and in terms of their contribution to the war effort they were no match for the hundreds who studied at the Bedford School or SOAS. On the other hand, their experiences give us a perspective on the ways in which the need for Japanese linguists was met in the United States. In this chapter, therefore, we will follow the careers of the five RNVR linguists while examining how the United States responded to their language deficit at the outbreak of war.

Machine gunner or intelligence officer?

Before the attack on Pearl Harbor, only a small number of Americans had shown any interest in the Japanese language. Japanese was, it is true, already being taught at eight universities in the United States, with a concentration at Harvard, Yale, Columbia University and the University of California at Berkeley. One of the few who were interested in studying the language was Robert Christopher, who started learning Japanese in his first year at Yale University in September 1941, just three months before the United States entered the war. Christopher's father had been a machine-gunner in the First World War, and he was convinced that America would soon be at war with Japan: 'When we go to war with Japan', he told his son, 'you will be better off as an intelligence officer than as a machine gunner.' That was undoubtedly true. In 1942, Christopher moved from Yale to continue his studies of Japanese in a more secure setting at Arlington Hall in Virginia, which was the US equivalent of Bletchley Park. Edwin Reischauer (1910–90), a Harvard professor of Japanese, had also moved to Arlington Hall, and he taught Japanese to Christopher and his classmates. Later in the war, Christopher was sent to Brisbane in Australia, where General MacArthur had his headquarters, and he served there as a translator in MacArthur's intelligence operation, as we will see in the next chapter.[2]

Robert Christopher, or perhaps I should say his father, was most unusual in anticipating the need for Japanese linguists in the event of war with Japan. Does this mean that the United States was in fact not as poorly prepared as Britain for the language war with Japan? The United States had, like Britain, a programme for sending military language students to Japan, so they provided at least a small pool of linguists to draw upon. Between 1908 and 1941, a total of ninety-nine officers from the Navy, the Army and the Marine Corps took advantage of the scheme and spent several years in Japan as language officers. Those who were there in the 1930s were often tailed and watched by the Japanese military police (Kenpeitai), as were members of foreign diplomatic missions. For foreigners, life in Japan was becoming increasingly dangerous. On 27 July 1940, eleven British residents in Tokyo were arrested, and two days later, one of them, the British Reuters journalist Melville James Cox (1885–1940), who had been asking awkward questions at press briefings and was accused of espionage, allegedly threw himself out of a window at the Kenpeitai headquarters to his death. He had unquestionably been brutally treated, but it remains unclear whether he was thrown out of the window or jumped to avoid further grilling. One month later, thirty-five US citizens were arrested. In the circumstances, it is surprising that the language officer programme continued as long as it did, but in the summer of 1941 it was closed down. By that time, some of the former language officers had turned to other duties and forgotten their Japanese. Just a few of them were working in intelligence and using their knowledge of the language. The most prominent of them were Sidney Mashbir (1891–1973) and Ellis Zacharias (1890–1961), who had both travelled to Japan in 1920 and spent three years there as language officers. They were later to play key roles as linguists at the end of the war, as we will see in later chapters.[3]

Another former language officer who proved of exceptional value was Gill MacDonald Richardson (1905–88), who ended his career as a rear-admiral in the US Navy. In November 1935, he went to Tokyo as a language officer and stayed for the usual three years, learning the language but also gathering naval intelligence. On one occasion, he recalled, he was about to enter a Japanese restaurant when he realized that he would have to take his shoes off, as is the norm in restaurants serving Japanese food. He hastily changed his mind and went elsewhere, for did not want to take his shoes off. The simple reason for that was that he had been illegally observing Japanese naval construction and had hidden his notes inside his shoes. When he got back to the United States in 1938, he worked on Japanese codes in the naval base at Pearl Harbor, and then he was sent to the US base on Corregidor, a fortified island at the entrance to Manila Bay. After the Japanese invasion of the Philippines in 1941, it became clear that the base would have to be evacuated, so in 1942 he escaped with other intelligence personnel by submarine to Java and then went on to Australia. Richardson, like Mashbir, Zacharias and others, had acquired good knowledge of Japanese during his years as a language officer, but apart from a handful of people like them, there was a real shortage of Japanese linguists, just as there was in Britain, and by 1940 some people were beginning to worry about the shortage.[4]

Yet surely there was no shortage, given that the United States had a huge potential asset in the form of hundreds of thousands of Japanese immigrants and their children living in America? From the 1890s, large numbers of Japanese migrated to the United States, mostly as unskilled workers, and that continued up to 1924, when the Immigration Act put an end to Japanese immigration. The children born to these Japanese migrants are known as Nisei (Japanese for 'second generation'), and in 1941 most of them lived on the west coast of America. They grew up and were educated in America, but they were subject to racial prejudice and sometimes outright hostility. For various reasons—to seek respite from the hostility, take advantage of the favourable dollar–yen exchange rate or escape from the difficulties caused by the Great Depression in the United States—some Nisei travelled to their parents' hometowns in Japan, with or without their parents, to attend high school or university. Their subsequent fates depended on where they happened to be on 7 December 1941. Those who were still in Japan were promptly conscripted into the Japanese Army, while those in the United States ended up in the US Army. For example, Takemiya Teiji (1923–2010), a Nisei who attended a school in Kumamoto, was conscripted into the Imperial Japanese Navy and later in the war was about to take part in a suicide boat attack when he was assigned to a team monitoring English-language broadcasts. At the end of the war, in late August 1945, he took part as an interpreter in the negotiations prior to the surrender ceremony on board the USS *Missouri*. On the other hand, another Nisei at the very same school, Thomas Sakamoto (1918–2013), had returned to the United States before the outbreak of war, and so he joined the Military Intelligence Service of the US Army. He served with General MacArthur as an interrogator and was on board the USS *Missouri* on 2 September 1945 to witness the surrender ceremony.[5]

Most of the Nisei were American citizens, but after Pearl Harbor panic-stricken doubts about their loyalty set in, and in 1942 those who were living on the west coast of the United States were forced to move inland irrespective of their citizenship, and they lost all that they owned. Over 100,000 of them were interned for the duration of the war. Thus, the Nisei were definitely not at first seen as an asset; on the contrary, they were regarded as a fifth column. Moreover, even those who could speak Japanese did not necessarily know how to read the script, and only a tiny handful had any knowledge of military Japanese. As a result, their existence was ignored when people began to consider how best to make linguistic preparations for war with Japan.[6]

It was in 1940 that the first efforts were made to prepare America linguistically for the possibility of war with Japan, and they were made by Reischauer, whose teaching in 1942 enabled Christopher to become an intelligence officer rather than a machine-gunner. Who was he and how did he, a Harvard professor, get involved?

Reischauer was born and raised in Tokyo, where his parents were missionaries. There were many American Protestant missionaries active in Japan from the 1860s onwards: their children usually grew up bilingual and, as we will see, they became a valuable pool of linguists during the war. Reischauer was unusual as the son of a missionary in that he took his competence in Japanese and his interest in Japan to a higher level: he completed a PhD at Harvard University in 1939 with a thesis on the travels of the Japanese monk Ennin in ninth-century China. He was to spend most of his life as a professor at Harvard, except for a posting as US ambassador to Japan from 1961 to 1966. By October 1940, he had become very much aware of the possibility of war with Japan, so he wrote a memorandum for the Navy pointing out that very few Americans knew the kind of Japanese used in military situations and hardly any could read Japanese that had been handwritten in a hurry. He had a possible solution, and that was to create a Japanese-language school to train linguists in advance, very much as the director of SOAS had argued, albeit to no avail.[7]

Surprisingly, Reischauer's warning did not fall on stony ground. That was because it landed on the desk of Lieutenant (later Commander) Albert Hindmarsh of the US Navy, and he needed little convincing. Hindmarsh agreed that there were indeed few competent Japanese-speaking officers available. The few universities that taught Japanese offered courses that seemed to him to be 'of the most impractical and academic character', and nobody had even thought to make a list of civilians competent in Japanese. So in December 1940, Hindmarsh submitted to his superiors a proposal for a nationwide survey of available Japanese linguists and for the establishment of a Navy Japanese School, which would be 'designed to produce junior Naval Reserve officers thoroughly competent in reading, writing, and speaking Japanese in quantity and quality sufficient to anticipate the demand ... particularly in the event of war between Japan and the United States'. In February 1941, his proposals were immediately accepted, and he began to build up a file of people with some level of competence in Japanese and then to plan a curriculum that would enable American academics to teach Navy students Japanese in a year. How on earth did Hindmarsh manage to get his proposal approved so quickly and without the need for extensive lobbying? To put it briefly, Hindmarsh was no ordinary naval lieutenant.[8]

Before he joined the Navy, Hindmarsh had himself been a professor of international law at Harvard University, and had already published two important books, *Force in Peace: Force Short of War in International Relations* (1933) and *The Basis of Japanese Foreign Policy* (1936), which revealed his concerns about the containment of expansionist policies with particular reference to Japan. While at Harvard, he was also a US Naval Reserve officer for intelligence duties. In 1937, he visited Japan as an exchange professor at the University of Tokyo, and he moved in lofty circles there. He even had conversations with Prime Minister Konoe Fumimaro and with Admiral Yamamoto Isoroku, who was the commander-in-chief of the Combined Fleet of the Imperial Japanese Navy when it launched its attack on Pearl Harbor four years later.[9]

On his return to Harvard, Hindmarsh not only presented a full report on his visit but also took the drastic but determined step of abandoning his professorship and joining the Office of Naval Intelligence of the US Navy. When Reischauer's proposal came across his desk, Hindmarsh was serving in the Far East Section, which was headed by Commander Arthur McCollum (1898–1976), who had been born in Japan to missionary parents, had spent three years in Japan as a language officer and had served as naval attaché in Tokyo. He, too, had good knowledge not only of Japan but also of the Japanese language, and he was also in the best position to appreciate the force of Reischauer's arguments. It was fortuitous that Reischauer's proposal landed on the desks of two officers who both had good knowledge of Japan and a thorough command of the language, but it turned out to be decisive.[10]

At the same time, in early 1941, the intelligence department of the Army was also starting to become concerned about the shortage of linguists. The Army and the Navy, therefore, put pressure on the American Council of Learned Societies to organize a conference of Japanese-language teachers to explore ways of improving language teaching for military purposes. The conference was duly held at Cornell University at the end of July 1941. Hugh Borton (1903–95), who had lived in Japan for four years and was teaching Japanese history at Columbia University, was tasked with organizing it, but he immediately hit an obstacle: the Army and the Navy were determined to exclude from the conference all teachers who had Japanese ancestry, even if they were American citizens. Borton considered these restrictions 'obnoxious' and managed to convince the Army and Navy that this would be self-defeating, for it was obvious to him that well-educated Nisei made the best language teachers. As a result of his representations, two Nisei with American citizenship were eventually invited, Henry Tatsumi (1896–1991), who taught at the University of Washington, and Joseph Yamagiwa (1906–68) of the University of Michigan, and they both went on to teach on the wartime language courses. Yet many others were excluded. This was not a good start, but for quite different reasons the conference was not a success: the representatives of the US Army and Navy found themselves at odds with the academics.[11]

What was the problem? 'It became obvious to all concerned', Hindmarsh wrote later, 'that the teaching methods and techniques in our universities were in a state of unmitigated confusion.' Hindmarsh, who—let us remember—was a former Harvard professor as well as a naval officer, was distinctly unimpressed. Instead, he outlined his own plan for an intensive course based on the textbooks written by Naganuma Naoe (1894–1974), who had been teaching American military language officers in Japan, but Hindmarsh's proposal was that the material be covered in one year rather than the usual three. Unsurprisingly, the university teachers were sceptical and did not agree that it could be done. The military delegates to the conference responded with dismay and anger. As one of them put it then and there, 'Well, gentlemen, you haven't got a thing that's any damned use to the government at all.' Despite all this, the representative of the American Council of Learned Societies remained convinced that the universities were a more credible provider of Japanese-language courses than the military, as he explained a few days later to the Rockefeller Foundation, which had provided the funding for the conference:

> I think that the degree of competence alleged to be attained by naval
> officers and others under the Naganuma method has been much exag-
> gerated, and that in all probability better results in just as quick a time
> can be reached by the Elisséeff–Reischauer combination [Serge Elisséef
> was a professor of Japanese at Harvard] or some modification of it.

As it turned out, he was wrong, and eventually the Navy proved
capable of running a successful Japanese-language school at Boulder.[12]

Far from being discouraged by the outcome of the conference,
Hindmarsh went back to his office in Washington with new resolve:

> We left the conference determined to do the job ourselves, because it
> was clear that the teachers had developed no practical methods, had no
> adequate teaching materials, no practical standards, were primarily
> interested in the Japanese language as a philological subject, and were
> unduly skeptical as to the feasibility of doing a job which we were
> certain had to be done.

Hindmarsh himself now drew up plans to run two Japanese courses
for Navy personnel, one at Harvard and the other on the Berkeley
campus of the University of California; these plans were approved by
his superior, McCollum, and authorization came through in August
1941. Time was running out, though they did not know it. The naval
attaché at the US embassy in Tokyo was instructed to procure fifty
complete sets of the textbooks used on the Naganuma course, which
arrived just in time, in September 1941. They were duplicated in
quantity for students to use, potential students were interviewed, and
the courses began on 1 October 1941, just two months before Pearl
Harbor was attacked.[13]

Remarkably, neither of these university courses lasted very long. By
May 1942, half the students on the Harvard course had failed their
examinations, and what is more, the Harvard teachers were stubbornly
refusing to use the prescribed Naganuma textbooks, preferring to use
their own. Hindmarsh therefore terminated the contract the Navy had
signed with Harvard. The course at Berkeley ran into difficulties of a
different kind. After the outbreak of war, most of the teachers disappeared. This was because they were Nisei, and early in 1942 all families
of Japanese descent, whether or not they were American citizens, were
removed from coastal areas and placed in internment camps inland.
Hindmarsh was going to have to think again, and the outcome was the

US Navy Japanese Language School at Boulder, which was a reincarnation of the course at Berkeley.[14]

Although Hindmarsh's early efforts to get courses up and running hit various snags, there were some individual success stories. One of them was Donald Keene (1922–2019), who attended the Berkeley course and became one of the first graduates of the US Navy Japanese Language School. He was later to become famous as a scholar and translator of Japanese literature at Columbia University. At the age of eighteen, he had read Waley's translation of the *Tale of Genji*, the classic Japanese novel written in the eleventh century, and he spent the summer of 1941 studying Japanese in a mountain retreat in North Carolina, simply out of a growing interest in East Asia rather than out of any premonition of war.

Shortly after the outbreak of war, Keene wrote to the Navy Department to volunteer for the Japanese Language School and soon started his studies at Berkeley. After finishing his studies in February 1943, he was sent to Hawai'i where he translated captured documents that seemed to him to be of no strategic value whatsoever. That was an unexciting start to his career as a naval translator, but he soon had more excitement than he had bargained for. He was sent from Hawai'i to the Aleutian Islands, which lie to the south-west of Alaska. Several of the islands had been occupied by Japanese forces, the only American territory to be occupied by Japan during the war, and Keene found himself taking part in an amphibious landing, as he described in his memoirs: 'We left the ship on rope ladders and boarded landing barges bound for the beach. I am not a courageous person, but I felt not the least fear of danger until suddenly I heard a terrible screaming.' What on earth had happened? Were Japanese troops ready and waiting with their machine-guns for the Americans? Not exactly: 'The ramp of the landing barge ahead of ours had dropped before the barge reached the shore, and the soldiers were thrown into the icy water. This was my first taste of war.' Once the islands had been retaken, there were ample documents to translate and prisoners to interrogate, but it was obvious that far more translators were going to be needed. Where were they going to come from?[15]

Soldier linguists

At the same time as Hindmarsh was developing his plans for a Navy Language School, other branches of the US military and the government were also beginning to tackle the language problem. On 1 July 1941, twelve carefully selected men were hurriedly admitted to the Marine Corps and sent to Hawai'i to begin a special course in Japanese. They all already had some experience of Japan and the Japanese language through birth, residence or a period of study there, so they were not complete beginners. After the attack on Pearl Harbor, the Marine Corps hastily moved its language school away from Hawai'i and instead established a Japanese school for enlisted men in San Diego, and later other schools in American Samoa and Saipan.[16]

The US Army, in turn, created in November 1941 a language school for male Nisei at San Francisco, the Military Intelligence Service Language School. The thinking was that it would be quicker to train Nisei, who could be expected to have some knowledge of spoken Japanese at least, than to train Americans who knew nothing of the language. The two criteria for admission were loyalty and language ability. Loyalty at this early stage was judged by the level of contacts candidates had with Japan, but later a formal requirement was introduced. Why was this necessary? As a result of changes in Japanese law in 1924, Japanese children who were born outside Japan were eligible for Japanese nationality, but the parents had to register the birth with a Japanese consulate; at the same time, it became possible for Japanese living outside Japan to renounce their Japanese citizenship. By 1941, around 70 per cent of Nisei in the United States had only American citizenship, but this means that 30 per cent were dual citizens, Americans by place of birth and Japanese by parentage backed up by consular registration. Those candidates for the language school who were dual citizens were now obliged, therefore, to swear allegiance to the United States and forswear any allegiance to Japan, thus renouncing their Japanese citizenship. When it came to language ability, however, there was a snag: it was found that most Nisei were so well assimilated into American society that only 10 per cent knew Japanese well enough to be accepted as students, and those capable of becoming teachers were fewer still. In May 1942, the Military

Intelligence Service Language School moved from San Francisco, where Nisei were no longer allowed to live, to Camp Savage near Minneapolis in Minnesota, and classes began there on 1 June 1942. The school was commanded by Colonel Kai Rasmussen, a Dane who had spent the years 1936–40 in Japan as a US Army language officer, but the other teachers were mostly drawn from the small pool of highly educated Nisei with a good command of both English and Japanese. Rasmussen and the other former US language officers were now finding that their linguistic expertise was valued by the Army, which was giving them important roles to play.[17]

As mentioned in the previous chapter, a number of Nisei worked alongside Storry and his colleagues in India and Burma. Although Storry, Allen and other British linguists mention the presence of Nisei in the Mobile Units and clearly appreciated their linguistic talents, they rarely bothered to mention their names. At least thirty graduates of the Military Intelligence Service Language School served with CSDIC(I) or SEATIC, in Delhi or in the field, but most are now nameless. One of the few exceptions is Henry Hideo Kuwabara (1919–2005), who served with the 36th Infantry Division in Burma (probably in one of the Mobile Units) and was awarded the British Empire Medal.[18]

By the end of the war, several thousand Nisei linguists had been trained at the Military Intelligence Service Language School, as well as a small number of white Americans who already had some knowledge of Japanese. The Nisei served in various theatres of the war, but they did so mostly as non-commissioned officers in small groups led by white American language officers. This was partly a result of racial discrimination and because of lingering doubts about their loyalty, but it was also believed that if Nisei were led by white officers, they would be unlikely to be taken for the enemy by regular soldiers who were not used to encountering Nisei. This was a serious consideration, for on a number of occasions Nisei linguists were indeed mistaken for Japanese infiltrators and narrowly avoided being shot. By 1944, Rasmussen had managed to arrange for some of his best graduates to be commissioned, but most continued to serve throughout the war as non-commissioned officers. In 1944, some Nisei women were finally admitted to the school as members of the Women's Army Corps, albeit in small numbers.[19]

The primary role of the Military Intelligence Service Language School was to train Nisei. Since there were insufficient white Americans with good enough knowledge of Japanese to lead them, in 1943 the Army established an Intensive Japanese Language School in Ann Arbor at the University of Michigan. The teachers here were mostly Nisei, but this was a school for white males who were to become officers, and Nisei were not accepted as students.[20]

What about the need for linguist cryptographers? Who was going to fulfil the role of Captain Tuck and teach Japanese telegraphese? Not long before the attack on Pearl Harbor, Reischauer, whose warnings in 1940 had proved so surprisingly effective, left Harvard for a spell at the State Department in Washington. In the summer of 1942, at the request of the US Army Signal Corps, he started running a top-secret course at Arlington Hall in Virginia. Arlington Hall had been a women's college, but it was taken over by the US Army Signal Intelligence Service in June 1942 and functioned like Bletchley Park as a secret cryptanalysis centre. Here, too, Nisei were not welcome, although some did serve at Vint Hill Farms, a cryptography school and intercept station in Virginia, a few miles to the west of Washington.[21]

Reischauer's courses, like Captain Tuck's at Bedford, concentrated on military vocabulary and the language of telegrams and wireless messages rather than the spoken language, and they were intended for cryptographers. The teachers were all either former missionaries or the children of missionaries. The students were specially recruited linguists, and they had been studying Japanese when the war broke out. Most of them had been studying at Harvard, Yale or Columbia, and they included Christopher, who had heeded his father's advice about not becoming a machine-gunner. Another was Henry Graff, who later became a professor of history at Columbia University, and his verdict on Reischauer's courses was succinct: 'He succeeded famously.' But as yet much less is known about the Arlington Hall courses than about the Bedford courses, and the story of the Arlington Hall endeavour is yet to be written.[22]

As far as I know, there were no British students at any of the US Army institutions or at Arlington Hall. At the US Navy school at Boulder, on the other hand, there certainly were British students, starting with those five RNVR officers, so we will now turn to the Boulder School.

Japanese at Boulder

In June 1942, the teachers and students at Berkeley, including Keene, were uprooted and sent to Boulder, a little way north of Denver in Colorado. Why Boulder? For one thing, it was far enough away from the west coast to be safe from any of the anticipated Japanese coastal raids; what is more, Boulder was a small town, and the school would attract less attention there. Perhaps the most important consideration, however, was that in Colorado there would be no problem about enrolling Nisei as teachers, for Nisei were not barred from living there.

The US Navy Japanese Language School became a very efficient operation once it had settled in its new location, and by the end of the war it had trained over 1,000 Japanese linguists. Unlike the US Army Language School, Nisei were not admitted as students, but as many as 150 Nisei were released from internment to teach at Boulder, for the students were divided into small classes and there were several courses running at the same time. There were no fixed criteria for the recruitment of students, but at first a large number of those who were accepted for the school had some connection with Japan already, and many of them had grown up in Japan as the children of missionaries— they formed a pool of students of a kind that was unavailable in Britain. Later on, when there were no more such students left, it was enough to be able to show evidence of linguistic gifts or academic excellence to gain admission. Most of the recruits were destined for the Navy, but some joined the Marine Corps, and, from 1943 onwards, ninety women from the US Navy Women's Reserve (known as WAVES, Women Accepted for Voluntary Emergency Service) were taught there too, albeit in separate classes.[23]

There can be no doubt that Boulder was a very successful operation, and, just as at Bedford, the outcome was down to one person. The courses were run by Florence Walne (1895–1946), a professor at the University of California, who had been born and raised in Japan and had taught there from 1916 to 1931. As Hindmarsh later acknowledged, 'she alone among the University teachers of Japanese in the summer of 1941, recognized the urgency, the practicability and the feasibility of doing the kind of job which eventually was done so well and to the tremendous advantage of the United States' effort in the Pacific Area'.[24]

The courses Walne ran were highly competitive and demanding. They were taught both by repatriated missionaries and by large numbers of Nisei, including some who still had Japanese citizenship and were therefore technically enemy aliens. The ready availability of Nisei teachers gave the Boulder courses an advantage over the SOAS courses when it came to providing instruction in spoken Japanese, and the commitment of the Nisei was warmly appreciated by the students. Nevertheless, the reception accorded the Nisei and their families in Boulder was sometimes far from welcoming. What is more, the parents of some of the students were appalled that their children were being taught by 'Japanese'. James Durbin, for example, wrote home frequently and soon had to confront this problem when it cropped up in the letters he received from his parents:

> I was quite surprised at your attitude towards the teachers. If you knew them I'm sure you would like them as much as I do. ... they work even harder than the students—they are willing and eager at any time whatsoever to help us as much as they can. All the ones I have [as teachers], and all the ones I know are fine people. ... All the Japanese I have met here are fine people and I like them—I see no reason why that shouldn't be[,] just because we are at war with their country.[25]

Unlike the Bedford and SOAS courses, the Boulder courses, which lasted for fourteen months, did not focus exclusively on military Japanese. The main textbook was the pre-war series of textbooks and readers produced by Naganuma, which the teachers at Harvard had been unwilling to use. These textbooks did not focus on military Japanese, so the Boulder graduates tended to have much smaller military vocabularies than the Bedford graduates. On the other hand, their courses were longer, and at the end they learnt how to read handwritten Japanese. They also worked their way through the *Navy Reader* (*Kaigun tokuhon*), which, in the 1937 edition, explained the role, organization and equipment of the Imperial Japanese Navy, and thus did serve to impart some basic naval vocabulary.[26]

Wavy Navy officers at Boulder

Let us now return to those five junior British officers. Why did they need to travel all the way to Boulder to learn Japanese? The easy answer is that they had all responded to an Admiralty circular calling for volunteers to learn Japanese, but it is still not clear why the Admiralty proposed sending men to the United States to learn Japanese in the first place. In 1943, Hindmarsh issued a press release about the US Navy Language School that stated that 'arrangements were made with the British Admiralty for the enrolment of a small number of British Naval officers in the Navy language course'. Again, in the official history of the US Navy Language School, which he wrote after the war, he implied that the initiative came from Boulder as part of the measures taken to increase the number of students, but I have so far been unable to find anything in the British Admiralty archives to explain the British response to this initiative. Perhaps it was a matter of cooperation between the two navies, coupled with the desire to create a small body of British naval linguists who would have contacts among their American counterparts and could act as liaison officers. One of them later did in fact serve as a liaison officer at the beginning of the Occupation of Japan, as we will see in chapter 11.[27]

In October 1943, the five Wavy Navy officers began their course at the US Navy Japanese Language School. They joined several hundred young American men and women, all recruited for the US Navy straight from university and studying the language in small classes. The course was demanding and relentless. Tuition was intensive, and there were weekly tests in which the students had to maintain an 80 per cent average in order to stay on the course—weaker students were ruthlessly expelled. After the first two weeks, all their conversations over lunch had to be in Japanese, and one of their teachers was always at table with them to make sure that the rule was obeyed. Occasionally, Japanese films were shown, presumably pre-war films that had been shown to Japanese communities on the west coast before the war, and attendance at these film-showings was compulsory. Few such films were available in Britain, so this gave the Boulder students access to an archive of the spoken language that the SOAS students did not have.[28]

The newly arrived British naval officers did not impress their American counterparts. One of the American students wrote to his parents:

> The main topic of conversation at the Language School right now is the arrival of five officers of the British Navy, who are here, like the rest of us, to plunge into the study of Japanese. They all look as if they have

been dug out of the recesses of the British Museum—small, thin, pale, and bespectacled.[29]

Who were these five weedy young men? One of them was William Beasley (1919–2006), who later in life was to become professor of Far Eastern history at SOAS and has left a detailed memoir of his wartime service, which I shall draw upon below.[30] After getting a degree in history from University College London, Beasley had joined the Royal Navy in late 1940 and was trained as a telegraphist. He was sent to sea on the destroyer HMS *Tartar* in 1941 as an ordinary seaman. He was on board when the *Tartar* hovered nearby as the British battleships *Rodney* and *King George V* finally put an end to the mighty German battleship *Bismarck* at the end of May 1941. He was also on board when the *Tartar* escorted the battleship *Prince of Wales* carrying Winston Churchill to his summit meeting with President Roosevelt off Newfoundland in August 1941, and when it took part in a number of operations off Norway and Spitzbergen. Beasley had certainly seen plenty of action at sea, but he had left the ship and was undergoing officer training in Portsmouth when he heard of the attack on Pearl Harbor. He was then posted to the naval base in Dartmouth and in 1943 was working on advance planning for land communications after D-Day when he collapsed from overwork. On finishing sick leave and returning to his desk, he fortuitously found an Admiralty circular calling for volunteers to learn Japanese and promptly volunteered, a step that changed his life.

Beasley tells us something of the other four in his memoir. Edward Alan Wilkinson (1922–2009) had also been in the thick of action. He was serving on one of the destroyers escorting the *Prince of Wales* off Malaya in December 1941 and watched as the great battleship was attacked and sunk by Japanese bombers. Andrew Birrell (1909–92) was the oldest of them all and, like Beasley, was already a lieutenant in the Navy. After graduating from Oxford in 1932, he had worked in Europe and had acquired knowledge of several European languages, but he had returned to Britain in a hurry in 1940 and joined the RNVR. He served on shore bases until he was sent to Boulder, and there he was appointed the senior officer of the British group of officers. Donald Gowing (1921–69) had studied history at King's College, Cambridge, but had interrupted his course to join the RNVR and had served in naval intelligence. Lastly, Edward Kennedy joined the RNVR half-way through his modern languages course at Cambridge. They had all responded to the Admiralty circular like Beasley.[31] Since rationing was in force in Britain, they may well have looked weedy to their better-fed American colleagues, but in fact they had considerably more naval experience than any of their fellow students at Boulder and several had already seen action on the high seas.

Beasley and his colleagues found that a degree of secrecy surrounded the Japanese Language School and its students. It was too big to be concealed from the community at the University of Colorado Boulder, but it kept a low profile and was referred to in the local newspapers as 'a naval unit on the university campus'.[32] However, it ceased to be a secret in December 1943, when the *New York Times* carried an article entitled 'Navy Men Learn Japanese in a Year'. The article reproduced verbatim the greater part of a press release issued by the US Navy, including a passage stating that it had become 'painfully obvious that the teaching methods and techniques in the Japanese-language courses in American universities were in a state of confusion'—the wording suggests that the hand of Hindmarsh was responsible for this press release. Thanks to the Navy's revolutionary scheme, the article reported, after twelve months of tuition 'the student was expected to read with fair ease a Japanese newspaper, to converse in Japanese with fluency and to handle the language in both its written and spoken forms with relative ease and facility'. Not included in the article was the proud conclusion to the press release:

> Through the program at the Navy Japanese Language School, the Navy has accomplished what was once believed to be impossible—the training of competent Japanese language experts in a mere twelve months. Know your enemy is a sound maxim, and our Japanese enemy can no longer barricade himself behind the complicated characters and syntax of his difficult language.

The newspaper article concluded by mentioning that 'All instruction is now concentrated at the University of Colorado', so the secret was out.[33]

This article in the *New York Times* attracted the attention of the British embassy in Washington, which had evidently been kept in the dark about the Boulder courses even though British officers were attending them. At this time, Sir George Sansom (1883–1965), who had served for many years at the British embassy in Tokyo and at various British consulates in Japan before becoming an academic historian of Japan, was doing wartime service as an advisor to the British ambassador in Washington. He was closely connected with GC&CS and while in Washington was working for the Special Operations Executive. When he was asked for his assessment of the article's claims, he wrote that in his opinion the article exaggerated the effectiveness of the US Navy courses and declared that the claims would only be true of the best students. All the same, he thought that disciplined hard work, intensive language work and 'carefully thought out methods designed to produce limited results for a specific purpose' might explain the success of the courses. Sansom's reaction was typical of those who had invested many years of hard effort to learn the language: sheer incredulity that intensive wartime courses could succeed in producing trained linguists in bulk in just one year. He would have been astonished, too, to learn what was being achieved at Bedford, but that was a secret to which very few were privy.[34]

Unaware of Sansom's opinion, Beasley and his colleagues were continuing their studies when, in 1944, some other Royal Navy officers were sent to join them. One of them was John Quine (1920–2013), who later became the head of MI6. Another was Stanley Heath, who obtained the second-highest grade average in the history of the Japanese Language School in Boulder but graduated in August 1945 just before the war ended. He was seconded to the US Navy and served in the Pacific. Doubtless he appreciated the better food in US Navy ships, but he probably missed the alcohol available on Royal Navy ships.[35]

One of the other students who joined in 1944, John Catt (1922–98), nearly caused an international incident. Like Beasley, Catt, too, had seen active service. He had served on the light cruiser HMS *Cairo* and while aboard had taken part in Operation Pedestal, the famous convoy that was sent in August 1942 to bring relief supplies to the besieged island of Malta. Later, he was one of the survivors when his ship was torpedoed by an Italian submarine and sank with the loss of twenty-four lives.

The problem with Catt was that he sported a beard. This was not a problem in the Royal Navy, but the US Navy preferred the clean-shaven look. In July 1944, the US naval lieutenant in charge of the men's dormitory at Boulder asked Beasley to have Catt shave off his beard. Catt declined to do so unless ordered to cut it off by a superior officer in the Royal Navy. Beasley wrote to the British Admiralty Delegation in Washington explaining the problem and pointing out that the lieutenant tended to look down on all the students, whether they were British or American. Hindmarsh intervened and wrote to the lieutenant saying that his attention had been drawn to 'what has become a *cause célèbre* in local circles, namely the present status of Catt's beard'. He explained, with some ingenuity, that Catt could not just shave off his beard since officers in the Royal Navy needed permission to change their appearance from the image that appeared on their identity documents. The British representatives in Washington, he added, 'would like very much to have Catt keep his beard'. So, although he diplomatically agreed that the beard looked odd, he suggested that Catt be allowed to keep it unless 'the situation is really causing harm to morale or to the efficient operation of the course'. This did the trick, and Catt kept his beard for the rest of his life.[36]

A third group of RNVR students reached Boulder in early August 1945, when it was still expected that the defeat of Japan was a long way off. Some of these, too, had already seen action at sea. But, as it turned out, they had all reached Boulder too late. Once Japan announced the decision to surrender on 15 August, their courses were terminated and they all returned home.[37]

As each group of students finished its course at Boulder, there was a graduation ceremony at which the valedictorian, the student with the best marks, gave an address in Japanese. On 16 December 1944, four of the six graduating men were British, and the valedictorian was British, too—perhaps Beasley. Unusually, the ceremony started out not with the US national anthem, as it did when the valedictorian was American, but with 'God Save the King', which the American student body had learnt to sing the day before. By this time, the RNVR students were no longer regarded as oddities 'dug out of the recesses of the British Museum': instead, they had won some respect and affection from their colleagues. One of them described Beasley as 'a wonderful raconteur, [who] entertained us with anecdotes about how to get along in the British Navy without really trying'.[38]

Boulder graduates at war

What happened to the American Boulder graduates when they went to war? The Marines needed to do basic physical training like all recruits to the Marine Corps. Some of them were sent to do a hasty course in how to read Japanese military documents at the Army Military Intelligence Language School. After that, they were sent into action in the Pacific islands, where they were Marines first and linguists second. Roger Hackett, who later in life became a historian of Japan, joined the 1st Marine Division early in December 1943 after he had finished his Boulder course. On 26 December, he landed with the first wave of Marines at Borgen Bay on the western tip of New Britain, a large island off the east coast of New Guinea. In other words, he landed as a combatant rather than as a translator: the translators who were attached to regular Army units tended to land only when the landing area had been secured. Other Boulder graduates were with the 2nd Marine Division when it landed on Tarawa in the Gilbert Islands (half-way between New Guinea and Hawai'i), and, as Roger Dingman put it, 'spent much more time fighting, carrying ammunition, pulling wounded men back, and trying to get medical help than they did interrogating'. When they could, they scavenged documents from abandoned Japanese corpses and translated them, and they interrogated the few prisoners the Marines took.[39]

The Boulder Marines were much closer to the brutal fighting than most of the British graduates of the Bedford or SOAS courses ever came to be. Two of them died in action and five were wounded. One of the Marines, Albert da Silva, owed his life to the Japanese Language School. In 1944, he landed on Mindanao in the Philippines and was travelling with a small US Army unit when it was ambushed. The bullets of the first salvo were stopped by the fat dictionaries that he and all the linguists carried around with them. Lucky to be alive, he dived under his jeep. He heard the Japanese officer order his men to kill the wounded and the prisoners, so da Silva rolled out from under his jeep into a stream and swam away. He was the only survivor.[40]

The Navy Boulder graduates, on the other hand, ended up in a variety of roles, as did their British counterparts: some were sent to the Office of Naval Intelligence in Washington where they worked on codebreaking, some to Hawai'i to work in a combat intelligence unit, some to the Intelligence Center, Pacific Ocean Area in San Francisco, and a few served as Radio Intelligence Unit officers on board ships, where they were under pressure to translate instantly the instructions given by enemy air attack coordinators. As for the women in the WAVES, since they were banned from serving overseas (and that applied even to Hawai'i), they were all sent to the Washington Document Center, a part of the Office of Naval Intelligence, where they were responsible for translating captured documents.[41]

As the war came to an end, the American Boulder graduates found themselves taking on new roles. During the Okinawa Campaign, the last step before the planned invasions of the Japanese homeland, several of them risked their lives trying to persuade Japanese civilians and soldiers to surrender rather than commit suicide. Two of the key roles, however, were not played by young Boulder graduates but by career Army and Navy officers who had spent years in Japan before the war. We encountered two of them earlier in this chapter. One was Captain. Zacharias of the US Navy, who had been a language officer in Japan in the 1920s, at the same time as Nave, and had then headed the Far East Division of the Office of Naval Intelligence in Washington. When war broke out, he was in command of a heavy cruiser, but in 1942 he returned to the Office of Naval Intelligence to engage in psychological warfare, culminating in a series of broadcasts he made to Japan from May 1945 onwards. These were recorded in Japanese and broadcast from Saipan, an island near Guam to the south of Japan, on the medium wave used by Radio Tokyo so that ordinary people could listen to them. In the broadcasts, he sought to impress upon Japanese listeners the catastrophe that was facing Japan following the defeat of Germany.

The other was Colonel Mashbir, who was a language officer in Tokyo at the same time as Zacharias and spent two further years there in 1937–9. In 1942, he was sent to Brisbane to join General MacArthur's staff, and there he set up ATIS, which will feature in chapter 9. As MacArthur's interpreter, he was present at the surrender ceremony aboard USS *Missouri* on 2 September 1945, and he also acted as the interpreter at General MacArthur's subsequent meetings with the Japanese emperor.

Once the Japanese government had announced on 15 August 1945 that they would accept the Potsdam Declaration and surrender, Boulder graduates became involved in negotiations for the surrender of countless island garrisons, and then they began to interrogate those who were suspected of war crimes. Finally, on 30 August 1945, when the British and American navies entered Tokyo Bay and took over the Japanese Navy base at Yokosuka, near Yokohama, to begin the Occupation of Japan, Boulder graduates were on hand to do the interpreting.[42]

The British Boulder graduates, on the other hand, returned to the bosom of the Royal Navy and then went in many different directions. Beasley, Kennedy and Wilkinson reported to British naval authorities in Washington, DC and were sent to Vancouver to undergo further training at the Canadian Army Language School. The Canadian school had opened in August 1943 and owed its existence to the efforts of Lieutenant-Colonel Brian R. Mullaly (1892–1965), an officer of the British Indian Army who had been a language officer in Japan from 1922 and had then spent the years 1939–41 as a military attaché in Tokyo. It is unclear why Beasley and his colleagues needed further training, especially at an Army school. It may well be that the Royal Navy did not know what to do with them. At any rate, as Beasley recalled, they took with them to Vancouver 'a sufficient supply of alcohol to supplement the resources of our hosts (Canada suffered from liquor rationing)'. They were put to work reading the Japanese infantry manual, which, Beasley drily noted, 'did not prove to be a subject of absorbing interest', and which had little to teach Navy officers. After that, they were sent to the US Navy Operational Intelligence School in New York, where they learnt how to interpret aerial reconnaissance photographs and gained experience in intelligence planning for landings on Japanese-held islands. Most likely, none of them ever had an opportunity to put these skills to use. After they had returned to Washington, Wilkinson was sent out to the Pacific with the bearded Catt and ended up in Japan in September 1945, after the surrender.[43]

Beasley, on the other hand, was flown to Australia and then to Manila to join ATIS. 'Manila turned out to be a disaster', he wrote: 'The city itself, which had been the scene of heavy fighting, was in many parts a shambles. The staff of A.T.I.S. were living under canvas at the racetrack.' Beasley soon moved out to Bilibid Prison in the hills 10 miles to the south of Manila. Funnily enough, most of the Japanese prisoners of war—and by this time many had been taken in the campaign to take back the Philippines—were held in a camp outside the

prison, while the prison itself was used as accommodation for the interrogators, mostly American but some from Australia or New Zealand
and a small number from Britain. Beasley did not find interrogating the
POWs professionally satisfying, for he found he could gather little
useful information from them. On the other hand, he was surprised at
how willing the prisoners were to talk:

> None of the [Japanese] naval prisoners who were sent to me were
> officers or petty officers or specialists of any technical kind, which made
> it unlikely that they would have information of importance, except by
> chance. On the other hand, they showed no reluctance to talk … they
> seemed too bewildered by what had happened to them to want to be
> obstructive in any way. They were anxious to talk about home and
> family, sometimes too much so for my purposes, and made no obvious
> attempt to be evasive about their military service.

He had just concluded that there was no operational intelligence to be
had from these captives when he was ordered to return to Sydney.[44]

In Sydney, he was told, without explanation, that he was to join the
British flagship, the battleship HMS *King George V*, near Okinawa. The
journey took a week, and by the time he reached his ship the atomic
bombs had been dropped on Hiroshima and Nagasaki. After the
Japanese decision to surrender, the *King George V* made its way through
the minefields into Tokyo Bay, with Japanese naval officers as pilots and
Beasley on board to interpret their sailing instructions, as we will see.[45]

The wartime careers of Beasley's British colleagues at Boulder are
much less easy to trace. Gowing, who for some reason left the course
early in May 1944, was sent to the naval shore base in Colombo, but
then early in 1945 he was sent to Sydney, where he presumably worked
in naval intelligence. On 1 April 1945, he was transferred to the
cruiser HMS *Swiftsure*, which became temporarily the flagship of Rear
Admiral Cecil Harcourt for the re-entry of British forces into Hong
Kong. After Harcourt had disembarked to become the administrator
of Hong Kong until the civilian administration could take over, the
Swiftsure went to Japan and on 18 October visited Nagasaki. Four sight-
seeing parties were organized, and in a colour film that has survived to
this day, Gowing can be identified talking with local Japanese.[46]

The British and American naval students underwent the same training at Boulder, but their subsequent careers were quite different. This

was partly because the Royal Navy was less involved than the US and Australian navies in the island-hopping campaign to oust the Japanese from the Pacific islands they had occupied, or in the hard-fought naval battles that gradually diminished Japanese naval power in the Pacific. Most of the RNVR students had already seen action before they ever went to Boulder, but by the time they reached the Pacific, the war was virtually over. By contrast, the US Navy and Marine Corps students mostly went to Boulder with no military experience whatsoever, but once they had graduated many of them found themselves in the thick of the action and often in danger.

It remains a mystery why Beasley and his RNVR colleagues were sent to the United States for their Japanese studies instead of being sent to SOAS. In the end, they graduated too late in the day to play much of a role in the war itself, but, as we shall see in later chapters, their talents came to the fore at the end of the war and in occupied Japan.

* * *

The RNVR officers at Boulder were the only British linguists trained in the United States so far as I have been able to discover, but this does not by any means signify that there were no other Britons in the United States engaged in the language war with Japan. In addition to Japan-experts at the British embassy like Sansom, there was also the British Admiralty Delegation in Washington, which kept abreast of the work of the various naval intelligence bodies in Washington and sent some of the translations they produced back to Britain along with Royal Navy assessments of the intelligence they contained. To give one example, in April 1943, the delegation sent the Admiralty in London a translation done at San Francisco of a captured document emanating from the Japanese Torpedo School. This provided an assessment of the efficacy of Japanese torpedoes fired in the Java Sea in 1942.[47]

At the same time, the British Political Warfare Executive, a clandestine body formed in 1941 by the Foreign Office to disseminate propaganda, maintained a mission in Washington, and this had a Japanese section. The mission's subsidiary office in Denver had the tasks of monitoring Japanese broadcasts and of broadcasting news and war commentary in Japanese in a wireless service aimed at Japan that was called the 'Voice of Britain'. Several Nisei were employed to read the texts live 'on air'. The head of the team producing the broadcasts in Denver was Wilfrid Wolters McVittie (1906–80), who had been in the British Consular Service in Japan from 1933 to 1940. His deputy from January 1944 was the extraordinarily long-lived Robert G. P. Weighton (1908–2020), who taught at a boys' school in Japanese-occupied Taiwan for the British Presbyterian Foreign Missions Committee from 1933 to 1939. He spent the years 1934–6 on a Japanese course in Tokyo and had good knowledge of Japanese, but he admitted that he was ignorant of Japanese military vocabulary. It was his job to prepare the texts for broadcasting, sometimes translations of press releases and at other times commentary on the progress of the war, but underlying the broadcasts were explicit instructions sent from London. On 6 February 1945, for example, the instructions were to emphasize Allied advances in all theatres of the war, to mention the impact of rising prices on the Japanese population and to note the fall of Manila to the Allies in the light of Japanese propaganda about the vital importance of the Philippines for safeguarding Japanese communications. English versions of the broadcasts were subjected to very careful scrutiny and in some cases criticism. On one occasion, for example, McVittie complained that a broadcast that mentioned the vast supply of superior aeroplanes available to the Allies failed to consider the likely response of Japanese propagandists, who would argue that the Allies relied solely on material superiority while Japanese airmen were braver and more skilful.[48]

On 16 August 1945, the day after news came of the Japanese surrender, the head of the Japanese Section, which had by this time moved from Denver to San Francisco, paid tribute to the efforts of his staff. He mentioned four Nisei named Hattori, Endō, Ono (or Ōno) and Dote, who 'followed the course of events [at the end of the war] with deep understanding' and 'interpreted [the news] in written words and "mike" [microphone] accents that I feel sure could not but make some impression on any hearers'. He also mentioned three British staff, Weighton, a Miss Hornby, whom I have not been able to trace, and Godfrey St George Montague Gompertz (1904–92), who had worked for the Rising Sun Petroleum Company in Japan and Japanese-occupied Korea before the war. But there is much that remains unclear about these broadcasts. Did the Nisei just read the texts out, or did they help make them linguistically suitable? What topics were covered in the broadcasts and what impact did they have? At present, it is not possible to answer these questions.[49]

9

FROM AUSTRALIA TO LEYTE GULF

Australia entered the Second World War on 3 September 1939, when the Commonwealth of Australia replicated Britain's declaration of war on Germany. Likewise, Australia declared war on Japan in December 1941. By the end of the war, almost a million Australians had served in the armed forces, campaigning in Europe, North Africa and the Pacific or working behind the scenes in Australia.

During the First World War, when many Australians lost their lives in the disastrous Gallipoli Campaign and on the Western Front, the fighting had taken place very far from the shores of Australia. This time it was different. Now Australia itself came under attack. Enemy action first reached the shores of Australia on 19 February 1942, when Japanese carrier-borne aircraft raided Darwin, at the north of the Northern Territory, killing more than 200 people, sinking ships in the harbour and destroying aircraft at the airport. A few months later, Japanese midget submarines attacked Sydney Harbour. There were raids on Townsville and other towns and cities on the east coast of Australia, too, and a large submarine surfaced off the east coast of Tasmania and launched a seaplane that flew over Hobart but did no damage. It is true that Japanese plans to invade Australia were abandoned in February 1942, but Australians were naturally unaware of that, and what was obvious was that the reach of Japan was now alarmingly close to Australia.[1]

It goes without saying that Australia was compelled to initiate Japanese-language training to deal with the threat, and in fact Australia had already done so, before Britain or the United States. But what does that have to do with this book, which is mainly focused on British personnel and their role in the language war? The answer is that, from the outset, British military and civilian linguists were active in Australia, as codebreakers, as intercept operators, as translators of captured documents and as interrogators of prisoners. What is more, the Australian War Memorial contains a unique archive of materials that throw light on all these activities, including some original captured documents. We will explore them later in this chapter.

Codebreaking in Australia

In 1940, Nave, now a commander in the Royal Navy, finally returned home to Australia. He was worn out by his years of work for the British government. We first encountered Nave in chapter 1, when he was already beginning to impress the Royal Navy because of his formidable cryptographic skills combined with a deep knowledge of Japanese acquired as a language officer in Japan. In 1925, the Royal Navy had 'borrowed' him from the Royal Australian Navy, ostensibly to act as an interpreter in Hong Kong. When he got there, he joined a small Royal Navy team starting serious work on Japanese naval codes and made valuable inroads into Japanese naval codes. Then in 1928 Nave was sent to London and put to work for GC&CS and in 1930 transferred to the Royal Navy: he was in a class of his own as a Japanese cryptanalyst, and the British government was loath to lose his rare capabilities. He and his former room-mate from Tokyo days, Shaw, were made to rotate postings, so that when one was in Singapore the other was at GC&CS. From 1937 onwards, Nave had been working under mounting pressure at the FECB in Hong Kong, and then, after the summer of 1939, in Singapore. But by this time he had begun to suffer from ill health, and it became clear that he could no longer work effectively in tropical or semi-tropical climates. Hence his return to Australia in 1940.[2]

Nave arrived back after an absence of fifteen years. What had changed in Australia during that time? For one thing, he found that Japanese codebreaking was being taken much more seriously in his home country. There was good reason for this. After all, Truk Lagoon (now Chuuk in Micronesia), which had passed from Germany into the hands of Japan after the First World War, lay not much more than 1,000 miles from Australia to the north-east of New Guinea. Truk was soon to be heavily fortified by Japan and equipped with as many as five airstrips. It became the Imperial Japanese Navy's formidable main base in the South Pacific: at one point in 1943, both the *Musashi* and the *Yamato*, the two largest battleships ever built, were anchored there. It is all too easy to understand, therefore, that as relations between Japan and the British Empire deteriorated in the 1930s, Australia became apprehensive about a possible outbreak of war with Japan.

In the absence of Nave, who had been poached by Britain, the Royal Australian Navy began to look for other talent. They picked on Lieutenant William McLaughlin, who had been a language officer in Japan from 1928. As early as the 1930s, the Navy had ordered McLaughlin to conduct courses for signallers in Japanese Morse and the Japanese language. In this respect, the Royal Australian Navy was well ahead of the Royal Navy or the US Navy. But these courses did not continue, and therefore they did not lead to the development of a cadre of experts. Consequently, by the late 1930s there was once again an acute lack of Japanese linguists and cryptographers in Australia. It was time to do something about this deficiency.[3]

It was in January 1940, nearly two years before the outbreak of war in the Pacific, that, with the encouragement of the Australian Army, a small group at the University of Sydney began to study Japanese codes. They were a curious group of brilliant individuals. The leader was Thomas Gerald Room (1902–86), who was professor of mathematics at the university. He was joined by Richard Lyons, who taught geometry, and by two classicists, Arthur Dale Trendall (1909–95), an expert on Greek vases, and Athanasius Treweek (1911–95), a lecturer in Greek. Treweek had two advantages over the others. First, he had been commissioned in the Field Artillery in 1932 and was now a major, so he had military experience, which the others had not. Second, he had started learning Japanese privately in 1937 in the expectation that Australia would soon be at war with Japan. There were few indeed in any of the future Allied nations who had the prescience of Treweek and acted upon it.[4]

In May 1941, Room and Treweek attended a meeting at Victoria Barracks in Melbourne. The director of naval intelligence, several Army intelligence officers and Nave were there, and the point of the meeting was to discuss the future of the little group at Sydney University. All were agreed that breaking Japanese diplomatic codes in Australia was feasible and that the group should make every effort to do so, particularly since, as the report of the conference warned, 'existing facilities at Singapore may not always be available'.[5] This was obviously a reference to the FECB, which had moved from Hong Kong to Singapore in 1939. But the way it was phrased is intriguing: it seems that those present had already concluded that Singapore was vulnerable to a Japanese attack. At any rate, with the agreement of Sydney University, the group moved to Melbourne to work under Nave in the Special Intelligence Bureau in August 1941. They had now exchanged their academic lives for the secret world of military intelligence, rather as Reischauer and Hindmarsh had done in the United States.

On 1 September 1941, shortly before the outbreak of war with Japan, Room was sent to Singapore to study the techniques used at the FECB. He was accompanied by Arthur Barclay 'Jim' Jamieson (1910–91), a lieutenant in the Royal Australian Navy who had been recruited by Nave as an intelligence officer earlier that year. Jamieson was well qualified for this role, for he had spent eight years in Japan from 1934 onwards, teaching English and working for the *Japan Advertiser* newspaper. It is a mark of his linguistic expertise that, in 1943, he produced a concise summary of written Japanese grammar as used in signals, together with a list of Japanese naval vocabulary. This familiarized students with the kinds of sentences they had to get used to if they were to be useful wartime translators, such as *raigeki ni yori chimbotsu seri* (sank as a result of a torpedo attack). Jamieson's booklet was sent to Bletchley Park, and there Lloyd, who was running Japanese courses for the Naval Section, thought so highly of it that he had 150 copies made for his courses. Jamieson was clearly in Nave's league as a linguist.[6]

Another aspect of Room's preparations for war was his decision, half-way through 1941, to begin learning Japanese. Again, it is difficult to name anybody in Britain or the United States who was so convinced that war with Japan was inevitable that they went to all the trouble of learning Japanese. On Christmas Eve 1941, after Room had completed six months of study, he wrote to the registrar of Sydney University: 'The two terms I have spent under Miss Lake have proved as useful in my present job as the twenty years' mathematics!' This was high praise indeed, but who was Miss Lake? She proved very hard to track down, but I finally found from the archives of the University of Sydney that her full name was Margaret Ethel Lake (1883–?). She was a lecturer in handicrafts at Sydney Teachers' College of Advanced Education, but she had also studied Japanese under Professor Arthur Sadler at the University of Sydney. After that, she had lived in Japan for more than a year, studying Japanese handicrafts and continuing her study of the language. Her teaching abilities must have been trusted, for whenever Sadler went on leave, she was appointed an acting lecturer and took over Sadler's teaching. He was on leave in April 1941, and that is how it came about that Lake was asked to run the concentrated course taken by Professor Room. After the war, she published a translation of the account of the capture of Singapore written by the notorious Colonel Tsuji Masanobu, who planned the attack on Malaya, and from this it is evident that she had thoroughly mastered the language.[7] Unfortunately, she has left very few traces and nothing more is known of her. I have been unable even to discover the year of her death.

From all this, it is evident that language training and codebreaking went hand in hand in Australia, just as in Britain and the United States. So far, Australia was self-sufficient in both linguists and codebreakers, at least to the extent that seemed necessary so long as Australia was not at war with Japan. Once war broke out and once, early in 1942, General MacArthur had set up his headquarters in Melbourne, intelligence and codebreaking in Australia were dominated by the US Navy and the US Army, but Australia retained its own capabilities, as we will see. What makes Australia stand out is that courses in Japanese for wartime purposes were started there well before the attacks on Malaya and Pearl Harbor, and well before similar courses were initiated elsewhere. Let us now turn to these.

Getting started with Japanese

The Royal Military College at Duntroon in Canberra began offering classes in Japanese as early as 1917, but in 1937 the authorities decided

211

to discontinue the teaching of Japanese. Given the growing tensions in East Asia following the Japanese invasion of China in that very year, it looks, with the advantage of hindsight, to be a case of bad timing. The decision to discontinue was made partly because the language was seen to be 'of little general cultural value', but also because it was thought that Japanese was 'almost a life-time study' and therefore that nothing was to be gained by teaching cadets just a smattering of the language. This decision had immediate consequences, for in response the minister of defence, Harold Thorby, became worried about the lack of qualified Japanese interpreters in Australia able to act in an 'emergency'—presumably this is an oblique reference to conflict. 'This represents', he stated, 'a very serious state of affairs, and I wish a scheme outlined for the encouragement and training of students in Japanese in the Services.' A committee was convened, and in January 1940 it submitted a detailed report proposing just such a scheme. By this time, however, the Australian government was preoccupied by the European war and the proposals were shelved. Although these plans came to nothing, they were put together well before military authorities in Britain, the United States and Canada had even begun to consider building up their Japanese-language capabilities.[8]

Wartime censorship had already been introduced in Australia in September 1939, but, as was also the case in Britain, it soon became apparent that there were not enough people with good knowledge of Japanese to do the work. Linguists were needed not only to check the despatches sent by Japanese journalists based in Australia but also to monitor private correspondence in Japanese. The Japanese population of Australia was, at not much more than 1,000 in all, much smaller than the Japanese populations in the United States or Canada, and a large proportion of the Japanese residents were employed either in the pearl-fishing industry in the Northern Territory or in the sugar cane industry in Queensland. Nevertheless, their correspondence needed to be checked in case they were either intentionally or accidentally passing information to their contacts in Japan. There was, then, an urgent need for more Japanese censors, so, in August 1940 the Censorship Office in Melbourne, which was under the supervision of Australian military intelligence, opened its own Japanese School.

The Japanese School in Melbourne was a bold initiative, particularly since neither Britain nor the United States had yet made any efforts to meet the linguistic deficit they would have to deal with if they found themselves at war with Japan. The school continued in operation until the end of the war, teaching written Japanese to both men and women whether they were civilians or in uniform. Although it was originally launched with a view to training censors, in the end it trained many people who had nothing to do with censorship, including Army students. The school was not exactly secret, but when the landlady of one of the Army students found some of his Japanese notes when she was cleaning his room, she called the police. They wondered if he was a spy, until they were able to confirm that he was legitimately studying the language.[9]

When it came to finding teachers for the school, no attempt was made to recruit Japanese Australians. As at first in the United States, they were ignored. This was partly because they mostly lived either in Queensland or Western Australia and were therefore out of sight and out of mind for military and political leaders in Canberra, but most likely racial prejudice and doubts about their loyalty also had a part to play. It is for the latter reason that Inagaki Mōshi (known in Australia as Inagaki Mowsey; born in 1883) was interned in December 1941 instead of being employed as a teacher. He had been appointed as an instructor at the University of Melbourne in 1919 and was in 1941 the only Japanese-born teacher of Japanese at an Australian university, but he spent the rest of the war in internment and was deported in 1947. It is clear from surviving papers in the National Archives of Australia that military intelligence had been keeping an eye on him for some time: they considered him to be of doubtful loyalty and thought that he had been deliberately sabotaging the teaching of Japanese in Melbourne beyond the elementary stage.[10]

Consequently, the first teacher at the Censorship School was instead John Shelton, a White Russian who had been raised in Japan. Early in 1942, Dorothy Selwood (1894–1971), who was born in Japan and had a Japanese mother, joined the school. She had lived in Japan until 1939, when she moved to Australia with her family, and she remained in charge of the school for most of its life.[11]

Some of the graduating students naturally went to work in the Censorship Office in Melbourne, which had created the school in the first place, but once Australia was at war with Japan many students headed in other directions. Let us take as an example one of the first students at the Censorship School, Norman Sparnon (1913–95). For no particular reason, he had become interested in Japanese and first went to the Berlitz Language School in Melbourne. The staff there told him that nobody had ever asked for Japanese before, so they were unable to help. Undeterred, be began learning Japanese privately in 1930 when he was just an eighteen-year-old. After the attack on Pearl Harbor eleven years later, Sparnon was hastily brought into the Army and sent to No. 1 Wireless Unit in Townsville, which was an intercept station located in northern Queensland and was therefore well placed to pick up Japanese signals. There were already two Nisei from the United States stationed there: they intercepted and transcribed messages sent *en clair*, and Sparnon's job was to translate them. Later he was nearly killed when he received a ricochet wound in the head during the operation to take Soputa in New Guinea, but he recovered and after the end of the war became a document officer at the trial of General Yamashita in Manila in 1946 before becoming an expert in the Japanese art of flower arrangement, or *ikebana*.[12]

The Censorship School trained a body of translators who, like Sparnon, were sent to No. 1 Wireless Unit in Townsville and similar units, but the translators did not work alone. The signals that needed to be translated were picked up by intercept operators like Jack Brown (1924–2013), who was also at No. 1 Wireless Unit in Townsville. In his memoir *Katakana Man: I Worked Only for Generals* (2006), he provides us with a glimpse of the intercept work done in the Wireless Units. His first eight weeks in Townsville were spent learning Japanese Morse, and like the other trainees he had to learn to take it at speeds twice as fast as the speed International Morse operators were normally required to deal with in training. The point of this was that from their first day on the job they needed to be able to take down every message they picked up, even those sent at high speed by expert telegraphists. If they failed to make the grade, they would spend the rest of the war on guard duty, as they knew too much about wireless interception to be allowed to return to ordinary units. The other operators Brown worked with included six women from the Women's Auxiliary Australian Air Force. They were not allowed to leave Australia, so when the Wireless Units moved overseas to be nearer to the advancing front lines, they were left behind. The intercept centre where they all worked in Townsville was a bomb-proof concrete building—on the outside, doors, windows and a veranda had been painted on the concrete to make it look like an ordinary weatherboard house. Inside there was air conditioning, a teleprinter connected to Central Bureau in Brisbane and scrambler phones, as well as the desks for the operators. The messages they took down had to be converted into *katakana*, decrypted and finally translated before being sent on to Central Bureau, which was yet another intelligence operation disguised by an innocent-sounding name.[13]

The Censorship School was the first institution in Australia to begin teaching Japanese for wartime purposes, but the outbreak of war with Japan inevitably led to greater awareness of the Japanese language in the Australian armed forces. The most extraordinary example of this is the 4th Australian Special Wireless Section, which was stationed not in Australia but far away in the Middle East, at Souq-el-Gharb in Lebanon. As soon as he heard of the attack on Pearl Harbor, Lieutenant Arthur Henry of the Australian Intelligence Corps began to 'think Japanese': from 27 December 1941, he began giving the men in his section instruction in Japanese Morse, more than a month before the first course began at the Bedford School.

With impressive enterprise, Lieutenant Henry procured three Japanese grammars in the bookshops of Beirut and learnt the method for recording Japanese Morse Code from the British signals intelligence base at Sarafand in southern Palestine. As a result, when the men in the 4th Australian Wireless Section returned to Australia, they were already equipped with the right skills to work at intercept stations or Central Bureau.[14]

The United States takes over signals intelligence

Once it had become obvious, early in 1942, that the US forces in the Philippines would not be able to withstand the fierce Japanese assault, General MacArthur had no choice but to order a withdrawal and make his escape from the US base at Corregidor, a fortified island at the entrance to Manila Bay. Travelling on 11 March 1942, first by torpedo boat and then by air, he, his family and his senior aides reached

EAVESDROPPING ON THE EMPEROR

Melbourne on 22 March 1942. He was followed by his intelligence staff, who were evacuated from Corregidor by submarines. They rapidly established themselves in Australia and began the task of planning MacArthur's return to the Philippines and the ultimate defeat of Japan. One of the consequences of the war was that the United States and Australia cooperated much more closely than they had ever done before. The cooperation extended to the development of a body of linguists and codebreakers.

By March 1942, there were already a number of people working on Japanese codes in Australia, as we have seen. Nave, Room and their colleagues were already at work in Melbourne, and there were several intercept stations at Darwin, Townsville and elsewhere. And then there were some British personnel who had escaped from the Far Eastern Combined Bureau just before the capture of Singapore, including Colegrave, Lieutenant Webb of the British Army and of course Arthur Cooper and his pet gibbon.

Ten male intercept operators from the intercept station at Kranji in Singapore had managed to escape, too, in the days before the surrender. They joined the Australian Special Wireless Group and were sent to work at the signals intercept station in Darwin. One of them was Lance-Corporal Geoff Day (1920–2005), who was born in Britain but remained in Australia after the war and has left a memoir of his wartime service. Since he and his colleagues, he wrote, were already familiar with Japanese Morse, it was their job to 'make experts' of the Australian signallers. The unit in Darwin was tasked both with intercepting encrypted messages, which they passed on to Melbourne, and with following the movements of Japanese forces to the north of Australia so as to give warning of imminent attacks. There were various ways of doing this: traffic analysis, which involved monitoring Japanese encrypted messages to see what could be deduced from their frequency, volume and direction; decryption of messages sent in low-level cyphers that were easy to break; and eavesdropping on the voice transmissions of Japanese pilots. These techniques often enabled them to forewarn RAAF units and thus to ensure that Japanese bombers were prevented from reaching their Australian targets. After a few months of exciting work in Darwin, Day was ordered back to the Australian Special Wireless Group headquarters in Melbourne to train newly recruited Australian men and women.[15]

The arrival of General MacArthur and his staff and the continuing build-up of US forces in Australia led to a major reorganization of intelligence organizations in Australia. Two new bodies were created in Melbourne, both of which were ultimately answerable to US commanders. One of them was the Central Bureau, which I will turn to below, and the other was FRUMEL (Fleet Radio Unit Melbourne), which was jointly run by the US Navy and the Royal Australian Navy and which absorbed the naval members of Nave's team in the Special Intelligence Bureau. FRUMEL was run by Lieutenant Rudolph Fabian (1908–84), a US naval intelligence officer who had escaped by submarine from Corregidor. His role was strengthened in October 1942, when FRUMEL was placed under the direct control of the US Navy and became answerable to Admiral Nimitz, the commander-in-chief of the US Pacific Fleet. Fabian, who was a skilled codebreaker but seems to have had an abrasive personality as an administrator, insisted that civilians such as Room and Trendall were surplus to requirements, despite their skills and experience. They therefore had no choice but to return to Sydney to resume their academic careers. Fabian also ejected Nave, despite his proven expertise and despite the fact that he was a naval officer of higher rank than Fabian. The reasons for Nave's ejection are not entirely clear, but it seems that Fabian objected to the fact that Nave was sharing intelligence with the Royal Australian Navy and also accused him of breaching security. At any rate, Nave moved to Central Bureau.[16]

FRUMEL was thereafter overwhelmingly American in character and personnel. Were there any British personnel? Rear-Admiral Richardson, an American linguist who worked at FRUMEL, recalled many years later that 'There were no Australian linguists at FRUMEL, but we were ably assisted by Lieutenant Commander Meriman of the British Navy, who had escaped from Singapore.' The implication is that Meriman was a linguist from the FECB, but since there is no Meriman in the Navy List, who was he? He may have been Commander Arthur Duncan Merriman, DSO (1901–68), who was assistant naval attaché at the British embassy in Tokyo from 1937 to 1939 and presumably learnt some Japanese there. By December 1940, he was engineering officer on the cruiser HMS *Suffolk* during the dramatic hunt for the *Bismarck* in the North Atlantic, for which he was awarded the DSO, and the Navy List suggests that he spent the rest of the war at sea. If Richardson is right, Merriman may have been detached and posted to the FECB in 1941 on account of his knowledge of Japanese, but some doubt remains.[17]

The most significant change introduced at FRUMEL in October 1942 was that it would no longer deal with Japanese diplomatic traffic. Nave and the other members of the Special Intelligence Bureau were informed that diplomatic traffic would be left to Washington and London. Arthur Cooper and several others protested vigorously against this decision, arguing that it would deprive Australia of valuable intelligence. The Military Intelligence Department of the Australian Army agreed, noting that Australia was able to intercept messages that were not picked up elsewhere, and considered that discontinuing work on diplomatic traffic would put Australia at a disadvantage.[18]

As a result, the Australian Army created a new body, opaquely named 'Special D Section', which would focus on decrypting Japanese diplomatic messages. It came under the chief of the General Staff of the Australian Army and occupied separate facilities in Melbourne. This was the most secret of the intelligence operations in Australia directed against Japan, possibly because it operated outside the US chain of command. For many years, its existence was denied and the papers were withheld, but thanks to the persistence of David Sissons, who was a member of the section from April to September 1945 and later worked at the Australian National University, some of the details have now come to light.[19]

The personnel working on the codes in D Section included Trendall and Treweek, both of whom were former members of Professor Room's group at Sydney University, several other classicists, and young Ian Smith, who later became professor of French at the University of Tasmania. Linguists and translators were needed to translate the decrypted messages, but the outbreak of war solved that problem, for some British personnel with a good knowledge of Japanese made their escape from Singapore to Australia. One of them was Arthur Cooper, who had arrived with his pet gibbon in March 1942 and stayed until December, when he returned to GC&CS at Bletchley Park. Others came from the British Consular Service in Japan, like Clement Hugh Archer (1897–1966), who had served in the British Army during the First World War and reached Australia in a roundabout way.[20]

From 1922 onwards, Archer had held a succession of British consular posts in Japan and its territories. In 1941, he had been ordered by the Foreign Office to investigate Japanese activities in Portuguese Timor, the eastern half of the island of Timor (now Timor-Leste), and to report on his findings to the Australian government, which was worried about Japanese infiltration so close to Australia. He arrived in Timor at the end of March and stayed for a month before making his way to Australia to make his report. He intended to stay for a short while and then proceed to the Japanese puppet state of Manchukuo in north-east China, where he had been appointed consul-general. But the Foreign Office postponed his posting for fear that he might be interned in the event of war, and in January 1942 he joined Nave's team and worked for D Section until December 1944. In January 1946, Archer returned to Japan as a member of the United Kingdom Liaison Mission in Tokyo, the forerunner to the post-war embassy.[21]

At least five other members of the British Consular Service in Japan worked for D Section, so it is clear that although it had a very secret existence, the secret was not kept from Britain. Apart from Archer, all the others had been in Japan when the war broke out. They were detained until July 1942, when a Japanese vessel took them to Lourenço Marques. There, they were exchanged for Japanese diplomats and civilians based in Britain. Some of the evacuees proceeded directly from Lourenço Marques to Australia, including Lloyd, whom we have already met as a teacher in the Naval Section at Bletchley Park. He worked for D Section until March 1943, when he returned to England and went to Bletchley Park.[22]

Finally, what was the role of Central Bureau? Like FRUMEL, Central Bureau was a cryptography operation under American control, but its focus was on the needs of the Allied armies and air forces. It was set up by MacArthur on 15 April 1942 and was staffed by US Army, Australian Army and RAAF personnel, with a sprinkling of British personnel as well. On 19 June 1942, the first batch of Nisei linguists arrived from the US Military Intelligence Service Language School, and they were followed by many others.[23]

In July 1942, MacArthur moved his headquarters north to Brisbane so as to be closer to the Japanese-occupied territories he was planning to invade, and Central Bureau moved there too in September. By late 1943, there were already over 1,000 men and women working in Central Bureau, mostly Americans and Australians. As the war progressed, detachments from Central Bureau moved to Hollandia (now Jayapura in Indonesia), to Leyte Island in the Philippines, and to San Miguel on the island of Luzon in the Philippines, so as to be closer to the front line and to MacArthur's headquarters, and finally, in September 1945, to Tokyo. If there were so many Americans and Australians there, what need was there for British personnel?[24]

Central Bureau recruits from the Bedford School

The fifth course at the Bedford Japanese School had begun in August 1943. At the end of January 1944, less than a month before the end of the course, Webb, now a major, visited the School. What did he want, the students might well have wondered. Before the war, Webb had been living in Japan as a British oil company executive, and he had learnt Japanese on the spot, living with a Japanese family. On the outbreak of war in September 1939, he went to Hong Kong to enlist and was then sent to Singapore, where he became an officer in the Intelligence Corps and ran the Special Wireless Section intercepting messages sent by the Imperial Japanese Army. He got out of Singapore with Arthur Cooper on 11 February, just four days before the British surrender, and reached Australia—before long, he was working in Central Bureau as a linguist, cryptographer and later administrator.[25]

According to Tuck, Webb's visit to the Bedford School caused 'great excitement', for he 'announced that he had been authorised to select twelve men to go out to Australia holding the rank of warrant officers'. The excitement was presumably due to the opportunity to visit Australia. Twelve men were selected who had all done better than average on the course. They were hastily put into uniform and were sent up to Wentworth Woodhouse, the Army training depot for the Intelligence Corps. Accompanying them as a reserve, in case anybody had to drop out, was one other fellow student, Alan Stripp. In his memoirs, Stripp says that they made careful preparations, for 'the rumour was that discipline there was rigid and the instructing staff thugs'. When they got to the depot, they found that this was an understatement. They had to get used to being screamed at, sworn at and generally 'broken in'.[26]

At the end of April 1944, Stripp went to Bletchley Park and the other twelve set sail in the *Queen Mary* across the Atlantic. They were fortunate, for the Americans running the ship treated warrant officers as officers and gave them first-class cabins, and the food, provided by the Americans, was plentiful—there was no shortage of bacon, eggs and jam, which were all strictly rationed in Britain. They crossed America by train and flew from San Francisco to Brisbane, stopping several times on remote islands to refuel.[27]

One of the twelve was Ray Eddolls, who had been awarded a scholarship in classics at Corpus Christi College, Oxford, before starting at Bedford. Many years after the end of the war, he recalled what happened to him:

> I arrived at Central Bureau in April, 1944, with eleven other youthful Oxbridge under-graduates, all disguised as Warrant Officers, Class II, and sweltering in British Army battle dress. We had been recruited from University for a six-month course in military Japanese at Bedford, and after selection for attachment to the Australian Army, had undergone a short period of square-bashing at the 'I' [Intelligence] Corps depot near Rotherham. ... My recollection of work at CB [Central Bureau] is rather vague, possibly because the daily routine of translation in the hut at Ascot Park [Brisbane] was overshadowed by the powerful impressions of life in the sub-tropics. I was delighted by the seemingly continuous sunshine, the wooden houses on stilts and the warmth of what the locals referred to as winter. I remember the small huts at Kedron Park [Brisbane], where we were accommodated until February, 1945, and heavy meat diet at the sergeants' mess there. I also recall the enormous cockroaches with which we shared tents beside the racecourse at Ascot before the great push north to the Philippines in mid-1945. We enjoyed our weekly days-off, often spending them at Redcliffe [a seaside resort north of Brisbane] or 'down the coast' at Surfers' [Surfers Paradise, a seaside resort to the south of Brisbane], which was easily reached by US army truck from Ascot. So idyllic was our life, in military terms, that I remember being puzzled by the remark of an Australian sergeant at Kedron who said he felt sorry for us. He was not being ironic though; we were very young, after all, and so far from mother's tender care.[28]

Eddolls returned to Oxford after the war and completed his degree, but Australia evidently made such a good impression on him as a twenty-year-old that he migrated to Australia in 1950. He subsequently

221

became a schoolteacher there and then worked as a civil servant for the Australian Department of Defence.

Eddolls said nothing about the actual work he did at Central Bureau. Was that because he simply could not remember or perhaps because he did not yet feel at liberty to divulge secrets? It certainly was not because there was any shortage of work for cryptanalysts and translators to do there, and a chance discovery gave them a lot of important work to do.

On 19 January 1944, the 9th Australian Division reached Sio, on the north-east coast of New Guinea. There, to their amazement, they found, lying in a deep water-filled pit, all the major code books of the Japanese Army high command. It was an extraordinary find. The code books all lacked their covers, and it seems that Japanese signals officers had handed the covers of the code books to their superiors as proof of their destruction. As a result of this deception, the Japanese high command remained completely unaware that the codes had been compromised. This fortunate discovery made it possible to read not only past messages in several different codes but also current messages.[29]

It goes without saying that all the decrypts resulting from this discovery then had to be translated. To deal with the demand, new translators were posted to Central Bureau in quantity in 1944. In addition to Eddolls and his colleagues, there were fresh translators from the RAF and the Royal Canadian Air Force. By this time, there were enough people on hand to organize the work more efficiently: scanners sorted the messages into one of four categories (Urgent, Operational Priority, Priority and No Priority), translators worked in teams of five, and then there were final checkers and lastly recorders, who filed copies of all the messages. By August 1944, the Translation Section at Central Bureau was translating on average fifty messages daily, rising to seventy-six in July 1945.[30]

Somehow or other, Captain Tuck and his students at the Bedford School were kept informed of the movements of the twelve sent out to Australia. In his final report, Tuck wrote:

> Their subsequent movements were followed with great interest, especially those of four or five who were sent ahead with forward units. The Course soon heard of Melinsky and Webster in Port Darwin; and of Hall, firstly in New Guinea and then landing in the

Philippines at Leyte, the only British representative with the American Forces. Melinsky later appeared in the landings on Borneo, together with Carson of Course VI.[31]

Unfortunately, Peter Hall (1924–2013) and William Carson took their secrets with them to their graves. Melinsky, on the other hand, who spent his post-war life as a priest in the Church of England, wrote up his experiences for his grandchildren.

On arrival in Brisbane, Melinsky was assigned to monitor the Japanese Naval Air Service. 'Our task', he recalled, 'was to decode and translate messages picked up by Wireless Units which listened to Japanese aeroplanes, flying anywhere from Tokyo to Singapore, and to their bases, and sent the messages to us in Brisbane.' These messages did not use Roman letters as the diplomatic codes did, but instead consisted of groups of two or four *katakana* letters sent in Japanese Morse. The meaning of these groups could only be ascertained by referring to a code book: here, the recipient might be told, for example, that ka-ka-ka-ka (the *katakana* syllable 'ka' four times) stood for 'battleship'. If you did not have the code book, then the message was meaningless. Thanks to that discovery at Sio and to the work of the codebreakers, the code books were available at Central Bureau. So all Melinsky had to do was turn to the code book he had been given, find the words encoded and then translate the text.

In June 1944, however, Melinsky had to leave the comforts of Brisbane behind, for he was posted to No. 2 Wireless Unit at Coomalie Creek near Darwin. The sixty men in the party slept in tents and showered in the open. He sat at a desk under a canvas awning stretched between two lorries, and as airmen brought messages picked up from Japanese aeroplanes he got to work decoding and translating them, dealing with around 100 messages a day, and working from 8.00 in the morning to 9.00 or 10.00 at night, with no days off for three months. The translations were then encrypted and sent by Typex to the intelligence staff at Central Bureau. The most exciting messages he dealt with, he recalled, were from aeroplanes that were escorting convoys. They invariably gave the position of the convoy, and the convoys were then subjected to Allied submarine attacks.[32]

By 1944, the war situation in the Pacific theatre had changed dramatically since the initial attacks in December 1941. At the end of

1942, Enrico Fermi had conducted the world's first nuclear chain reaction at the University of Chicago, which was to have fateful consequences for Japan in August 1945. In the following year, 1943, Japanese forces finally pulled out of Guadalcanal in the Solomon Islands after five months of bitter fighting. They were subsequently forced to abandon more and more of the territories they had occupied, from the Aleutians in the north to Guam and the Mariana Islands farther south.

Now was the moment for MacArthur to launch his campaign to retake the Philippines. The campaign began on 20 October 1944, with amphibious landings on the coast of Leyte Island. The landings were preceded by heavy bombardment from six battleships and met with little opposition. As usual, the official histories of the campaign do not mention the interpreters, translators or intelligence officers, but they were definitely on Leyte by 24 October, for on that day a captured Japanese private was interrogated about the tanks in his tank company, and on 28 October other Japanese prisoners were interrogated about the forces confronting the American troops. Some, but not all, of the interrogators were American Nisei. Translators were needed too. As in India and Burma, many Japanese officers who were killed in action were found to be carrying battle orders and maps, all of which needed translating and assessing.[33]

One of the British translators involved in the Philippines was Donovan Richnell (1911–94), an RNVR officer who was awarded the US Bronze Star for his wartime service and later became director general of the British Library Reference Division. He had been sent on a Japanese course at SOAS and was then posted to Brisbane to join ATIS, of which more below. He spent four months there on translation training, learning Japanese military language and working on a Japanese air raid precautions manual. He was then assigned to the headquarters of the US Army 10th Corps and took part in the landing on Leyte. Once ashore and settled in a plantation, he began dealing with the huge quantities of documents brought in by the fighting soldiers: some were dispositions of troops or requisition orders for ammunitions and equipment, but most were disappointingly routine military forms. Almost all of the material was handwritten and illegible unless it had been kept dry; very little was encrypted. The Nisei in his unit did the preliminary sorting and translating, so Richnell's task was to check that their translations were correct and in good English before they were passed on. If the documents were important, he first gave an oral summary to the staff intelligence officer.[34]

How many other British personnel were there at Central Bureau? There is no way of knowing, but a surviving photograph with captions gives some clues. It shows one representative of each of the nine armed services working there, including the Australian Military Forces, US Army, Royal Canadian Air Force, RAAF, US Women's Army Corps, the Women's Auxiliary Australian Air Force, and the Australian Women's Army Service. Also included were the British Army, represented by Warrant Officer Richard Bellingham, and the RAF, represented by Sergeant David Eunson. The first is probably a mistake for Bernard Bellingham (1924–95), a Bedford graduate who is known to have worked at Central Bureau. But who was Eunson? He was in fact David Alexander Eunson (1925–99), who went to Kirkwall Grammar School in the Orkney Islands, joined the Kirkwall Air Training Corps and then, after studying classics for one year at Edinburgh University, joined the RAF. Probably because of his background in classics, he was selected for one of the phonetics courses for RAF personnel at SOAS, did outstandingly well and then went out to Australia. What exactly did he do at Central Bureau and how many others were there from SOAS like him? We shall probably never know the answers to either of these questions.[35]

In addition to translators like Richnell, wireless operators, cryptographers and intelligence personnel were also needed in large numbers. It was in the autumn of 1944 that the plans were made for the invasion of Leyte Island, the first stage in MacArthur's campaign to retake the Philippines, which were an American possession. This was to be an all-American affair, but Brigadier-General Spencer B. Akin (1889–1973), who was the chief signals officer on General MacArthur's staff, turned to Australian signals staff to form a wireless unit in the invasion force. To this end, twenty-four wireless operators and intelligence personnel were withdrawn from No. 1 Wireless Unit, which was now based at Biak (New Guinea), and were flown to Hollandia to join the huge landing force preparing for the invasion. None of them knew where they were heading. Several days after the invasion fleet left Hollandia, an announcement was made that Leyte was the goal. Akin personally briefed them and introduced them to the senior American officers preparing for the invasion, even though most of them had the lowest ranks in the Australian Air Force and only two of them were officers. Akin took six of them, five Australians and Peter Hall of the Bedford School, on his own communications vessel, while the rest went on a tank-landing ship with the Wireless Unit's three wireless trucks. During the six or seven days it took for the convoy to reach Leyte, the six who went with Akin were under constant pressure as they monitored all the Japanese bomber, fighter and air-base frequencies night and day. There were, after all, a lot of generals afloat, and they did not want any nasty surprises. Jack Brown, an expert RAAF intercept operator on the tank landing ship, found it a worrying experience:

> During the day the heat on deck was unbearable, but it was quite pleasant at night. Standing on the deck one could look in any direction and see ships close together and stretched to the edge of the horizon. At night I worried a bit that the other ships were too close to us. If these ships slowed or changed course, or if it rained, they may not be seen and we could be rammed.

He found it too hot to sleep below decks, and when he tried to sleep on a jeep tied down on the deck he was drenched by a tropical shower.[36]

On 21 October, the day after the first troops went ashore on Leyte, the Wireless Unit personnel landed at Tacloban to join the headquarters of the landing force and they pitched their tents. There they monitored air operations of the Japanese Army and Navy, including kamikaze attacks. But the most urgent messages they were handling concerned the troop transport convoys that were bringing desperately needed reinforcements for the beleaguered Japanese defenders into the port of Ormoc. These convoys were escorted by aircraft, which, as Melinsky put it, 'obligingly gave full information of the ships' movements and particularly their estimated time of arrival'. As a result, he continued, 'American aircraft were alerted and gave them a warm welcome.' On 11 November, 'an entire troop-laden convoy was destroyed'. Brown had a more dramatic landing the following day: a Japanese aircraft came to strafe the beach just after he had got ashore, and he had to run for his life to the trees. It was to be a while before they would feel safe, for the invasion forces were constantly being bombed or strafed. Just in case, the Wireless Unit personnel were all

Fig. 51: David Eunson (1925–99), George Aspden and James Tait (L to R) at Central Bureau in Brisbane. Eunson had done one of the courses at SOAS, and the same was true of the other two. (Courtesy of Jim Eunson)

Fig. 52: Members of No. 1 Wireless Unit of the Royal Australian Air Force on Leyte Island in the Philippines. All those shown are Australian personnel except for Warrant Officer Peter Hall, a graduate of the Bedford Japanese School, who is squatting in the front row, second from left; squatting on the far right is Leading Aircraftman Jack Brown, who later published his memoirs as *Katakana Man: I Worked only for Generals*. A full list of all the names can be found on the website of the Australian War Memorial (https://www.awm.gov.au/collection/C51231). (Courtesy of the Australian War Memorial, photograph P00514.001)

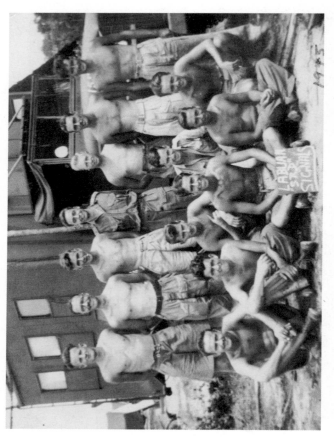

Fig. 53: Members of SRD (Services Reconnaissance Department) Signals unit attached to the Allied Intelligence Bureau on Labuan, British North Borneo, in 1945. Most are unidentified Australians. Fourth from left in the back row, fully clothed, is George Walter John Eade (1913–99), who was a Lieutenant in the Royal Corps of Signals; fifth from left in the back row and the first two on the left in the front row are unidentified British personnel. Eade's name does not appear among the surviving lists of those who did SOAS courses and I have been unable to find out anything more about him. (Courtesy of the Australian War Memorial, photograph P01134.001)

Fig. 54: This photograph was probably taken by Lieutenant Ernest Ballard Beath (1920–2001) of the US Navy. He completed a Japanese course at the US Navy Japanese Language School at Boulder, Colorado, and then became a translator for a succession of Admirals. He was serving as Admiral Joseph 'Jocko' Clark's translator on the aircraft carrier USS *Hornet* in 1944 when two 'Betty' (Mitsubishi G4M) bombers were shot down and the documents were presumably taken from the crew after they had been taken prisoner or from their corpses. In the centre can be seen a photograph of Emperor Hirohito on his white horse; there are also family photographs, pay-books and assorted other military documents. (Courtesy of University of Colorado Boulder Libraries; Roger Pineau collection Box 7, Folder 23, Item 9)

Fig. 55: The sun sets behind Mt Fuji on 27 August 1945, as seen from USS *Missouri* anchored in Sagami Bay, outside Tokyo. Ships of the US Third Fleet and the British Pacific Fleet are in the distance. Closest to the camera, in the centre right beneath Mt Fuji, is HMS *Duke of York*, with HMS *King George V* beyond and to the right of her. (Official U.S. Navy Photograph, now in the collections of the National Archives, Washington: 80-G-490414 Sagami Wan, Japan)

Fig. 56: A still from the Pathé newsreel 'Tokyo Bay' (1942). On the deck of the battleship HMS *King George V*, William Beasley is addressing the Japanese pilot who has come on board to provide directions through the mine-infested waters and who is being restrained by ratings. (Courtesy of British Pathé Ltd)

Fig. 57: Envelope of a letter written by Paul J. Sherman of the US Navy on board the USS *Missouri* on the day of the surrender. A special postmark was used that day to mark the occasion. (Courtesy of University of Colorado Boulder Libraries; Paul J. Sherman papers Box 1, Folder 2)

THE DIMINUTIVE JAPANESE ENVOY, ACCOMPANIED BY HIS INTERPRETER, ARRIVING ON BOARD THE "SWIFTSURE," TO DISCUSS SURRENDER, BEING INTERROGATED.

Fig. 58: An unnamed Japanese envoy and his interpreter arriving aboard HMS *Swiftsure* to discuss the surrender of Hong Kong. (*Illustrated London News*, 22 September 1945, p. 317)

Fig. 59: The surrender of Singapore on 15 February 1942. From left to right, Major Cyril Wild carrying the white surrender flag, Brigadier Thomas Newbigging (1892–1968) carrying the Union Flag, Lieutenant-Colonel Sugita Ichiji (later General, 1904–93) with an unidentified Japanese behind him, Brigadier Kenneth Torrance (1895–1958) and Lieutenant-General Arthur Percival. They are heading for their meeting with General Yamashita and the photograph was taken by a Japanese official photographer. The flag carried by Newbigging, which was secretly preserved by Wild throughout the war, is now in the Imperial War Museum (FLA 2449). (© Imperial War Museum (HU 2781))

Fig. 60: Colonel Cyril Wild (1908–46) giving testimony in a post-war war crimes trial, as shown on the cover of James Bradley's biography (1997). He had lived in Japan before the war and was a POW on the Burma-Siam railway. (Courtesy of Woodfield Publishing, Bognor Regis)

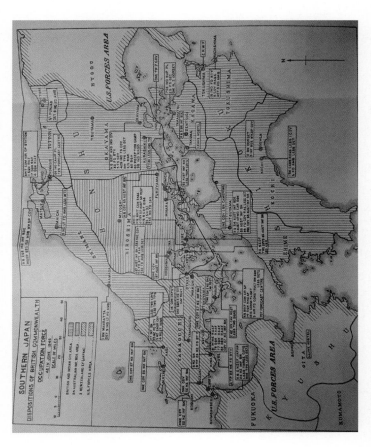

Fig. 61: Map showing the disposition of the British Commonwealth Occupation Force units in western Japan taken from Rajendra Singh, 'Post-war Occupation Forces: Japan and South-East Asia', in Bisheshwar Prasad (ed.), *Official History of the Indian Armed Forces in the Second World War 1939–45* (Combined Inter-Services Historical Section India & Pakistan, 1958), map following p. 100.

Fig. 62: The booklet *Know Japan* given to members of the British Commonwealth Occupation Force in 1946. This copy was given to James Sutherland (1926–2019), who completed the 8th course at the Bedford Japanese School and was then sent to the Wireless Experimental Centre, Delhi. After the end of the war, he did a field security course in Karachi and then took part in the British Commonwealth Occupation Force. (Courtesy of the late James Sutherland)

Fig. 63: James Sutherland at home in Peebles in November 2019.

Fig. 64: Sergeant James Sutherland on leave at the famous bridge in Iwakuni. (Courtesy of the late James Sutherland)

Figs. 65a and 65b: Publicity photograph of Takamine Hideko, a film star, with James Sutherland's Japanese inscription on the back reading 'Lover … Jock'. (Courtesy of the late James Sutherland)

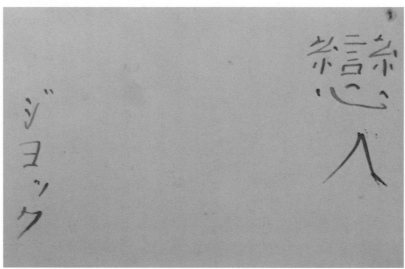

Fig. 66: 'A few of the dangers of Japan': a page from James Sutherland's wartime photograph album. (Courtesy of the late James Sutherland)

Fig. 67: James Sutherland (on the extreme left) with some of his colleagues in the Japanese countryside near Kobe. Most of the others are Royal Australian Air Force personnel. (Courtesy of the late Professor Michael Screech)

Fig. 68: James Sutherland outside the Combined Services Detailed Interrogation Centre barracks in Kure. (Courtesy of the late James Sutherland)

Fig. 69: Some of the Japanese women who were employed to cook, clean and wash for the CSDIC staff in Kure. (Courtesy of the late James Sutherland)

issued with cyanide capsules to use if captured. It was, of course, of the highest importance to prevent the Japanese forces from discovering how successfully their secret communications were being read, and there was no knowing what a captured intelligence officer or intercept operator might reveal under interrogation or torture.[37]

Hall of the Bedford School was the only known British participant in the Leyte landings. Before being sent to Hollandia, he had already participated in the New Guinea Campaign, serving there with Australian Wireless Units at Port Moresby and other locations, some of the time operating under canvas. A photograph of his Wireless Interception Group was taken on Leyte in December 1944 by General MacArthur's official photographer, and a copy was given to each of them with a message of appreciation for the role they had played, personally signed by General Spencer Akin. In the middle of 1945, Hall met up with other members of his group of linguists from Bedford when he finally got to San Miguel in the Philippines, now a suburb of Manila.[38]

As he explains in his memoir, Melinsky followed a different route to San Miguel. In April 1945, he flew to Morotai Island in what is now Indonesia. From there, he took part in the seaborne invasion of Borneo with a detachment of No. 4 Wireless Unit. After a ten-day voyage, the fleet reached Borneo on 10 June. There was a naval bombardment and then the assault troops went ashore. By the early evening, Melinsky and his unit were ashore and preparing for work, and the next day they resumed their decoding and translating work. Some days later, a group of desperate Japanese soldiers who had exhausted their ammunition were led by their officer on a rampage through the Allied lines with their bayonets and swords. They managed to kill several US and Australian soldiers before they were caught on the beach, where they promptly killed themselves. Melinsky realized afterwards that he had been lucky, for they had run right past his tent. On 17 July 1945, by which time there was little work to do on Borneo, he was sent to No. 6 Wireless Unit at San Miguel, near Manila. There he met up with Hall. They discovered that their unit was to be the only non-American unit given the honour of participating in the invasion of Kyushu, which was planned to take place on 1 November. One can imagine their delight.[39]

MacArthur's linguists

FRUMEL and Central Bureau were primarily intelligence and cryptography operations, and they were subordinate to the US Navy and to General MacArthur respectively. Once the fight back against Japanese expansion began, it became obvious that there was also going to be a need for a body of linguists to deal with prisoners and documents. The Australian Army responded to this need by establishing its own Combined Services Detailed Interrogation Centre (CSDIC) in Melbourne, in July 1942, just two months after a body with the same name was established in Britain for the interrogation of German and Italian prisoners of war. The personnel attached to CSDIC were all linguists who were already in the armed services, but they now received extra training in the techniques of interrogation. The Australian CSDIC had a short life, however, for it was soon absorbed into a much larger organization that was answerable to MacArthur. This was by now a familiar pattern.

The Allied Translator and Interpreter Section (ATIS), which was established in Brisbane on 19 September 1942, was described in the secret US history of intelligence operations as 'possibly the most important single intelligence agency of the war'. In the Pacific, it certainly fulfilled a number of key roles that depended on knowledge of Japanese. As the American and Australian forces under MacArthur worked their way up from Australia to Japan via New Guinea, the Philippines and many smaller islands, it was ATIS men who interrogated prisoners of war, sorted captured documents and translated the important ones, and disseminated the intelligence gained from them. It was also ATIS personnel who ran propaganda and psychological warfare operations designed to induce Japanese troops to surrender.[40]

ATIS was led for most of its wartime existence by Colonel Mashbir, a former US Army language officer. Although under American command, ATIS was from the beginning an Allied enterprise. In addition to personnel from the US Army, US Navy and (US) Women's Army Corps, there were personnel from a bewildering variety of armed services of numerous Allied nations: from the UK, the Army, Royal Navy, RNVR and RAF; from Australia, the Army, Royal Australian Navy, Royal Australian Naval Volunteer Reserve (RANVR), RAAF,

Australian Women's Army Service, Women's Royal Australian Naval Service, and Women's Auxiliary Australian Air Force; from Canada, the Royal Canadian Navy, Royal Canadian Naval Volunteer Reserve (RCNVR) and RCAF; from New Zealand, the Royal New Zealand Navy, Royal New Zealand Naval Volunteer Reserve (RNZNVR) and New Zealand Expeditionary Force; from the Netherlands, the Royal Netherlands East Indies Army, Royal Netherlands East Indies Navy and Netherlands Forces Intelligence Section; the Chinese Army and the Indian Army.[41]

There were also a few misfits, such as Arthur Pappadopoulos (1922–2011). His Greek father and Russian mother had fled to Yokohama from Odessa in 1920 and there they lived until March 1941, when they moved to Australia. After the attack on Pearl Harbor, Arthur and his father joined the Australian Army, but at first little notice was taken of the fact that both had a good knowledge of Japanese. It was only when Arthur astonished his superiors, by identifying the Japanese planes that attacked Port Hedland in the northern part of Western Australia on 31 July 1942, that his skills overrode his status as an alien. He joined ATIS in March 1943.[42]

Colonel Mashbir himself wrote the official history of ATIS, but it is by no means representative of the whole range of ATIS activities. In fact, Mashbir only covered the US Army-related activities of ATIS, and the same is true of the surviving records, or at any rate of those that have been released. This is a serious shortcoming. As a result, the contributions of the Allied Naval Forces Unit, which was commanded by Lieutenant-Commander Lionel Francis Hopkinson of the Royal Navy, who had escaped from Singapore to Australia early in 1942, and of the Allied air force unit, which was commanded by Wing-Commander Gordon Allman of the Royal Australian Air Force, are completely missing from the official history and are currently impossible to assess. The only conclusion that can be drawn is that the official history, which after all was published by the General Headquarters of the US Army in Tokyo in 1948, is heavily weighted towards the contribution of the US Army. A more balanced history of ATIS is yet to be written.[43]

At the beginning, ATIS was staffed by a contingent of trained Nisei linguists who had arrived in Australia in June 1942 and by the Australian members of CSDIC in Melbourne. They were followed by several consignments of Boulder graduates and, in 1943, by more than 100 Nisei graduates of the Army language school at Camp Savage. By March 1944, the staff numbered 178, by January 1945 there were 487, and by July 1945 as many as 1,802. But these figures, which come from the American official history, include only US service men and women and the numbers of others are unknown. The only information on the others so far available is the list of ATIS members contained in the internal telephone directory for MacArthur's headquarters. This excludes all linguists on attachment to units in the field, but it does at least provide some names, and the ranks shown make it evident that almost all those in the Allied Air Forces Unit were Australian or British.[44]

All new linguists attached to ATIS were graded on arrival, with only those who could handle all forms of handwritten Japanese being graded 'A'. This made sense, for 70 per cent of the documents recovered for translation were either in 'running script' (*sōsho*) or the semi-cursive script (*gyōsho*), which were usually written in a hurry and were difficult to read, and these tended to be of the highest intelligence value.

The sharp end of ATIS was the small parties of linguists whose job it was to accompany the invasions of Japanese-held territory. These Advanced ATIS (ADVATIS) units dealt with documents retrieved on the battlefield, just as Allen and Storry were doing in India and Burma. Pappadopoulos was trusted enough to be sent off with one of the ADVATIS units and went ashore at Luzon where he searched bodies for documents:

> I came across the body of a soldier wearing a captain's badge of rank. The head and upper torso were blown away, obviously hit by a bazooka-type weapon. In his pocket we found the operations order [for a raid on Allied HQ] that provided complete data on the mission, its timings, routes of approach and withdrawal, and to which was appended the battle map.[45]

By December 1944, ATIS had a produced a manual on the exploitation of captured Japanese documents. This included photographs of various types of documents and maps, which were accompanied by translations and explanations to guide translators and intelligence officers. Storry had a copy in Burma, so it was evidently circulated beyond

ATIS circles. In his preface to the manual, Mashbir explained why captured documents were so valuable:

> The Japanese written language is one of the most difficult in the world
> ... amounting almost to a cryptographic system. The Japanese military
> authorities are well aware of this and, in practice, tend to place undue
> reliance upon the security offered by their language alone. In the earlier
> campaigns in the South West Pacific Area conventional field security
> measures appear to have been neglected, possibly upon the assumption
> that even if the Allied forces did capture Japanese documents, they
> would be unable to translate them.

Valuable they may have been, but they were often in poor or disgusting condition: 'Many are taken from battlefields, crashed airplanes, graves, sunken ships and foxholes. They are apt to be torn, defaced, water-soaked, soiled with body fat or blood, or charred and, consequently, difficult or impossible to read in that condition.' It was therefore worth some effort to render them legible. From July 1944, five women from the American Women's Army Corps under a WAC officer began working full time on document-restoration, applying the civilian skills of archivists to documents retrieved on the battlefield. Unlike civilian archivists, they needed to work in a hurry, and they knew that the documents had come from dead men, as was sometimes obvious from the fresh blood stains.[46]

In most theatres of the Second World War, very little survives of the process of deriving intelligence from battlefield documents. The original documents were not kept, nor were the translations or even the intelligence reports based on them. Yet in the Australian War Memorial in Canberra one batch of documents gathered on the battlefield or from abandoned Japanese positions has survived intact. This gives us a glimpse of the kinds of materials that the ATIS men were handling in New Guinea, the Philippines and the Pacific Islands and that Storry, Allen and their colleagues were handling in India and Burma.[47]

This batch of documents includes some printed materials, such as manuals and rule books given out to soldiers before they left Japan, military gazettes giving news of promotions and a booklet containing the text of imperial rescripts (proclamations issued in the name of the emperor). Most of it, however, consists of manuscript material, such as operational orders, soldiers' diaries, unit diaries, unit personnel lists, sick lists, personal letters, postcards (unposted) and photographs with handwritten captions on the back. Some of these documents provided tactical information, such as a handwritten document that had been mimeographed and marked 'top secret', which concerned the maritime transportation of men and materiel to territories occupied by Japan in the southern Pacific. Others instead provide us with glimpses of the lives of Japanese troops far from home, such as the diary of an unnamed medical officer covering the month of January 1945 and a duplicated handwritten letter dated 8 December 1943 and sent to frontline soldiers by a head teacher in Gifu to remind them what an honour it was to serve the emperor. Did the recipients wonder how much honour there was in being malnourished, prey to tropical diseases and under constant attack by a better-armed foe? Did they comment wryly to their comrades about how easy it was to write about 'honour' from the comfort of the home front?

Again, although none of Allen's wartime translations seem to have survived, many of the translations produced by ATIS translators as well as many ATIS interrogation reports are preserved in the Australian War Memorial. Unfortunately, it is not possible to match these with the names of individual translators or interrogators, for the names that appear at the end of each translation or report are those of the officers in charge, and the translators are either not named or are identified either by numerals, such as '#702', or by initials, such as 'Translator: ASK/GKR'. Most of the ATIS translators were American, it is true, but there was also a large Australian contingent and there were Britons like Richnell and others from Canada, New Zealand and other countries as well, but their contributions cannot now be identified.[48]

What can we learn from the interrogation reports that they produced? Sometimes, they were very detailed and provided information that was of tactical importance. For example, on Christmas Day 1944, second-class Private Matsuishi Minoru (twenty-three), an artillery observer from Okayama in southern Japan, was captured in the hills between Ipil and Albuera on Leyte Island in the Philippines. He was interrogated on the last day of the year by 'interpreter #701'. The report runs to twenty pages and notes that Matsuishi was 'of high intellect'—before being captured, he had been ordered to search for food but had then got lost: 'His observation and knowledge of Art[iller]y matters were above average. He was very cooperative, friendly, and appreciative. He even volunteered information of great tactical value.' Others had nothing of value to impart, but the interrogation reports instead reveal something of the psychology of the prisoner. For example, near Albuera an unnamed private from Nagoya, aged twenty-one, was captured on 11 December 1944, when it was obvious that Japan was not winning the war. He was interrogated two days later by interpreter #702. He said that he had been advancing through a grove when he was concussed by a shell. When he came around, he realized that he had been captured. He was intending to commit suicide by biting off his tongue but changed his mind on seeing an interpreter. The desperate preference for death rather than capture was common to many Japanese soldiers, but why did this young man change his mind? It may have been because the interpreter was a Nisei and so had a familiar Japanese facial appearance, or it may have been simply that the interpreter had sufficient command of Japanese to reassure him that he was in a familiar linguistic world and would be able to communicate. As it happens, this prisoner had no information of value to impart and said that 'he was unlucky not to have been killed by the shell', but his change of mind suggests that he had assumed that if captured he would find himself in the hands of white American or Australian troops who did not speak a word of Japanese. Perhaps that assumption goes some way towards explaining why captivity was so unappealing that soldiers would rather bite their tongues off.[49]

By comparison with the interrogation reports, the translations were less immediate, both because they took more time to produce and because the documents were sometimes already old when they were found. In the Battle of Milne Bay at the eastern end of New Guinea (25 August to 7 September 1942), a mostly Australian force defeated a Japanese invasion attempt; this was the first significant Allied victory on land in the Pacific. In the aftermath, a number of documents were found that the Japanese had left behind, and Sparnon, the first Australian Army man trained in Japanese at the Censorship School, was sent to Milne Bay to translate them. Among the mass of papers he found waiting for him was the diary of an unnamed Japanese who had been marooned on Goodenough Island with some companions and was awaiting rescue by submarine. His diary records the highs and the lows of their wait:

17/9/1942: Air raids every day since the 12th. We wait every day for our planes to arrive, but they have not yet come. All the troops are pessimistic, but there is nothing that can be done about it. Physical strength has been weakened and malaria is developing. Under present conditions, with lack of hygiene and medical care, we will all be wiped out by the end of the month.

4/10/1942: Since we now have foot and medical supplies, everybody is on top of the world. In the afternoon, the rations were distributed. The evening meal was a bit late, but at any rate, we had boiled rice. Truly, the Japanese people and rice are one and the same thing. We soothed our stomachs with rice for the first time in 42 days.

The story behind these diary entries is the destruction of Japanese convoys bringing supplies to the troops. Japanese signals concerning the movements of convoys were being intercepted, decrypted and translated and then submarines were sent to torpedo them or bombers to subject them to aerial bombardment. The last entry reveals the euphoria when supplies finally did manage to get through.[50]

Later in the war, lack of food became a serious problem for the Japanese troops, as is clear from other diaries that provide evidence about the morale of Japanese troops and the difficulties they were facing. For example, a soldier's diary found near Tolibao on Leyte Island on 13 December 1944 was translated four days later, possibly because of the valuable information it provided about the lack of food for the Japanese troops. The unnamed soldier, who frequently mentions the casualties caused by artillery and air bombardment, recorded: 'Dispatched two men … to forage for food. Replenishment of rations is difficult. One meal per day. … Enemy strength is overwhelming but our morale is high.'[51] Yet the progress of the war was also becoming a source of anxiety, as is revealed by the following extracts from Shioya Yoshio's diary written in late summer 1944 on islands to the north-west of New Guinea:

13 July. Heard that Nagoya had an air raid, also that the Emperor has issued a proclamation that the enemy fleet is to be destroyed. I wonder if Japan Proper is now in a precarious position. [First inklings that Japan is heading to defeat]

20 July. Wireless News: Hollandia [now Jayapura in Indonesia]. Our airplanes met about 50 enemy airplanes and shot down 40 of them.

Our losses were 2 airplanes. This seems like a lie. It seems unbelievable. [No longer believes his own side's propaganda]

20 October. All I worry about nowadays is concealment. I can't even hang my wash[ing] out to dry. [Diminished fighting spirit]

In January 1945, the diary of a soldier was found near Pahagan in the Philippines:

> A year ago today is the day that I was inducted. That is a regrettable day that I left everything worthwhile. Today I heard the first step of a new life. I heard the voices and footsteps of American soldiers and my heart leaped. Instead of fear I find that I feel a certain fondness. I can not help but think that those voices have come to save me. ... The leaders of Japan should know that this war will end in defeat.

Sentiments like these he could only confide to his private diary. It would have been suicidal to voice such views in front of his officers.[52]

Other documents were of more immediate importance. A mimeographed file of papers was found in Hollandia on 28 April 1944—titled 'Sketches of Operational Airfields West of Hollandia', it was compiled on 31 February 1944 and marked 'Military Most Secret'. This gave the lengths of the runways and included sketches of the airfield locations, which the translator traced from the original documents on tracing paper, adding translated captions. This document enabled the Allied air forces to ferry personnel and supplies to New Guinea by air. Again, after the invasion of Leyte, the handwritten operational orders for the defence of Japanese positions issued by the commanding officer, Hokoda Keijirō, were found at Dagami. Hokoda's expectations of where the Allies would land were correct, but he did not anticipate that landings would be made simultaneously in two different places. As with many Japanese battlefield orders, Hokoda's orders were drawn up by hand, communicated to other units orally or by telephone and finally circulated in mimeographed copies of the original handwritten orders.[53]

What contributions did all these translations and interrogations make to combat operations? As we have seen in Burma, sometimes a direct connection can be made that links intelligence gathered on the field as a result of linguistic expertise with subsequent military operations. The official history of ATIS anticipated this question and gave a number of concrete examples. Here are two of them:

On 17 January 1943, the main enemy perimeter to the south of Giruwa [New Guinea] was still intact although it was being approached by three columns of Australian and American troops. At 2300 hours on the night before the planned Allied attack, a wounded prisoner was captured and taken to the portable field hospital at Soputa. This prisoner revealed that the American reconnaissance patrol had failed to discover the main Japanese strong point earlier that morning. He gave a detailed disposition of enemy troops and automatic weapons covering the approaches along the Soputa Track, the exact position of enemy headquarters within the perimeter, and the enemy strength as well as the exact locations of all land mines planted on the track. At 0100 hours this information was in the possession of the Commanding General of the 7th Australian Division who, after conference with the Commanding Officers of the United States 163rd Infantry and the 18th Australian Brigade, shifted the plan of attack as a result of which the enemy strong point was captured and occupied by dawn.

On 22 October 1944, X Corps captured four sketches, one of gun positions north of Dulag, Leyte, and three of San Roque, Catmon Hill Area Leyte, containing gun and coastal defense positions. Exact tracings with translations were supplied to XXIV Corps prior to attack on these positions. At the same time, two sketches were captured at Tacloban, Leyte, which showed the disposition of the enemy 16th Division.[54]

These pages of the official report were obviously designed by Colonel Mashbir to justify the existence of ATIS. There can be no doubt that ATIS translators and interrogators did indeed provide valuable battlefield intelligence, but what use was made of it is usually difficult to discern.

The typed ATIS translations and interrogation reports were duplicated and circulated to a limited number of military bodies. For example, the copies of the *ATIS Bulletins* in the Australian War Memorial were evidently those sent to naval headquarters, for the names of all ships have been underlined with a red crayon. The distribution of such material obviously carried the risk that the enemy would learn of the activities of ATIS and perhaps take steps to ensure the destruction of documents instead of simply assuming that the Allies would have nobody who could read them. Japanese intelligence reports were carefully monitored for signs that the secrecy had been penetrated. But there was never any sign that the Japanese were even aware of the existence of ATIS, despite the gigantic quantities of material produced by ATIS. By July 1945, ATIS had published 12,500 interrogation reports, scanned and summarized over 33,000 documents and translated and published over 16,000 of them. These figures come from Mashbir's official history, but it is not clear if they include translations and interrogations done by personnel other than those in the US Army.[55]

A small number of the ATIS reports were for very restricted distribution, and that was because they concerned Japanese intelligence operations. One example is a report on the interrogation of Sakieda Ryūji, who was captured on 11 March 1943 on Goodenough Island, in the Solomon Sea to the east of New Guinea. He had been working in an intelligence and interception unit and provided his ATIS interrogators with priceless information about Japanese wireless procedures and enciphering routines and even provided a list of technical terms used by signallers in the Imperial Japanese Army. Most copies of this report were sent to Central Bureau, but it also reached London in the form of a photographed copy.[56]

The ATIS headquarters in Brisbane closed down in June 1945, but ADVATIS linguists continued to be active in the Philippines until the end of the war. From September 1945, ATIS became a component of the US Occupation force in Japan, but by that time it consisted entirely of American personnel and was based in Tokyo. For most of its existence, it had been a multinational Allied enterprise, and it is a great pity that only the contributions of the US Army are celebrated in the official history.

* * *

Australia was the first of the Allied powers to introduce courses in Japanese to remedy the linguistic deficit, and this happened well before the attacks of December 1941. Moreover, the mathematicians and classicists of the University of Sydney were, like Nave, engaging with Japanese codes and ciphers well before the outbreak of war and acquiring sufficient knowledge of the language in the process. Once the war with Japan was fully under way, the need for linguists to deal with documents found on the battlefield and with prisoners of war became acute, and at this point the linguistic battle involved all the Allies.

Americans, and particularly Nisei, dominated, but there were also many Australians. The British contribution is best documented in the case of the refugees from Singapore, of the consular officials who were repatriated from Japan and of the Bedford graduates who joined the Central Bureau, but there were others in ATIS whose identities are now unknown and whose activities are difficult to pin down. As the war with Japan came to an end, many of them had to turn their skills to surrender negotiations and then to the business of policing the Occupation of Japan, as we will see in the following chapters.

10

THE END OF THE WAR IN THE PACIFIC

On 7 May 1945, the BBC interrupted its scheduled radio broadcast with a newsflash. All German armed forces on land, sea and air had unconditionally surrendered to General Eisenhower, the Supreme Allied Commander. That was enough to bring crowds on to the streets of London, but it was on 8 May that the real celebrations began, not only in Britain but in Western Europe, Australia and the United States, while in the Soviet Union and New Zealand the end of the war in Europe was celebrated on 9 May.

In Britain, 8 May was a warm and sunny day, and there were street parties in many towns in England, Northern Ireland, Scotland and Wales. The joy is captured in commemorative photographs taken in cities, towns and villages to preserve the moment for posterity, and in L. S. Lowry's painting of the VE Day celebrations. Prime Minister Churchill addressed the crowds in Whitehall in person, and the whole population on the radio, and he stood on the balcony of Buckingham Palace waving to the huge crowds in the Mall with King George VI, Queen Elizabeth and Princesses Elizabeth and Margaret. The day on which the war ended was one of those moments people remember for the rest of their lives, and ever since, Victory in Europe Day, or VE Day, has been celebrated every year on 8 May.[1]

Yet not everybody was celebrating in 1945. At the Yalta Conference of February 1945, Churchill, Roosevelt and Stalin had agreed on post-war spheres of influence, and since Poland formed part of the Soviet sphere of influence, Poles like my father, who had fought alongside British armed forces in the Battle of Britain, in the Allied advance on Rome and in many other campaigns, felt betrayed. Moreover, the war was not completely over, and many more were still to suffer and to die. Both Churchill and President Truman, who had just succeeded Roosevelt, warned in their speeches that the war was only half won, for Japan had yet to be defeated.

For the men and women engaged in the war on the other side of the world in May 1945, the end of the war still seemed a long way off. Japan was undefeated and did not seem likely to be defeated any time soon. At the Supreme Allied Command South East Asia in Ceylon, Lieutenant-Colonel Thomas Winterborn (1909–85) of the Intelligence Division was weighing up the future course of the war. He had spent three years in Japan as a language officer from 1935 and before returning home in 1938 had spent a month attached to a Japanese infantry regiment; owing to his linguistic skills and intellectual gifts, he had spent the war in intelligence roles. He considered that Singapore would not be retaken until early 1946 and that the Japanese armed forces would go on fighting in the hope that something would turn up to avert defeat. On the other hand, he thought that some Japanese 'will already have started thinking of what they can save from the mess'. For the time being, however, there was no alternative but to take the war to its logical conclusion. In fact, detailed plans had already been drawn up for the invasion of the Japanese mainland. The Allies expected that the invasion would be fiercely resisted and were bracing themselves for huge numbers of casualties. The last act of the war against Japan was scheduled to start on 1 November 1945 with Operation Olympic, an amphibious assault on the island of Kyushu, to be followed by Operation Coronet, an even larger assault on Honshu near Tokyo, beginning on 1 March 1946.[2]

Interpreters had already been assigned to accompany the invasion forces, and one of them was Robert Christopher. We encountered him earlier when he was starting to learn Japanese at Yale in September 1941 on his father's advice so as to avoid becoming a machine-gunner. After he had completed his studies, he was sent to join Central Bureau in Brisbane, and he moved with the advance parties up to the Philippines:

In the spring of 1945, when I had moved up to San Miguel [Luzon, Philippines], I was astonished to receive a letter from Yale University asking if I was coming back to school since the war was winding down. I was scheduled to go with the troops as an interpreter in operations Olympic and Coronet to invade Japan. I was worried about being dead, never mind going back to school. I was relieved when the U.S. dropped the atomic bomb and Japan surrendered.[3]

Grant Goodman was also relieved to hear the news about the atomic bombs. He had been interrogating Japanese prisoners as an American member of ATIS since the beginning of July and had three times taken part in trial runs for Operation Olympic. Each time, he and his fellow interpreters had to fill their backpacks with the heavy dictionaries they needed and practise climbing up the nets on to the transport ships. For him and for many others, the fear of many months of dangerous war-time service suddenly vanished.[4]

In July 1945, Churchill, Stalin and Truman met in Potsdam, Berlin, to set the terms for Japan's surrender. The Potsdam Declaration, issued on 26 July, called upon the Japanese government to surrender, warning that 'The alternative for Japan is prompt and utter destruc-tion.' The declaration was translated into Japanese, and the Japanese text was made known to the Japanese population both by radio trans-missions and by millions of leaflets dropped by bombers. The Japanese government did not respond. On 6 August 1945, the city of Hiroshima was devastated by the first atomic bomb. Three days later, the city of Nagasaki met the same fate, and a third bomb was being prepared for use on another city later in the month. In Hiroshima and Nagasaki together, more than 100,000 people were killed instantly, and many tens of thousands more died in the days and months that followed.

Even before the bomb was dropped on Nagasaki, the Soviet Union declared war on Japan and immediately invaded Japanese-occupied Manchuria. On 10 August 1945, the Japanese government decided to accept the terms of the Potsdam Declaration and communicated its decision to the Allies via Switzerland. The announcement led to cele-brations in Piccadilly Circus and outside the White House in Washington, DC, and Allied troops celebrated in Paris, Berlin, Manila and many other places. On 15 August, the emperor used his first ever radio broadcast to announce Japan's decision to surrender, and that led to further celebrations.

The formal surrender ceremony, however, had yet to take place. With the agreement of the British, Chinese and Soviet governments, President Truman designated General MacArthur as Supreme Commander for the Allied Powers with the authority to accept the surrender of the government of Japan. MacArthur was still in Manila, and now he awaited the arrival of a Japanese delegation to discuss the details of the surrender.

On 19 August, a small group of Japanese military representatives arrived in Manila for this purpose. Among them was a young Nisei lieutenant. He could have been on either side. He had studied at New York University but had been in Japan when the war broke out and so had been conscripted into the Japanese Army. The delegation brought with them sheaves of documents, all of course written in Japanese. As requested beforehand, the documents covered the dispositions of Japanese troops throughout the Japanese Empire, the identities of those in command, the locations of the camps where Allied prisoners were kept and the location and operational condition of airfields within Japan. The Japanese delegation was confronted with an Allied team that consisted of twelve men, nine of whom were linguists serving with ATIS. It was their job to translate into English the materials that the Japanese party had brought with them but also to translate into Japanese the nine proclamations that MacArthur had issued to initiate the Occupation of Japan after the surrender ceremony. By 23 August, the ATIS translators had translated, checked, mimeographed and published the entire collection of documents apart from the maps.[5]

On 27 August, a fleet of Allied ships, from Britain, the United States, Australia and New Zealand, steamed gingerly into Tokyo Bay. Why gingerly? For the very good reason that Japanese coastal waters were still mined. Japanese pilots came aboard several of the larger ships to guide the fleet safely through the treacherous waters. Leading the way into Tokyo Bay was the Japanese destroyer *Hatsuzakura*, with guns depressed, breeches open and torpedo tubes empty. It was followed by the destroyer HMS *Whelp*, with Prince Philip of Greece (later the Duke of Edinburgh) as second-in-command, and then came the battleships USS *Missouri*, USS *Iowa*, HMS *Duke of York* (the flagship of the commander-in-chief of the British Pacific Fleet, Admiral Sir Bruce Fraser), HMS *King George V* (the flagship of Vice-Admiral Bernard

Rawlings, Fraser's second in command), and six more US battleships, plus a host of lesser vessels including the light cruiser HMS *Newfoundland*, the flagship of Rear-Admiral Patrick Brind.[6]

Beasley, who had learnt his Japanese at Boulder, was on board HMS *King George V* and recalled what happened when the Japanese pilots came on board his ship:

> Two [Japanese naval officers] came to *King George V*, one a navigation specialist, the other, a fact not at once apparent, his interpreter. I met them as they came aboard—an event my mother saw on newsreels, to her immense delight ['Tokyo Bay', a Pathé newsreel issued in 1945]—and took them to the conning tower, where they were to stay under guard while I relayed to the bridge the navigational information they provided. I explained this to them. The navigator ... though clearly disappointed that he would not be allowed on the bridge, gave the impression of being much more flattered at having been chosen to bring in the British flagship than chagrined at his country's defeat. His younger companion had little to say on any subject, whether in English or Japanese.

Once the *King George V* was safely at anchor, Vice-Admiral Rawlings, who had served as naval attaché in Tokyo from 1935 to 1938 but had limited knowledge of the language, addressed the two Japanese in English, and it fell to Beasley to translate his speech into Japanese:

> Its theme was that the Royal Navy had contributed to the training and development of the Japanese navy throughout modern times; for Japan to have attacked Britain in the war just ended was therefore contrary to the respect a pupil should show to his teacher; it was, in fact, a breach of Japanese tradition. I did my best to put this into adequate Japanese but the task was beyond my powers and my vocabulary. The result was painfully clumsy.

These were the last official duties Beasley performed at sea. But his war was not yet over, as we will see in the next chapter.[7]

Although the Japanese decision to surrender had been broadcast on 15 August, it was not until 28 August that the first Allied troops set foot in Japan—apart, that is, from Allied personnel in Japanese prisoner of war camps. MacArthur flew in on 30 August, and on the same day Admiral Nimitz and Admiral William Halsey of the US Navy, along with large numbers of Allied sailors and marines, landed at Yokosuka, a little to the south of Yokohama, and took over the Japanese naval base there. A few days later, on 2 September, General MacArthur was to preside over the official surrender ceremony aboard the battleship USS *Missouri* with representatives of all the Allied nations. But who was going to represent Japan, if not the emperor himself?

On the Japanese side, nobody wanted to take on the duty of representing Japan at the ceremony on the *Missouri*. In the end, Shigemitsu Mamoru (1887–1957), the foreign minister, represented the government and General Umezu Yoshijirō (1882–1949), who was chief of the Army General Staff and had vigorously opposed the surrender, represented the armed forces. Both of them were subsequently convicted of war crimes at the International Military Tribunal for the Far East (Tokyo Trials).

Accompanied by nine other officials from the Foreign Office and the War and Navy Departments, Shigemitsu and Umezu were driven to Yokohama past 'miles and miles of debris and destruction', as Kase Toshikazu (1903–2004) recalled. At the time, he was one of the Foreign Office officials in the party, but he was later to become Japan's first ambassador to the United Nations. He was, incidentally, the uncle of Yoko Ono, the artist and peace activist who married John Lennon in 1969. At Yokohama, the military officers were required to leave their swords behind before proceeding to the *Missouri*, which was anchored 18 miles offshore. Once aboard the *Missouri*, Kase remembered, 'A million eyes seemed to beat on us with the million shafts of a rattling storm of arrows barbed with fire.' The Japanese representatives were, however, astonished by the tone of MacArthur's opening words:

> We are gathered here, representatives of the major warring powers, to conclude a solemn agreement whereby peace may be restored. The issues, involving divergent ideals and ideologies, have been determined on the battlefields of the world and hence are not for our discussion or debate. Nor is it for us here to meet, representing as we do a majority of the peoples of the earth, in a spirit of distrust, malice, or hatred.

They had not expected anything so magnanimous. Once all the official representatives had signed the instrument of surrender, there was a fly-past of 400 B-29 bombers and 1,500 carrier planes, which demonstrated the overwhelming power still available to the Allies in the Pacific.[8]

Alongside the VIPs, Colonel Bashir, the head of ATIS, was present on the *Missouri* as MacArthur's personal translator.[9] Also present was Paul Sherman, an American Boulder graduate, who took advantage of a special postmark in the ship's post office reading 'Japanese formal surrender, U.S.S. *Missouri*, Tokyo Bay, September 2 1945' to send a letter home. Gowing, one of the RNVR officers trained at the US Navy Language School in Boulder, was probably also on board. Beasley was on the *King George V*, and, he wrote, 'like many others I listened to a running commentary on it broadcast to the fleet'.[10]

In addition to the ceremony on board the USS *Missouri*, there were many local surrender ceremonies in the various territories occupied by Japan during the war. Some of these were carried out by British forces with British interpreters on hand. In August, a British fleet consisting of sixty-one ships, including the two aircraft carriers HMS *Indomitable* and HMS *Venerable*, HMS *Swiftsure* and one other cruiser, four destroyers and eight submarines, assembled in Subic Bay in the Philippines, and on 30 August it made its way into Hong Kong harbour to take over control from the Japanese garrison commanders. Rear-Admiral Harcourt was in command with his flag on the *Indomitable*, but he transferred his flag to the *Swiftsure* for the entry into Hong Kong harbour. He made this transfer for the simple reason that as an aircraft carrier the *Indomitable* would be vulnerable to mines. In the event, the danger came from a different direction, for as the fleet approached the harbour some Japanese suicide boats were seen to be leaving their moorings. Harcourt ordered his carriers to launch their aeroplanes and destroy them. Later the surviving members of the suicide boat crews were rounded up and captured. Once the fleet was finally safely at anchor, Japanese envoys came aboard the *Swiftsure* to discuss the surrender arrangements.[11]

On 16 September, Harcourt took the surrender of Vice-Admiral Fujita Ruitarō, who signed with brush and ink and then affixed his personal seal. Harcourt then remained ashore as administrator of Hong Kong until April 1946. At the surrender ceremony, it was Captain (later Admiral Sir) John Eccles (1898–1966), the captain of the *Indomitable*, who explained the surrender terms to the Japanese party. As a young lieutenant, he had been sent in 1921 to the School of Oriental Studies (now SOAS) in London to learn Japanese; he later spent several years as a language officer in Japan and underwent intelligence training at GC&CS. Unlike most language officers, whose subsequent career gave them little opportunity to use their knowledge, for several years he served as an interpreter and intelligence officer, but then he resumed his career afloat and from 1943 served on the aircraft-carrier *Indomitable*. The caption to the official photograph of the scene states that 'He [Eccles] speaks fluent Japanese and has been responsible for many of the surrender arrangements.' Lower-ranking interpreters and translators rarely rate a mention, but it is unlikely that the fleet reached Hong Kong without several junior interpreters, including perhaps British graduates of the Japanese Language School at Boulder, on hand to facilitate the practical arrangements.[12]

The role of junior service interpreters is apparent from the initial negotiations prior to the surrender of Japanese forces in Lower Burma. Allen states that he 'took part personally in a number of surrender negotiations'. He may have been the interpreter when Japanese envoys from Singapore flew to Rangoon, escorted by Spitfires, to make prior arrangements for the surrender of Singapore. Once the preliminary arrangements had been agreed, the 5th Indian Division set sail for Singapore, uncertain whether there would be resistance or opposition. There were still 96,000 Japanese troops on Singapore, but the division would only have 10,000 men on the ground in the first three days. On 4 September 1945, the day before the landing, a conference was held on board the heavy cruiser HMS *Sussex*, the flagship of Rear-Admiral Cedric Holland. Along with Major-General Robert Mansergh of the 5th Indian Division, he and other senior officers met the Japanese commanders for the first time to finalize the arrangements. Representing Japan were General Itagaki Seishirō, commander of the Japanese 7th Area Army, and Vice-Admiral Fukudome Shigeru; when they reached a final agreement on the surrender terms, Fukudome grinned but Itagaki wept. British linguists were present to do the interpreting, but they are not named. The following morning, landing craft took the troops ashore to bring the Japanese Occupation to an end, and among them was de Moubray, who, as mentioned in chapter 3, was there reunited with his parents.[13]

Cortazzi, who on leaving India had been attached to the 14th Army as the personal interpreter to General Dempsey, found himself in

Singapore having to interpret at a meeting between a brigadier on Dempsey's staff and General Itagaki. This was a difficult assignment:

> At one point, I asked General Itagaki to explain something which I had not properly understood. The [brigadier] then bawled me out and told me that my job was not to ask the General questions but to interpret word for word what he said! Fortunately, one of the Japanese side's interpreters helped me out of this difficult moment.

He was present for the surrender ceremony on 12 September, but the interpreting on that occasion was done by Major Arthur Arab of the British Army, who had lived almost all his life in Japan and before the war was employed as the Japan agent of R. H. Macy & Co. of New York, and by Wing-Commander Boyce, whom we encountered in chapter 7 when he was working in India as a translator and expert on Japanese air terminology.[14]

The formal surrender of all Japanese forces in South East Asia at Singapore on 12 September was one of the final duties undertaken by SEAC under Mountbatten. Beforehand, Mountbatten had summoned Field Marshal Terauchi from his headquarters in Saigon to make the formal surrender of Japanese forces in the South East Asia theatre, but Terauchi pleaded ill-health following a stroke. Mountbatten's doctor went to Saigon and confirmed that this was indeed the case, so the surrender was signed instead by General Itagaki once he had shown written evidence of the authority vested in him by Terauchi. However, in a letter Mountbatten wrote in October to Major-General Douglas Gracey, commander-in-chief of Allied Land Forces in French Indochina, he made it clear that 'until Terauchi has handed over his sword the surrender cannot be regarded as complete', adding that 'no Japanese officers whatsoever are being allowed to return to Japan with their swords'. Terauchi's swords were hurriedly sent to him from Japan, and on 30 November 1945 he surrendered them in Saigon. Terauchi was subsequently transferred with a skeleton staff to Singapore on 13 February 1946 and died of another stroke on 12 June 1946 while detained at Renggam POW camp in Johore.[15]

Meanwhile, Laurence Cohen (1923–2006), a Bedford graduate who had subsequently served at Kilindini and HMS *Anderson* in Colombo, was one of the small British party that received the surrender of the large Japanese garrison at Penang. Lieutenant Albert Corey, who had done his Japanese at SOAS, was on hand as interpreter when Major Wakō Hisanori of the Japanese 28th Army handed over his sword to Lieutenant-Colonel O. C. Smyth of the Gurkha Rifles prior to local surrender negotiations somewhere in northern Burma.[16]

The surrender of Rabaul, New Britain (now part of Papua New Guinea), was overseen by Captain Anthony Buzzard (1902–72; later rear-admiral) in command of the aircraft carrier HMS *Glory*, which was accompanied by the sloops HMS *Amethyst* and HMS *Hart*. General Imamura Hitoshi and Vice-Admiral Kusaka Jin'ichi, as commanders in chief of the Japanese South East Army and Fleet respectively, boarded the *Glory* on 6 September. They were disarmed on arrival and treated as prisoners. Their surrender was accepted by Lieutenant-General Vernon Sturdee, the commander of the 1st Australian Army, watched by 1,000 officers and men of the *Glory* lined up on the flight deck. 'After signing', it was reported, 'General Imamura spoke at some length, expressing his appreciation of the consideration shown him in negotiations and asking assistance to relieve the bad conditions his troops were in.'[17] Who conducted the negotiations and who did the interpreting? The record does not say.

Despite the capture of Rangoon at the beginning of June, the war in Burma did not end on 15 August. Up to the summer of 1944, Allen recalled, 'the Japanese were a hard and ruthless enemy that you feared and took very seriously if you valued your life'. After that, things were different: 'my only feeling for the Japanese I saw was one of compassion. I felt sorry for them—I didn't think they could do anything ultimately harmful at all—the notion of fear had gone completely'. After the capture of Rangoon, there were still substantial Japanese fighting units at large, weakened though they were by sickness, foot-rot, lack of food supplies and sheer exhaustion. Some of them managed to break-out across the Sittang River and begin the trek south to Moulmein, but they lost at least half their men in the process to illness, enemy (i.e., Allied) action or the swollen waters of the Sittang, and they had lost any means of communicating with each other. Consequently, many units did not hear the emperor's message on 15 August announcing that Japan would capitulate.[18]

It fell to Fred Kagawa to tell them about it. He was a Canadian Nisei, who had just been posted to the Canadian Intelligence Corps in

Rangoon, and he was absorbed into SEAC's Psychological Warfare Broadcasting Unit, a multinational unit in Rangoon. His job was to translate the day's news into Japanese, including the dropping of the atomic bombs, the emperor's broadcast and the hopeless situation of the Japanese armies in retreat. Then he had to sit in front of a microphone and broadcast it, in the hope that Japanese units with a radio would be listening and would realize that the war was over.[19]

The war was over for the combatants, but it was not over for the linguists. As those who had studied at Bedford, Karachi and SOAS were soon to discover, they were needed to screen surrendered Japanese troops, investigate war crimes and take part in the Occupation of Japan. And the same was true of many of the personnel in ATIS and SEATIC. Some of them, as we will see, were anxious about their likely reception in Japan, but in the event they found the Occupation something of an anti-climax.

11

FINISHING THE JOB

At last it was time to be demobbed and to go home. Men and women in uniform now did just that, beginning their long journeys home by ship or by aeroplane. But there were many who were not yet free to return to their loved ones. However much the translators and interpreters may have wanted to go home, they still had a kaleidoscope of work to do. After all, who else could interpret at war crimes trials involving Japanese? Who else could screen and interrogate surrendered Japanese personnel in all the far-flung parts of the short-lived Japanese Empire? And who was going to police the Occupation of Japan if not them?

For many of them, this meant acquiring new language skills. It also meant coming face to face with the 'enemy' for the first time, at first in reclaimed parts of the former Japanese Empire, like Burma, Singapore, the Philippines and the many islands of what is now Indonesia, and then in Japan itself. Some of those who had studied Japanese at the Bedford School or at SOAS were keen to visit Japan for the first time and actually volunteered to postpone their demobilization for the opportunity to serve in the British Commonwealth Occupation Force (BCOF) in post-war Japan. Even so, they were not sure what they were going to find. Were the defeated Japanese going to be resentful, hostile or even violent? What dangers awaited them in Japan, and what kind of work would they have to do? These sorts of questions preyed on their minds, but when they got there, they found that there was little or no trouble from the Japanese population and there was little meaningful work to be done.

As we will see, it was not until 1946 that BCOF reached Japan to begin its work there. Before that, the interpreters and translators found that they were fully occupied. After the surrender, they were screening Japanese troops before allowing them to return to Japan and interrogating many officers for the information they could provide. Some were involved in war crimes trials, while others went to Japan to open up the British embassy again or to investigate Japanese technological developments during the war. In this chapter, we will see how the linguists' skills were used once the pressure of the war was removed and how they found Japan when they finally got there.

Historical interrogations

When the war ended, the first task for Allied linguists was screening. Hundreds of thousands of Japanese military personnel were being held in camps after they had surrendered. They were trapped overseas, and they, too, wished to go home. But Japanese military personnel were not allowed to return to Japan unless they had been screened, and that was a job that only interpreters could do, for very few Japanese soldiers could speak English. 'What is your rank, what unit are you attached to, where were you fighting, what was your role?' The object of these questions, of course, was ultimately to identify individuals who may have been responsible for the torture or killing of Allied prisoners of war or of the local population. The linguists had 'stop lists' to help them identify wanted individuals. Storry relied on one that gave their names and ranks, the crimes they were accused of and where the crimes had been carried out, in most cases the Burma–Siam Railway. Storry also kept the notebook in which he kept notes on his interrogations as he did them. [1]

Louis Allen and Stanley Charles had been in the thick of the action in Burma as translators and interrogators. The war came to an end before they reached Rangoon, so they changed roles and personally interrogated about 600 surrendered Japanese soldiers. Many of them were, as Allen recalled, 'rotting with disease', especially *beri-beri*, dysentery and malaria. 'They could have killed me at any time', he said, 'but I never felt the least disquiet.' Allen and Charles were on the lookout for any evidence of atrocities committed against the Burmese population or against British or Indian prisoners of war, and they paid particular attention to Japanese personnel who had been connected with intelligence work or with the Indian National Army or the Burma Independence Army.[2]

All the same, they considered that their main task when conducting these interrogations was rather to investigate and write up the history of the Burma Campaign relying upon the testimony of the Japanese generals and staff who were available in the camps in Burma. This was also Allen's main concern in November and December 1945, when he interrogated members of the Kenpeitai in Rangoon Gaol. Here, too, his purpose was historical, and he left the investigation of atrocities and war crimes to the specialist teams who would interrogate them later. He admitted, nevertheless, that he felt uneasy interrogating Kenpeitai personnel because of the personal risk: many of them knew that they were likely to face the death penalty and had nothing to lose.[3]

It may seem surprising that Allen and Charles were focused on history. It was not because they were professional historians—they were not—but rather because Japanese units destroyed all their paperwork before they surrendered. They had had plenty of opportunity to do so, since there was a gap of two weeks or more between the emperor's surrender broadcast on 15 August and the various surrender ceremonies in Japan, Singapore, Hong Kong and elsewhere. The instructions given to Japanese forces surrendering in Singapore included the following:

> All demolitions, destruction, damage and sabotage of all kinds whatsoever are prohibited. In particular, the following are to be placed under guard until taken over by British Forces: ... All documents, records, archives, cyphers and codes, both Military and Civil. This is to include those prior to the Japanese occupation and during it.[4]

By that time, however, it was too late: most Japanese documents had already been destroyed. This was, therefore, the only opportunity, before Japanese personnel returned to Japan, for the Allies to examine the Japanese perspective on the campaign that had just ended and to discover what Japanese commanders had known about Allied movements in the campaign.

The desire for information from the Japanese side came from the Allied commanders. They wanted to know how effective their intelligence had been, where they had caused the enemy most problems and how successful their attempts to disguise their own intentions had been. There were lessons to be learnt for the future, and to that end they needed to derive as much information from the defeated Japanese as they could before it was too late.

General Gracey, who took over French Indo-China from the Japanese occupying forces, was one of the commanders who took historical investigations seriously. In Saigon, he requested the commander of Japanese forces in South East Asia, Field-Marshal Count Terauchi Hisaichi, to provide a detailed account of Japanese operations since the beginning of the war. Terauchi furnished his account in October 1945, still styling himself as 'Supreme Commander, The Japanese Expeditionary Forces in Southern Region'. This was by now an empty title, of course. Terauchi's account was naturally written in Japanese, so it was edited and translated by a team of unnamed translators and then printed in Rangoon in December 1945. The editors cast doubt on the accuracy of Terauchi's account in a few places but explained that, 'Having destroyed all their official records, the Japanese wrote these three documents from memory.' Similarly, the editor of a report on the history of the Japanese 38th Division in Indochina, based on the testimony of three Japanese generals, notes that they only had their memory to rely upon. The destruction of records was widespread, and that gave some urgency to the task of extracting the details from Japanese officers. This was a task that required translators and interrogators to shift gear from assessing the tactical value of the material that came before them, as they had been doing for months and years, to exercising judgement about the accuracy of the information they were being given.[5]

There was a similar historical focus in the interrogations conducted by Cortazzi in Singapore. Over several months in 1946, he undertook a lengthy series of interrogations and translations focusing on the air forces of the Japanese Army and Japanese Navy in South East Asia. He compiled a detailed report, but he was, he admitted, hampered by the fact that for the early part of the war, most of the participants had either died or returned to Japan. Also, he was unable to interview members of Japanese forces operating in Siam, French Indo-China, Java or

Sumatra (now in Indonesia). All the same, through his interrogations he discovered what he considered was a marked difference between the air forces of the Japanese Army and the Japanese Navy. Senior officers in the Navy Air Force, he found, were often former aircrew, and this gave them a good understanding of air power. In the Army Air Force, on the other hand, he found that 'semi-efficient, unenterprising dull-witted staff officers who had mainly been transferred from ground units and knew nothing of the air arm' tended to be in charge and failed to appreciate the potential of air power. He also found that, in general, Japanese air intelligence and signals security were very poorly developed and that there was a chronic lack of supplies, which was caused by Allied attacks on Japanese merchant shipping. Some of his findings were no different from what intelligence officers had suspected during the campaign, but he was able to confirm that Allied attempts to disrupt the Japanese supply chain had been effective and to explain why the Japanese Navy had performed better in the air than the Japanese Army.[6]

Many of the interrogations conducted in the months after the end of the war resulted in reports of a similar kind, not focused on war crimes but rather on the organization, tactics and movements of Japanese units during the war. The interrogations of Kenpeitai personnel conducted by Allen and others led to a detailed report that described the organization of the Kenpeitai in Burma, their role in Japanese intelligence organizations, the disguises they adopted in the field and so on. As the author of the report drily concluded, 'Personnel interrogated professed to have no knowledge of atrocities committed.'[7]

All these historical reports constituted a huge feedback loop. They gave commanders insight into their successes and failures and helped them understand the impact on the enemy of the decisions they had taken. What is unfortunately hidden from our view is the precise lessons drawn. What, for example, did General Gracey think of Field-Marshal Terauchi's report? What new perspectives on the campaign did it give him? To these questions we have no answers.

Technical interrogations

In the immediate aftermath of the war, interrogations were conducted with a view not only to gaining a better understanding of the campaigns recently fought but also to acquiring specialist knowledge from Japanese personnel. For example, after two junior Japanese officers and one warrant officer who had been involved in the handling of codes and cyphers surrendered at Singapore, they were promptly interrogated by Flight-Lieutenant H. Salter, who had done one of the SOAS courses. All three he described as 'most helpful and co-operative': they gave a lot of information about the Type 97 Coding Machine, which was known to the Allies as 'Purple', and provided drawings labelled in Japanese, as well as information about other cypher systems used by the Imperial Japanese Navy. Salter's report went to the Admiralty in London: Was the information of any value or was it simply filed away? It is now impossible to tell.[8]

The same is true of the much more extensive investigation of all the scientific and technological developments that had taken place in Japan during the war, which in some cases involved the removal of machinery and equipment to the United States for further examination. This is one of the least well-known consequences of the end of the war. The investigation was led by the United States, which established the US Naval Technical Mission to Japan (NavTechJap) on 14 August 1945, the day before the war ended. The focus was on developments likely to be of interest to the US Navy or the Marine Corps, and the investigations involved not only the examination of material and documents but also the interrogation of Japanese naval and civilian personnel. Obviously, this meant that the staff employed on NavTechJap investigations had to have either technical or linguistic qualifications.

On 23 September 1945, NavTechJap investigators entered Sasebo harbour on the island of Kyushu to begin their work. Sasebo had been a major naval base and arsenal for the Imperial Japanese Navy, so it was an appropriate place to start. Other groups of investigators were sent straight away from there to the naval arsenals at Yokosuka and Kure, but teams were soon in operation at relevant locations throughout Japan. Most of the NavTechJap officers were from the US Navy or the US Naval Reserve, but there were also some from the Army and the Marine Corps. Furthermore, as the official history noted, there 'was a delegation of approximately 23 British technical specialists and language officers, an able and experienced group which cooperated effectively on many difficult investigations'. Who were these people and what did they find?[9]

The official history of NavTechJap lists twenty-five participating officers of the Royal Navy or the RNVR, the senior British officer being Captain Robert James Dunbar Bald (1902–57), a Royal Navy gunnery expert. Among his team were four of the Royal Navy language students from Boulder, including Catt whose beard had caused ructions. They were sent to join a team in Sasebo, and Catt acted as the interpreter for a group examining Japanese meteorological instruments. Most of the other names on the list were probably naval officers with technical expertise, such as Commander G. J. Stewart. He was a Royal Navy engineering officer and co-authored the report on the Japanese 18-inch guns and mounts that had made the *Yamato* and the *Musashi* the most powerful battleships in the world. Among the other British translators was Richnell, who, as we have seen, went ashore at Leyte as an interpreter with ATIS. In an oral account of his war, he referred briefly to his experiences with NavTechJap. The end of the war found him in Manila, he said, and by that time he had a lot of experience as a translator and interrogator under his belt. He was recalled to ATIS headquarters in Brisbane and then sent out to Japan to work for NavTechJap in Kure. He was the only Briton in a team that consisted mostly of American engineers; they visited factories and naval bases and impounded some technical equipment for further examination.[10]

By early 1946, the mission had completed its investigations in Japan. The NavTechJap teams seized in all more than 3,000 documents and sent them back to the United States for translation and analysis. They also seized 15,000 pieces of equipment, which were also sent back to the United States, including two 18.1-inch guns weighing 180 tons each, which were shipped back from Kure. The end result of all this activity was the production of a large number of technical reports, which are now to be found in the US Navy Department Library in the Washington Navy Yard. Some reports identify 'new, unique, or superior design by the Japanese', while others conclude that the United States had nothing to learn from Japan or, in the case of electronics, was in fact far ahead of Japan. Copies were sent to Britain, but I have so far been unable to locate them. In 1948, however, somebody in the Home Office borrowed the NavTechJap reports on the medical consequences of the dropping of atomic bombs on Hiroshima and Nagasaki and made extracts from them.[11]

The named authors of the reports are mostly US naval or Army officers, but in some cases RNVR linguists were named as translators and/or interpreters, and in a few instances Royal Navy experts contributed to the research and the writing of the reports. 'Welding in Japanese Naval Construction', for example, was written by Construction Lieutenant James A. H. Paffett RN and a US Navy civilian technician, assisted by Lieutenant R. Cunninghame RN, who had done one of the SOAS courses, as translator and interpreter. The report was largely negative, in the sense that it found there was little to learn from Japanese welding, but several dozen Japanese publications had been covered and five Japanese experts had been interviewed, and the report runs to fifty pages.[12]

Although NavTechJap was overwhelmingly an American enterprise, technical experts and linguists from the Royal Navy were also involved. Were they included because their expertise was valued, or was it just a bit of naval diplomacy, for which the British men who had been trained at Boulder were a perfect fit? Probably the latter. It is difficult to gauge the impact these investigations had on the United States or Britain. Wherever the investigators found evidence of what the official report called 'new, unique, or superior design by the Japanese', it is only to be expected that these designs were adopted by the American and British navies, but I have not been able to find any proof of that. Just how much of a technology transfer was there, I wonder?

War crimes

According to Allen, he and Charles did try to identify war crimes suspects when they were screening Japanese troops in Burma, but he states that they left the detailed interrogation of suspects to specialist teams. Allen provides no further details of these specialist teams, but it is inconceivable that they did not include linguists acting as interpreters. I have so far been unable to discover their identities, but as a result of their investigations eighty-five war crimes suspects were identified in Burma, and under British auspices some forty trials were held, sometimes with multiple defendants, in Rangoon, Mandalay and Maymyo in 1946–7.[13]

Meanwhile, war crimes trials were being held elsewhere under American auspices. One of the most significant was that of General

Yamashita Tomoyuki, which began in Manila on 29 October 1945 and
concluded on 7 December with a sentence of death, which was carried
out on 23 February 1946. He was accused of 'command responsibility'
for his failure to prevent atrocities inflicted by his troops on civilians in
the Philippines and was the first to be accused of war crimes by omission. This itself was a precedent that formed the basis of subsequent
war crimes trials, but more significant from the perspective of this
book is the fact that the interpreting arrangements for the trial were
chaotic. The three US Navy and Marine officers assigned to the trial
declared that they were not sufficiently competent and recommended
that Nisei linguists be used instead. The Nisei linguists, unsurprisingly,
had inadequate knowledge of legal terminology in Japanese and English
(after all, they had been trained for warfare, not for the courtroom).
In the end, the trial went ahead, with the Nisei linguists being unoffi-
cially helped by Yamashita's personal interpreter, who had been educated at Harvard but was himself a prisoner of war. The conduct of
Yamashita's trial did not bode well for the interpreting arrangements
at the more important trials still to come.[14]

In April 1946, the hearings of the International Military Tribunal for
the Far East (the Tokyo Trials) began. There were Britons, Australians,
Canadians and New Zealanders on the judges' bench and among the
prosecutors, but not among the defence lawyers or the interpreters. In
fact, so far as I have been able to discover, not one British linguist was
involved. What is even more surprising is that most of the interpreters
at the trials were officials at the Japanese Ministry of Foreign Affairs.
To be sure, they were supervised by American monitors, but in some
cases the monitors did not have a strong command of Japanese. In fact,
Takeda Kayoko points out that the higher the rank of the monitor, the
poorer his (for they were all men) linguistic competence was likely to
be. In this respect, the situation in Tokyo was not so different from the
interpreting arrangements at the Nuremberg Trials. Attempts to
recruit German translators and interpreters in Britain for war crimes
work failed to meet the targets, and in the end the courts and the
Occupation authorities relied upon native speakers of German with a
good command of English. Similarly, in the case of the Tokyo Trials,
Japanese citizens were used rather than trained American interpreters.
This was probably because American interpreters had not performed

well at the Yamashita trial and at other trials held in Yokohama. But why was the quality of the interpreting such an important issue? The overriding concern for the Allies at Nuremberg and Tokyo was that the trials be conducted with dignity and with the appearance of fairness. It is surely for this reason that, for the first time, the Allies turned not to their own interpreters but to German and Japanese citizens, who could not be accused by the defendants of incompetence or bias. This explanation cannot, however, be found in documents relating to the trials, possibly because it did not need to be spelled out once the policy decisions had been made about how the trials were to be conducted.[15]

In addition to the Tokyo Trials, war crimes trials were held in the Philippines, China and other parts of the former Japanese Empire, and in these cases Allied interpreters were usually involved, both in the pre-trial interrogations and in the trials themselves. One of the leading British interpreters involved in war crimes trials in the initial phase was Colonel Cyril Wild (1908–46), who survived three and a half years as a prisoner of war on the infamous Burma–Siam Railway. He was in a unique position, both in terms of his Japanese linguistic skills and of his personal experiences as a prisoner of war. He had not been a language officer before the war and did not attend either the Bedford School or SOAS, so how did he acquire his knowledge of Japanese?[16]

In 1931, Wild was studying classics at Oxford, but he abandoned his course half-way through to accept a job with the Rising Sun Petroleum Company in Japan. He attended a language course in Japan, as was expected of the company's expatriate employees, and throughout his years in Japan he continued to make efforts to improve his knowledge of the language. In 1940, after the outbreak of war in Europe, he returned home and joined the Army, which at first sent him to Northern Ireland. To the War Office perhaps this seemed the best place to send a Japanese linguist. Eventually, good sense prevailed: he was sent out to Singapore as an interpreter and intelligence officer. When the meagre British and Commonwealth garrison could no longer hold out against the Japanese forces that had invaded Malaya and rapidly fought their way down to Singapore, the British commander, Lieutenant-General Arthur Percival, had no option but to surrender. In order to finalize the terms of the surrender, Percival and three other men passed through the Japanese lines to their fateful meeting with the

Japanese commander, Lieutenant-General Yamashita Tomoyuki. Wild was one of them, as Percival's interpreter, and it was he who carried the white flag as he walked alongside Percival through the Japanese lines. Wild was the only one of those four who was also present at Singapore on 12 September 1945, when General Itagaki Seishirō, on behalf of Field Marshal Terauchi, surrendered all Japanese forces in South East Asia to Mountbatten.

During the intervening years between 1942 and 1945, Wild was a prisoner of war, first in Singapore and then on the Burma–Siam Railway. During his period on the railway, he worked tirelessly to do what he could to lighten the punishments meted out to the prisoners and to stand up for all who were forced to work in the terrible conditions on the railway, as many subsequently testified. After the Japanese surrender, Wild was free once again, but instead of heading home to England he went back to Singapore and applied himself to the task of investigating war crimes suspects.

Wild flew to Manila, for example, to interview Lieutenant-General Yamashita, whom he had first met during the surrender negotiations in February 1942 but who was at the end of the war in overall charge of Japanese forces in the Philippines. Wild formed the impression that Yamashita was telling the truth when he disclaimed any knowledge of the atrocities that had taken place during the Malaya Campaign. Nevertheless, as Wild was fully aware, the prosecution was to argue that, as commanding officer, Yamashita bore responsibility for the behaviour of the men under his command even if he had neither ordered nor known of the atrocities. Yamashita was indeed found guilty and was hung, but the verdict remains controversial.[17]

In December 1945, Wild was at last reunited with his family in England. In February 1946, he returned to Singapore, this time with his wife, to continue his investigations. He personally arrested some members of the Kenpeitai and other suspects, and he gave evidence in some war-crimes trials that took place in Singapore and Tokyo (the International Military Tribunal for the Far East). For example, he was a witness at the trial of Sergeant Aoki Toshio, who was accused of mistreatment of British POWs at Songkurai Camp on the Burma–Siam Railway in November 1943. At the trial in February 1946, which ended in a guilty verdict and a sentence of three years' imprisonment, one of the pieces of evidence was Wild's translation of Aoki's confession. Aoki had dictated this confession to Wild and an Australian lieutenant-colonel, L. F. G. Pritchard, at Outram Road Jail in Singapore in October 1945, and Wild had written down an English version then and there.[18]

Wild's knowledge of Japanese had proved indispensable for the surrender negotiations in Singapore in February 1942, for his attempts to stand up for those labouring on the Burma–Siam Railway and for his post-war work as interrogator. He had survived more than three years as a prisoner of war. In 1946, he was on his way back from Hong Kong to Singapore, to participate in war crimes trials for which he had prepared much of the evidence, when he died in an aeroplane crash. It was a tragic end to a life in which he had had to face the most extreme tasks that any interpreter can be asked to deal with.

Some of the linguists we have met in previous chapters also became involved in war crimes trials. Bawden, one of the Bedford graduates, was one of them. When the war ended, he had been in HMS *Anderson* in Ceylon with nothing to do. In early December 1945, he was sent to Hong Kong along with two other Bedford graduates. Later he recalled what happened to him there:

> We reported to an intelligence office where, again, there was no real work to do. However, I remember very clearly spending some days at the Supreme Court, supervising Japanese internees who were translating depositions for a war crimes trial which was in progress. Even at the time, it seemed to me that this particular trial was a rather dubious procedure, and the verdict a foregone conclusion. I was invited to witness the subsequent hangings, but declined the privilege. Hong Kong was in those days a ravaged city. Most of the houses above harbour level had been looted, right down to the doors and window frames, apparently in the interlude between Japanese collapse and the British resumption of authority.

Another Bedford graduate, Ian Willison, also spent some time in Hong Kong translating materials for war crimes trials and then did similar work in Tokyo. Unlike Wild, Bawden and Willison had never themselves been prisoners and perhaps for this reason were less convinced by the trials.[19]

Linguist interrogators

For many months after the Japanese surrender, linguists were busy screening, translating and interrogating. Those who had studied at the Bedford School and then worked as codebreakers were less well prepared for this kind of work, since they had been trained for documentary work. Nevertheless, some Bedford graduates found themselves assigned to interrogation work in SEATIC, which moved from Delhi to Singapore on 20 September 1945 and later to Johore Bahru, just across the strait from Singapore.

One of the most enviable tasks for the linguists fell to Robinson, who had been one of the key figures at the WEC in Delhi and had risen to the rank of major. He was given the job of collecting the codebooks from Japanese units, as had been agreed under the terms of the surrender on 2 September. The point of this exercise was not only to prevent Japanese units from continuing to communicate with each other in code but also to enable the codebreakers to decrypt the messages they had not been able to decrypt earlier. Robinson was provided with an aeroplane and an escort, and he travelled to the various countries that had been occupied by Japanese forces, gathering all the codebooks he could find. According to his colleague Lloyd-Jones, he had somehow acquired an ability to speak polite Japanese by this time. This made his mission easier, since in several destinations he and his escort were the first Allied soldiers the Japanese troops had seen. When he arrived on one of the islands that now form part of Indonesia, his Japanese hosts showed him a well-stocked wine-cellar left by the Dutch and urged him to have as much of its contents as he liked loaded on to his plane. Lloyd-Jones, who told this story, failed to say whether Robinson took up this offer.[20]

One Bedford graduate who needed retraining was Joseph Ward. He completed the last course, which ended in September 1945. By that time, work on Japanese coded messages at Bletchley Park had come to an end. He was sent to Karachi to do a course in spoken Japanese, and when that was finished he and his fellow students were, he recalled, 'put into teams engaged in the screening of Japanese prisoners-of-war and war crimes investigation', but he did not feel that he had sufficient command of Japanese:

For my part, occasional screenings of prisoners-of-war were hampered by my non-fluency in Japanese, except where the interviewee turned out to be fluent in English. I explained my difficulties to my commanding officer ... and I was (thankfully) relieved of further interrogation work. ... For a few months thereafter I was engaged in investigating allegations of war crimes by Japanese soldiers against local (Malayan) citizens, which could generally be done in English or through interpreters.

He was subsequently sent to Burma to work in a war crimes court. 'None of my duties in this period required any knowledge of the Japanese language', he noted, 'though I found such knowledge helpful, eg when checking original documents.'[21]

Whitehorn also did the Karachi course, and after he had finished it, he was promptly put to work:

Our next move was by flying boat to Singapore via Calcutta. I was housed at Johore Bahru, across the causeway from Singapore island on mainland Malaya, in colonial style houses which had been turned into an officers' mess. From there we travelled into Singapore daily to a translation centre. We were supposed to help with the translation of the diary of the head of the Japanese Military Police in Bangkok. He had written it in minute characters, but he sat there obligingly re-writing it into more legible characters and explained things which we didn't understand, even though this was likely to be used in evidence against him as a war criminal. I don't think that we who had just finished the language course contributed anything to the exercise.[22]

From the recollections of Ward and Whitehorn, it is clear that graduates of the Bedford and Karachi schools were mostly out of their depth when it came to interrogating prisoners and dealing with situations requiring a good command of spoken Japanese.

By contrast, the SOAS graduates were well prepared, even for interrogating high-ranking Japanese officers, provided they had done one of the eighteen-month courses. Two such SOAS graduates were Allen and Cortazzi, who in 1946 interrogated Lieutenant-Colonel Fujiwara Iwaichi (1908–86) at Changi Gaol in Singapore. Fujiwara had risen to prominence as the founder of the 'Fujiwara Kikan' or 'F-Kikan', which was a special operations unit assisting independence movements in British India, Malaya and the Dutch East Indies. At the request of Allen and Cortazzi, Lieutenant-Colonel Fujiwara wrote down his views on various topics such as the Imphal Campaign and the Indian National Army, and these essays were translated and published in a SEATIC bulletin. The significance of these essays lay in the fact that India's future status was by no means settled. After 1941, the Indian National Army had encouraged resistance to British rule in the hope of putting an end to British control over India. Now that the war was over, Britain could no longer ignore the passion for Indian independence, but it was not until 1947 that Britain announced that India would become an independent country. When Fujiwara was being interrogated, all this still lay in the future.

The same issue of the SEATIC bulletin that carried Fujiwara's historical essays also included one he had written entitled 'The Policy That Should Be Taken for the Construction of a New Japan'. This was included by the translators as an illustration, as they put it, 'of the mind of a typical Japanese officer of high rank who obviously intends to have a say in his country's future'. In the essay, Fujiwara made no attempt to disguise his beliefs:

> In the light of Japanese history and character, I believe that a system centred around the Emperor is absolutely necessary for justice, order and unity. Because one group of politicians between the Emperor and the people abused their powers, the Communists try to show that this was the fault of the Imperial system.

In other words, like many others, he was hopeful that the pre-war political system could continue in the future. He concluded his essay with the claim that 'Japan has the mission of protecting East Asia from the Communist menace.' In this respect, too, it is evident that the war had not made much of a difference to his views. By this time, 1946, Japanese communists had been released from Japanese prisons and for the first time the Japanese Communist Party became a legal entity. In the longer run, however, the party became a victim of the Cold War when the Japanese government aligned itself with US policy towards the Communist world, a policy change that doubtless pleased Lieutenant-Colonel Fujiwara.[23]

Another senior Japanese officer who was interrogated by members of SEATIC was Colonel Hayashi Hidezumi of the Kenpeitai, who was chief of staff to Lieutenant-General Tsuchihashi Yūichi in French Indo-China. He was interrogated by Major Arthur Newington (1923–88) in

265

Saigon. Newington already had a lot of experience by this time. He had done a Japanese course at SOAS and had later worked in one of the Mobile Sections moving eastwards through India and Burma until the Japanese surrender. According to Allen, he was regarded as one of the best Japanese speakers at SEATIC and also as a capable interrogator. During the interrogation, Newington discovered that Colonel Hayashi had not thrown away his diary. This was unusual, but he may have decided to retain it because he had written the entries in the cursive 'grass script' (*sōsho*) that he might have assumed no foreigners would be able to read. Newington, at any rate, could not read it, so he had Hayashi write it out in more legible form. There was an obvious danger here: Hayashi might rewrite it rather than just transcribe it. To avoid such a possibility, Newington got two young translators, John McEwan (1924–69) and Ian Graeme-Cook (1924–59), to check that what Hayashi wrote down matched what was written in his diary. What Newington did not know was that, before handing his diary in, Colonel Hayashi had already gone through it obliterating with black ink any compromising passages, a fact that Allen learnt from Hayashi himself when he met him in Tokyo many years after the end of the war. It was in this way that Hayashi managed to evade prosecution.[24]

The two young translators who checked Hayashi's transcription, McEwan and Graeme-Cook, would not have been able to read the passages Hayashi had obliterated with ink and perhaps did not realize the significance of the deletions. All they could do was check that the transcription matched the diary, and, not surprisingly, they found that it did indeed match. As former 'Dulwich Boys', McEwan and Graeme-Cook were both well trained in reading handwritten Japanese, but McEwan had done exceptionally well. His final report from SOAS was outstanding, and his RAF report shows that he was well equipped to deal with the demands of the job: 'he is extremely keen and hardworking, and has acquired a very good knowledge of written Japanese. He is one of the few translators in SEATIC competent to translate all categories of Japanese documents.' According to his obituary, 'he was mentioned in despatches from Burma for deciphering a crucial but seemingly undecipherable message in execrable handwriting', but I have not been able to confirm this. What is certain is that, in September 1945, he went to Saigon with General Gracey, who took over French

Indo-China from the Japanese occupying forces led by General Tsuchihashi, and it was there that he checked Colonel Hayashi's transcription of his diary. McEwan is reported by one of his former colleagues to have conversed with (interrogated?) Field-Marshal Count Terauchi Hisaichi, either in Saigon or, after February 1946, in Johore, but unfortunately no further details have yet come to light. It is, sadly, so often the case that the contributions made by individual linguists can now no longer be traced. [25]

Britain and Japan during the Occupation

Since the Allies had expected that Japan would not surrender until they had actually invaded the Japanese mainland, planning for the Occupation of Japan was not well developed when the war ended. In August 1945, the US government declared that the 'United Kingdom, China and the Soviet Union have a responsibility to participate with the United States in the Occupation and military control of Japan and the obligation to assume a share in the burden.' At that stage, the US government was clearly thinking of a multinational occupation, just as in the case of Germany, which was divided into zones under the control of the Soviet Union, the United States, Britain and France. In the case of Japan, President Truman decided that General MacArthur, who had been appointed Supreme Commander of the Allied Powers (SCAP), would be in overall control. The Occupation of Japan, therefore, was bound to be politically and organizationally dominated by the United States, which had played the leading role in the war against Japan. It soon became clear that the Soviet Union would not participate in the Occupation if it meant accepting MacArthur's overall control, and that China would not participate because of growing domestic conflict between the Nationalists and the Communists. What role, then, was left for Britain to play in the Occupation, and who was going to represent British interests in post-war Japan? [26]

Unlike most of the other British personnel who were in Tokyo Bay for the surrender ceremony on 2 September 1945, Beasley and Gowing, both Boulder graduates, were sent ashore right away. They were among the first British personnel to set foot in Japan after the end of the war, but each had a different job to do.

Beasley stayed at first in Yokohama and then went to the US Naval Headquarters at Yokosuka as British naval intelligence liaison officer. He recalled in his memoirs that he found it easy to slot into his new role: 'The job was made easier by several circumstances; my American training; the presence of several former Boulder students on the intelligence staff; the fact that I arrived with a case of whisky at a time when supplies of alcohol were desperately short.'[27] Once again, it seems, Beasley had smoothed his way with a crate of booze. Beasley wrote his memoirs many years after the end of the war, and as a historian, he was well aware that his memory was an unreliable witness. Yet it seems unlikely that he made up those occasions when he used alcohol to smooth his way.

Beasley shared a house in Yokosuka with two American Boulder graduates, and together they worked on a detailed examination of the contents of the Japanese naval base. He also had to interpret for NavTechJap specialists sent out from Britain in search of technical information. He heard rumours of possible uprisings against the occupying forces, but they turned out to be completely without foundation. What struck him much more forcefully was the poverty, and the desperation with which people were willing to sell treasured possessions in order to be able to buy food and survive. When he had finished his assignment in Yokohama, Beasley was posted to the Naval Intelligence Section of the British Liaison Mission in Tokyo. The Liaison Mission served as Britain's official representation in occupied Japan until the British embassy resumed its functions in 1952, when peaceful relations between Japan and the Allied Powers (but not the Soviet Union) were restored. Beasley's job there was to gather information on political and economic developments in Japan for inclusion in the monthly report to London. In March 1946, he was recalled to London and sent on leave pending demobilization. His war was finally over.[28]

Gowing, on the other hand, went straight to Tokyo and was based there in the former British embassy until early 1946. His journey from Yokohama to the embassy, which still lies opposite the Imperial Palace, was sobering:

Wherever one looks in Yokohama, Kawasaki or Tokyo it is the same story—a scene of almost complete and utter destruction. ... Along the whole length of [the] Tokaido highway from Yokohama to the

Imperial Palace, I don't think I saw more than half a dozen buildings completely intact. ... Having lost our way in a city where every road is so battered as to look like every other, we finally drove round the moat surrounding the Imperial Palace (itself burnt to the ground by sparks from the city fires), past the shells of the once arrogant War and Navy Departments, past the ruins of the Foreign Office and the grim charred shell of the Ministry of Justice ... and drove through the imposing iron gates into the British Embassy compound. In distinct contrast not a window was broken and the Coat of Arms over the entrance shone out bright and triumphant, having been covered with an old sack for over 3 years.

Gowing's role, until April 1946, was to serve as secretary to the chief political advisor in the United Kingdom Liaison Mission.[29]

Both Beasley and Gowing thus ended up in the former British embassy buildings, but what had happened to the embassy during the war? The embassy compound had, surprisingly, remained intact, including the Royal Coat of Arms over the entrance, which, Gowing tells us, was left in place throughout the war but covered with a sack. The embassy was looked after throughout the war by Swiss diplomats, who had an increasingly difficult time as bombing raids increased and food supplies dwindled. The Swiss handed over the embassy to a Foreign Office official who had served in Japan before the war. His name was Dermot MacDermot (1906–89), and he was of Irish aristocratic descent. MacDermot had recently arrived in Manila to reopen the British consulate-general there but on 25 August was ordered to Japan on 'special service'. He arrived in Japan on 1 September 1945 on HMS *Whelp*, the first British ship to enter Yokohama since 1942; the vast and normally busy harbour was, he reported, completely deserted and empty apart from two small freighters, a sunken aircraft carrier and an American hospital ship. He reopened the British consulate in Yokohama and sent his first despatch back to London before making his way on to Tokyo.[30]

MacDermot's official position in Japan was Foreign Office representative with the commander-in-chief of the Pacific Fleet, and once he had restored the embassy compound to British control, it was immediately taken over as a naval shore station. MacDermot remained at the embassy and established contacts with American Occupation officials but, as he complained in November, 'Since leaving Manila I have received no guidance whatever regarding British interests in or policy towards the Allied occupation of Japan.' In 1946, the Royal Navy left the embassy compound and it then became the United Kingdom Liaison Mission in Tokyo. By then, MacDermot had returned to Manila as consul-general.[31]

Who was this Dermot MacDermot? He had first been to Japan in 1920 as a student interpreter in the Japan Consular Service and held a number of consular posts in Japan in the period up to the outbreak of war. He was repatriated from Japan in 1942 via Lourenço Marques and subsequently served for most of the rest of the war in Australia and the United States in non-diplomatic capacities. In Australia, he worked at Central Bureau, General MacArthur's codebreaking organization. In late 1943 and early 1944, he seems to have been working at the British Political Warfare Mission outpost in Denver, Colorado, which was responsible for propaganda directed towards Japan, but then he was transferred elsewhere. He was most likely being used for his knowledge of Japanese and his familiarity with Japan, but he disappears completely from the records until the end of the war. He remained in Japan until 1946 as the senior Foreign Office representative at the Liaison Mission and later served as British ambassador to Indonesia and then Thailand, but there is undoubtedly something of a mystery about his wartime activities. It is difficult to believe that his knowledge of Japanese was wasted, but what was it being used for? Once again, it has proved extremely difficult to throw any light on the wartime activities of an individual participant.[32]

The Occupation of Japan was from the outset going to be under the control of General MacArthur, who would have absolute power to act as he saw fit. The US government agreed that a contingent of British Army personnel would participate in the Occupation, but the Chiefs of Staff in London insisted that Royal Navy and RAF units participate as well, and that Commonwealth personnel be included. After protracted negotiations, it was eventually agreed that a British Commonwealth force consisting of British, Indian, Australian and New Zealand units would participate under the command of the chief of the Australian General Staff, Lieutenant-General John Northcott. Finalizing the arrangements took several months, and as a result it was not until February 1946 that the first BCOF units arrived in Japan, nearly six months after General MacArthur set up his Occupation headquarters in Tokyo. The military government of the whole of Japan remained the responsibility of the United States, but the BCOF was given responsibility for demilitarization, destruction or disposal of Japanese military equipment and munitions, reception and processing of returning Japanese troops and fulfilling the decrees of SCAP in one designated area of Japan far from Tokyo. The prospects for having any influence on the Occupation were slim.[33]

BCOF was made responsible for the western extremity of Honshu, including Tottori, Shimane, Yamaguchi, Hiroshima and Okayama Prefectures, and the whole of the island of Shikoku. Initially, BCOF consisted of over 35,000 military personnel, of whom 32 per cent were Australian, 28 per cent British, 27 per cent Indian and 12 per cent were from New Zealand. The air force contingent was based in Iwakuni, but otherwise BCOF had its headquarters in Kure, a port city near Hiroshima. Kure had been Japan's largest naval base and naval dockyard, and as a result was heavily bombed in 1945. In 1946, it was still 'a ruin of bombed buildings and twisted webs of girders', as Allan Clifton, an Australian translator, described it; 'the houses were ramshackle and facilities primitive', and the black market was 'a great sprawling collection of rickety booths on a wide bomb-cleared space'. Clifton was shocked to find that many women had turned to prostitution out of sheer necessity, most poignantly one who had lost her husband and all four of her children in the atomic bomb blast in nearby Hiroshima.[34]

Since BCOF needed to have Japanese-speakers on hand to manage relations with local mayors and police chiefs, and translators to monitor the press, many Australian and British linguists were posted to Japan to cover the language gap. That was not necessarily an enticing prospect. Clifton was apprehensive before he reached Japan. How would the defeated Japanese respond to their conquerors? Would he be safe? James Sutherland, a Bedford graduate who had actually volunteered to take part in the Occupation, felt the same and wondered if he had been right to volunteer. They wondered if their presence would be resented, or if they would even be attacked. In the end, they were both relieved and surprised to find that none of the Japanese they met seemed to show any signs of resentment; on the contrary, they went out of their way to be helpful. This was a fairly universal experience: some put it down to obedience to the emperor's broadcast at the end of the war, others to war-weariness and a recognition that Japan was in no position to continue fighting. So far had the pendulum swung that, when Clifton saw former soldiers of the once mighty Imperial Japanese Army returning home, he felt only sympathy: 'No one watching them could fail to feel stirrings of pity for them. An Allied interpreter went among them, offering a cigarette here and there.'[35]

The tasks awaiting the interpreters were varied and demanding. Clifton was sometimes required to act as a court interpreter when Japanese defendants were brought before the British Military Court, and at other times he was searching out weapons and other military equipment that had been hidden in the last two weeks of August between acceptance of the Potsdam Declaration and the arrival of the first Allied troops. He also found himself translating love letters between Australian soldiers and Japanese women, and even facilitating negotiations with Japanese prostitutes.[36]

How did the members of BCOF adapt to living in defeated Japan? In 1946, a well-illustrated manual, *Know Japan*, was published 'to provide members of the British Commonwealth Occupation Force with some of the essential background to an understanding of Japan and its people', as Lieutenant-General Northcott, the commander-in-chief, put it in his preface: 'Although we may not like the Japanese people', he wrote, 'we must learn something of their history and customs, so that we can help them to make themselves fit to take their place alongside the other peoples of the civilized world.' The policy on fraternization was severe: 'You must be formal and correct. You must not enter their homes or take part in their family life. Your unofficial dealings with the Japanese must be kept to a minimum.' Despite all this, however, the ninety-four pages of the manual had nothing to say about the war. There was, it is true, a photograph of the devastation of Tokyo in 1945 and some dismissive comments on State Shinto (the nationalistic religion of Japan up to the end of the war), on Bushido (a militaristic form of the Way of the Warrior, which had earlier been a code of behaviour for samurai) and on the militarization of schools in pre-war and wartime Japan. On the other hand, the rest of the manual contained photographs of a castle amid cherry blossoms, a tea ceremony and a sumo tournament, and reproductions of several woodblock prints, including, on the cover, a print of Mt Fuji by Hiroshige. There was even a mention of the *Tale of Genji*, 'a masterly work that describes in great detail the mannerisms, art, and wit of the Court of that period'. In other words, it resembles a guide for cultural tourists more than anything else and is completely different in tone from the propaganda film directed by Frank Capra, *Know Your Enemy: Japan*, which was released in August 1945. This is certainly curious. The compiler of *Know Japan* evidently knew a lot about Japan and had affection for its cultural traditions; he or she may well have had personal experience of Japan in the 1930s, when the military were becoming increasingly dominant in Japanese society. What is clear, at any rate, is that the compiler was well disposed towards Japan and that this was the approach that the BCOF authorities wanted to inculcate.[37]

The official BCOF policy on fraternization was actually much stricter than US policy and extended even to Emperor Hirohito (1901–89; now known by his posthumous name as Emperor Shōwa) himself. During the war, Allied propaganda treated him much the same as Hitler and Mussolini, but General MacArthur decided to grant him immunity from prosecution. This decision was controversial, and the debate over Hirohito's war responsibility has continued ever since. Be that as it may, after the end of the war he put himself much more in the public eye and attempted to rally the battered population. In November 1947, he visited western Japan, which lay within the area of BCOF's responsibility. A notice was issued in the name of the commander-in-chief of BCOF that no units were to make any official recognition of the visit and no personnel were to attend any functions in an official capacity; in any case, the emperor would not be visiting any BCOF bases. When the governors of Yamaguchi and Hiroshima Prefectures informed BCOF that there was a plot by Korean communists to assassinate the emperor and requested that military police be provided to protect him, the reply they received was that protection of the emperor was a purely Japanese responsibility and BCOF would not help. In the event, the emperor's visit passed without incident, and he addressed a huge crowd in Hiroshima.[38]

BCOF in effect refused to have anything to do with the emperor's visit. In daily life, however, the BCOF's fraternization policy was hard

273

to enforce. After all, those who did the cleaning, washing and ironing for the military personnel were mostly local Japanese women, and it is clear from the photographs kept by members of BCOF that good relationships were established with them.[39]

Who were the linguists participating in BCOF? When the war ended, all US linguists had been withdrawn from ATIS so that they could participate in the Occupation as a corps of American linguists operating under General MacArthur. In September 1945, therefore, the Australian armed forces began to prepare for future needs during the Occupation of Japan. As a first step, CSDIC, which had first been established in Melbourne in 1942 and then absorbed into ATIS under General MacArthur, was reconstituted, this time on the island of Morotai (now part of Indonesia) with the objective of training a corps of interpreters for Occupation needs. At this stage it consisted entirely of Australian linguists who had been trained at the Royal Australian Air Force language school in Sydney, which had begun operating in July 1944 with teaching provided by Margaret Lake of Sydney University, whom we encountered in chapter 9 when she was teaching Professor Room; Professor Sadler and a new member of staff, Joyce Ackroyd (1918–91), had also done some of the teaching. These RAAF linguists now underwent some retraining on Morotai to enhance their knowledge of conversational Japanese. Australian CSDIC units reached the BCOF area of Japan on 23 February 1946, and within a month eleven officers had also arrived from SEATIC, including two RAF and six British Army intelligence officers. By July, CSDIC also included four Canadians, three of whom were Nisei, and the number of personnel was over eighty. But there is no surviving list of the BCOF linguists, so how many there were altogether is unlikely ever to be known.[40]

The linguists in BCOF were responsible for gathering a wide range of intelligence from a variety of sources, including newspapers and private letters. Sergeant J. B. Bennett of the Canadian contingent reported on a demonstration that had taken place, with the permission of BCOF, in Hiroshima on 28 May 1946. There had been around 3,000 people present, and from a loudspeaker mounted on a lorry, speakers had protested about the unfair distribution of rice and food and the poor distribution of clothing, and claimed that farmers were holding back rice to sell on the black market. Some representatives of the dem-

onstrators saw the governor of Hiroshima Prefecture and demanded
the dismissal of the Kure police chief on the grounds that his behaviour
during the war had been ruthless. On the other hand, Lieutenant
S. H. Parker of the Royal Welch Fusiliers, who had been trained at
SOAS, noticed an article in a local newspaper that he thought worth
translating and noting. It stated that 'Due to the food emergency,
school pupils are becoming increasingly unfit to assimilate education
due to empty stomachs.' This threatened to diminish the efficacy of the
reformed education system, which was supposed to inculcate a respect
for democratic principles.[41]

Personal letters were of course monitored, too, and they were
translated if they were 'thought to contain matter adversely reflecting
on sentences administered by War Crimes Court and treatment [of
prisoners] whilst detained in the Compounds'. One woman wrote to
her husband, 'Let us repeatedly try as hard as we can to get revenge in
the era of our children or grandchildren. Do you think we can reap
vengeance 50 years from now?' She was evidently thinking that Japan
should in the future take revenge for its defeat. A man detained at
Rabaul wrote to a female correspondent in Kumamoto (his fiancée?),
'My trial took place in May and I was sentenced to 2 years' imprisonment. But I do not regret this in the slightest nor am I disappointed but
rather regard it as an honor.' What action was taken in these cases, if
any, is unknown. There seem to have been few letters containing such
sentiments, either because not many Japanese were thinking about
revenge or because people were too wise to mention such feelings in
their correspondence.[42]

On the other hand, on 30 April 1949 a woman submitted a petition
to BCOF, which was translated as follows:

> I can offer no excuse for the fact that my son, Niimi Masao, on the 30th
> Dec., 1948, entered an Occupation Force railway carriage at Hiroshima
> station without permission and I am deeply grateful for the lenient
> sentence of 3 years imposed by the Court on the 26th of April.

She was referring to the special carriages that were attached to crowded
Japanese trains for the exclusive use of Occupation personnel: Japanese
were forbidden to use them. She pleaded for her son to be allowed to
return home out of consideration for the circumstances of his family,
for his father had been killed by the atomic bomb, his younger brother

aged seventeen earned a pittance in a brewery and his sister was a maid, so without her son 'we can barely eke out a living'. There is now no way of knowing if her petition was treated with sympathy, as it ought to have been.[43]

There are no lists of the British personnel working at CSDIC in Kure, so they are mostly beyond our reach. I managed to find a few survivors, and from their accounts we can get a glimpse of what there was for them to do. One of them is Professor Nish, then a young lieutenant in the Intelligence Corps, who had learnt his Japanese at the School of Japanese Instruction in Simla/Karachi. After the end of the war, Nish worked in Singapore, in a team translating the handwritten diaries of a Japanese general. What he had learnt in India was mostly military Japanese, which was useful for dealing with the military material he was translating in Singapore but not of much use in occupied Japan. Furthermore, he had learnt little about Japan itself and felt unprepared to work in Japan. On arrival in Kure, he was relieved to be called to the office of the American Military Government to be briefed about the recent history and current situation in Japan. Then he got down to the job of scanning the local newspapers and making translations of articles that were of interest to BCOF. In the autumn of 1947, he was posted to the island of Shikoku. British Occupation forces had already been withdrawn from Shikoku, so, until he left Japan in 1948, he was working entirely on his own. He was mostly cooperating with the local Japanese police who were dealing with problems such as rice distribution and the status of Korean and Chinese residents.[44]

Another Briton working at CSDIC was Sutherland, who had learnt his Japanese at Bedford. It took me a long time to find him, for after retiring from his practice as an accountant he moved from Edinburgh to the Borders town of Peebles. I stayed there for two days, since he had an extraordinary recall of the past and, in addition, had kept a lot of material from his days with the WEC in Delhi and BCOF in Kure. He got out his photograph albums from 1946. When sticking in each photograph, he had written a caption underneath identifying the place and the people shown. He told me that after leaving Bedford he had been sent as a sergeant to the WEC in Delhi, where he was mostly decoding messages using a captured code book. He was perfectly capable of doing the translations, but he was required to leave translation to the officers. Occasionally, he said, he did do some translations nevertheless, and he recalled having translated one sent by Japanese forces in Malaya requesting 50,000 condoms. After the end of the war, he was sent to the Indian Army Intelligence Corps Training Centre in Karachi to do a Field Security course, but since the focus was on war-time security it seemed to him pointless. From May 1946 to November 1947, he was in Kure, along with several other Bedford graduates, and was a member of a field security team. They were lodged in wooden huts formerly used by Japanese naval officers, and since most of their colleagues were Australian, they were provided with Australian rations, and these, he was glad to find, were much better than what he had been used to in wartime Britain and India. Kure was in ruins except for the cinema: Sutherland went to see all the Japanese films he could, and he fell for the film-star Takamine Hideko (1924–2010). When I interviewed him in November 2019, barely a month before his death, he showed me with a grin several commercial photos of her that he had bought in Kure in 1946. On the back of one of them, he had written two words in Japanese, Jock (his nickname in the Army) and *koibito* (lover): she was his pin-up girl.[45]

Sutherland had to admit that there was not a great deal for him and his colleagues to do, at least from a security point of view. One day, however, there was a panic. All the telephones in Kure had gone dead. This was obviously a case of sabotage, his superiors thought. His col-league Michael Screech, another Bedford graduate, was sent off to investigate. Without much difficulty, Screech found the place where the underground telephone wires had been dug up and cut. Was it sabotage? Not exactly. What had happened was that the young son of a local farmer had come across the wires by chance. It was just the thing he thought his father needed, so he cut off a length and took it home, innocently unaware that he had cut off all telephone communi-cations in Kure.

Sutherland and his colleagues were also responsible for checking the security in the camps used by the Occupation forces for accommoda-tion. Sometimes they found holes in the fences, but again these were not cut by hostile Japanese. Instead, they were cut by Occupation troops who wanted to get out at night without passing the guardroom. One day, an Intelligence Corps officer told Sutherland's section to visit various schools in and around Kure to check that forbidden topics were not being taught, such as glorification of the Japanese armed forces, and that there were no wartime textbooks in use that had been banned by the Occupation authorities. They obediently set off for the nearest school, only to discover that it was a Japanese public holiday and all the schools were closed, a fact that the intelligence officer was unaware of. Another time they were told to go around the local brothels, using a list provided by the Kure police chief. Their job was to check that the women were not there against their will: each had to give name, age and religion, which were duly written down. From all this, it is difficult not to get the impression that, whatever his expectations had been beforehand, his duties were in fact rather unimportant.

Not far from Kure was Hiroshima. Sutherland told me that the consensus at the time was that nothing would grow there because of the radiation from the atomic bomb. Some of his colleagues suspected that MacArthur had assigned this area to BCOF because Americans did not want to get too close to Hiroshima. On his first visit in June 1946, Sutherland found green shoots growing. There were also street stalls, where he bought a hanging scroll and a silk kimono, and even a bookshop where, as a loyal Scot, he bought a copy of *The Life of Burns* with notes written in the margins by a Japanese reader. On another visit, he came across some boys playing baseball in the ruins. There were indeed signs of recovery and regeneration if you looked for them, he recalled.

Leslie Phillips also visited Hiroshima. He had begun his Army life in January 1945, when he was seventeen. He had already been accepted for a course at SOAS, but first he had to endure six weeks in Glasgow undergoing basic training. After eighteen months, at the end of 1946, he and his fellow students were shipped out to Japan via Singapore, where several hundred Japanese prisoners of war, with 'absolute dejected appearances', came on board to be repatriated:

> Going through the Inland Sea heading to Kure, we could very clearly see the absolute devastation [caused by] the atom bomb dropped on Hiroshima a couple of years previously. Most of the islands were devastated, some had a few pine trees on the side sheltered from the blast—all of this miles away from the target.

This was a shocking introduction to Japan. After Phillips docked at Kure in June 1947, he joined CSDIC and found that he was required to read and translate the local newspapers, marking up any items that might be of importance to the occupying forces, such as murders, fires and possible black-market activity. Later he was assigned to an Australian unit on the island of Shikoku investigating the black-market in fish and vegetables. Again, none of this was threatening or serious, but that probably came as a relief to those who had been worried about how the defeated Japanese would react.[46]

Nish, Sutherland and Phillips were all in the Army. What about the RAF and Royal Navy personnel? Here information is even scantier, but I did find a few survivors. One of them was Bawden, who had been at Bedford and went to Japan as a naval member of BCOF. Earlier he had been at HMS *Anderson* in Ceylon translating decrypts of messages and then in Hong Kong supervising Japanese internees who were translating documents for war crimes trials:

> We were really only waiting for demobilization, but before that happened I went to Japan, taking passage in a fast mine-laying cruiser. Going through the Inland Sea we could see at every turn evidence of the last days of the Japanese navy—the coast seemed to be littered with sunken ships. In Kure I lived on board ship, the town being completely wrecked. Again, there was little to do. I belonged to a unit called Disposal of Enemy Equipment, and looking back I can only remember going round the countryside by jeep looking wisely at dumps of paint and such like. I paid a couple of visits to Hiroshima, not far away. It was still, in April 1946, quite devastated, though superficially the damage looked similar to that in Kure. Life had already begun again, with shops and stalls springing up.[47]

So Bawden is yet another who had little work of any significance to do in the Occupation.

One person on the RAF side was Cortazzi, who in June 1946 managed to get a transfer from Singapore to the British Commonwealth Air Contingent in Iwakuni, south-western Japan. It will by now be unsurprising that he found there was nothing for an intelligence officer to do there, so he was assigned to security duties. 'As there was no obvious security threat', he recalled, 'we had to look for one.' This meant checking schools to make sure that there were no vestiges of wartime militarism, but it soon began to seem pointless: 'We regarded the rules against fraternization with the Japanese as increasingly stupid and irrelevant and ignored them as much as we dared.' His excuse for doing so was that he needed to meet people in order to monitor potentially subversive activities. He stayed there until December 1946, when he was posted to Yonago in Tottori Prefecture to take command of a Provost and Security Flight, which consisted mostly of RAF policemen. Their job was to ensure that Occupation personnel dressed and saluted properly and generally behaved themselves, but they did also concern themselves with the black-market and prostitution. Overall, Cortazzi's verdict was that the security role he played was meaningless and that BCOF fulfilled no useful purpose.[48]

In 1947, the make-up of BCOF underwent profound changes. Owing to the partition and independence of India and Pakistan, all the Indian Army troops returned home. What is more, by April 1948 almost all the British members of BCOF had also left. For the next few years, BCOF consisted almost entirely of a large Australian contingent and a much-reduced New Zealand contingent.[49]

During its short life, BCOF provided a large number of wartime linguists with employment and the opportunity to visit Japan, but in later life their recollections of that period lack the excitement, urgency and sense of purpose that their wartime work had given them. And they were hard put to think of anything important or significant that they had done in Japan. All the same, many of them were drawn to the Japan that they had only studied from a distance and they returned in later life, in some cases often. Sutherland visited Japan with his wife in the 1970s, while Cortazzi spent most of his diplomatic career there.

* * *

During the latter stages of the war, huge quantities of Japanese documents were recovered by American troops, and those that were not urgent were shipped back to the United States for translation in Washington, DC. In June 1944, the Far East Section of the Office of Naval Intelligence in Washington began publishing translations for limited distribution. This process continued throughout the war and in later years, too. A few of them were used when compiling official histories, but the remainder were translated for the sake of completion and had little light to cast on the conduct of the war.[50]

By contrast, most of the British translations of Japanese documents undertaken during and after the war were done in India, Burma and East Asia. However, in 1946 Captain Tuck of the Bedford School had his swan-song when he was asked to take charge of a group required to translate captured Japanese materials at the Royal Naval College, Greenwich. Some of the translators were former Bedford students, and others had done one of the courses in the Naval Section at Bletchley Park; Philip Vennis (1925–99), who spent his post-war life as a school-teacher, was a junior officer in the RNVR and had probably done his Japanese at SOAS. John Cook recalled his six months in Greenwich:

> It came as a welcome surprise to be sent suddenly to Greenwich to meet some old friends from Course IX and a few new translators to work under Captain Tuck's direction. It was a mark of his concern for his old students and of the respect the authorities held for him that he had arranged for us to work only in the mornings—we spent the rest of each day watching the cricket at Lords and generally relaxing—and to be generally treated as rather special residents. We enjoyed all the privileges of the College, including dining in the Painted Hall on the weekly guest nights when we were joined by visiting admirals and invited celebrities. I think there were just 10 or 12 of us translators. My recollection is that the material we worked on was of minor significance but that was not our concern. We regularly started the morning's work by collectively solving *The Times* crossword.

Cook was demobbed in the autumn of 1946 and went to Cambridge, to take up the scholarship in classics he had been awarded in 1943. In later life, he taught classics in schools and ended his career as director of education in Edinburgh.[51]

By 1952, the British linguists scattered all over the world had returned home. Collectively, they had demonstrated the effectiveness of the various wartime courses they had attended. Gradually, however, the wartime courses slipped into oblivion, their contribution forgotten.

12

LOOKING BACK

In the end, the insatiable demands of the Allies for Japanese linguists were met, despite the culpable lack of preparation beforehand and the ad hoc nature of the courses. In Australia, the United States, Britain, India, Mauritius and finally Canada, training programmes were put in place, teachers were found and altogether several thousand men and women learnt enough Japanese to be dependably employed as translators, interpreters and interrogators.

Although the truncated wartime language courses succeeded in imparting enough Japanese to complete beginners to enable them to function effectively and to learn more on the job, it is important not to forget that in the Pacific and in the Burma Campaign large numbers of well-trained Nisei were on the job as well. Many of them had superior abilities in spoken Japanese or in reading handwritten documents, but few of them were commissioned officers. Some of their British or American officers acknowledged the contribution made by the Nisei, yet they generally failed to mention their names.

Again, the success of the courses should not obscure the smaller numbers of Americans, Britons, Canadians and Australians who already at the outbreak of war had a much deeper knowledge of the language than the beginners: people like Lloyd, the Australians Nave and Selwood, and the Americans Walne and Mashbir. There were in fact several dozen British linguists who were well equipped to work with

Japanese in December 1941. Some of them were former language officers or former members of the Consular Service in Japan, who had all undergone rigorous training and had lived in Japan for at least three years. They were taken on by Bletchley Park and by several intelligence organizations in Australia. As Loewe, now the sole survivor of the first course at Bedford, acknowledged to me, 'Their knowledge of Japanese was infinitely superior to ours.' They were not the only ones. Various British residents of Japan before the war, like Andrews, Divers and Cyril Wild, also had a formidable command of the language, but Andrews and Wild became prisoners of war in February 1942 and exercised their knowledge as intermediaries between their fellow prisoners and the Japanese camp authorities.[1]

Did Japanese intelligence officers ever realize that their language was not the natural code that some thought it was? Was it known in Japan that the Allies were devoting considerable resources to their language, that handwritten Japanese documents were being read on the field of battle and that eavesdroppers could understand what pilots were saying as they approached their targets? It is impossible to give definite answers to these questions, but in all cases the probable answer is 'no'. At any rate, there is no clear sign that any measures were taken to safeguard communications, as they should have been if there had been any grasp of how successful the Allies' language training programmes had proved to be. It was probably only during the Occupation of Japan, when large numbers of American, Australian, Canadian and British Japanese-speakers landed in Japan, that Japanese became aware of the Japanese-language training courses overseas. Since these linguists were needed in Japan precisely for their language skills, there was no need to draw a veil over their language training any more, but back in Britain some were still concerned about secrecy, especially at Bletchley Park.

As the end of the war drew nearer, the authorities at Bletchley Park began to realize that the provisions of the Official Secrets Act were not sufficient to preserve the secrecy of the work done on Japanese messages. They were very anxious to prevent the Japanese from finding out that their wartime messages had been decrypted. Why should they have been so anxious? Part of the explanation lies in the desire to keep everything done at Bletchley Park during the war secret, so as not to draw attention to Britain's prowess at codebreaking in the uncertain post-war world. Another factor was probably the desire not to undermine the military defeat inflicted by the Allies on Japan by suggesting that the intelligence war was more important.

One of those who came up against the anxieties at Bletchley Park was Chadwick, whom we have met earlier when he switched from working on Italian codes to Japanese. He had undergone a Japanese course in the Naval Section at Bletchley Park, and at the end of it, he wrote, 'We were warned that if ever we went to Japan, we should not attempt to speak the language, since the forms we knew would reveal the kind of texts we had studied.' An unsigned and undated memorandum, which was probably written early in 1945, makes it clear what precisely the anxieties were:

> The following point is I think worth consideration in connection with keeping secret the purpose and nature of the special knowledge of Japanese 'telegraphese' which has been acquired during the war by members of the three services and by civilians. ... As the war develops, and after Japan's defeat, it is virtually certain that students who have undergone this training in 'telegraphese', but who have learnt no colloquial Japanese, will come into contact with Japanese nationals. ... On the assumption that it is felt to be desirable, and that it is thought to be possible, to conceal after the war the fact that Japanese ciphers have been read, the precautions that could be taken with this object seem to be the following.
>
> (a) explicit warning to all who have been trained in 'telegraphese'
> (b) some instruction in colloquial to be given by non-Japanese to anybody likely to come into contact with Japanese nationals
> (c) if worst comes to worst they should explain that they acquired knowledge through reading plain language intercepts (press, commercial, etc).

In light of Chadwick's recollection, it is clear that the warning he was given related to this memorandum, but the anxieties were probably misplaced, for 'telegraphese' was not a form of the language that was unique to encrypted messages. In Japanese as in English, abbreviation and omission were a common feature of telegrams, for by reducing the number of words you reduced the cost. At any rate, it is doubtful if this warning served any purpose or was even heeded by those to whom it was addressed. But they certainly did take the Official Secrets

Act seriously, and it was only in the 1970s that they began, reluctantly, hesitantly or eagerly, to tell their stories.[2]

In the United States and Australia, it was in 1941 that the fear of war with Japan impelled the authorities to inaugurate courses in Japanese. Britain did so only after the outbreak of war, as we have seen, and Canada much later. Since cogently argued warnings were being sent time and again to the War Office and Foreign Office by the British ambassador in Japan and by the director of SOAS, it is puzzling that these warnings fell on such stony ground. Why did the War Office not heed the warnings? Why was no action taken before December 1941? No definitive answer can be given, but complacency and over-confidence in the supposed impregnability of Singapore must have played a part, and probably a racist assumption of the inferiority of the Japanese armed forces was at work, too. Certainly, there were few indeed who could have predicted not only that Singapore would fall into Japanese hands in less than three months but also that the British and Indian troops in Burma would be forced to retreat all the way to India.[3]

The British wartime courses in Japanese should have started much earlier. It was not that the War Office was unaware in general terms of the advantage of having some knowledge of foreign languages. After all, tests in German had been introduced at the Woolwich Academy in 1855, and later, languages were included in the curriculum at Sandhurst, to say nothing of the language officer scheme that sent officers to Japan for several years. The problem was largely one of scale. During the Second World War, intelligence work involved not just interrogating captured enemy personnel but also gathering documents, monitoring telegraphic and radio transmissions and listening in to air-to-ground communications, and all these interceptions required linguists in much larger numbers than in earlier conflicts. The War Office, like its counterparts elsewhere, failed to anticipate the much greater needs that would be generated by radio communications, and in any case was concentrating on the European war until late 1941.[4]

The British armed forces continued to take language learning seriously after the war, particularly during the Cold War. The Joint Services School for Linguists, which was established in 1951, taught Russian to around 5,000 National Servicemen before it closed down with the end of conscription. Despite the successes of the wartime and post-war courses as factories for the mass production of linguists, they were not matched in later decades by any similar government commitment to language learning. In the United States, the National Defense Education Act became law in 1958, at the height of the Cold War, and explicitly targeted foreign language studies for financial assistance, with the exception of Latin and Greek. More recently, in 2005, the Defense Language Office was created within the US Department of Defense to maintain language and regional experience. In Britain, by contrast, and despite the publication of various government reports into the teaching of Middle Eastern, South Asian and East Asian languages, the decline in language learning has been stark and the impact of so-called 'market forces' on the teaching of all languages in schools and universities in Britain has been disastrous. As in the years before the outbreak of the Second World War, the official neglect of languages in Britain has proved difficult to overcome.[5]

The men and women we have met in the course of this book were in most cases familiar with French, German and Latin and a few had exposure to other languages. In order to learn Japanese, they were uprooted from what was linguistically familiar and comfortable and were made to learn a language completely different from anything they had encountered so far. They did surprisingly well, but what long-term effect did their experiences have on them?

Many of the wartime linguists returned to civilian life and resumed where they had left off, putting their knowledge of Japanese and their experiences of warfare firmly behind them. Captain Lloyd-Jones returned to Christ Church, Oxford, to complete his degree in classics. In 1960, he was appointed Regius Professor of Greek at Oxford and was knighted in 1969. He spoke about his wartime experiences to his children and his pupils. His son recalls:

> He once intercepted a message which led to the destruction of a whole battalion of Japanese troops, ambushed by Gurkhas thanks to his work. Someone came from HQ and told him that and he was then allowed to wear the Army (combat?) flash on his uniform as an honour. I asked, 'Did you think about the widows and orphans?' He replied, 'Not at the time, it was them or us. But years later I did think about it and feel some remorse.' (or words to that effect).

He never went to Japan (though his son did), but in later life he did put together a memoir, which I have quoted from extensively in previous chapters.[6]

Many of the other classicists who had been recruited for Bedford also returned to the fold after the war. Among them were Russell, who became professor of classical literature at Oxford; John Anderson (1924–2015), who became professor of classical archaeology at the University of California, Berkeley; and Chadwick, who taught at Cambridge and became famous for his decipherment of the Mycenaean script Linear B with Ventris. Some switched to other fields, like Maurice Wiles (1923–2005), who became Regius Professor of Divinity at Oxford. Most of them, however, did not become university teachers, pursuing instead careers in other fields after they had completed their degrees. Some became teachers, like David Eunson of Kirkwall, who spent his life as a classics teacher in the Orkney Islands and in Scotland, while Ward became a civil servant. Sutherland became a chartered accountant in Edinburgh, but he welcomed Japanese visiting Edinburgh to his home and kept many mementos of Japan.

Most of the linguists saw much more of the world during the war than they would ever have expected. Many, indeed, had never before been abroad when they were sent to India, Ceylon or Australia. For some, this was an eye-opening experience. Archdale, who led her band of Wrens trained in Japanese Morse to Singapore, ended the war in Australia and decided to stay there. In 1946, she became principal of the Women's College at Sydney University, and in 1958 she became headmistress of Abbotsleigh, an independent girls' school in Sydney. There she reformed the curriculum, introducing sex education and physics and shifting the emphasis from British history to Australian history. She was not the only one to find Australia an attractive option after wartime service there. Eddolls, who had done one of the Bedford courses and had worked at Central Bureau in Brisbane during the war, returned to Oxford to complete his degree and then in 1950 emigrated to Australia, where he worked as civil servant for the Department of Defence. Carson, who had also been at Bedford and Central Bureau, did not even bother to return to Oxford to complete his degree: after emigrating to Australia, he worked as a farm labourer for two years and then for the rest of his career worked as an administrator for the University of Western Australia and then Sydney Hospital.[7]

What is striking is how many of them had distinguished careers in later life. Newcombe of the Naval Section at Bletchley Park became a barrister, a British representative at the United Nations and a delegate to the European Parliament and was given a life peerage as Baroness Elles of Westminster. Parker, one of the Dulwich Boys, became chairman of the British Railways Board and was knighted; he was also the chair of the committee that produced the Parker Report in 1986 into the future teaching of Oriental languages in British universities. Kerry became the Treasury solicitor and was knighted, and Richnell, one of the few Britons who took part in NavTechJap, became director general of the British Library Reference Division. De Moubray, who reached Singapore in August 1945 to be reunited with his parents, became the chief economist at the Bank of England. Many of them received honours, and a large number were elected fellows of the British Academy, including some who have appeared in this book—Bawden, Beasley, Blacker, Chadwick, Cohen, Dore, Hunter, Laslett, Lloyd-Jones, Robins, Russell, Screech and Wiles. The distinction achieved by many of the linguists in later life is more than anything else an indication that those who selected them made the right choices: they did indeed manage to pick out the best of those available.

A considerable number of the linguists were so struck by their experiences of learning Japanese and using it during the war and afterwards that their lives were turned in a new direction and they spent their future careers engaged with Asia. That was the case with Cortazzi, who did a degree in Japanese at SOAS after the war and then became a diplomat. After retiring as British ambassador to Japan in 1984, he was for many years chairman of the Japan Society of London and wrote many books on Japan. There were other diplomats, too. Lloyd, who had taught on the courses in the Naval Section at Bletchley Park, returned to his former profession and became ambassador to Laos. And Ronald Kidd (1926–2003), who had done one of the RAF courses at SOAS and later worked at SEATIC, did a degree in Japanese at Cambridge and later served at the British embassies in Seoul and Tokyo.[8]

Nish, who started learning Japanese at Simla, returned to Edinburgh University to finish off his degree in history, but for the remainder of his career he was a professor at the London School of Economics with a particular interest in Anglo-Japanese relations in the twentieth century. Kenneth Gardner (1924–95), who did one of the SOAS courses during the war, returned to SOAS after the war to get a degree in Japanese and spent his career at the British Library, taking good care of the Japanese collection there.[9]

Without the contributions of those who decided to make a career of Japanese studies, the study of Japan and Japanese in British universities would never have taken off—this was true of the United States, as well. Geoffrey Bownas from the Bedford School became professor of Japanese at the University of Sheffield; Storry became professor of Japanese studies at the University of Oxford; Blacker, Ceadel and McEwan all taught at Cambridge, while O'Neill and Beasley joined Daniels at SOAS. Dore, one of the Dulwich Boys, became a distinguished sociologist of Japan and taught at Sussex University and other institutions. McClellan, who had been born in Kobe and was repatriated to Britain in 1942, did a degree in history at the University of St Andrews and then pursued his career in the United States, finally becoming Sterling Professor at Yale.

Several turned their attention to other parts of East Asia. Robinson, who married Lloyd-Jones' sister, did a degree in classical Chinese at SOAS and then lectured there in Far Eastern history. Loewe, David Hawkes and Twitchett all became distinguished scholars of China, following a similar trajectory, while Rutt, who was a missionary in Korea and later a bishop, became a well-known translator of Korean literature and scholar of Korea. Allen returned to the study of French literature and became reader in French at the University of Durham, but he was best known as a historian of Japan and the Second World War, especially the Burma Campaign in which he took part, and as a broadcaster on programmes such as *Round Britain Quiz* and the arts review *Kaleidoscope*. He was also active in both the European Association for Japanese Studies and the British Association for Japanese Studies, of which he was president in 1980.

Allen and several others who took part in the war as linguists later played significant roles in furthering reconciliation and mutual understanding between Britain and Japan. In retirement, Allen was involved in an enterprise to sponsor contacts and exchange visits between Japanese and British ex-servicemen who had served in Burma. Charles, who had also served in Burma, was for many years a member of the Burma Campaign Fellowship Group, which worked for reconciliation between former enemies.

Many retained an affection for Japan, such as Sutherland and Screech. To what was this due? Paul Gore-Booth (Baron Gore-Booth, 1909–84), who spent more than four years at the embassy in Tokyo until he was repatriated in 1942, offered an explanation in his memoirs:

> The great majority of foreigners, even those who might have been subjected to ill-treatment under interrogation, refused to be turned against the Japan they had known. There was something about the beauty of the country, and the way of life of this unique, serious people that made those who had lived there feel they could forgive much and that, when the current aggressive madness had been purged, they would like to come back.

It was for that reason that his parents-in-law returned to Japan after the war, and that he himself later renewed his acquaintance with Ōta Saburō (1905–?), who as a Foreign Ministry official went to the British embassy on 8 December 1941 with the declaration of war. But Gore-Booth was writing of foreigners who had lived in Japan before the war, like Captain Tuck, and perhaps also of those who had worked in Japan during the Occupation. By contrast, those who had suffered on the Burma–Siam Railway or in other camps knew nothing of the country or its people apart from what they had themselves experienced, so it was understandably much more difficult for Allen and Charles to effect reconciliation between former captives and their captors.[10]

Some of the linguists found themselves at odds with the dominant narrative of the war. McEwan took what was considered at the time to be the unfashionable view that not all Japanese soldiers were war criminals. Allen considered that he had

> an extreme case of vicarious bad conscience. He [McEwan] had done nothing to harm the peoples of the East personally, quite the opposite. But he was one of a people, of a nation, which in his view had wreaked havoc upon the East, and somehow he felt *he* had to make amends.

Similarly, Clifton wrote in 1949:

> For some time after my return to Australia I was hesitant about express-ing opinions that ran counter to the current popular mood, and I

deferred to private prejudices born of lost sons, husbands, and close friends. But I do so no longer. All the libraries of hate-books, all the ostracism and unforgiving exclusionism will not bring back one dead soldier or salve the wounds of the maimed: it could dig the graves of their children.

He wrote instead about rapes perpetrated by members of BCOF and the sexual licence they took in their relations with Japanese women.[11] Allen was criticized for trying to write the history of the Burma Campaign even-handedly, but he grasped one of the outcomes of the war very clearly: 'In the long perspective, difficult and even bitter as it may be for Europeans to recognize this, the liberation of millions of people in Asia from their colonial past is Japan's lasting achievement.'[12]

Very few of the many people mentioned in this book received any kind of honour or recognition of their contributions to the war effort. Allen, Beasley, Storry, Twining and all the others I have mentioned had to content themselves with the knowledge that they had risen to the extraordinary challenges confronting them and had acquitted themselves well. There were a few exceptions: from SOAS, Firth was awarded an OBE for having devised the phonetics courses, but there was nothing for Edwards, who had organized and run the courses in the Far East Department throughout the war. From Bletchley Park, Marie-Rose Egan, who had been working at GC&CS before going to the Bedford School, was awarded an MBE in 1946, Josh Cooper a CMG in 1943 and Tiltman a CBE in 1944: all three of them were said in the official announcements to be simply 'employed in a department of the Foreign Office'. Very belatedly, Nave was awarded an OBE in 1972.[13]

On the other hand, none of the linguists who completed the Japanese courses and served in the field lost their lives as a result of enemy action. By contrast, at least twenty US Army linguists died in action, most of them on Okinawa in 1945; all but one of them were Nisei. Keene had a close shave during the Okinawa Campaign:

> Early one morning I was standing on deck when I noticed in the sky a black point that seemed to be growing larger. After a time I realized that it was a kamikaze plane, obviously heading toward my ship, the largest transport in the convoy. I stared at the plane unable to move. I would probably have been killed if on its downward path the plane had

not struck the top of the mast of the next ship and plunged into the water. A slight miscalculation on the pilot's part had saved my life.

Captain Paul V. Halley of the Canadian Army was not so fortunate: on Christmas Day 1944, while broadcasting propaganda to Japanese forces in India, his jeep was hit by a shell and he was killed. Storry and his companions at Imphal were certainly in great danger, and so were Hall and the others who went ashore at Leyte, but they all survived. A few were killed in aircraft crashes as they made their way home at the end of the war, it is true, and, as we have seen, many young Wrens who had been trained in Japanese Morse lost their lives when their ship was torpedoed in the Indian Ocean.[14]

The end of the war came as a relief to the pilots, sailors and troops on the front line, but it also involved a major adjustment for those who had worked in the intelligence war, as Norris recalled:

> In retrospect, Bletchley did not seem to us at the time to be at all strange, once we had experienced a few weeks of initiation; it very soon became part of our lives; it was normality itself, and it seemed as if it was set to go on for ever. What was unnerving was when everything stopped so abruptly: it was the world outside, to which we now had to adapt, that was strange and foreign; it felt as if part of our own being had suddenly died, and the mental shock was probably akin to that experienced by a hospital patient following an amputation.

Norris visited Bletchley Park again in 2001 and was much moved: 'I got the sensation that what had changed most was the total absence of any of my own little band with whom we had all been so very closely bonded; I felt like a ghost moving among silent ghosts.'[15]

I have lived with these ghosts for several years while writing this book, trying, sometimes in vain, to catch glimpses of their lives. The French Nobel prize-winner Patrick Modiano once wrote of a small party held in Paris during the war just before a photographer friend disappeared: 'Remembering that evening, I feel a need to latch onto those elusive silhouettes and capture them as if in a photograph. But after so many years, outlines become blurred, and a creeping, insidious doubt corrodes the faces. So many proofs and witnesses can disappear in thirty years.'[16] So many more have disappeared since the end of the war in 1945.

APPENDIX 1

SOAS STUDENTS OF JAPANESE

The Dulwich Boys

There is no official list of the students on the State Scholarship course, known as the Dulwich Boys. The information below comes from the Combined Cadet Force record cards at Dulwich College Archives and from The National Archives (ED 54/123); I have also used ancestry. co.uk and forces-war-records.co.uk to supplement the information. Entries in brackets are missing from Dulwich College Archives, presumably because they did not join the Combined Cadet Force. Sources of the information are given in parenthesis.

Name	Recruited	Left
(Bates, Peter Edward Gascoigne) CBE (1924–2005)	1/5/1942	29/7/1943
Joined the Intelligence Corps and served in India and Burma. Took part in the Occupation of Japan and wrote a book about it. (Recorded interview in sound archive at IWM)		
Church, Henry John Melchior (1924–82)	1/5/1942	16/12/1943

Joined the RNVR and served on HMS
Lanka in Colombo.

Cotes, William Luxon (1924–89) 1/7/1942 16/12/1943

Joined the Intelligence Corps.

(Currie, Gordon)

Joined the Intelligence Corps.

De Moubray, Guy Laurence Layard 1/5/1942 16/12/1943
(1925–2015)

Joined the Intelligence Corps.

(Autobiography, *City of Human
Memories* (Stanhope: Memoir Club,
2005))

Dore, Ronald Philip (1925–2018), 1/7/1942 16/12/1943
CBE, FBA

Taught at SOAS during the war and
then became a scholar of Japan. His
academic career began at SOAS, but
he subsequently held positions at the
University of British Columbia, the
Institute of Development Studies at
Sussex University, the Technical
Change Centre at Sussex, the Institute
for Economic Growth in Delhi,
Imperial College, Harvard University
and Massachusetts Institute of
Technology.

Farthing, Roger David Hadfield 1/5/1942 16/12/1943
(1924–2004)

Joined the Intelligence Corps.

Greenland, Francis Laffan (1924–2001)	1/5/1942	16/12/1943
Joined the Intelligence Corps.		
Hore, Michael Fane (1925–77)	1/5/1942	16/12/1943
Joined the Intelligence Corps and was a major in 1947. (*The Times* 13/5/1947, p. 7)		
Inglis, Kenneth Andrew David (1924–)	1/5/1942	1/4/1943
Joined the RAF.		
Judd, Jean-Pierre (1924–2012)	1/5/1942	16/12/43
Joined the RNVR and served on HMS *Lanka* in Colombo.		
Kay, George Robertson (1925–2000)	1/5/1942	29/7/1943
Joined the Intelligence Corps. Served with Major Stanley Charles in No. 2 Mobile Section in India/Burma.		
Long, Richard Arthur Kingslow (1925–77)	1/5/1942	16/12/1943
Joined the Intelligence Corps.		
Mason, David Charles (1924–2001)	1/7/1942	16/12/1943
Joined the Intelligence Corps.		
McEwan, John Robertson (1924–69)	1/7/1942	1/4/43
Joined the RAF. He graduated from SOAS with a degree in Japanese in 1948 and was immediately appointed to a lectureship at the University of		

Cambridge. (Peter Kornicki, 'John
McEwan (1924–1969): Scholar of
Japanese at Cambridge University', in
Hugh Cortazzi (ed.), *Britain and Japan:
Biographical Portraits*, vol. 10)

(Nelson, Terence Edwin
(1924–2003))
Joined the Intelligence Corps.

O'Neill, Patrick Geoffrey   1/5/1942   16/12/1943
(1924–2012)

Joined the RNVR and later became
professor of Japanese at
SOAS. (Biography by Phillida Purvis in
Hugh Cortazzi (ed.), *Britain and Japan:
Biographical Portraits*, vol. 8)

Parker, Peter, Sir (1924–2002)   1/5/1942   29/7/1943

Joined the Intelligence Corps and
served in India and Burma, reaching
the rank of major. After the war, he
read history at Lincoln College,
Oxford. He became chairman of
British Rail in 1976 and was knighted
in 1993. (Obituary in *Daily Telegraph*,
30/4/2002)

Pearce, Donald Joslin (1924–)   1/7/1942   29/7/1943

Joined the Intelligence Corps and served
until 1947. Went to the United States
in 1949 and became naturalized as a US
citizen in 1952. Completed a degree at
George Washington University in 1953
and spent his career as a librarian.
(Biography on prabook.com)

Pike, John (1924–)   1/5/1942   19/7/1943

Joined the Intelligence Corps and
served in Malaya after the end of the
war. Completed a degree in PPE at
Oxford and joined the Colonial
Service. Ended his career as registrar
of the London School of Economics.
(https://www.questia.com/library/
journal/1G1–147927924/
from-british-military-intelligence-to-
financial-secretary)

Rock, Matthew (1924–)   1/5/1942   16/12/1943

Joined the Intelligence Corps.

Scamell, Hugh Arthur (1924–2007)   1/5/1942   16/12/1943

Joined the RNVR and served on HMS
Lanka in Colombo.

Scanlon, Peter (1924–)   1/5/1942   16/12/1943

Joined the RNVR and served on HMS
Lanka in Colombo.

Sherwood, Peter Barlow (1924–89)   1/5/1942   16/12/1943

Joined the RNVR and served on HMS
Lanka in Colombo.

Stephens, Henry Robert (1924–)   1/5/1942   29/7/1943

Joined the Intelligence Corps.

Walters, Francis Raymond   1/7/1942   16/12/1943
(1924–2017)

Joined the RNVR and served on HMS
Lanka. Completed a degree at Balliol

College, Oxford, in 1949 and then
trained for the ministry in the Church
of England. (*Parish Matters* (The United
Benefice of Woodhouse, Woodhouse
Eaves & Swithland), February 2017,
pp. 20–1)

Wilson, Alexander Galbraith (1924–2014)	1/7/1942	1/4/1943

Joined the Intelligence Corps. After the
war, he did a degree in English at Oriel
College, Oxford. In later life, he became
famous as the composer and lyricist
Sandy Wilson, whose biggest success
was *The Boy Friend*, which opened in
1954. (Obituary in *The Guardian*,
27/8/2014; autobiography *I Could Be
Happy* (London: Joseph, 1975))

Students on later SOAS courses

Only the State Scholarship course, known as the Dulwich Boys, is well
documented. The records that were kept in the former Far East
Department at SOAS appear now to have been destroyed. There were
three types of course: those for interrogators and those for translators
in the Far East Department and those in the Phonetics Department.
Incomplete lists of the names of those in the Army, RAF and Royal
Navy (including women) who did courses in the Far East Department
and the Phonetics Department are preserved in SOAS Archives
(SOAS/REG/01/01/05), but they do not cover the last year of the
war. There is also in The National Archives (HW 67/4) a report on
the Translators III course giving the marks achieved by each student,
and Hugh Norris gives the names of all those on Translators II in his
'Memoir', p. 41. There are some further records of those who did
courses in the Phonetics Department in The National Archives (HW
41/139, HW 14/60). Since several hundred students completed
courses in Japanese at SOAS, it is clear that many names are missing.

APPENDIX 1

It is now difficult or impossible to discover how they put their skills to use during the war. One example is John Russell, 4th Earl Russell (1921–87), the eldest son of Bertrand Russell. After graduating from Harvard, he joined the RNVR and then in 1944 was on an interrogators' course at SOAS, but where he was posted after that is a mystery. (Hugh Norris, 'Memoir', p. 50; Bertrand Russell, *Autobiography of Bertrand Russell (1914–1944)* (New York: Bantam Books), p. 327)

APPENDIX 2

THE BEDFORD JAPANESE SCHOOL

Biographies of all the students at the Bedford Japanese School I was able to trace are given in Kornicki 2019. Since then, I have been able to identify a further three, and their details are as follows.

Brown, Peter (1925–) (eighth course)

Exhibition in English, Selwyn College, Cambridge. After Bedford, he was sent to the Japanese Forces Section, Bletchley Park, as a lance corporal; in late 1944, he was commissioned and sent to the Middle East to take command of a small independent signals unit. He returned to civilian life in 1947 and returned to Cambridge, where he completed his degree and underwent teacher training. He subsequently taught English and then was headmaster of several schools in succession. (Information provided by Mr Brown in an email, 7 October 2019)

Draper, Alan Gregory (1926–) (eleventh course)

Scholarship at The Queen's College, Oxford. After Bedford, he served in the RNVR and then joined the Civil Service, becoming in 1988 the director of the Defence Procurement Management Group at the Royal College of Military Science. (*Who's Who*)

Sutherland, James Summers 'Jock' (1926–2019) (eighth course)

After Bedford, he was sent to the WEC, Delhi, India; after the Japanese surrender, he was sent to Karachi, where he passed a Field Security

Course. He then volunteered to go to Japan as part of BCOF. He spent one year in Kure, near Hiroshima, and then four months in Kurashiki, as a member of a Field Security Section. After demobilization in 1947, he became a chartered accountant in Edinburgh and was senior partner of his firm when he retired to Peebles in 1988. (Information provided by James Sutherland in an interview on 5 September 2019)

APPENDIX 3

SIMLA AND KARACHI STUDENTS

No documentation appears to survive of the School of Japanese Instruction that opened at Simla and was later transferred to the Intelligence Corps Training Centre at Karachi. The following are known to have attended the school:

Mason, Richard (1919–97)

After a stint working for the British Council, he entered service in the RAF and served from 1939 through 1944. Attached to the 14th Army as an intelligence officer, he was taught Japanese in a three-month crash course taken in India so as to be able to serve as an interrogator of prisoners of war in India and Burma. He wrote *The Wind Cannot Read* and the *The World of Suzie Wong*, both of which became successful films. Lived in Rome for the last forty years of his life. (Obituary in *The Guardian*, 15 October 1997)

Lyons, Algernon Islay de Courcy (1922–93)

He was at Grenoble University when the Second World War broke out. He made a daring escape over the Pyrenees, was caught and imprisoned in Spain but managed to escape and work his way back to England, where he joined up and served in the RAF for the rest of the war. He served first in North Africa, and then he was sent to India to learn Japanese in three months. He later became a photographer and novelist. (Wikipedia)

In the possession of John Whitehorn, there is a photograph labelled 'School of Japanese Instruction: July 1946'. The reverse of the photograph identifies the location as Karachi and identifies those present. See fig. 44.

APPENDIX 4

RNVR OFFICERS AT THE US NAVY JAPANESE LANGUAGE SCHOOL

The following British naval officers studied at the US Navy Japanese Language School at the University of Colorado Boulder. The first line in each entry gives the dates of entry and graduation (where available) according to the records in the University of Colorado Boulder Archives.

William Gerald Beasley (1919–2006). Entered 26 October 1943 and graduated 16 December 1944. His wartime activities feature in this book. In later life, he became professor of Far Eastern History at SOAS, was elected a fellow of the British Academy and was awarded the CBE. (Beasley, 'Traveller to Japan')

Andrew E. Birrell (1909–92). Entered 23 October 1943. He attended Wadham College, Oxford, 1928–32. From 1933 onwards, he worked in various parts of Europe for a British manufacturing company and in the process acquired fluency in French and German and a working knowledge of Polish and Hungarian; he fled Europe in 1940 and joined the RNVR. He served ashore until 1943; at Boulder, he was appointed the senior officer of the first British group. After Boulder, he was appointed to the staff of Captain Hugh Roy MacGregor Laird, RN (1899–1953), who was in charge of naval intelligence for Admiral James Somerville, the British naval representative on the Combined Chiefs of Staff in Washington, DC. His superior officer was Commander R. Leggatt, RN, 'who had originally recruited, at the Admiralty in

307

London, the candidates for the Japanese course at Boulder' and who had been stationed in Japan for some years before the war.

(Letter from Birrell of 1 April 1982 in UCB archives, Roger Pineau Collection, 3–4)

John Catt (1922–98). Entered 11 May 1944 and graduated 5 August 1945. Catt's wartime activities feature in this book. He entered Trinity Hall, Cambridge, in 1946 and graduated with a degree in natural sciences in 1948. He then taught at Woodberry Forest School in Virginia from 1948 to 1954, when he returned to the UK. In 1959, he founded the educational publishing company that still bears his name, which he sold in 1987. (Letter he sent to Roger Pineau on 26 January 1988: UCB archives, Roger Pineau Collection, 29–7; letters in Roger Pineau Collection, 9–11; biography on the website of the publishing company he founded: http://www.johncattbookshop.com/john-catt-60.)

Donald James Graham Gowing (1921–69). Entered 26 October 1943 and left the course in May 1944 before graduating, for reasons that are unclear. In the autumn of 1939, he entered King's College, Cambridge, as a bass choral scholar studying history. In 1941, he joined the RNVR as an ordinary seaman and in due course was commissioned and sent to Boulder. According to Beasley, Gowing 'fell by the wayside' and did not complete the course, and he was not one of the four who graduated in December 1944. He married the distinguished scientist Margaret Gowing in England on 7 June 1944. His later wartime activities feature in this book. In 1946, he joined the Covent Garden Opera Company and later worked at the Treasury and the Musicians' Benevolent Fund but remained an active opera singer. (Obituary in *King's College Annual Record*, 1970, p. 37; Gowing's Royal Navy service record; Beasley, 'Traveller to Japan', pp. 52, 55; UCB Archives, William J. Hudson Collection 2–15, photocopy of letter from Beasley dated 18 April 1993; TNA, ADM 53/121916, log of HMS *Newfoundland*; for the film of *Swiftsure* in Nagasaki (Gowing is the officer in dark glasses), see https://www.youtube.com/watch?v=nqzoWo1yOVQ)

Stanley Victor Heath (1921–81). Entered 8 September 1944 and graduated August 1945. He entered Sidney Sussex College, Cambridge, in the autumn of 1940 with a scholarship in classics and completed the

APPENDIX 4

first year with first-class honours. He left to enrol in the RNVR and then served on convoy duties in the North Atlantic. Later he was stationed at HMS *Glendower*, a training establishment in North Wales. After Boulder, he was seconded to the US Navy and briefly served in the Pacific before landing in Japan as a member of NavTechJap. He returned to Cambridge in 1946 but left later the same year without completing his degree and after working for Shell for four years in Buenos Aires he became an American citizen in 1955 and worked for Revlon in New York, Tokyo and Hong Kong. (*The Interpreter* 60 (2003); Sidney Sussex College Archives)

Thomas Troy Holles (1925–2012). Entered 8 August 1945 and withdrew. He went to King Edward VII School, Sheffield, and became a midshipman in the RNVR in April 1944. He probably left Boulder as soon as the war ended, for on 21/8/1945 he became engaged to WRNS Margaret Jane Brierley in 1945, whom he married; in 1960, they sailed to Sydney with their three children but returned to Britain in 1963. (*The Times* 21/8/1945; information from his son, Roger Holles)

Victor Wallace Jaffray (1919–77). Entered 8 August 1945 and withdrew. Lived in Scotland. In 1956, he was commissioned as a flying-officer in the RAF Volunteer Reserve Training Branch. (*Supplement to the London Gazette*, 28 August 1956, p. 4921)

Edward Arthur Gilbert Kennedy (1920–2002). Entered 30 October 1943 and graduated in November 1944. He entered Pembroke College, Cambridge, in 1938 to read modern languages, but in 1941 he joined the RNVR and served on the training ship HMS *Eaglet*. On leaving Boulder in the autumn of 1944, he reported to Washington, DC with Beasley and Wilkinson; they were then sent to Vancouver to undergo further training at the Canadian Army Language School in Vancouver and then at the Intelligence School in New York before returning to Washington. While at Boulder, he married WAVE Margarite Dagmar Hofstra. After the war, he finished his degree and graduated in 1946, and then moved to Belfast in Northern Ireland, where he spent his whole career in government service. (Letter Wilkinson sent to Roger Pineau on 26 January 1988: UCB archives, Roger Pineau Collection, 29–7; letter from Beasley of 15 November

1987, UCB archives, William J. Hudson Collection, 5–7; *The Interpreter*, Reunion 2002 2a)

Miroslav Stanley Lansky (1925–2014). Entered 8 August 1945 and withdrew. He was born in London to Czech parents. In 1943, he entered the RNVR, but since he was still too young he spent Trinity Term studying PPE at Balliol College, Oxford. He began his basic training with the Royal Navy in October 1943. On 20 November 1943 as an ordinary seaman he joined the heavy cruiser HMS *Norfolk* at Scapa Flow, which formed part of the escort for Russian Convoy JW55B to Archangel. On 26 December, HMS *Norfolk* engaged the German battlecruiser *Scharnhorst*, which was eventually sunk by other ships in the convoy. In January, he was sent for officer training and then served on HMS *Cassandra* when it was torpedoed on 11 December 1944 and on HMS *Venomous* when it accepted the surrender of German naval forces at Kristiansand in Norway on 15 May 1945. He was then sent to Boulder but after the surrender of Japan returned to Britain and was discharged from the Navy in March 1946. He returned to Oxford, completed his degree and after postgraduate study at the University of Virginia joined the United Nations as a translator in 1955. In 1961, he joined the United Nations office in Geneva. (Biography at http://www.holywellhousepublishing.co.uk/MiroslavLansky.html)

Hugh Macintosh. Entered 11 May 1944 and withdrew. He came from Greenock, Scotland, but has not been identified.

Donald Redpath Menzies (1912–94). Entered 13 December 1943 and withdrew. After leaving school, he had spent more than three years in China working as a reporter for the *Peking Chronicle* then in Japan working for *The Japan Advertiser* for a year, before returning to Canada in 1938. He already spoke Chinese and to a lesser extent Japanese. Served in the RCNVR from 1943 to 1946. After Boulder, being Canadian, he transferred to the Canadian Army Language School in Vancouver when it opened nine months after he entered Boulder. He was sent to Melbourne and served with the Royal Navy on the battleship HMS *King George V* as Japanese interpreter and translator, but by the time he got there the atomic bomb had already been dropped. Reported to Vice-Admiral Rawlings and was surprised when the admiral spoke some words of Japanese to him. Went ashore at Yokosuka as translator on

310

30 August, the first Canadian naval officer to set foot on Japan after the surrender. In 1950, he was living in Chicago as Canadian vice-consul. (Letters from Menzies of 21 April and 19 September 1982 in Roger Pineau Collection, 3–4; *The Crowsnest* 8, no. 3 (1956), p. 19)

George Morris. Entered 8 August 1945 and withdrew. He came from Southampton, but has not been identified.

John Quine (1920–2013). Entered 11 May 1944 and withdrew. He was commissioned in the RNVR in 1942 and volunteered for service in the coastal forces. He operated in motor torpedo boats and in 1943 was on several occasions in action off the Dutch coast. After the end of the war, he was, along with Catt and Wilkinson, attached to NavTechJap (the US Navy Technical Mission in Japan) in Sasebo. At the end of the war, now a member of the Secret Intelligence Service (MI6), he interrogated several senior Japanese figures. He then served in Tokyo from 1947 to 1953 as an MI6 officer attached to the British embassy keeping an eye on the Soviet embassy. He served later in Warsaw, Pretoria and Mauritius, but he is most famous for his role in 'breaking' the Soviet spy George Blake in 1961. (*The Interpreter* 208 (2015); obituaries in *The Daily Telegraph*, 12 June 2013, *The Times*, 2 May 2013)

Derek Percival Scales (1921–2004). Entered 8 August 1945 and withdrew. He was born in England but lived in Australia, and in 1943 he was a lieutenant in the Royal Australian Navy serving as a liaison officer on the Free French Force destroyer, *Le Triomphant*. After the war, he returned to Australia where he had grown up and died in Canberra. He was professor of French at the Australian National University and published *Aldous Huxley and French Literature* (1969). (AWM, P05103.006 and P05103.004)

John English Synnott (1917–82). Entered 11 May 1944 and withdrew. He joined the Royal Navy Volunteer Reserve in 1942. He graduated from Downing College, Cambridge, in 1949 with a degree in English. He went on to teach English in Algiers, Stockholm, Uppsala and Rambouillet. (Obituary in *Downing College Alumni Association Newsletter*, 1983)

Edward Alan Wilkinson (1922–2009). Entered 11 November 1943 and graduated in late 1944. On leaving Boulder in the autumn of 1944, he reported to Washington, DC with Beasley and Kennedy; they were then sent to Vancouver to undergo further training at the Canadian Army Language School in Vancouver and then at the Intelligence School in New York before returning to Washington. He was then sent with Catt to the Pacific via Australia and New Guinea and landed at Yokohama in September 1945. Along with Catt and Quine, he was attached to NavTechJap (the US Navy Technical Mission in Japan) in Sasebo. He left Japan in March 1946 and worked in the Ministry of Defence until his retirement in 1982. (Letter he sent to Roger Pineau on 26 January 1988: UCB archives, Roger Pineau Collection, 29–7)

APPENDIX 5

EVE EDWARDS' TOUR

In 1946, Professor Eve Edwards, who had been head of the Far East Department at SOAS and responsible for all the wartime courses, made an extensive tour of East and South East Asia under the auspices of the Air Ministry and SEAC. The objective was 'to follow up the training of Service candidates by studying on the spot the result of the training they had received'. 'The results of her investigations', reported her obituarist, 'were included in a very detailed report which received full approval from the Services concerned.'[1] Unfortunately, the full report has yet to be found, if indeed it has survived, but the list of those she met on her travels has survived in a truncated copy in the old Colonial Office records.[2] From this list, I have extracted the names of those who are identified as having studied Japanese; some of them are not known from any other sources, but others are mentioned in the pages of this book. They are identified in her report by their initials only, but I have added given names where known. She also identified their current occupation and the courses they had done using the following abbreviations:

SC=Service Course
SSC=State Scholarship Course (i.e., Dulwich Boys)
CAC=Civilian Affairs Course
CC=Civilian Course

Captain J. D. Blount, translator, International Prosecution Section, SCAP (SC)

Captain S. Brickley, c/o War Crimes, Tokyo (SC)

A. A. L. Brown, SEATIC, Johore Bahru (SC)

Flying-Officer J. E. C. Brown, BCAIR [British Commonwealth Air Forces of Occupation], Iwakuni (SC)

Squadron-Leader W. G. Cheeseman, CSDIC, Kure (SC)

Major W. Clarke, War Crimes, Tokyo (instructor in Japanese)

Flight-Lieutenant Hugh Cortazzi, Area Security Office, Iwakuni (SC)

Captain Gordon Currie, GSO III, Intelligence Corps HQ, BCOF (SSC)

Flying-Officer P. J. Davies, Legal Office, Iwakuni (SC)

Captain Guy de Moubray, SEATIC, Singapore (SSC)

Captain C. E. Field, SEATIC, Singapore (SC)

Captain Francis Laffan Greenland, SEAC, Singapore (SSC)

Squadron-Leader J. W. W. Graham, RAF SO, SEATIC (SC)

Captain Ian Gordon Graeme-Cooke, translator SEATIC, Johore Bahru (SSC)

Ex-Sub/Lieutenant James Peter Hobson, translator, ATIS, Tokyo (SSC)

Lieutenant J. C. Hartley, translator SEATIC, Singapore (SC)

Captain Michael Fane Hore, SEATIC, Singapore (SSC)

Lieutenant R. Johnston, in transit (SC)

Captain George Robertson Kay, translator SEATIC, Singapore (SSC)

Lieutenant Louis Levy, SEATIC, Singapore (SC)

Major F. E. Mostyn, War Crimes Commission, Singapore (SC)

Captain David Charles Mason, SEATIC, Singapore (SSC)

Flight-Lieutenant John Robertson McEwan, SEATIC, Singapore (SSC)

Captain Terence Nelson, ALFSEA [Allied Land Forces, South East Asia], Singapore (SSC)

Captain A. J. Newington, SEATIC, Singapore, and War Crimes Commission, Japan (SC)

Major J. Nicholson, SEATIC, Singapore, and War Crimes Commission, Japan (SC)

Captain John Pike, ALFSEA, Singapore (SSC)

Flying-Officer H. I. Parker, BCAIR, Japan (SC)

Captain Matthew Rock, SEATIC, Singapore (SSC)

Captain D. Rose, SEATIC, Singapore (SC)

APPENDIX 5

Captain R. Rowley, SEATIC, Singapore (SC)
Joseph Roggendorf, Sophia University, Tokyo (CC)
Captain Peter Scanlon, SACSEA, Singapore (SSC)
Captain J. Taylor, War Crimes Commission, Singapore (SC)
Flying-Officer T. Townsend, BCAIR, Japan (SC)
Lieutenant C. Versteegh-Meulemans RN, c/o Port Directorate, Kure
  (SC)
Major A. White, SEATIC, Johore Bahru (CAC)
Sub/Lieutenant Francis Raymond Walters, in transit (SSC)

NOTES

PROLOGUE: BRITAIN AT WAR WITH JAPAN

1. Seki 2006, chapter 3; Hack and Blackburn 2004, p. 83.
2. McNaughton claims that, 'In the early months of the war the Allies had lost many experienced intelligence personnel with the fall of Hong Kong, Singapore, and the Netherlands East Indies' (McNaughton 2006, p. 78), implying that it was British and Dutch intelligence staff who were captured. In fact, some US intelligence staff were captured in the Philippines. McNaughton also claims (p. 160) that many British military language officers became prisoners of the Japanese in 1941 but he cites no sources; the only ones known to me who became PoWs are a handful who reached Singapore in 1941 and did not manage to escape, and a couple in Hong Kong, who will all be mentioned later in this book.
3. Derek Taunt, who worked in Hut 6 at Bletchley Park, is unusual in mentioning the work of the translators: Taunt 2001, pp. 80, 83. See also Ralph Erskine's comments in Chadwick 2001, p. 111.
4. Footit and Tobia 2013, pp. 27–8, 35–6; McLelland 2015, pp. 145–8.
5. In his history of GCHQ, John Ferris claims that for the period up to 1945 'the evidence already is in the public domain' (Ferris 2020, p. 4). This is not strictly true: for example, many of the papers concerning the Naval Section at Bletchley Park in TNA in file HW 8/37, and other papers concerning Bletchley Park during the war in files HW 14/24, 14/27, 43/4–5, 43/20, 43/31–3, 43/42, 43/53, etc., have been retained by GCHQ and are not in the public domain.

1. JAPAN MUST FIGHT BRITAIN

1. In his introduction to Cooper 2018, Galambos provides a biography of Cooper. For the suggestion that Cooper spent some time in Japan, see

TNA, HW 4/30, typed comments by N[igel] d[e] G[rey], 10/11/1949. In *My Friend Tertius*, a book for children on Cooper and Tertius, Corinne Fenton has Cooper and Tertius arrive in Fremantle on a freighter and then travel to Melbourne by train. Galambos' account of the submarine arrival is based on that of Cooper's son. According to Jenkins 1992, p. 158, Cooper did indeed arrive by submarine, along with two British consular officials who knew Japanese, Henry Archer and Herbert Graves. Professor Arthur Dale Trendall, who worked with Cooper in Australia in 1942, stated in an interview in 1990 that Cooper had arrived by submarine, but in an interview in the same year Athanasius Treweek, who also worked with Cooper, stated that he had arrived by steamer: Ball and Tamura 2013, pp. 117, 133. It is unclear if the submarine story is true, although three of the five accounts mentioned above state that he arrived by submarine. Arthur Cooper featured in a BBC *Look Stranger* programme (https://www.youtube.com/watch?v=eu8rEJBRSRA&feature=youtu.be), but he has nothing to say there about his life except to state, misleadingly, that he worked for the Foreign Office.

2. TNA, HW 4/30, Nigel de Grey, summary of a talk given by Cooper, 10/11/1949; corroboration of the claims made by Cooper is attached in the form of extracts from GC&CS papers; these sources do not mention Webb's presence.

3. For Webb, see Ballard 1991, p. 163, and Smith 2000, p. 102. For Webb's role in Australia, see chapter 9.

4. Hotta-Lister 1999 and Itoh 2001. For a *Punch* cartoon on the Alliance, see https://en.wikipedia.org/wiki/Anglo-Japanese_Alliance#/media/File:Punch_Anglo-Japanese_Alliance.jpg.

5. Kornicki 2010.

6. Bywater 1925, pp. 75, 98.

7. Honan 1990, chapter 16. The copy of Ishimaru Tōta's book, *Nichiei hissenron* (1933), which Guy Rayment used for his translation *Japan Must Fight Britain*, is preserved in Cambridge University Library and contains Rayment's signature and various marginal notes. There is a strong possibility that this copy was given to Rayment by Admiral Yamamoto Isoroku when he was in London in 1934; see Koyama 2018, chapter 1.

8. For superb coverage of this period, see Best 1995 and 2002 and Iguchi 2010.

9. On royal visits, see Kornicki, Best and Cortazzi 2019; on language officers, see Kornicki 2016 and Best 2002, who gives lists of Army, Navy and RAF language officers on pp. 94–5, 108; hereafter, references to language officers and the years they were in Japan are based on Best's lists. On Shand, see Koyama 2016.

10. On the US scheme, see Packard 1996, pp. 365–71, and Bradford 2002;

Packard provides details of their subsequent duties. On the Australian scheme, see NAA, MP 472/1, 5/18/6582.

11. Shaigiya-Abdelsamad 2015; Baker 2003; Kennedy 1924.

12. NAA, MP 472/1, 5/18/6582, esp. Murdoch to Nave 1/9/1920 and M. Miyata to Navy Office, Melbourne, 20/3/1919; also, memo of 29/6/1916. Nave was taught by M. Miyata, a 'teacher of Japanese in New South Wales'. See also Pfennigwerth 2006, pp. 22–33.

13. CACC, Denn 1/4, untitled typescript dated 2/12/1944 on the development of GC&CS from 1919 to 1939, pp. 4, 8.

14. CACC, Denn 1/4, untitled typescript, p. 8; Denniston 1986, pp. 55–6; Ferris 2020, pp. 121–9.

15. Smith 2000, chapter 2; Pfennigwerth 2006, pp. 32–9.

16. Smith 2000, p. 64.

17. For the Admiralty's appreciation of the successes achieved despite the difficulties posed by the language and Japanese Morse, see Straczek 2008, p. 82.

18. TNA, ADM 116/3114, Dickens memo of 26/10/1933.

19. *An English–Japanese Dictionary of the Spoken Language*, originally compiled by Ernest Satow and Ishibashi Masakata in 1876; the third and fourth editions, revised and expanded by Hobart-Hampden and Parlett, were published in 1904 and 1910 respectively. The fourth edition was reprinted in the United States in 1942 to answer wartime needs.

20. TNA, ADM 223/297, NID, vol. 42, p. 2; Straczek 2008, pp. 90–1, 95. Bennett had also served as air attaché in Tokyo and had undergone training at GC&CS; after the war, he continued to serve in the RAF and retired as a group captain. On FECB, see Smith 2000, chapters 3–5.

21. TNA, FO 371/22192/4200, Craigie to Halifax, 19/3/1938. For the view that three years were necessary, see also TNA, ADM 1/7728, memorandum by J. H. Gubbins, 20/10/1904, ADM 116/3114, memorandum by H. W. Woodward, 9/9/1933, ADM 116/2349, naval attaché, Tokyo, to director of Naval Intelligence London, 12/1/1923, and ADM 116/2351, recommendation of 1925.

22. https://rsgb.org/main/blog/news/silent-keys/2018/11/28/jack-moseley-g2ciw-2018/

23. Herbert and Des Graz 1952, vol. 1, pp. 33–4, 366–9; SOAS Archives, Turner to Lord Scarbrough, 1/10/1945.

24. TNA, FO371/27953, Craigie to Foreign Office, 5/12/1940, 24/3/1941.

25. TNA, FO371/27953, Craigie to Foreign Office, 26/4/1941, 1/7/1941.

26. Liddell 2009, vol. 1, pp. 24, 131, 150–2, 157, 164, 173.

27. Liddell 2009, vol. 1, pp. 178, 200–2. The quotation comes from TNA, PREM 3/252/5, Churchill to Eden, 17/9/1941. Transcripts of Sempill's

monitored telephone and mail communications are contained in KV 2/872 (these are photocopies: the originals have been withheld). Commander McGrath perhaps refers to Donal Scott McGrath (1891–1978), who was a commander in the Royal Navy, but I know nothing of the case referred to by Churchill.

28. Information from his son, David Lloyd.
29. SOAS archives, SOAS/WW/01/01/03: Hartog to Simon, 23/1/1939. Cf. TNA, WO 32/4356, Hartog to French, 31/1/1939. The Englishman was Commander Noel Everard Isemonger RN (1883–1951), who qualified as a Japanese interpreter in 1909 and joined the school in 1921 as a teacher of Japanese, and the 'Japanese assistant' was Yoshitake Saburō (d.1942).
30. *Report of the Governing Body, Statement of Accounts and Departmental Reports for the Year Ending 31st July 1942* (SOAS, 1942), p. 15.
31. TNA, CO 859/5/5, Harlech to Chatfield, 13/11/1939 and 11/12/1939; Turner to Brooks and Turner to Harlech, 9/12/1939; Brown 2016, p. 84.
32. SOAS archives, SOAS/WW/01/04/01, Chatfield to Harlech, 10/1/1940.
33. On the director's efforts and of his frustration in the face of the government's poor response to his warnings, see SOAS archives, R 24/6, Ralph Turner to Scarbrough, 1/10/1945; Brown 2016, pp. 84–5.
34. Phillips 1967, pp. 34–5; unfortunately, the sources are not identified, and I have so far been unable to trace this correspondence in TNA.
35. TNA, WO 208/226, Major-General Grimsdale, military attaché at British embassy Chungking, to Lieutenant-Colonel B. F. Montgomery, War Office, 10/4/1944.
36. Best 1996 and 1997. For Grimsdale's views, see the memoir he wrote in 1947, which is in the IWM (Documents 8251a): the COVID-19 lockdown has prevented me from consulting this, so I have relied on the summary provided on the website.
37. Firth 1945, p. 38.
38. Funch 2003, pp. 39–41; Binkley 2011, pp. 17–21; see also Dingman 2004 and TNA, FO 371/41792. For further details, see chapters 8 and 9.

2. HUSH-HUSH: WHAT'S GOING ON IN BEDFORD?

1. Interview with Michael Loewe, Cambridge 2019. For the questions asked at interview, see also Melinsky 1998, p. 4; Denham 1993, p. 264; Stripp 1989, p. 4.
2. For biographies of all the Bedford students, see Kornicki 2019. On Mary Tate, see Oswald Tuck Papers, diary entries for 10 and 12/2/1942 and

the Bletchley Park Roll of Honour (online); Tuck states that she was in the ATS, but this is incorrect. Her husband, Norman de-la-Poer Tate (1908–79), whom she married in 1936, was a major in the Royal Corps of Signals based in Singapore, where he was taken prisoner in mid-February 1942. In October 1942, her brother, Patrick Reid, who was a prisoner of war in Germany, made a daring escape from Colditz Castle and managed to reach the safety of Switzerland. Mary's sister, Nora Naish, provides some glimpses of their lives in *Passage from the Raj: Story of a family, 1770–1939* (Chipping Sodbury: Champak Press, 2005). In the *Daily Telegraph* of 7/5/2014, there appeared a rare wartime photograph of Wrens working at Bletchley Park: Mary is in the second row on the right, next to the two circled Wrens with her face showing clearly above those of two Wrens in the front row. In TNA (HW 3/152), there is a brief history of the WRNS at Bletchley Park written in October 1945 by Superintendent (i.e., Captain) Edith Blagrove (1895–1979), who became the commanding officer of the Wrens there on 2/5/1944.

3. CACC, Tuck 5/3; Kornicki 2019, pp. xvi, 93.
4. Melinsky 1998, p. 4.
5. TNA, HW 14/26, 'Books on the Japanese Language in Possession of the War Office, 1 Jan 42'; WO 106/5695, 'Report on Visit to Korea and Manchukuo by Lieut J D P Chapman R.E.'; WO 106/5656, report on attachment to the 13th Infantry Regiment in Kumamoto dated 7/3/1935. For MI2c reports on Japan in 1934, see WO 106/5498. The subsequent career of John Denys Percival Chapman is a mystery, but according to TNA, CAB 81/92, he was attached to SEAC when he made a report to the War Cabinet Joint Intelligence Subcommittee on 15 February 1944; he was awarded a CBE in 1949 and retired as a colonel in 1956.
6. On Tiltman, see Clabby 2007, Erskine and Freeman 2003 and Nicoll 2004. Tiltman, 'Some Reminiscences' (written *c.*1965–68), p. 5.
7. Tiltman, 'Some Reminiscences', pp. 6–7; Erskine and Freeman 2003, pp. 295–6. On Marr-Johnson's command of Japanese, see West 2005, pp. 366–7. Marr-Johnson's first name is given as 'Peter' in Smith 2000, but this is incorrect.
8. *The Quarterly Army List*, December 1941, vol. 2, p. 3574. The Navy had fifteen officers listed as Japanese interpreters at the time: *The Navy List for December 1941*, p. 1598. According to the *Indian Army List*, January 1942, p. 2258, there was one Japanese interpreter in the Indian Army.
9. TNA, HW 42/9, 'Proposals Based on Meeting Held at B.P. on 27th December 1941', p. 3. Birch served with the RNVR during the First World War and then taught history at Cambridge; he left the university to become an actor, but in September 1939 he joined the Naval Section at Bletchley Park.

10. On the Dulwich scheme, see the next chapter.

11. TNA, HW 67/3, typescript 'The Japanese Language Course at Bedford' by John Tiltman, dated 26/6/1942. See also Tiltman, 'Some Reminiscences', p. 9. On the Inter-Service Special Intelligence School, see TNA, HW 50/78, 'Notes on ISSIS (Inter-Service Special Intelligence School)', and HW 43/13, Frank Birch, *G.C.&C.S. Naval SIGINT*, vol. Va, p. 155, n. 2.

12. According to TNA, HW 67/2, 'Rough Notes on a Suggested Course in Japanese', 24/12/1941, Captain Reginald Divers had also given some thought to a course in Japanese, but his suggestions, which may have been intended for Tiltman, were very basic. Divers had been working for the Rising Sun Petroleum Company in Japan before the war (TNA, FO 371/27953, Craigie to Foreign Office, 26/4/1941) but joined the Army and was sent to Bletchley Park; he was later sent to India.

13. This myth is widespread: it appears, for example, in the memoirs of one of Tuck's students, David Leonard Stockton (Magdalen College Archives, Oxford: MC: P175, p. 38), in Jarvis 2005, in Smith 2000, pp. 119–20, in Stripp 1989, p. 139 (and, on p. xiv, in Christopher Andrew's preface to the same volume), and in many other secondary sources. The quotation is from Ferris 2020, p. 419; none of the few teachers of Japanese in SOAS in 1941 were experts in Japanese poetry.

14. CACC, Tuck papers 5/5: Tuck, 'Bedford Japanese School', p. 1. For a full transcript of Tuck's history, see Kornicki 2019. Unless otherwise mentioned and indicated in the notes, the account of the Bedford School that follows is based on this history.

15. Andrew 1985 and 2001.

16. CACC, Tuck 1/5, entry for 19 July 1906. In the Oswald Tuck Papers, there is a commemorative photograph of a gathering of Japanese and British naval officers, with Admiral Tōgō in the centre, on some unrecorded occasion, probably in 1909 when Captain (later Admiral) Charles Dundas was naval attaché; Tuck is standing behind Dundas, whose assistant and interpreter he became in 1908.

17. On Tuck, see TNA, FO 371/87/88, ff. 531–6, 20/11/1906; ADM 1/7728, Gubbins to Macdonald, 10/1/1904 [*sic*: 1905]; Jarvis 2005; Kornicki 2019; Oswald Tuck Papers, cutting from the *Evening News* of 8/10/1937 giving an account of his career. In a lecture he gave in August 1943 (TNA, HW 8/125), Tuck stated that he last set foot in Japan in 1906; this was a typo, a lapse of memory or deliberate obfuscation.

18. Oswald Tuck Papers, diary entries for 24/3/1941 and 30/6/1941.

19. Oswald Tuck Papers, diary entries for 16–17, 22/12/1941, 3/1/1942.

20. Oswald Tuck Papers, diary entry for 13/1/1942.

21. TNA, HW 67/3, John Tiltman, 'The Japanese Language Course at

Bedford', dated 26 June 1942. Grose's name does not appear in Tuck's history but is mentioned by Sir Hugh Lloyd-Jones, who was on the first course at Bedford, in his 'Memoir of WWII Service'. Given the large number of students from Christ's College, it is likely that Lloyd-Jones was right. On cryptography and the classics, see Richmond 2001–2. On the Australian classicists and Japanese, see chapter 9.

22. Oswald Tuck Papers, diary entries for 23 and 26/1/1942.
23. The information on Dashwood in this and the following paragraphs comes from Dashwood 1987, pp. 128–32. Barrow, 'Autobiographical Memoir 1924–1946'. For the backgrounds of the others, see the biographies in Kornicki 2019.
24. For the lives of the people named, see Kornicki 2019.
25. These quotations and details come from Tuck's own history of the Bedford school, reprinted in Kornicki 2019. The characters come from the cards kept by Leslie Phillips and preserved in SOAS Archives.
26. M. Larry Okino, *Practical Standard Japanese with Military text* (South Pasadena, CA: P.D. and Ione Perkins, 1943).
27. In Bletchley Park Archives (OEF 3625), there are files of such cables dating from October and November 1941, approved by either Tuck or Arthur Waley and subsequently used for teaching at the Bedford School by Tuck and Ceadel. Notes were added and then duplicated for the use of students.
28. Interview with Michael Loewe, 2019. Tuck, 'Bedford Japanese School' (Kornicki 2019, p. 4); Oswald Tuck Papers, diary entry for 4/6/1942.
29. Wilkinson, 'My Life Story', p. 19; Ward, 'Notes by Joseph Haggitt Ward on Army Japanese Course at Bedford, Apr 1945–Sep 1945, and Subsequent Service'. Tuck's diaries show that he was a discerning listener and much enjoyed concerts of classical music.
30. TNA, HW 67/3, 'Japanese Language Course at Bedford'.
31. Denham 1993, p. 266; Oswald Tuck Papers, diary entry for 27/6/1942. At the end of 1942, Godfrey gave Tuck a certificate, which he kept in his diary: it states that Tuck had conducted himself 'very much to my satisfaction. A very able teacher of Japanese whose enthusiasm has infected his pupils. Has made a very valuable contribution to the war effort.'
32. Stripp 1989, p. 141; Oswald Tuck Papers, diary entries for 16–17/7/1942. Gibson was the best-performing student on the first course; he later went out to Delhi and became a major in the Intelligence Corps.
33. Wilkinson, 'My Life Story', p. 18; letter from Charles Bawden, 2/1/2016; letter from David Bentliff, 14/12/2015; letter from Donald Russell, 12/11/2015.
34. Patrick Field papers.

35. TNA, HW 41/138, 'Japanese Students', 21/1/1943.

36. Barrow, 'Autobiographical Memoir 1924–1946'.

37. Joseph Ward's story is based on 'Notes by Joseph Haggitt Ward on Army Japanese Course at Bedford, Apr 1945–Sep 1945, and Subsequent Service'.

38. CACC, Tuck 5/1, 5/2, 5/5; Bletchley Park Archives, D1315–001; TNA, HW 41/138, 'Report on Japanese Class iv/July 5–Dec 20 1943'; for Ceadel's attitude towards women on the Bedford courses, see CACC Tuck 2/9, Hawkes to Tuck, 16/11/1945.

39. TNA, HW 8/37, 'Japanese Language Training', 'Future of Japanese Language Course at Bedford'.

40. Axelrod 1945, p. 41; Kornicki 2019, p. 39; Okumura 2012, p. 6.

41. For the visits, gifts, letters, post-war visits to Oxford and Cambridge, see the records in CACC Tuck 1/10 and 1/11. The letters of Soskice and Goldberg are to be found loose in 1/10 and they are dated 4/6/1945 and 27/2/1944 respectively. On Jews at Bedford and Bletchley Park, see Sugarman 2005.

42. Donald Russell, letter to the author, 12 November 2015; Hugh Lloyd-Jones, 'Memoir of WWII Service'; telephone interview and exchange of emails with John Cook, 2019; interview with Michael Loewe, 2019. See also Oswald Tuck Papers, diary entry for 22/6/1943.

43. Kornicki 2019, p. 12; Oswald Tuck Papers, diary entry for 15/6/1942.

44. CACC, Tuck 1/10, entry for 2/6/1943; Oswald Tuck Papers, diary entries for 1/6/1943, 3/10/1943; Bletchley Park Archives, D-1315–001, 'Notes on Japanese Grammar', 4/9/1942.

45. TNA, HW 41/139, Typex message from Central Bureau Brisbane addressed to Brigadier [James Rene] Vernham [deputy director of military intelligence, War Office] at GC&CS, 23/7/1945; CCAC, Tuck 1/10, entry for 28/7/1945.

46. CACC, Tuck 2/9, D.D.(N.S.) Frank Birch to Tuck, 7/12/1945. A copy was still available at GC&CS when the official (but unpublished) histories of the naval section were written after the war: it is referred to, for instance, in TNA, HW 43/13, Frank Birch, *G. C. & C. S. Naval SIGINT*, vol. Va 'The Organisation and Evaluation of British Naval SIGINT', Part IV Japanese, p. 156. There ought to have been a copy in HW 8/37, which contains various papers collected by Frank Birch covering the period July to December 1945 and includes some correspondence with Tuck, but Tuck's report is not among the papers; a surprisingly large number of items in HW 8/37 have been retained by GCHQ, but the historian at GCHQ has informed me that Tuck's report is not among them nor is it elsewhere in the GCHQ archives.

3. THE DULWICH BOYS AND THEIR SUCCESSORS

1. De Moubray 2005, pp. 45–6, 74–5; a recording of an interview with Guy de Moubray is available on the SOAS website: https://www.soas.ac.uk/centenary/alumni-profiles/1940s/guy-de-moubray.html. His mother's diary and other papers are in the Imperial War Museum, but I have been unable to consult them owing to the closure of the IWM research room during the COVID-19 pandemic.
2. The quotation is from Karnad 2015, p. 49.
3. TNA, ED 54/123, Hartog to Butler, 14/1/1942. For the earlier efforts, see pp. 000–000.
4. TNA, ED 54/123, W. H. Ottley of the War Office to Board of Education, 17/1/1942.
5. Dulwich College Archives, *College Governors' Minutes 1942*, minutes of a meeting of the General Purposes Committee on 6/2/1942, pp. 2, 16, and 'Notes on a Conference Held in Room 329, War Office, on Thursday, February 5th, 1942, to Discuss Details of This Proposed Scheme for State Bursaries in Certain Rare Languages'. TNA, ED 54/123, Turner to permanent secretary, Board of Education, 11/2/1942; Piggott 2008, p. 268.
6. TNA, ED 54/123, 'Memorandum to Headmasters: Scholarships in Oriental Languages', 14/2/1942. See the cuttings from the *Birmingham Post*, the *Schoolmaster* and the *South London Advertiser* preserved in the SOAS archives: SOAS 23/2.
7. TNA, ED 54/123, '[Report on] Scholarships in Oriental Languages', 31/3/1942; '[Report on] Scholarships in Oriental Languages [Scotland]', 23/4/1942. *Report of the Governing Body, Statement of Accounts and Departmental Reports for the Year Ending 31st July 1942* (SOAS, 1942), p. 15. For the tests, see de Moubray 2005, pp. 45–7.
8. TNA, ED 54/123, 'State Scholarship Courses, Japanese, Report, March 31st, 1943'. According to Kenneth Inglis, who was also from Scotland and who, after finishing the Japanese course, joined the RAF, there were aptitude tests at the interviews and applicants were assigned their languages: personal communication, 23/11/2014. O'Neill 2001, p. 1; de Moubray 2005, pp. 47, 75–6.
9. Daniels 1963, pp. 18–19. Daniels' report on the wartime courses at SOAS is reprinted in Kornicki 2018. For the students in 1941, see the list in SOAS Archives, SOAS/REG/01/01/04: in addition to those mentioned, three others were listed, one doing a PhD, one a businessman and one who had earlier studied Chinese, but it is not clear if these three were following courses. Retrospective surveys of the wartime courses can be found as 'Wartime Special Courses', in the *Report of the Governing Body, Statement of Accounts and Departmental Reports for the Year Ending 31st July 1945* (SOAS,

1945), pp. 47–8, and in *Report of the Governing Body, Statement of Accounts and Departmental Reports for the Year Ending 31st July 1946* (SOAS, 1946), pp. 55–8.

10. Ōba 1995, p. 47; Dore 1994; Allen 1990, p. 26; de Moubray 2005, p. 55.

11. On Canada, see Feir 2014, pp. xviii–xix, 22, 40–2, 56; Roy 1977, pp. 198–200. The Vancouver school was run by Colonel Brian Reginald Mullaly, who had been a military attaché at the British embassy in Tokyo and spoke Japanese. On 22 December 1941, just a few days after the Pearl Harbor attack, Llewellyn Carlyle Fletcher (1900–80), a Canadian who had been professor of English at Keio University in Tokyo from 1927 to 1931, volunteered his services to the Canadian government as a speaker of Japanese, but they were not wanted. On the treatment of Japanese Canadians during the war, see Adachi 1991.

12. Ito 1984, pp. 153, 158–9, 212–32; on Peter Yamauchi, see Fukawa 2005. The National Nikkei Museum in Burnaby BC has a collection of documents and artefacts relating to the Yamauchi family. On Matsuyama, who changed his name in 1946 to Eric Maxwell and worked for Gee Lawson Chemicals, see TNA, FO 371/23571, and Takeda 2018, p. 90; I am grateful to his son, Ken Maxwell, for having provided further information. A photograph of him teaching one Private Lewis Japanese conversation appeared in *The Illustrated* magazine on 13/10/1945, p. 11 and is reproduced in Brown 2016, p. 88.

13. SOAS 2007, p. 24. For the Japanese spoken by the Japanese Canadians, see TNA, HW 41/138, 'Japanese: Interrogators Courses' (January 1943), p. 3 (although anonymous, this knowledgeable report makes no mention of Daniels by name and so was probably written by him): 'We are hampered in the teaching of a good pronunciation by the fact that none of the N.C.O. instructors [i.e., the four from the Canadian Army] speaks standard Japanese. The two who speak it as natives speak two different dialects, and the third, although his Japanese is near-standard, has a trace of European accent.' Matsuyama may have been the one said to have spoken near-standard Japanese, given that he was working at the Imperial Hotel.

14. Ōba 1995, p. 21; Itoh, 2001, pp. 98, 163, 184, 195. The husbands of British citizens did not acquire British citizenship through marriage. On Yanada, see Oba and Kaneko 2015 and Oswald Tuck Papers, diary entry for 8/12/1941. For details of all the teachers, see Daniels' report reprinted in Kornicki 2018.

15. Best 2013; Blacker 1991; Piggott's energetic correspondence with Lord Hankey, chancellor of the Duchy of Lancaster, on British policy towards Japan, can be found in TNA, CAB 63/177; his own copies of this cor-

respondence are in the Imperial War Museum (Documents.15214). Piggott's *The Elements of Sōsho* (i.e., Japanese handwritten 'grass script') was published in Yokohama by Kelly and Walsh in 1913.

16. For the biographical details, see Kornicki 2018; TNA, HW 41/138, 'List of British Subjects of "Tatsuta Maru" with Some Knowledge of Japanese'. Cahusac was later in India on intelligence duties with 359 Wireless Unit: TNA, AIR 29/163/A, 359 Wireless Unit.

17. One of them, John Hindley, who learnt Turkish and then spent the war in the Middle East, was the inspirational teacher who later taught me Latin and Greek at school.

18. The record cards of all the students, giving some details of their military training, are preserved in Dulwich College Archives; see appendix 1. TNA, ED 54/123, typed report of a visit to Dulwich made by F. W. D. Bendall of the Board of Education on 7/7/1942; this includes the daily timetable of the students. Sandy Wilson recalled: 'such petty restrictions as not being allowed to smoke and having to go to bed at a certain time were more than we could stomach'; Wilson 1975, p. 75. See also de Moubray 2005, p. 49. *The Alleynian* 71, no. 493 (February 1943), pp. 4, 9; Lawrence Breen, 'Autobiography'.

19. TNA, ED 54/123, 'Dulwich Students: Finally Agreed Division of Chinese and Japanese Students between the Three Services 4.3.43'. According to de Moubray 2005, p. 56, the students were given no choice out of the three services. For details of the teaching, probably derived from interviews, see Ōba 1995, chapter 2.

20. *Report of the Governing Body, Statement of Accounts and Departmental Reports for the Year Ending 31st July 1944* (SOAS, 1944), p. 41; Dulwich College Archives, *College Governors' Minutes 1943–44–45*, minutes of a meeting of the General Purposes Committee on 5/2/1943, p. 3.

21. IWM, Sound 12314, recording of an undated interview with Radcliffe; Sound 12068, recording of an interview with Beverton made in 1991.

22. TNA, HW 4/24, 'Interpreters in Japanese', pp. 20–7; HW 41/138 'Minutes of Meeting of the Inter-Services Committee for Language Training', 17/9/1943: the members were Wing-Commander Patrick Guimaraens, Major A. L. S. Harris of the Royal Marines and Major Astley Sparks, who was later replaced by Major S. Aston. Hugh Norris, 'Memoirs', p. 38.

23. Aspden, 'Memoirs'.

24. TNA, HW 4/24, 'Interpreters in Japanese', pp. 20–7; a shorter version is ADM 223/297, NID, vol. 42, pp. 55–7, R.T.B. [Barrett], 'Interpreters in Japanese'.

25. Daniels, *Dictionary of Japanese (sōsho) Writing Forms* (London: Lund Humphries, 1944).

26. TNA, HW 41/138, untitled memo from the RAF section at GC&CS, 4/7/1943; minutes of meeting at SOAS on 19/7/43. After the war, Rideout became professor of Oriental studies at Sydney University, Australia, from 1948 to 1949; he was then appointed professor of Chinese at the University of Hong Kong in 1950, but in the same year he disappeared after a short walk and was found floating dead in the sea; an Australian newspaper report of his death quotes a colleague of his to the effect that he had been an MI5 agent during the war, but it is not clear if he was still engaged in secret work. The coroner's verdict was misadventure, but questions remain. *The Sunday Herald* (Sydney), 9/4/1950, p. 3; Brown 2016, p. 88, n. 20; Sima 2015, pp. 12–14.

27. TNA, HW 41/138, untitled memo from the RAF section at GC&CS, 4/7/1943; HW 41/138, Turner to J. Cooper, 9/9/1943; SOAS Archives, SOAS 24/6, Turner to Lord Scarbrough, 1/10/1945; obituary of Firth by N. C. Scott in *Bulletin of the School of Oriental and African Studies* 24 (1961): 413–18.

28. TNA, HW 41/138, Wing-Commander W. W. Williams, list of men on #2 Japanese WTI course, beginning 4/1/1943; HW 41/139, 'Japanese W.T.I. Training at Newbold Revel', 2/2/1944. The reports on the various RAF courses at SOAS can be found in HW 41/138 and 139.

29. TNA, HW 41/138, 'Reference Sheet' from director of naval intelligence to assistant chief of Air Staff (Intelligence), 24/7/1943, and Guimaraens to de Grey, 31/7/1943; SOAS Archives, SOAS 24/6, Turner to Lord Scarbrough, 1/10/1945.

30. Hugh Norris, 'Memoirs', pp. 37–8, 41–2, 53a.

31. TNA, HW 41/138, Air Ministry [probably Wing-Commander Guimaraens] to Turner, 30/7/1943. Jack Carnochan (1918–2004) was an expert on West African languages and became professor of phonetics at SOAS (obituary in the *Guardian*, 13/9/2004); Beatrice Honikman (1905–97) was an expert on African languages (obituary in *The Phonetician* 83 (2001): 23–4); Eugénie Henderson (1914–89), an expert on South East Asian languages, became professor of phonetics and a fellow of the British Academy (*ODNB*); Eileen Whitley (née Evans, 1910–88) taught phonetics at SOAS; on Mackay and Robins, see Kornicki 2019.

32. Firth 1945, pp. 38–9. It is not clear who 'our oriental scholars' were: he may have meant SOAS teachers of Chinese and Japanese, but he might instead have meant others such as Sir George Sansom or Arthur Waley, who were the most famous scholars of Japan at the time.

33. Firth 1945, pp. 38–9. Obituary of Firth in *Bulletin of the School of Oriental and African Studies* 24 (1961): 413–18, and of Hartog in *Journal of the Chemical Society* (1948): 901–3.

34. TNA, HW 41/139, 'Report on W.A.A.F. Translators (vi): Combined Course'; Eileen Mary Barker papers. See also Smith 2015, chapter 9.
35. SOAS archives holds the papers of Leslie Philips, including his unpublished autobiography.
36. SOAS archives, SOAS/REG/01/01/06; the documents are dated 13/11/1945 and 25/9/1945, but see also the statistics in SOAS/REG/01/01/05.
37. TNA, HW 41/139, 'Report on R.A.F.T. viii'; George Aspden, 'Memoirs'.
38. Daniels in Kornicki 2018; TNA, HW 41/138, 'Japanese: Translators' Courses; Review of Six Months' Work' (January 1943).
39. Obituary of Edwards by Walter Simon in *Bulletin of the School of Oriental and African Studies* 21 (1958): 219–24.
40. TNA, HW 4/24, 'Interpreters in Japanese', pp. 26–7.
41. TNA, HW 4/24 'Interpreters in Japanese', p. 25; IWM, Sound 12314, recording of an undated interview with Radcliffe.
42. TNA, HW 41/139, 'List of Documents at SOAS'.
43. De Moubray 2005, pp. 45–6, 74–5; email from Guy de Moubray, 19/11/2014; *The Straits Times*, 11/9/1945, p. 2. Brett-James 1951, pp. 432–3, describes the landings; he does not mention de Moubray, but that is because he never names interpreters or intelligence officers. Peter Bates, who was also attached to the 5th Indian Division, similarly claimed to have been the first British officer ashore at Singapore in 1945: IWM, Sound 19531, recording of an interview with Peter Bates made in 1999.

4. HMS *PEMBROKE V*, ALIAS STATION X, ALIAS BLETCHLEY PARK

1. On Anderson, see TNA, HW 53/4, Richards to Hastings, 23/3/1945; Juliet Norton Newlands, 'Wartime Service of Elizabeth Helen Anderson 1906–1993'. Her cousin, Margaret Mary Moncrieff 'Madge' Anderson (1904–88), graduated from St Andrew's University and joined the Foreign Office in 1927; she worked at Broadway, the headquarters of MI6 and the pre-war location of GC&CS. In August 1939, she married Frederick Winterbotham, an RAF officer working for MI6 who became responsible during the war for the distribution of Ultra intelligence. It seems likely, therefore, that 'Madge' was already working for MI6 when she recruited Elizabeth.
2. Nigel West, introduction to Liddell 2009; Peter Hennessy, 'Restrictions Eased on Codebreaking Secrets', *The Times*, 14/1/1978, p. 1
3. Liddell 2009, 1:236, 19/3/1942.

4. TNA, HW 43/78, Nigel de Grey, 'Allied Sigint: Policy and Organization', appendix 3, pp. 9–11, 18–20.

5. TNA, HW 8/28, John Lloyd to Commander McIntyre, 30/8/1943; HW 8/29, a P.S.S. written by somebody identified only by illegible initials, 2/9/[1943].

6. Footitt and Tobia 2013, pp. 44–5.

7. Patrick Field kept both the typed test paper and his translations, with corrections made by one of the teachers, and they form part of his collection of wartime papers: I am indebted to him for his generosity in making them available to me.

8. Maffeo 2016, p. 140; Budiansky 2000, pp. 36–7; Prados 1995, p. 82. For illustrations, see https://oztypewriter.blogspot.com/2014/08/the-crypto-underwood-typewriter.html.

9. TNA, HW 42/7, 'Recommendations on the Use of Special Typewriters for Japanese Morse Traffic', minutes of a meeting on 16/7/[1942]; HW 8/29, memo of 25/11/1943, 'Suggested Improvements in the Imperial Model KANA Typewriter prior to Further Production'; HW 67/4, Lt. de Laszlo to Tiltman, 14/9/1942.

10. TNA, HW 42/7, 'Procedure Adopted for Learning Underwood Code Machine (Typewriter) for the Purpose of Japanese Reception' (undated, probably 1942 or 1943); Day 2003; Smith 2000, p. 118 (letter from Juliet Tasker, née MccGwire).

11. Smith 2000, pp. 189–90 (interviews with Maurice Wiles and Elsie Griffin, née Hart); obituary of Vlasto in *The Independent*, 22/8/2000; Wiles 1993, p. 285.

12. TNA, HW 41/138, letter from Professor T. S. R. Boase for Josh Cooper to Professor Edwards, 29/7/1943; Wiles 1993, p. 285. Boase (1898–1974) had an interesting war at GC&CS and Cairo; he later became vice-chancellor of the University of Oxford.

13. TNA, HW 3/156, 'A History of the Japanese Military Intelligence Section' (anonymous; undated but covers the summer of 1943 to the summer of 1945); the 'Final Allocation of Personnel' comes at the end and presumably reflects the situation in August 1945. On Daphne C. S. Seamark, see the Bletchley Park Roll of Honour and the obituaries of the Bedford Girls' School Association (https://community.bedfordgirlsschool.co.uk/obituaries).

14. TNA, HW 8/55, Commander J. P. McIntyre RN, 'The Evolution of N.S. IIJ and N.S. IIIJ', Naval Section Historical Memorandum no. A.I.b. (19), pp. 4, 39; HW 8/51, Hugh R. Foss, 'The Origin and Development of N.S. I J', Naval Section Historical Memorandum no. A.I.b. (1), pp. 4–5, 19, 33, and appendix p. 164 (list of linguists). After the war,

Brain served as ambassador to Cambodia and then to Uruguay and was knighted.

15. TNA, HW 50/78, 'Japanese Linguists in the Naval Section Who Had Trained at SOAS'. Some students were also sent from Colombo to take a special three-month course in the Naval Section: HW 3/131, Naval Section, Central Office Note no. 95, 'Japanese Language Courses, 25 September 1944'.

16. IWM Sound Archive 19099, interview with Beryl Cubitt Lawry (1923–2009); Blacker 1993; Cortazzi 2017. In an interview recorded by Bletchley Park in 2017 and retained in Bletchley Park Archives, Nora Malvin's daughter, Mrs Helen Hopper, read out some extracts from her mother's memoir entitled 'Canopy'; these are transcribed in a written account of the interview, 'Kenneth and Nora MacLaren', in the Bletchley Park Archives.

17. TNA, HW 8/60, Miss S. P. Gibson, 'The Records Party (Japanese)', Naval Section Historical Memorandum no. A.I.b. (24), pp. 5–6. See also Ferris 2020, p. 442.

18. *ODNB*; John Dunn and Tony Wrigley, 'Thomas Peter Ruffell Laslett 1915–2001', *Proceedings of the British Academy* 130 (2005): 109–29; Smith 2000, pp. 214–15 (interview with Peter Laslett). For lists of the names of Naval Section personnel trained at SOAS, see TNA, HW 50/78 (reprinted in Kornicki 2019, pp. 100–5) and HW 3/131, Naval Section, Central Office Note, Japanese Language Courses.

19. TNA, HW 8/62, Naval Section Historical Memorandum no. A.I.b.(26), J. O. Lloyd, 'The Japanese Language School (Long Course)', pp. 4–5, 15.

20. Snell 2007, pp. 37–45; obituary in *The Times*, 13/12/1980, p. 12. Morris wrote an account of his experiences in *Traveller from Tokyo* (1943). For the other lectures, see TNA, HW 8/125, typescript copies of preliminary lectures given in August 1943 for Naval Section Japanese course. On Grice, see Chapman 2007, p. 21, and obituary in *The Times*, 30/8/1988, p. 12.

21. TNA, HW 43/14, Frank Birch, *G.C.&C.S. Naval SIGINT*, vol. Vb, p. 520, quoting N.S. Historical Memorandum (Japanese) no. 19, p. 51; HW 8/27, F. B. [Frank Birch], 'Japanese Translators', 5/4/1943.

22. Author's interview with David Lloyd, London, 10/3/2020. After the war, John Lloyd served as consul-general in Osaka/Kobe and then San Francisco, and ended his career as ambassador to Laos. He was awarded the CBE. From documents cited in Straczek, 'Origins and Development', p. 298, it appears that he worked at Central Bureau before returning to Britain.

23. TNA, HW 8/63, Naval Section Historical Memorandum no. A.I.b.(27),

A. T. Watson and Henry Reed, 'The Japanese Language School (Short Courses)', p. 16; HW 8/32, Lloyd, 'Naval Section Japanese School'.

24. TNA, HW 8/29, 'Japanese Course: Report for Month Ending September 30th, 1943'. For the personnel on other courses, see HW 8/32, Naval Section, Central Office Note no. 141, 'Japanese Language Course, 19 August 1944'; HW 3/131, Naval Section, Central Office Note no. 95, 'Japanese Language Courses, 25 September 1944', and Central Office Note no. 94A, 'Japanese Language Courses, 29 September 1944'. For the identities of these and others who did the Naval Section courses, see Kornicki 2019, pp. 100–9. For the textbooks, see HW 8/120, 121, 122.

25. Wyatt, 'Kitty Wyatt's Reminiscences of Her Time at Station X: Bletchley Park'. From December 1942, Wrens at Bletchley Park were said to have been posted to HMS *Pembroke V*: see Superintendent Edith Blagrove, 'History of the Wrens at GCCS', 6/10/1945 (TNA, HW 3/152), which provides the numbers of Wrens at Bletchley Park and its outposts.

26. Author's interview with Elizabeth Hely-Hutchinson, London, 23/1/2019.

27. Rozanne Colchester (née Medhurst), 'Bletchley Park 1942–1945: Italian and Japanese Air Sections'; Robert McCrum, 'Women Spies in the Second World War', *The Observer*, 7/11/2010.

28. Chan 2014, p. 253.

29. TNA, HW 50/78, 'Japanese Linguists in Naval Section' (undated, but 1944).

30. The following quotations are taken from Chadwick's memoir, 'A Relatively Peaceful War', pp. 69–82. His published account, Chadwick 2001, is briefer, although it includes some details deliberately omitted from his earlier memoir, especially names. For a biography, see J. T. Killen and A. Morpurgo Davies, 'John Chadwick 1920–1998', *Proceedings of the British Academy* 115 (2002): 133–65.

31. The consuls were Ronald Watts and Leonard Pickles (1916–83): Watts had joined the British Consular Service in Japan in 1937 and Pickles in 1939; Pickles served in Japan as consul-general in Tokyo after the war, while in 1947 Ronald George Henry Watts became first secretary at the British Liaison Mission in Tokyo, which took the place of an embassy until 1952, when full diplomatic relations were resumed. Nicol had been a Japanese translator in the Naval Section since February 1941 (TNA, HW 8/51, Typescript: H. R. Foss, 'The Origin and Development of N.S. I J', Naval Section Historical Memorandum no. A.I.b. (1), p. 4), but he had never been a language officer or served in the embassy in Tokyo, so it is unclear how he acquired his knowledge of Japanese.

32. TNA, HW 43/65, 'The History of the Japanese Air Intelligence Section

October 1943 to October 1945', p. 17; IWM, interview with Pamela Margaret Bagnall (1922–), Sound 28456.

33. TNA, HW 14/60, 'Japanese Courses from Scratch'; HW 41/139, 'Those at Present Studying Japanese with Arthur Cooper (17.12.1944)'.

34. Tiltman, 'Some Reminiscences', pp. 9–10; TNA, HW 14/60, 'Japanese Phonetics'. See the obituary of van Praag in *The Independent*, 7/6/1993.

35. TNA, HW 41/138, untitled memo from the RAF section at GC&CS, 23/3/1943, and Firth, 'Report on Personnel of First Course after Seven and a Half Weeks Training', 3/12/1942.

36. TNA, HW 41/138, Wing-Commander W. W. Williams, station commander, RAF Newbold Revel, to Air Ministry, 1/1/1943; on the three Bedford graduates who were among them, Alabaster, Bell and Darlow, who all worked in India on Japanese air-to-ground communications, see Kornicki 2019.

37. For a detailed account of Ōshima's life and the decryption of his dispatches, see Boyd 1993. The National Institute for Defence Studies (Bōei Kenkyūsho) in Tokyo admitted to me after some persistent questioning that they possess a number of interviews with Ōshima recorded on tape after the war; they finally agreed to allow me to listen to them, but said that they did not have a machine on which I could listen to them. Fujiyama 1989, pp. 115–17, 147–8.

38. Drea 1992, p. 10; TNA, HW 8/51, H. R. Foss, 'The Origin and Development of N.S. I J', Naval Section Historical Memorandum no. A.I.b. (1), p. 3; NARA (NR4632 ZEMA37 38221 19390000; National Archives identifier 2811397), 'Report of Technical Mission to England', 11/4/1941. According to a report cited in Budiansky 2000, p. 179, the Americans formed the impression that the British had given up on Purple.

39. Beasley, 'Traveller to Japan', pp. 80–1. Dower 1999, p. 39, writes of the destruction of files and 'bonfires of documents' at the end of the war, but offers no sources. The lack of almost all the originals makes it impossible to judge the accuracy of the translations, of course. The suggestion that mistranslations led to a misinterpretation of Japan's motives in 1941 is debunked in Iguchi 2010, pp. 88–9.

40. TNA, WO 208/4703, memo dated 31/8/1944. According to a quotation included in the Japanese version of his Wikipedia biography and also in an article entitled 'Chūdoku taishi Ōshima Hiroshi bannen no kotoba' in the *Asahi shinbun* on 10/11/2018, when Ōshima, at some point after 1955, was invited by the ruling Liberal Democratic Party to stand as a candidate for the Diet, he replied, 'I have misled the country. It is not permissible for such a person to assume public office again'; the source

of this quotation is not provided, and I have so far been unable to track it down.

41. Nakagawa 2014.
42. Bōei Kenkyūsho, Chūō Gunji Gyōsei sono ta 95, 'Bōchō ni kansuru kaisō chōshuroku' (handwritten transcripts of interviews with Ōshima Hiroshi conducted in November 1959 by Major-General Kubo Muneharu and others), interview no. 5, pp. 1086, 1088.
43. NARA, National Archives identifier 12087386, Ōshima interrogations: typed document dated 3/12/1945.
44. Smith 2000 pp. 224–8; Ferris 2020, p. 260; TNA, WO 208/4703.
45. TNA, HW 8/52, R. G. H. Watts, 'The Japanese Naval Attache Machine Party (translation) (J.N.A.20)', pp. 3–4, 7; letter from Donald Russell, 12/11/2015.
46. TNA, HW 8/52, Watts, 'Japanese Naval Attache Machine Party', pp. 9–10, 12; on Norman, see Kornicki 2019, pp. 102, 108.
47. TNA, HW 8/52, Watts, 'Japanese Naval Attache Machine Party', pp. 25–6.
48. TNA, HW 8/52, Watts, 'Japanese Naval Attache Machine Party', p. 28; HW 23/348, decrypts ULTRA/ZIP/SJA/1601, /1605 and /1611.

5. MAURITIUS IN DANGER

1. On the Clandon Park War Hospital, see https://www.surreyinthegreat-war.org.uk/story/clandon-park-war-hospital/. On Evelyn, I have relied on an interview with the Twinings' younger son, Professor William Twining, in Oxford on 11/1/2019 and on the DuBuisson Papers (Surrey History Centre, Woking), especially 9307/1/1/10, 'War Time Activities in Mauritius' (undated notes written by Evelyn DuBuisson after the war) with an appreciation of her work dated 23/8/1944 and signed by forty colleagues, and 9307/1/1/14, typescript of the address delivered at Evelyn's funeral by Helen DuBuisson's son, William Twining, on 14/3/1983. 'War Time Activities in Mauritius' is the source of all quotations attributed to Evelyn in this chapter; it was probably written in the 1970s at the request of Darrell Bates, who was writing a biography of Twining, and it tells us very little about her own role.
2. Turner 1961, pp. 7–11.
3. *British Medical Journal*, 17/6/1944, p. 823; Jackson 2001, p. 139. Jackson was the first to uncover Twining's wartime organization.
4. On the history of Mauritius in the twentieth century, see Jackson 2001, esp. chapters 2 and 3, from which most of the information in this section is taken.
5. Twining Papers (Bodleian Library, Oxford) Box 22/2, Twining to mother,

17/5/1942. On the racial tensions on the island, see Jackson 2001, pp. 108–11.

6. Twining Papers Box 22/2, Twining to his mother, 4/8/1941, 20/2/1942 and 10/4/1942. On Twining, see also Darrell Bates 1972; Bates' book contains no indications of sources but was based on interviews with members of the Twining family and on Twining's papers. Twining produced a typewritten autobiography towards the end of his life, which is now in the possession of his son, but he omitted his years in Mauritius, presumably because, at the time of his death in 1967, Bletchley Park and wartime decryption were still covered by the Official Secrets Act.

7. On the U-boats, see Paterson 2004. In 1934, the Admiralty had foreseen a role for Rose Belle in time of war, but nonetheless it was closed down: TNA, ADM 116/4463, memoranda of 25/8/1934, 21/2/1938. NHB, *C-in-C Eastern Fleet War Diaries*, vol. 12, ff. 112, 217, 260–1.

8. TNA, CAB 79/18/31, minutes of War Cabinet meeting of 25/2/1942; CAB 80/34/53, 'Defence Plan for Mauritius', presented to Chiefs of Staff Committee, 23/2/1942; Jackson 2001, pp. 53, 59–60.

9. Turner 1961, pp. 116–17, 131, 142–3; NHB, *C-in-C Eastern Fleet War Diaries*, vol. 11, f. 187.

10. Hinsley 1981, vol. 2, p. 85; Thomas 1996. *The Times*, 11/2/1942, p. 3, 'U.S. "Dissatisfied" with Vichy'. See also Rosenthal 1944, pp. 42–5.

11. On the Battle of Madagascar, see the previous note; on the capture of Réunion, see NHB, *C-in-C Eastern Fleet War Diaries*, vol. 11, f. 292.

12. Herbert and Des Graz 1952, 1:545.

13. Evelyn DuBuisson, 'War Time Activities in Mauritius'; the mention of Indonesia is odd—it is probably a mistake for Indo-China. Herbert and Des Graz 1952, 1:257–8; Twining Papers Box 23, May to Agatha [Twining], 26/4/1940.

14. NHB, *C-in-C Eastern Fleet War Diaries*, vol. 9, ff. 308, 367, 446, etc.

15. A small selection of the reports circulated in the United States is preserved in the NARA archives (Maryland): see record identifiers 2148787 and 2148788. Herbert and Des Graz 1952, 1:258, 546; TNA, HW 14/39, 'Government of Mauritius to Secretary of State for the Colonies', 4/6/1942.

16. NHB, *C-in-C Eastern Fleet War Diaries*, vol. 9, ff. 125, 370, 447, vol. 10, ff. 177, 214, 250.

17. NHB, *C-in-C Eastern Fleet War Diaries*, vol. 10, ff. 144, 174–5, 177–8, 213, 345.

18. Herbert and Des Graz 1952, 1:258; TNA, ADM 223/505, R. T. Barrett, 'German Success against British Codes and Cyphers', p. 15. Barrett's piece is odd: it is mutilated, somebody has added in pen 'based on report

by [Commander W. G. S.] Tighe' [RN] and the date 29/8/1948, and the final section on the Y organization in Mauritius has nothing to do with the title of the document.

19. Herbert and Des Graz 1952, 1:258; TNA, HW 61/16, Twining to Blanketing [Censorship Department, London], 20 February 1943, paragraph 23.

20. Martial 2001. In Jackson 2001, p. 41, Vaughan is said to have been a Japanese speaker, but this is incorrect: Jackson cites Smith, *Emperor's Codes*, p. 199, but Smith refers to 'a botanist from the colony's agricultural department', and that was Harry Evans.

21. Stamberg 1998, pp. 83–4, 102–3.

22. TNA, HW 61/16, minutes of a meeting of the 'Y' Board held on 5 August 1943 and 'Extracts from "Report of an Intelligence Reconnaissance of Indian Ocean Island Bases Carried Out by Major W. H. B. Oldham (G.S.I., G.H.Q., India) between 12th March and 20th May, 1942"', paragraphs 11–15. See also the memorandum dated 18/1/1942 in HW 14/27, which shows how much the Mauritius interceptions were valued.

23. TNA, HW 53/4, Twining memorandum, 1/5/1944; obituary in *The Times*, 30/9/1983.

24. Obituary, *Daily Telegraph*, 11/6/2002; see also the obituary in *The Times*, 26/7/2002, p. 32.

25. TNA, HW 42/7, governor of Mauritius to secretary of state for the colonies, 18/9/1942; D. Stopford Adams in Downing Street to Brigadier A. L. Harris, 26/9/1942. TNA, HW 42/9, G.O.C. in C., E. Africa, to the director of military intelligence and the director of naval intelligence, London, 12/11/1942.

26. TNA, HW 42/7, Denniston to Harris, 5/10/1942; HW 42/9, chairman 'Y' Board to G.O.C. in C., E. Africa, 19/11/1942. The listening service at RAF Flowerdown in Hampshire could pick up some Japanese traffic, but this only amounted to 120 signals a day: TNA, HW 8/27, Lt Dugmore to Frank Birch, 'Flowerdown Interception of Japanese Traffic', 29/4/1943.

27. TNA, HW 61/16, Twining, 'Mauritius: Notes on the Derivation of Intelligence from Plain Language Intercepts', 9/8/1943.

28. Twining Papers Box 22/1, Evelyn to Mrs Twining, 18/10/1942.

29. TNA, HW 61/16, Twining, 'Mauritius: Notes on the Derivation of Intelligence from Plain Language Intercepts', 9/8/1943.

30. TNA, HW 23/835 and 836, weekly intelligence reports from 9 September 1943 to 14 June 1945; HW 23/837, Weekly Intelligence Report no. 107, Mauritius, week ending 15/4/1943.

31. TNA, HW 61/16, War Office to G.O.C. in C. E. Africa, 27/11/[1943].

32. TNA, HW 61/16, 'Notes on Mauritius Listening Service', and Twining to [Brigadier A. L.] Harris in London, 26 November 1943; HW 61/17, Twining to Denniston, 26/10/[1943].

33. TNA, HW 61/16, 'Memorandum on Mauritius Listening Service', 10/11/1943; telegram of 2/9/1943 from Blanketing [Censorship Department] to Chesor [Twining]; HW 62/10, Twining, 'Mauritius: Japanese Linguists', 30/8/1943.

34. TNA, HW 61/16, Twining, 'Mauritius: Notes on the Derivation of Intelligence from Plain Language Intercepts', 9/8/1943, p. 5.

35. TNA, ADM 223/505, R. T. Barrett, 'German Success against British Codes and Cyphers', p. 15 (see note 18, above).

36. CACC, Tuck 5/5, 'Bedford Japanese School'; TNA HW 62/11, Richards to Hastings, 23/3/1945; Robert Milne Sellar archive; Dashwood 1987, pp. 128–31.

37. On Hely-Hutchinson, HW 53/4, Richards to Denniston, 15/5/1944; she was not the 'lady' about to get SOAS training referred to in HW 62/10, telegram from Chesor Mauritius to Blanketing London, 11/11/43. Interview with Elizabeth Hely-Hutchinson, 23/1/2019.

38. Robert Milne Sellar archive, letters of 23/5/1944 and 30/9/1944 to his brother, Pat.

39. Dashwood 1987, pp. 130–1.

40. TNA, HW 62/11, telegram from GC&CS to Mauritius, 25/5/1944.

41. TNA, HW 61/16, Twining, 'Mauritius: Notes on the Derivation of Intelligence from Plain Language Intercepts', 9/8/1943, p. 5; HW 62/11, Twining to Travis, 2/2/1944.

42. TNA, HW 53/4, Richards to Denniston, 15/5/1944.

43. TNA, HW 53/4, Elizabeth Anderson to Denniston, 10/7/1944; HW 62/11, Richards to Captain E. G. Hastings, 23/3/45.

44. TNA, HW 62/10, Chesor to Blanketing 'For Shaw from Sellar', 9/1/1944, and Twining to Sayer, 12/1/1944; HW 53/4, Richards to Denniston, 15/5/1944; HW 62/11, telegram from Admiralty to C-in-C Eastern Fleet, 26/3/44; HW 8/30, 'Y Coverage of Japanese Naval and Naval/Air High Frequencies Transmissions', 25/1/[1944], and C-in-C Eastern Fleet to Admiralty, 16/3/1944.

45. Victor Frederick Lemprière graduated in 1922 from Exeter College, Oxford, with third-class honours in classics; he taught at Hirosaki High School (now Hirosaki University) from 1923 to 1926: https://www.hirosaki-u.ac.jp/rft/foreign_teacher.htm. Probate on his estate was granted in 1948 in Jersey (Jersey Archive, D/Y/A/120/94).

46. TNA, HW 53/4, Richards, 'Japanese Linguists', 17/8/1944 (this provides assessments of the abilities of all those handling Japanese traffic).

47. HW 62/11, Richards to Sayer, 4/5/1945.

48. Robert Milne Sellar archive, postcard from Réunion, 24/8/1945; TNA, HW 62/11, Travis to Richards, 15/8/1945, and telegram to GC&CS, 20/8/1945.
49. Email from Robin Sellar, 15/12/2018. Wires 1999.
50. TNA, HW 61/16, Twining, 'Mauritius: Notes on the Derivation of Intelligence from Plain Language Intercepts', 9/8/1943, p. 5; TNA HW 53/4, Richards to Denniston, 21/7/1944.
51. NHB, *C-in-C Eastern Fleet War Diaries*, vol. 10, ff. 174–5, 214, 250.
52. TNA, HW 30/6, p. 920, Takaoka Marine Products Co. to Saigon, 2/10/1944; Batey 2001, p. 96.

6. THE BACKROOM BOYS—AND GIRLS

1. Lloyd-Jones, 'Memoir of WWII Service'. Other quotations relating to Lloyd-Jones in this chapter are from this memoir. The story about the bomb falling on Bedford is also mentioned in Tuck's account: Kornicki 2019, p. 23.
2. TNA HW 4/24, R. T. B. [Barrett], *H.M.S. Anderson and Special Intelligence in the Far East*, typescript. Shaw, *History of Far East Combined Bureau and H.M.S. Anderson*, chapter 2, pp. 1, 10. For lists of all the language officers sent to Japan from 1917 onwards, see Best 2002, pp. 94–5, 108. These lists are the source of all further references to language officers sent to Japan.
3. Shaw, *History of Far East Combined Bureau and H.M.S. Anderson*, chapter 2, p. 1; TNA, HW 43/78, Nigel de Grey, *Allied Sigint: Policy and Organization*, chapter 7 'India and the Far East', pp. 15–16.
4. For a photograph of the farewell party showing the Wrens in their new tropical uniform, see IWM, Photographs A3254 and A3255 (https://www.iwm.org.uk/collections/item/object/205137668).
5. SLNSW, MLMSS 9091, Betty Archdale Papers, Box 5, untitled memoir by Elizabeth Miller, pp. 54–60, 104, 139–40. Miller names the other nineteen (Joyce Allingham, Monica Armstrong, Joan Barber, May Blood, 'Bunch' Burrows, Betty Dart, Jean Epps, Margarete Finch, Marjorie Finlay, Lily Gadd, Gwen Heap, Margaret Hodgson, Phil Holmes, 'Jackie' Jackson, Henrietta Marshall, Eileen Moorley, Enid Monson, Rene Skipp, Joan Sprinks) and the ten who followed later (May Atkinson, Freda Bonar, Beryl and Mollie (Mary) Crace, Pamela Gray, Betty Hopson, Joan Peters, Jean Porter, Penny Rodgers and Kathleen Thompson). Miller has little to say about their work and only obliquely refers to their knowledge of Japanese Morse, describing it as 'special training'; presumably she still considered herself bound by the Official Secrets Act. In November 1942, she was commissioned and became a 3rd officer. Joan Barber (later Joan

Dinwoodie) made it clear later that they were taught Japanese Morse before departure: IWM, Sound 24207, recording of an interview conducted in 2002; WWII People's War, extracts from Dinwoodie's diary (https://www.bbc.co.uk/history/ww2peopleswar/stories/55/a5679255.shtml); there is a photograph of Dinwoodie at Kilindini, Kenya, on the cover of Gwendoline Page 2003.

6. On Archdale, see Macpherson 2002, pp. 125–53; obituary in *The Guardian*, 16/2/2000; Smith 2000, p. 63; and Fletcher 1989, pp. 33, 42. Towards the end of the war, she became a 1st officer (i.e., lieutenant-commander) and was stationed at the Royal Naval headquarters in Melbourne in charge of 300 Wrens.

7. SLNSW, MLMSS 9091, Betty Archdale Papers, Box 5, untitled memoir by Elizabeth Miller, pp. 109, 190, 192, 195–6, 198.

8. TNA, ADM 223/297, NID vol. 42, pp. 2, 5. On the situation in Singapore before the withdrawal, see Smith 2000, pp. 9–13.

9. On the decrypt, see Denham 1993, pp. 274–5.

10. SLNSW, MLMSS 9091, Betty Archdale Papers, Box 5, untitled memoir by Elizabeth Miller, pp. 247, 255–7.

11. TNA, ADM 223/297, NID vol. 42, p. 6.

12. Shaw, *History of Far East Combined Bureau and H.M.S. Anderson*, chapter 6 (by Captain Keith), p. 1.

13. TNA, ADM 223/297, Captain H. R. Sandwith, 'Report on Special Intelligence', 9/12/1942; TNA, ADM 223/297, NID vol. 42, appendix A, 'Remarks by Burnett on his Visits to London and Washington in Connection with Japanese Special Intelligence'.

14. On the breaking of JN40, see the obituary of Brian Townend in *The Times*, 2/3/2005, p. 75. On the sinking, Shaw, *History of Far East Combined Bureau and H.M.S. Anderson*, chapter 6 (by Captain Keith), p. 2. See also Smith 2000, p. 150.

15. Denham 1993, pp. 269–72. The other two chosen were Laurence Cohen and Douglas Wynn Davies.

16. CACC, Tuck 1/10, letters from Hugh Denham in Kilindini and Cohen in Colombo, 25/6/1943 and 9/11/1943; Denham 1993, pp. 269–72.

17. SLNSW, MLMSS 9091 Betty Archdale Papers, Box 5, untitled memoir by Elizabeth Miller, p. 230.

18. On the sad story of the *Khedive Ismail*, see Crabb 2015, which includes several pictures of the ship and the survivors. The identification of eight of the WRNS victims as Typex operators comes from Smith 2015, p. 233, but he gives no source and I have so far been unable to confirm this. For Crace, see SLNSW, MLMSS 9091, Betty Archdale Papers, Box 5, untitled memoir by Elizabeth Miller, p. 264; the name of Beryl Merrill (née Crace) appears on the war memorial in Skendleby church in

Lincolnshire. Statements made by survivors, who attest to the rapidity of the sinking and the terrifying experiences they had, can be found in Crabb 2015 and TNA, WO 361/491.

19. Shaw, *History of Far East Combined Bureau and H.M.S. Anderson*, p. 75.

20. TNA, HW 50/78, 'Japanese Linguists in Naval Section G.C. & C.S. and at Anderson' (undated, but from internal evidence clearly 1944). In comments on the secret official history made in 1953 by Commander Colegrave, he is critical that the history is 'largely concerned with arguments and excuses in favour of the large duplication effort at Bletchley at the expense of the more important British operational effort under the Commander-in-Chief, Eastern Fleet at Colombo': TNA, HW 43/13, Frank Birch, GC&CS Naval SIGINT, vol. Va, 'The Organisation and Evaluation of British Naval SIGINT, Part IV Japanese', 'Remarks by Cmdr. E. H. Colegrave, R.N., July 1953'.

21. TNA, HW 4/31, monthly report of 1/10/1944; TNA, HW 8/37, 'Officer Commanding Anderson' (July 1945). Although not complete, the Bletchley Park Roll of Honour (https://bletchleypark.org.uk/roll-of-honour) records the names of most who worked at Bletchley Park during the war.

22. Smith 2000, pp. 211–12 (correspondence with Dorothy Smith, née Robertson).

23. IWM, Sound 30423, interview with Stowers recorded in 2007.

24. TNA, HW 4/31, monthly report of 31/10/1944.

25. Bawden, 'Charles Roskelly Bawden: An Academic's Life', p. 6.

26. TNA, HW 4/24, 'H.M.S. Anderson and Special Intelligence in the Far East', p. 8.

27. TNA, HW 43/73, 'Draft History of Signals Intelligence Service in India and Colombo' (January 1944; with pencilled corrections and additions), p. 1. Marr-Johnson was sent to Japan as a language officer in 1933 and was still there in 1936: Best 2002, p. 108, and N. M.-J. [Nancye Marr-Johnson], 'The Honourable Taxi-Ride', *Saint Christopher's Review* 20 (September 1945): 5.

28. TNA, WO 208/5128, 'Memorandum by the "Y" Committee', 7/5/1942.

29. WO 208/5054: 'Administrative History of Wireless Experimental Centre'; Smith 2000, p. 241 (interview with Michael Kerry).

30. There are copies of *Hello Chaps! This is Delhi*, which was printed at the Times of India Press in Bombay, in the late James Sutherland's papers and in the IWM. On the ATS and WAAF contingents, see De Grey, 'India and the Far East', p. 45, and TNA, WO 208/5054, 'Administrative History of Wireless Experimental Centre'. The WEC magazine, entitled *Saint Christopher's Review*, was edited by Company Sergeant-Major

H. Transfield and was issued monthly by St Christopher's Chapel at the WEC; Sergeant D. Singh's essay on her experiences is contained in issue 20 (September 1945), p. 11.

31. TNA, HW 67/4, 'Employment of Cryptographers in India', GHQ India to Tiltman, 19/11/1942. On the organization of the WEC, see Smith 2000, pp. 162–4. On the initial problems, see Beckhough 1995, p. 15; Harry Beckhough was an intelligence officer who joined the WEC at the end of 1942.

32. West 2005, p. 366. This information appears to have come from Frederick James Maugham Marr-Johnson, whose father was a cousin of Patrick and who, when I interviewed him, confirmed it. Erskine and Freeman 2003, p. 295. Patrick Marr-Johnson was originally known as Patrick Marr Johnson, without a hyphen, but he changed his name in 1938: *The Times*, 27/4/1938, p. 4. For his impressions of the products of the Bedford School, see TNA, HW 67/4, Marr-Johnson to Tiltman, 20/11/1942. Reginald Divers (1907–89) worked for the Rising Sun Petroleum Company in Japan but on the outbreak of the war joined the Intelligence Corps of the Army and on Christmas Eve 1941 drew a rough plan for a Japanese course: TNA, FO 371/22192, 'List of British Subjects in the Tokyo Consular District Capable of Serving as Interpreters in the Japanese Language', and HW67/2, 'Rough Notes on a Suggested Course in Japanese', 24/12/1941.

33. Lloyd-Jones, 'Memoir of WWII Service'; Balliol College Archives, letters from Noyce to Grimble dated 29/2, 13/3, 23/8, probably 1944.

34. TNA, WO 208/5151, WEC interrogation reports.

35. Smith 2000, pp. 230–1, 241 (interviews with Michael Kerry); obituary of Kerry, *The Times*, 21/5/2012, p. 47. The photograph is in the Philip Taylor papers.

36. Smith 2000, pp. 245–6; TNA, HW 43/73, 'Draft History of Signals Intelligence Service in India and Colombo' (January 1944; with pencilled corrections and additions), p. 43. According to the operations record book of 355 Wireless Unit (TNA, AIR 29/162A/6), it moved to Comilla on 12/3/1945 and stayed there until the end of June, so the episode described must have taken place during that time.

37. Thacker 2014; Philip Taylor diary, 'Movements'. The diary of 368 WU in TNA, AIR 29/163/A/4.

38. 'Inside Burma with the RAF', newsreel made in December 1944 by British Movietone for Indian News Parade. On Bell, see Kornicki 2019. The personnel working in 355, 357, 358, 359, 367, 368, 369 and 370 Wireless Units are named in the unit diaries in TNA, AIR 29/163.

39. For more details and an illustration, see Bou 2012, p. 81.

40. TNA, WO 208/5054, 'Administrative History of Wireless Experimental

Centre'; 'The Rise of W.E.C.', *Saint Christopher's Review* 20 (September 1945): 12–16; Stripp 1989, p. 46.

41. TNA, HW 50/34, typescript 'VHF R/T Training: Naval' (includes references to letters of 6/4/1944 and 31/10/1944 from Captain Keith at HMS *Anderson* on their performance).
42. TNA, AIR 29/162A/7, appendix 1.
43. TNA, AIR 29/162A/7, appendix 3.
44. TNA, HW 4/5.
45. TNA, HW 4/5.
46. For the names of those who had completed military courses at SOAS, see SOAS Archives, SOAS/REG/01/01/05 and appendix 1.

7. ON THE FRONT LINE IN BURMA

1. Karnad 2015, p. 61. The posters are in the National Army Museum, London; they can also be seen here: https://qz.com/india/1599799/japans-world-war-ii-poster-propaganda-against-britain-in-india/.
2. Allen 1984, pp. 153–5. In 2017, NHK World produced an account of the Imphal Campaign entitled *The Battle of Imphal*, which can be found on YouTube. It contains interviews with survivors and introduces newly discovered documentary material.
3. On the sinking of the *Kuala*, see *The Times*, 17/6/1942, p. 5, and http://www.roll-of-honour.org.uk/evacuation_ships/html/ss__kuala_history.htm. The quotations come from Storry's diary (IWM, Storry Papers, Box 1, 2/2); see also Storry 1986, pp. 65–9.
4. IWM, Storry Papers, Box 1, 5/5 and Box 2, 8/6; Storry 1986, pp. 69–77.
5. IWM, Storry Papers, Box 2, 8/5, untitled Q&A typescript dated 18/2/1960. Sometimes photographs were among the documents recovered from corpses; a number are preserved in the Storry Papers, Box 1, 6/1. See also Allen 1984, p. 396; Storry 1986, pp. 164–5. For British practices, see Hastings 2015, p. 51.
6. Brett-James 1951, p. 390. The bilingual questionnaire is in the IWM, Storry Papers, Box 1, 5/7; Storry Papers, Box 2, 8/5.
7. Storry Papers, Box 2, 8/5. See also Evans and Brett-James 1962, pp. 79–80: since Storry's account in 8/5 is dated 1960, it is clear here and elsewhere that Evans is quoting Storry. The assessment of Storry by Lieutenant-Colonel G. A. Stephenson is in the Storry Papers, Box 1, 5/31.
8. The programme, with a colour-printed cover, is in IWM, Storry Papers, Box 4. Contingents from the Royal Navy, the Royal Indian Navy, the Burmese Navy, the Army, the Indian Army, the US Army, the Chinese Army, the RAF and the US Air Force paraded in front of Mountbatten.

9. Purvis 2005, pp. 345–6.

10. Allen 1984, p. 506; Allen 1973, pp. xv, 241.

11. Allen 1984, pp. 506–9. Allen writes of himself in the third person as Lt. Levy, using his original surname. *The London Gazette*, 3rd supplement, issue 37730, 17/9/1946, p. 4706 (under the name Levy).

12. Allen 1984, p. 509; Purvis 2005, p. 351; Mountbatten 1951, p. 181.

13. Storry Papers, Box 1, 2/2, Diary, early February 1942; Christine Wass, 'From Sandon to Changi', *The Essex Countryside*, June 1985, p. 47.

14. *The Times*, 21/3 and 26/3/1940. On Andrews, see the previous note and Christine Wass, 'Eric Leicester Andrews: Memorial Altar of Changi', *FEPOW Forum* (September–October 1985): 10–11. These two articles seem to be based on information provided by Eric Andrews' daughter, Beryl Saltmarsh, who lived in Sandon.

15. TNA, WO 106/2617, telegram from Wavell to CIGS, 18/12/1941.

16. For information about his life in captivity, I am indebted to Martin Andrews, his grandson, who has made family papers available to me. Some further information is also available on the website of the Adam Park Project http://www.adamparkproject.com

17. IWM, Sound 32318, undated recording of an interview with Drower; Drower 1993, pp. 39–41, 51–84; obituary in *The Times*, 3/9/2007, p. 44. In January 1939, Ambassador Craigie compiled lists of British residents in Japan with some knowledge of the language, and these included a number of people who might be described as 'commercial representatives', to use Drower's term, but none of these names can be found in the Army Lists for 1942: TNA, FO 371/23571/2580, Craigie to Lord Halifax, 8/2/1939.

18. Obituary in *The Times*, 7/8/1998, p. 23. The names of Intelligence Corps officers who became POWs in Malaya/Singapore or were wounded there are given in *Notes of Interest*, no. 4, 1944 (printed by the Intelligence Corps), pp. 17–18 (I am grateful to the Military Intelligence Museum, Chicksands, for having sent me a photocopy during the COVID-19 lockdown). Andrews, Drower and Wild are listed, and among the others are Harold Winter Atcherley (1918–2017), who wrote *Prisoner of Japan: A Personal War Diary, Singapore, Siam & Burma 1941–1945* (2012), and Arthur Vacquerie Cramsie (1915–2002), who wrote *Guest of an Emperor* (1987); neither of them were Japanese linguists, although Cramsie, who had lived in Singapore before the war and knew Malay, joined FECB.

19. Evans and Brett-James 1962, pp. 76–9; TNA, FO 643/34, 'C.S.D.I.C. (India) Red Fort Delhi, Information Section Report No. 1' (25/1/1943).

20. TNA, WO 208/3463, 'Note on C.S.D.I.C. (I) Mobile Sections' (28/10/1943). IWM, Storry Papers, Box 1, 5/22 and Box 2, 8/5. The

first of these two lists in the Storry Papers gives the full complement of No. 1 Mobile Section, including the Nisei (Harold Hanaumi and Henry Tsuchiyama), but as language officers includes only Storry and Lt. Peter Evsievievich Kostiloff, a White Russian who had been in the Shanghai Defence Force. The second list gives the names of six officers (Captains R. P. Brown, Cecil Arab, Richards, Yorke and, from SOAS, J. H. Watkins) and states how they came to know Japanese. Neither gives a date but they clearly belonged to different phases in the history of the section; it appears from Evans and Brett-James 1962, p. 76 that it is the second list that applies to the Battle of Imphal. On Peter Edward Gascoigne Bates and No. 4 Mobile Section, IWM, Sound 19531, a recording of an interview with Bates made in 1999.

21. The file in question is TNA, WO 203/3940.

22. Evans and Brett-James 1962, p. 82.

23. Evans and Brett-James 1962, pp. xii, 75, 79, 83; Allen 1984, pp. 184–5, 220.

24. Allen 1984, pp. 396, 506. The two linguists were Major Stanley T. Charles and George Robertson Kay—Charles did one of the wartime Japanese courses at SOAS while Kay was a 'Dulwich Boy'. There is an obituary of Charles in *The Burma Campaign Society Newsletter* 13 (2008): 7. According to Allen 2010, pp. xxi–xxii, the commanding officer of No. 2 Mobile Section was Major 'Chips' [Spencer John] Bardens who had been born in Kobe to a family that had long lived in Japan and who spoke Japanese but had minimal knowledge of the written language; Cecil Arab had been a Kobe businessman and succeeded Bardens. Cecil's brother was Arthur Arab, who interpreted at the Japanese surrender ceremony in Singapore; their family, too, lived in Japan before the war.

25. Cortazzi 1998, pp. 28–9. Major Eric Crane and his family had returned to Britain before 1941: Balin 2009, p. 174.

26. Dredge, 'History of SEATIC', p. 5. Unless otherwise stated, the information about SEATIC in this section comes from Dredge's account. Since for most of its existence SEATIC was under US command, many of the SEATIC files are kept in the United States (NARA, Maryland, National Archives identifier 6483847), but the files only concern US SEATIC staff.

27. Allen 1984, pp. 394–5, 464–5.

28. TNA, AIR 40/2172, 'Captured Enemy Documents Report No. 13: Fragments of Three Diaries Written by Two N.C.O.'s and One Officer of 12th Hikōsentai [Squadron] during the Period 29.7.42 to 22.3.43', dated 5/5/1943; quotations from 26/7, 29/7 and 25/11/1942. On the abandonment of the plan to invade Australia, see Frei 1991, pp. 165–6.

29. On Boyce, see Pardoe, 'Captain Malcolm Kennedy and Japan', n. 214. After the war, Boyce was a member of the British International

Prosecution Section at the Tokyo Trials, and in 1949–51 he was a first secretary at the British embassy in Tokyo. His *Japanese Air Terms* was published in Calcutta by the British Ministry of Information in two volumes in 1944 and 1945.

30. TNA, HS 1/186, London Report [from SOE in the United States], 26/2/1945. Takeda 2018, pp. 178–86, 193–4; Ito 1984, pp. 167, 182; Robinson 2011, pp. 216–17. Donald Hayden Thurston Mollison was the grandson of James Pender Mollison (1844–1931), who went to Yokohama from Glasgow in 1867 and worked for a tea exporting company that was eventually renamed Mollison & Co. There is a photograph of Donald Mollison in the Nikkei Museum (http://www.nikkeimuseum. org/www/item_detail.php?art_id=A32808) and there are further photographs in his Special Operations Executive personal file (TNA, HS 9/1047/1). Names and photographs of the twelve Japanese Canadians in the first batch and the twenty-three in the second batch, all of whom were sent to India, are to be found in TNA, HS 1/186.

31. Dredge, 'History of SEATIC', pp. 2–3.

32. Dredge, 'History of SEATIC', pp. 7–8.

33. IWM, Storry Papers, Box 1, 4/9 and 5/15. According to Dredge, 'History of SEATIC', p. 1, the school at Simla was founded in 1942.

34. Phillips 1995, pp. 13–15; obituary in *The Daily Telegraph*, 26/3/2004.

35. Ian Nish kindly showed me his copy of the book of handwritten documents produced in Simla. In 1944, the school also published a *Vocabulary of Common Japanese Words with Numerous Examples and Notes*.

36. TNA, WO 208/226, telegram from the Joint Intelligence Committee (London) to the director of military intelligence, SACSEA, India, 14/9/1945; van der Bijl 2013, pp. 103–4.

37. CACC Tuck Papers, Tuck 2/9, letters of John Healy to Tuck 19/11/1945, 18/3/46. CAC Tuck Papers, Tuck 2/9, letters of John Healy to Tuck 19/11/1945, 18/3/46. Emails from John Pole, who was one of those on Course X who was flown out to Karachi. On the Kuala Lumpur war crimes trials, see Smith 1997.

38. Joseph Ward, 'Notes by Joseph Haggitt Ward on Army Japanese Course at Bedford, Apr 1945–Sep 1945, and Subsequent Service'.

39. John Whitehorn, 'Memoirs'.

40. John Whitehorn, 'Memoirs', p. 9; Joseph Ward, 'Notes by Joseph Haggitt Ward on Army Japanese Course at Bedford, Apr 1945–Sep 1945, and Subsequent Service'. The photograph is in the possession of John Whitehorn and on the back carries a key. For Dicker, see Kennedy, *The Diaries of Captain Malcolm Duncan Kennedy, 1917–1946*, entries for 7/7/1923, 13/2/1926, 22/10/1926, and Dredge, 'History of SEATIC', p. 5.

41. Interview with Nish, 6 May 2016; Nish, *Collected Writings of Ian Nish*, part 1 (Folkestone: Japan Library, 2011), pp. viii–x; quotations from Kendrick 2004 and the preface to the American edition of *Kenkyusha's New Japanese–English Dictionary* (Cambridge, MA: Harvard University Press, 1942). Nish also has a copy of *Fuzambo's Comprehensive English–Japanese Dictionary*, similarly published by Harvard in 1942. Interview with Nish, 6/5/2016; Nish, *Collected Writings of Ian Nish*, part 1, pp. viii–x; Kendrick 2004.

42. TNA, CAB 79/37/19, minutes of meeting of Chiefs of Staff Committee, 17 August 1945, pp. 329, 337–9. Present were Field Marshal Sir Alan Brooke (chief of the Imperial General Staff), Marshal of the Royal Air Force Sir Charles Portal (chief of the Air Staff) and Admiral of the Fleet Sir Andrew Cunningham (chief of the Naval Staff).

43. SOAS Archives, SOAS/REG/01/01/05, 'Far East Department, Air Ministry, Japanese Service Students, 1941–42' and 1942–43 (he appears as R. L. Mason); Allen 1984, p. 623; Storry 1986, p. 81; Isobel Montgomery, 'Writer Who Found Suzie Wong: Richard Mason', *The Guardian*, 15/10/1997, p. 16; Ōba 1995, pp. 25–6, 45, 117–20. Mason probably first came across this poem in Basil Hall Chamberlain's *A Handbook of Colloquial Japanese* (1888). Chamberlain's translation of the poem is 'Even a board stuck up and inscribed with the words "It is strictly prohibited to pluck these blossoms" is useless as against the wind, which cannot read', which is clumsier than Mason's: Chamberlain, *A Handbook of Colloquial Japanese*, 4th edn (London: Crosby Lockwood, 1907), p. 488.

44. Mason 1946, pp. 16, 26, 33, 36–7.

45. Bayly and Harper 2004, p. 260; http://hollywoodjapanfile.blogspot.com/2014/04/the-wind-cannot-read-1958.html. The film was directed by Ralph Thomas. On Aiko Clarke at SOAS, see Kornicki 2018, p. 316, and on her background and work at the BBC, see Ōkura 1983, pp. 122–4.

8. THE WAVY NAVY IN THE UNITED STATES

1. Beasley, 'Traveller to Japan', pp. 48–9, 52; quotation from a letter that James Durbin sent to his parents from Boulder in 1943, in UCBA, Ross H. Ingersoll papers 1–1, p. 25.

2. Maneki 2007, pp. 42–5. On Japanese studies in the United States before the war, see Jansen 1988.

3. Dingman 2009, p. 3; McNaughton 2006, pp. 17–18; Packard 1996, pp. 365–71. On the US Navy's language students in Japan before the war, including Mashbir and Zacharias, see Slesnick 2006, chapters 1 and 2, and

Bradford 2002. Joseph Rochefort and Edwin Layton, who also studied in Japan, both became brilliant cryptanalysts during the Second World War. Binkley 2011 is an illustrated history that includes many photographs of pre-war and wartime Japanese learning in the US armed forces. On Cox, see Cortazzi 2013; on the arrest of US citizens at the end of August 1940, see *The New York Times*, 30/8/1940, p. 7.

4. Maneki 2007, pp. 73–5; Maffeo 2016, pp. 432–5.
5. McNaughton 2006, pp. 387, 392. The stories of Takemiya and Sakamoto are told in Takeda 2018, pp. 12–18. On Sakamoto, who interpreted for President Eisenhower in 1961 during his visit to Okinawa and ended his career as a colonel in the US Army, see http://www.svcmoaa.org/Memoriam/COLTomSacamoto.htm. On the situation of the Nisei in the United States, see Azuma 2005.
6. On the internment of Japanese Americans, see Robinson 2001 and Lyon 2012.
7. Hindmarsh, 'Navy School of Oriental Languages', pp. 1–2; Dingman 2009, p. 2.
8. Hindmarsh, 'Navy School of Oriental Languages', pp. 1–2.
9. Dingman 2009, pp. 5–9.
10. Dingman 2009, pp. 5–9.
11. Borton 2002, pp. 76–7. There is a full list of those who attended the conference at the University of California Berkeley Bancroft Library, CU-5, University of California, Office of the President records, circa 1885–1975, series 2, 1941, item 487. Apart from Reischauer, Borton, McCollum, Hindmarsh, and representatives of the American Council of Learned Societies, the Rockefeller Foundation, the Department of Justice and the Federal Communication Commission, those who attended were: William Acker (George Washington University), Serge Elisséeff (Harvard), Charles Fahs (Claremont College), Col. William Friedman, Harold Henderson (Columbia), George Kennedy (Yale), Major Wallace Moore (Military Intelligence, US Army), Henry Tatsumi (University of Washington), Florence Walne (University of California) and Joseph Yamagiwa (University of Michigan).
12. Hindmarsh, 'Navy School of Oriental Languages', pp. 2–3; McNaughton 2006, p. 24; Dingman 2009, p. 12. Mortimer Graves (administrative secretary of the council) to David Stevens of the Rockefeller Foundation, 30/7/1941: Rockefeller Archive Center, Rockefeller Foundation records, projects, RG 1.1, series 200.R, box 197, folder 2365 (available online at https://rockfound.rockarch.org/digital-library).
13. Hindmarsh, 'Navy School of Oriental Languages', pp. 2–3 (see pp. 9–11 for a complete list of the textbooks and dictionaries provided to each student). For lists of the students, see Slesnick 2006, pp. 78–9.

14. Hindmarsh, 'Navy School of Oriental Languages', pp. 2–3.
15. Keene 2008, pp. 26–41 (quotation from p. 39). For the relations between the two Navy language officers and the Nisei linguists during the Aleutian Campaign, see McNaughton 2006, pp. 168–9.
16. Dingman 2009, pp. 10, 12, 15–19; Slesnick 2006, pp. 178–207.
17. Loureiro 2001, p. 386; Williams, pp. 184–5. On the US Army and other language training programmes, see McNaughton 2006, pp. 20–31, chapter 4 and *passim*, and Slesnick 2006, chapter 8. Slesnick was himself a Marine Corps language officer during the war, while McNaughton is an outstandingly well-researched study. On the Nisei, see Lyon 2012, pp. 18, 48–9, 75–6.
18. Ichinokuchi 1988, pp. 171, 211. Kuwabara's papers are in the Go For Broke National Education Center, Los Angeles, California, but I have not been able to see them.
19. On American Nisei serving with British forces in India, see McNaughton 2006, p. 276.
20. McNaughton 2006, pp. 147–50.
21. McNaughton 2006, pp. 216–17; Reischauer 1986, pp. 85–95.
22. Letter from Graff to the editor, *The New York Times*, 9/9/1990, p. 24; Packard 2010, pp. 74–5; Reischauer 1986, pp. 85–95. Prados 1995 is a lengthy account of US intelligence operations against the Japanese Navy but has very little to say on the problem of the shortage of linguists.
23. The archives of what was properly called The Navy School of Oriental Languages (since there was a separate Chinese course) were destroyed after the war, but Hindmarsh's detailed report on its activities, which was probably written in 1946, includes numerous appendices that include official correspondence, graduation programmes, extracts from newspapers, photographs and the text of a play written and produced by the students. See also Dingman 2009. On the Nisei teachers, see Arntson 2014.
24. Obituary in *University of California: In Memoriam, 1946* (available online at texts.cdlib.org). She resigned in September 1944 owing to ill health and a few months later married Samuel Farquhar, so she appears in some sources as Florence Walne Farquhar.
25. UCBA, Ross H. Ingersoll papers 1–1, letter from James Durbin to his parents, 1943, p. 11.
26. Dingman 2009, pp. 21–2, 24–5, 42, 46, 54, 61; Ross Ingersoll, 'Naval Training School (Japanese): An Overview', in UCBA, Ross H. Ingersoll papers 1–3; Abe 1938. The Naganuma textbooks were reprinted by Yale University in 1943.
27. Hindmarsh, 'Navy School of Oriental Languages', p. 22, and appendix 42, p. 6.

28. Dingman 2009, p. 32. According to emails received from David Pole, students on Course X at Bedford were shown two Japanese-language films

29. From a letter that James Durbin sent to his parents from Boulder in 1943, in UCBA, Ross H. Ingersoll papers 1–1, p. 49.

30. The story of William Beasley is based on his unpublished account, 'Traveller to Japan', dated 2002. Archives relating to the US Navy Language School are kept at Boulder, Colorado, and David M. Hays of the University of Colorado Library kindly provided me with a list of all the RNVR students at Boulder.

31. Beasley, 'Traveller to Japan', p. 48. On Birrell, see a letter he wrote on 1/4/1982, in UCBA, Roger Pineau papers, 3–4, 'JLOs from Great Britain'. On Gowing, see also MacLeod 2012, p. 70.

32. Ross Ingersoll, 'Naval Training School (Japanese): An Overview', in UCBA, Ross H. Ingersoll papers 1–3, p. 10.

33. *New York Times*, 12/12/1943, p. 58; Hindmarsh, 'Navy School of Oriental Languages', appendix 42 contains the full text of the press release (quotation from p. 8).

34. TNA, FO 371/41792. On Sansom and GC&CS, see Ferris 2020, p. 116; Sansom's wartime Special Operations Executive personnel file is in TNA (TNA, HS 9/1310/4), but I have been unable to see it owing to the COVID-19 lockdown.

35. See appendix 4 for details of all the British students at Boulder. On Heath, see *The Interpreter* 60 and 69a (2003).

36. Beasley's letter and Hindmarsh's reply are both reprinted in Hindmarsh, 'Navy School of Oriental Languages', appendix 56; the identification of Beasley as the author of the first is based on a carbon copy of the letter in UCB archives, Roger Pineau Collection 9–11.

37. See appendix 4.

38. UCBA, Sidney DeVere Brown Collection 1–1, letter to his brother Stanley, 16/12/1944; H. Morris Cox, 'Brits in Boulder', *The Interpreter* 44 (1 May 2002). According to Beasley, 'Traveller to Japan', p. 55, the four graduates were Birrell, Kennedy, Wilkinson and himself. On Gowing, see appendix 4.

39. Dingman 2009, pp. 67, 73, 75–6, 83–4.

40. Colonel John C. Erskine, USMCR (Ret.), 'Language Officers Recall Combat Roles in the Pacific', *Fortitudine (Bulletin of the Marine Corps Historical Program)* 15, no. 4 (1986): 23–4. Erskine was a Boulder graduate. The da Silva story as told to David Hays is in *The Interpreter* 119 (2008). For Nisei deaths while in service, see McNaughton 2006, pp. 283–4.

41. Dingman 2009, pp. 100–12, 123–4, 129; McNaughton 2006, p. 221.

The Washington Document Center was established in February 1945 following discussions between American, Australian, British and Canadian military representatives.

42. Zacharias 1946, pp. 351–75, 399–424; Dingman 2009, pp. 138–44, 162–3, 164–6, 170–85.

43. Beasley, 'Traveller to Japan', p. 55; UCB archives, Roger Pineau Collection 29–7, letter from Wilkinson of 26/1/1988. On the Canadian Army Japanese Language School (formally known as S-20 Pacific Command Japanese Language School), see the 'Standing Orders' written by Major A. P. McKenzie, MC, the commanding officer, in November 1944 (TNA, HS 1/186); Ito 1984, pp. 212–32, and Feir 2014, pp. 45–7, 54–7. Most of the students who went through the course were from the Canadian Army (202), but there were also some from the Canadian Women's Army Corps (14), the Royal Canadian Navy (9), the Royal Canadian Air Force (2) and the Royal Australian Air Force (1) in addition to the four from the RNVR.

44. Beasley, 'Traveller to Japan', pp. 58–9.

45. Beasley, 'Traveller to Japan', pp. 60–2.

46. TNA, ADM 53/122353, log HMS *Swiftsure*, August–October 1945. The colour film can be seen at https://www.youtube.com/watch?v= nqzoWo1yOVQ; Gowing is the one wearing dark glasses.

47. TNA, ADM 1/12647.

48. Weighton 2008, pp. 301–5; Weighton replaced McVittie's deputy, a Mr McDermott (possibly the Dermot MacDermot who will be mentioned in chapter 11). Obituary of Weighton in *The Guardian*, 8/6/2020. In 1941, Ambassador Sir Robert Craigie in Tokyo listed Weighton as competent in Japanese: TNA, FO 371/27953, Craigie to Foreign Office, 26/4/1941. McVittie became British ambassador to the Dominican Republic after the war. For the instructions and the criticism, see TNA, FO 898/285, London Far Eastern Directive no. 19, 6/2/1945, and 'Comments on Japanese Programmes January 5th to 11th [1945]'. None of the broadcast scripts are included in this file, and their whereabouts, if they have survived, are unknown to me.

49. Quotation from TNA, FO 898/285, Hugh MacMillan to director, 16/8/ [1945]. I have not so far been able to identify the four Nisei. Gompertz later became an expert on Korean ceramics and donated his collection to the Fitzwilliam Museum, Cambridge.

9. FROM AUSTRALIA TO LEYTE GULF

1. Jenkins 1992, pp. 201–24. For the dismissal of plans to invade Australia, see Frei 1991, pp. 165–6.

2. On Nave, see Pfennigwerth 2006. See also the excellent account in Bou 2012, pp. 15–23.
3. Straczek, 'Origins and Development', pp. 126, 133–4, 172–3.
4. On Room and the Australian codebreakers working on Japanese signals, see Hirschfeld and Wall 1987 (the quotation comes from p. 581), McPhee 1998, Merrillees 2001, Donovan and Mack 2002, Ball and Tamura 2013, Dufty 2017 and Funch 2003. The account of an interview with Treweek in 1990 is contained in Ball and Tamura 2013, pp. 131–4.
5. Cited by Sissons 2013, pp. 17–19.
6. Sissons 2013, p. 19; Jenkins 1992, pp. 45–6; TNA, ADM 223/496 'Establishment of a Special Intelligence Section in Australia'; HW 8/125, typescript 'Basic Japanese', 1/9/1943, by Paymaster Lieutenant A. B. Jamieson RANR; HW14/90, handwritten note by J. O. Lloyd, 21/10/1943.
7. On Lake, see Jones 2017; Ajioka and Tornatore-Loong 2011, p. 47, n. 16; University of Sydney Archives, staff card for Lake, Margaret Ethel; Straczek, 'Origins and Development', pp. 189–90. The original English title of Lake's translation was *Singapore, the Japanese Version* (Sydney, 1960); it was later reissued by Oxford University Press, Singapore. Sadler himself was not involved in any of the work relating to Japanese decrypts, partly because his wife was half-Japanese and partly because he was thought to lack discretion: Merrillees 2001, p. 8; Straczek, 'Origins and Development', p. 190.
8. NAA, A816, 44/301/9, 'Royal Military College: Changes in Curriculum, etc', 3/12/1937; 'Minute by Minister [of Defence Harold Thorby]', 28/7/1938; 'Study of Japanese Language in the Services: Report of Sub-committee', 11/1/1940; etc. Takeda 2018, pp. 126–33, examines the proposals in detail. See also Funch 2003, pp. 12–16.
9. Funch 2003, pp. 36–50.
10. On Inagaki, see Nicholls 2007, pp. 79–80, and the papers contained in NAA, A367, C73350, 'Inagaki Mowsey Moshi'. His Australian wife Rose had died in 1943, but their daughter Murako remained in Australia.
11. IWM, Sound 25574, recording of an interview conducted in 2003 with Frederick Alexander Arblaster, an Australian NCO who studied at the Censorship Office Japanese School and then worked throughout the war as a Japanese linguist. Arblaster implies in his interview that Selwood looked Japanese; she was married to a missionary, Frederick James Selwood, but her mother was Japanese, Mary Mitsu Sakurai Pigott, whose grave is in Yokohama Foreign General Cemetery. Funch 2003, pp. 39–48.
12. Miles, 'History of the Operations', pp. 5–7, 9, 13, 33, 37 (interview

with Sparnon). Alison Broinowski, 'Sparnon, Norman James (1913–1995)', *Australian Dictionary of Biography*, National Centre of Biography, Australian National University (http://adb.anu.edu.au/biography/sparnon-norman-james-21619/text31832).

13. Brown 2006, pp. 14–16, 21; Bleakley 1991, pp. 49–51. There was a numerical limit placed on the number of Australian servicewomen permitted to serve outside Australia, and as a result no women from Central Bureau were allowed to leave the country: Dufty 2017, p. 336. For a picture of the camouflaged concrete building, see Bleakley 1991, p. 69. John (Jack) Ashton Morse Bleakley (1922–2016) joined the RAAF in 1942 and served with No. 1 Wireless Unit in Townsville and later in several locations in New Guinea.

14. Ballard 1991, pp. 134–5.

15. Ballard 1991, p. 146; Smith 2000, pp. 112–14 (based on Day's unpublished memoirs). According to a communication from Geoff Day in the *Central Bureau Intelligence Corps Association Newsletter* (Australia), June 2002, p. 6, the other intercept operators who travelled with him from Singapore to Australia were J. Lang, D. Seager, H. Finch, G. Connor, J. Bloomfield, J. Davis, O. Jones, F. McGuire and G. Gamlin; they all served out the war in Australia, the Pacific Islands and the Philippines. On his escape from Singapore on 31 January 1942, see Day 2003.

16. Sissons 2013, pp. 22–5; Smith 2000, pp. 109, 169–70; Duffy 2017, pp. 175–8; Straczek, 'Origins and Development', pp. 297–8.

17. Maneki 2007, p. 75. He may have got the name wrong: working as a linguist at ATIS was Lieutenant-Commander Lionel Francis Hopkinson of the Royal Navy, who had indeed escaped from Singapore to Australia early in 1942.

18. Sissons 2013, p. 23; Straczek, 'Origins and Development', p. 298.

19. Sissons 2013, pp. 22–5.

20. When I worked as a lecturer in Japanese at the University of Tasmania from 1978 to 1982, Ian Smith was my head of department, but he never mentioned his wartime work on Japanese codes, presumably because he still felt bound by the Official Secrets Act. Smith's own account of his wartime work in the section, written as a letter in answer to a query from Sissons in 1990, is in Ball and Tamura 2013, pp. 125–30. Details of staff from Ball and Tamura 2013, p. 89.

21. Archer's report is in NAA, A981, TIM P 9. He found less evidence of Japanese penetration than he had been expecting but noted the suspicion that there was a secret Japanese radio transmitter in operation.

22. Kornicki 2019, pp. 100–1. The others were Hubert Ashton Graves (1894–1972, later Sir Hubert), who was in Japan from 1924 onwards and after the war served as ambassador to Vietnam; Dermot MacDermot

(1906–?), who joined the service in 1929; Richard Leslie Cowley (1897–?), who joined in 1919 and after repatriation served as a consul in Brazil until he was seconded for work in Australia; Henry Raywood Sawbridge (1907–90), who joined the service in 1930, and after repatriation served in the Foreign Office before being sent to Australia; and Edward Thomas Biggs (1914–?), who joined in 1938 and from 1942 to 1944 was serving in Kilindini until he was seconded for work in Australia. Details of their careers are taken from the Foreign Office List for 1941 and successive years. In 1939, Graves was consul general in Kobe and was gathering information about the Japanese Navy: Arthur Page 2008, pp. 25–7.

23. McNaughton 2006, pp. 78, 124–5, 179.
24. On the formation of FRUMEL and Central Bureau, see Bou 2012, chapter 2, and Drea 1992, pp. 15–25. Drea is a well-researched examination of the work of MacArthur's intelligence operations, and he provides a detailed account of MacArthur's use of ULTRA intelligence obtained from decrypts in his campaigns; a shortcoming is that he wrongly assumes that all the breaking of Japanese codes during the war was done by Americans.
25. Ballard 1991, p. 163; Dufty 2017, p. 138.
26. Melinsky 1998, p. 14; Tuck, 'Bedford Japanese School' (Kornicki 2019, p. 25); Stripp 1989, pp. 10–12.
27. Ballard 1991, p. 163.
28. Ballard 1991, p. 195.
29. Dufty 2017, pp. 257–66. For an illustration showing the nature of the find, see Bleakley 1991, pp. 112–13.
30. Ballard 1991, p. 194.
31. Tuck, 'Bedford Japanese School' (Kornicki 2019, p. 25).
32. Melinsky 1998, pp. 20, 36–9.
33. Cannon 1954, pp. 135, 141, 250–1.
34. IWM, Sound 10095, recording of interview with Richnell in 1988; obituary in *The Independent*, 22/2/1994.
35. The photograph is in Ballard 1991. Eunson's name appears in the list of those who took the Air Ministry Phonetics Course at SOAS in 1943–4 in SOAS Archives, SOAS/REG/01/05, and his results are in TNA, HW 41/139, RAF VIII Phonetics Course, 22/1–29/3/1944 (he was the only student to be placed in the first class, and his report said he was 'good all round' and had 'a good ear'). His nephew, David Partner, who provided the other information, told me that Eunson said nothing about the years 1945 to 1947, when he was demobbed, except that he was 'clearing up'.
36. Melinsky 1998, pp. 44–5; Brown 2006, pp. 75, 77, 80; Dufty 2017,

pp. 297–305. See also the recollections of Bleakley, who fails to mention Hall, in Bleakley 1991, pp. 176–81.

37. Melinsky 1998, pp. 44–5; Brown 2006, pp. 81, 87.

38. Hall reported on his activities to Captain Tuck: see Tuck, 'Bedford Japanese School' (Kornicki 2019, p. 25). His responses to an interview in 2005 are summarized in Bou 2012, p. 67, and the photograph is item P00514.001 in the Australian War Memorial (in the front row, Jack Brown is on the far right and Peter Hall second on the left, in an Australian slouch hat): for the inscription and the identities of all of them, see Brown 2006, pp. 128–9, and Bleakley 1991, pp. 190–1.

39. Melinsky 1998, pp. 52, 56–63, 65–6; Dufty 2017, pp. 327–8.

40. General Headquarters, *A Brief History of the G-2 Section, GHQ SWPA and Affiliated Units*, p. 63; Gilmore 1995 and 2004.

41. General Headquarters, *Operations of the Allied Translator and Interpreter Section*, p. 58.

42. Page 2008, pp. 51–4, 66–9

43. Miles points out (Miles, 'History of the Operations', pp. 17–18) that ATIS was first commanded by Colonel Karl F. Baldwin and then, three weeks later, Colonel Sydney F. Mashbir took over; a history of ATIS written in 1944 by Captain Charles Henry Reichardt was suppressed, and the official history (General Headquarters, *Operations of the Allied Translator and Interpreter Section*), which was written by Mashbir but edited and revised by Captain Alexander W. Grey of the Australian Imperial Forces, credits Mashbir with both the origins and development of ATIS. What is indisputable is that the two Army compilers made hardly any mention of the work of the naval and air force sections anywhere in the two volumes of the official history. The roles of Mashbir and Grey in the compilation of the official history are mentioned in small print on the title page. On the Naval Section, see General Headquarters, *Operations of the Allied Translator and Interpreter Section*, p. 9.

44. General Headquarters, *Operations of the Allied Translator and Interpreter Section*, appendices 3 and 9, and p. 7. For a list of the Nisei taken to Australia by their commander, Major David Swift, in June 1942, see Dunn 2018, pp. 10–11. Dunn provides a useful summary of the activities of ATIS with a bibliography but no footnotes; included are some valuable appendices reprinting reports on interrogating techniques and other matters and lists of ATIS staff. Page 2008 is an excellent account of an Australian linguist's career at ATIS and includes many photographs of Japanese prisoners taken from the collection of the Australian War Memorial. A photocopy of the telephone directory, dated May 1944, is in the MacArthur Memorial Library and Archives in Virginia, and the

ATIS staff are listed on pp. 63–9; Professor Allison Gilmore kindly provided me with a PDF.

45. Miles, 'History of the Operations', p. 34; Page 2008, p. 326.

46. *The Exploitation of Japanese Documents* (ATIS Publication no. 6, 14/12/1944; I used the copy in IWM, Storry Papers, Box 4, but the manual is also reprinted in General Headquarters, *Operations of the Allied Translator and Interpreter Section*, vol. 1, appendix 5), pp. 1, 7; General Headquarters, *Operations of the Allied Translator and Interpreter Section*, p. 12.

47. AWM, AWM82 1/3/2, 1/3/14, 1/3/39; all the documents are now scanned and viewable on a CD-ROM at the AWM. For further details, see https://www.awm.gov.au/collection/C1424606

48. According to Page 2008, p. 103, every ATIS translator had a code number, and on reports this was usually followed by the initials of the typist. There is a complete set of ATIS reports on microfiche in LHC.

49. AWM, AWM54 423/4/8, File 2.

50. On Sparnon's role, see Miles, 'History of the Operations', p. 14 (based on an interview with Sparnon); AWM, AWM55 3/1, *ATIS Current Translations*, p. 14 (18/1/1943).

51. AWM, AWM54 423/4/9, File 2.

52. AWM, AWM55 2/1, ADVATIS translation 1 (30/11/1944); AWM54 423/4/8 File 1.

53. AWM, AWM54 423/4/116, *ATIS Bulletin* 1002 (7/5/1944); AWM55 2/1 ADVATIS translation 1 (30/11/1944).

54. General Headquarters, *Operations of the Allied Translator and Interpreter Section*, pp. 44–50.

55. AWM, AWM55 1/1, *ATIS Bulletins* no. 1 (29/10/1942); General Headquarters, *Operations of the Allied Translator and Interpreter Section*, appendix 8.

56. TNA, WO 208 /5151, ATIS Limited Distribution Interrogation Report #3, 8/7/1943.

10. THE END OF THE WAR IN THE PACIFIC

1. Lowry's painting is in Kelvingrove Art Gallery and Museum, Glasgow. For contemporary photographs of the celebrations of VE Day and VJ Day, see the Imperial War Museum's website (https://www.iwm.org.uk).

2. TNA, WO 208/524, Winterborn to Lieutenant-Colonel B. F. Montgomery at the War Office, 24/4/1945. The document to which Winterborn was responding is unfortunately not included.

3. Maneki 2007, p. 45.

4. Goodman 2005, pp. 30–1.

5. General Headquarters, *Operations of the Allied Translator and Interpreter Section*, pp. 13, 36–7; Miles, 'History of the Operations', pp. 35–6; McNaughton 2006, pp. 387, 392.

6. Recollections of W. J. Stonebridge, a stoker on board HMS *Whelp*: https://www.bbc.co.uk/history/ww2peopleswar/stories/90/a3509390.shtml

7. Beasley, 'Traveller to Japan', pp. 60–2. Donald Menzies, a British Boulder graduate who was posted to the *King George V* as a Japanese interpreter, mentioned his surprise when Rawlings spoke some words of Japanese to him: UCB archives, Roger Pineau Collection 3–4, letters from Menzies of 21/4/1982 and 19/9/1982. For a list of the Allied ships present on 2 September 1945, see https://en.wikipedia.org/wiki/List_of_Allied_ships_at_the_Japanese_surrender. Beasley, 'Traveller to Japan', pp. 60–2; Stillwell 1996, pp. 53–5. Stillwell notes that Missouri was President Truman's home state and that his daughter christened the ship; it is possible that was the reason for the choice of the ship as the setting for the surrender ceremony.

8. Kase 1950, pp. 4–12; the quotations come from this account. The author of this book, Kase Toshikazu, was one of the party that travelled to the *Missouri* for the ceremony. His son, Kase Toshiaki, is a controversial historical revisionist who contests, among other things, the accepted account of the Nanjing Massacre.

9. According to the Deck Log Book of the USS *Missouri* (entry for 2/9/1945), the representatives of the United Kingdom were Admiral Sir Bruce Fraser, Captain A. D. Nicholl, Commodore R. H. Courage, Commodore A. P. Cartwright, Surgeon Lieutenant G. E. Cayman and Lieutenant V. C. Merry; the representatives of the British Pacific Fleet were Vice-Admiral Sir H. B. Rawlings, Rear-Admiral E. J. P. Brind, Commodore J. P. L. Reid, and Lieutenants G. E. Cook and E. B. Ashmore: a facsimile of the original (US National Archives Identifier: 595157) is available online at https://catalog.archives.gov/id/595157/2/public?contributionType=transcription. However, the list is incomplete.

10. Dingman 2009, pp. 164–6; Beasley, 'Traveller to Japan', pp. 60–2. For the postmark, see the envelope in UCB archives, Paul J. Sherman Collection, 1–2. According to Gowing's obituary in *King's College [Cambridge] Annual Record* (1970), p. 37, he was serving as staff officer (intelligence) 'on the Staff of the U.S. Naval Commander [Admiral Chester Nimitz] and was aboard the flagship when General MacArthur received the surrender'. He was actually on the staff of Rear-Admiral Brind, but from 1/7 to 23/9/1945 he was serving on board HMS *Newfoundland*, which was indeed present at the surrender ceremony in Tokyo Bay, and he may well have accompanied Brind to the ceremony.

11. Kirby 1969, pp. 283–8. For the suicide boat men, see the photographs in IWM, Papers of Cecil Harcourt, Documents 14003, album of photographs.

12. Harcourt 1947, pp. 7–8. On Eccles, see http://www.navy.gov.au/biography/admiral-john-arthur-symons-eccles. In the official Admiralty photograph of the surrender, he is standing behind Vice-Admiral Fujita: TNA, CO 1069/456, p. 7; however, a photograph in the IWM (Papers of Cecil Harcourt, Documents 14003) shows him seated at the table explaining the terms, presumably in Japanese. The delay in holding the surrender ceremony was due to Generalissimo Chiang Kai-shek's insistence that the Japanese surrender of the China theatre in Nanjing take place first; Chiang Kai-shek appointed one Chinese (Major-General Pan Hwa-kuei) and one American representative (Colonel Adrian Williamson) to take part in the ceremony: see TNA, ADM 116/5354.

13. Allen 1976, p. xiii; Allen 1984, p. 538; Allen 2010, p. xxii; Brett-James 1951, pp. 427–33; the plate facing p. 435 reproduces photographs from the Imperial War Museum showing the landing craft approaching and then landing at Singapore.

14. Cortazzi 1998, p. 30, and email from Cortazzi, 31/3/2015.

15. Singh 1958, pp. 206, 214; LHC, General Sir Douglas Gracey Papers, Gracey 4/13, Mountbatten to Gracey, 31/10/1945, and Gracey to Mountbatten, 9/11/1945.

16. CACC Tuck 1/11, 'Diary of the Japanese Translation Party', entry for 10/4/1946; IWM, photograph SE 4612. For a detailed account of the surrender negotiations conducted by interpreters, see Page 2008, pp. 410–29.

17. TNA, ADM 1/18165.

18. Allen 1990, p. 26.

19. Farquarson 2002, pp. 208–9.

11. FINISHING THE JOB

1. IWM, Storry Papers, boxes 3 (notebook) and 4 (Provisional Stop List).

2. Allen 1990, pp. 26–7. There is an extant film of Allen interrogating surrendered Japanese personnel at Shwegyin in Burma (Myanmar), to the north-east of Rangoon: IWM, JIN 120.

3. Allen 2010, pp. xxii–xxiii, xxxi.

4. TNA, ADM 116/5562, 'Prohibition of Destruction'.

5. LHC, Gracey Papers 6/4, Terauchi to Gracey, 20/10/1945; 6/13, *The Japanese Account of Their Operations in Burma* (Rangoon: HQ 12th Army, December 1945); 7/8, SEATIC report no. 249 (25/5/1947)—this was the last report published by SEATIC. LHC, Gracey Papers 6/5~10 consist

of a number of detailed reports on Japanese operations at the end of the war compiled, translated and typed at Phnom Penh in November 1945; each carries a red seal reading 'Fukutomi' and that probably signifies that the compiler was Major-General Fukutomi Banzō, chief of staff of the Japanese 11th Army at the end of the war.

6. TNA, WO 208/5151, 'Report on Air Interrogations from F/O H.A.H. Cortazzi, RAF Section, SEATIC', 22/3/1946; Cortazzi email to author, 31/3/2015.
7. TNA, WO 203/6305, SEATIC Intelligence Bulletin 227 (19/1/1946), issued under the name of Lt/Col. Dredge.
8. TNA, ADM 223/801, report by Lt. Boyd, 30/11/45.
9. Grimes, *History of the Mission* (quotation from p. 3); Packard 1996, pp. 162–3.
10. Grimes, *History of the Mission*, p. 45. The other three with Catt were Heath, Quine and Wilkinson. Catt's name is mentioned in NavTechJap report X-17, while Stewart was the co-author of report O-45(N); IWM, recording of an interview with Donovan Thomas Richnell made in 1988, Sound 10095.
11. TNA, HO 228/2.
12. Grimes, *History of the Mission*, pp. 9, 11. PDFs of the reports are available at http://www.fischer-tropsch.org/primary_documents/gvt_reports/USNAVY/USNTMJ%20Reports/USNTMJ_toc.htm. The welding report is S-91(N).
13. Cribb 2016 and the other chapters in von Lingen 2016; Cheah 2017. The identities of the interpreters can probably be ascertained from the South East Asia war crimes files in TNA (WO 325), but the COVID-19 lockdown has prevented me from seeing them.
14. Takeda 2010, pp. 69–72. An account of the trial by one of the Nisei and some photographs are contained in Ichinokuchi 1988, pp. 142–50.
15. Takeda 2010, pp. 27–30, 53, 59–61, 68–9, 124, 129; Footitt and Tobia 2013, pp. 114–16, 120.
16. The account of Cyril Wild is based on Bradley 1997.
17. On the controversial issues, see Ryan 2012.
18. TNA, WO 235/817, trial of Sergeant Aoki Toshio. There was an interpreter present at the trial but no name is given.
19. Bawden, 'Charles Roskelly Bawden: An Academic's Life'; interview with Ian Willison, 29/10/2015.
20. Hugh Lloyd-Jones, 'Memoir of WWII Service'.
21. Ward, 'Notes by Joseph Haggitt Ward on Army Japanese Course at Bedford, Apr 1945–Sep 1945, and Subsequent Service'.
22. Memoirs of John Nevile Whitehorn.
23. Allen 2010, pp. xxviii, xxxii–xxxiii; Allen 1976, pp. 151–5. Fujiwara

described himself as the 'Lawrence of Arabia of South-East Asia'. See SEATIC Bulletin 240 (9/7/1946), especially 'Introduction' and pp. 58–61 (quotations from p. 59) and Fujiwara 1983.

24. Allen 2010, pp. xxxii–xxxiii, xxxvi; interview with Christian van Nieuwerburgh. Newington's real name was Arthur van Nieuwerburgh; he was Belgian, but his mother was British, so he fled to England when Germany invaded Belgium in 1940. He changed his name to Newington during the war, as he did not appreciate being taken for a German. After the war, he resumed his Belgian citizenship and changed his name back to van Nieuwerburgh. He was demobbed in Japan and remained there for some time, marrying a Japanese woman; he then spent twenty years in Lebanon as a French–Japanese translator for Toshiba but was murdered in 1988.

25. The reports are cited in Ōba 1995, p. 154. The source cited is Daniels' *The War-Time Courses*, but the one extant copy of Daniels' report does not contain the personal reports, and they are probably now lost: see Kornicki 2018. McEwan's name does not appear on this page of Ōba's book or in the accompanying RAF report, but the identification seems certain as only two of the students joined the RAF, and McEwan, as well as being reserved, was on the refresher course mentioned earlier in the report. Obituary in the *Annual Report* (King's College, Cambridge; 1970), p. 45. On Saigon and the meeting with Terauchi, see Willie Minto, 'John MacEwan [*sic*], "Mac", R.A.F.'. William Minto did an Air Ministry course at SOAS in 1943–4: SOAS Archives, SOAS/REG/01/01/05.

26. Bates 1993, p. 253.

27. Beasley, 'Traveller to Japan', p. 63.

28. Beasley, 'Traveller to Japan', pp. 63–9; Dingman 2009 and accompanying photograph. Beasley's house in Yokosuka, which came with a garden and two servants, became a home away from home for other Boulder graduates at Thanksgiving and Christmas.

29. Letter from Donald Gowing of 14/9/1945 in possession of Nik Gowing.

30. On MacDermot's role in Manila from May 1945, see TNA, FO 369/3348 and his biography in the *Foreign Office List*, 1947. MacDermot's informal account of his arrival in Japan is contained in *Japan and Dependencies: Political and Economic Reports 1906–1960*, vol. 17, 'Japan: Political Reports 1945–1953' ([Slough]: Archive Editions, 1994), p. 17. His first dispatch from Japan, dated 3/9/1945, indicates that he first took over the British consulate in Yokohama before proceeding to Tokyo: TNA, FO 371/46510.

31. TNA, FO 371/46510, dispatch of 21/11/1945 addressed to J. C. Sterndale Bennett, the head of the Far Eastern Department at the Foreign Office.

32. See Figgess' account in Cortazzi 2001, pp. 5–10; Bates 1993, p. xvii. Sir Dermot Francis MacDermot, KCMG CBE, who was also known as The MacDermot and the Prince of Coolavin, served in Australia (December 1942 to March 1943) and at Washington, DC (April 1943 to February 1944), according to *The Foreign Office List and Diplomatic and Consular Year Book* (1951), pp. 361–2. However, Robert Weighton recalled that a 'Mr McDermott', whom he had known in Taiwan when the latter was acting consul there, was assistant head of the British Political Warfare Mission in Denver until the spring of 1944 (Weighton 2008, p. 302); if this was Dermot MacDermot, then he may in fact have been working for the mission, which had its headquarters in Washington but broadcast from Denver. According to Gore-Booth 1974, p. 115, he and MacDermot worked together in Lourenço Marques to help those who had been repatriated resume their onward journeys. A document cited in Straczek 'Origins and Development', p. 298, makes it clear that in Australia he worked at Central Bureau. MacDermot was given a CBE in 1947 for his work at the Liaison Mission. There appear to be no records of HMS *Return*, which was the name given to the embassy in its capacity as a naval shore station in late 1945, in TNA. Some Australian naval ratings were also attached to HMS *Return*: see the account of Roy Scrivener at the Australians at War Film Archive, http://australiansatwarfilmarchive.unsw.edu.au/archive/171-roy-scrivener

33. TNA, CAB 79/37/19, minutes of the meeting of the Chiefs of Staff Committee, 17/8/1945, pp. 324–5; Bates 1993, pp. 11–43, 66–7, 71–2, 257. See also Nish 2011.

34. Clifton 1950, pp. 7–8, 24–5, 46. For a map showing the distribution of the various contingents of the BCOF, see Singh 1958, map following p. 100.

35. Clifton 1950, pp. 44, 85.

36. Clifton 1950, pp. 21–5, 74–5, 97, 107. On the concealment of military equipment, see the report in *The Times*, 6/1/1948, p. 3.

37. British Commonwealth Forces, *Know Japan* (1946); there is a copy in the Imperial War Museum. The full text of the policy on fraternization is contained in Singh 1958, pp. 60–1, where it is stipulated that members of the BCOF should not take part in any sporting or athletic contests with Japanese.

38. AWM 114, 423/2/1; Bates 1993, pp. 111–21; Nish 2011, appendix 6.

39. The albums of James Sutherland are one example.

40. AWM 114, 130/2/52, typed outline of CSDIC activities 28/9/1945–30/6/1946, dated 3/7/1946. James Sutherland's papers include a typed CSDIC bulletin dated December 1946 that gives the names of all the per-

sonnel and their units. On the RAAF language school, see Funch 2003, pp. 51–75.

41. AWM 114, 423/10/5, intelligence reports dated 3/6/1946 and 18/6/1946. The former mentions the involvement of Japanese communists, who were also the subject of other reports in AWM 114, 423/10/2.

42. AWM 114, 423/10/11, extract from letter no. 4 from Itō Shigeo in War Crimes Compound, Rabaul, to Mis Matsutani Sachiko in Kumamoto (21/7/1947), report of 10/4/1947 including one undated letter from Ozaki Toki of Saoka-mura in Kōchi Prefecture to her husband.

43. AWM 114, 423/10/11, petition of 30/4/1949 from Niimi Kazue.

44. Nish 2011, pp. 3–4, 6–7. This book contains many translations he did in 1946 from material relating to the war with commentary added and photographs taken by the author in Japan at the time.

45. Interviews with James Sutherland in Peebles, 5/9/2019 and 5–6/11/2019.

46. SOAS Archives holds the papers of Leslie Philips, including his unpublished autobiography.

47. Bawden, 'Charles Roskelly Bawden: An Academic's Life'; letter from Bawden, 2/1/2016.

48. Cortazzi 2013 (quotations from pp. 136–7); Cortazzi email to author, 31/3/2015.

49. Bates 1993, p. 172.

50. See the guide to the translations written by Dr Greg Bradshaw of the NARA, College Park, Maryland: https://text-message.blogs.archives.gov/2014/10/24/exploitation-of-captured-japanese-documents-by-the-far-eastern-section-foreign-intelligence-branch-of-the-office-of-naval-intelligence-op-16-fe-1944-1946

51. Kornicki 2019, pp. xix–xx; emails from John Cook.

12. LOOKING BACK

1. Loewe 1993, p. 262.

2. Chadwick, 'Relatively Peaceful War', p. 71; TNA, HW 41/139 'Top Secret and Confidential', undated, unsigned.

3. Ferris 1993.

4. McLelland 2017, pp. 43–4.

5. Footitt and Tobia 2013, p. 178; McLelland 2015, pp. 182–3. The reports I am referring to are the Scarborough Report (Independent Commission of Enquiry into Oriental, Slavonic, East European and African Studies in the UK, 1947), the Hayter Report (An interdepartmental Commission of

Enquiry on Oriental, Slavonic, East European and African Studies, 1961) and the Parker Report (Speaking for the Future, 1986).

6. Email from Ralph Lloyd-Jones, 5/3/2019.
7. Obituary of Archdale, *The Guardian*, 16/2/2000; for Eddolls, and all other Bedford graduates, see the biographies in Kornicki 2019.
8. Obituary of Kidd in *Queens' College* [Cambridge] *Record* 2004, p. 55.
9. Obituary of Gardner in *The Independent*, 1/5/1995.
10. Obituary of Charles in *The Burma Campaign Society Newsletter* 13 (September 2008): 7; Gore-Booth 1974, pp. 104–7 (quotation from p. 114).
11. Minto, 'John McEwan'; Allen 2010, p. xxxiii; Clifton 1950, p. xiv (preface written in 1949).
12. Allen 1976, p. 162.
13. Supplements to the *London Gazette* nos. 36033 (28/5/1943), p. 2421, 36309 (31/12/1943), p. 20 and 37412 (9/1/1946), p. 292. According to Ferris, Egan had been working in Cairo with the legendary Emily Anderson (1891–1962), and together they had 'ravaged Italian cryptosystems'; it may have been for this work that Egan was honoured: Ferris 2020, p. 440.
14. Slesnick 2006, p. 275; Keene 2008, p. 44; Feir 2014, pp. 46–7.
15. Norris, 'Memoir', p. [58]; letter from Norris to Fries, 1/4/2001, attached to his memoir.
16. Modiano, *Suspended Sentences: Three Novellas*, trans. Mark Polizzotti (New Haven: Yale University Press, 2014), p. 32.

APPENDIX 5: EVE EDWARDS' TOUR

1. Obituary by Walter Simon in *Bulletin of SOAS* 21 (1958): 222; TNA, WO 208/226, telegram War Office to SEATIC, 29/7/1946.
2. TNA, CO 129/616/1, 'Report on a Six Months' Tour of South East Asia, the Far East and Australia, August 1946–February 1947', by E. D. Edwards, dated 18/9/1947.

BIBLIOGRAPHY

Institutional archives

Australian War Memorial, Canberra (AWM).
Balliol College Archives, Oxford.
Bletchley Park Archives.
Bodleian Library, Oxford.
Bōei Kenkyūsho (National Institute for Defence Studies), Tokyo.
Churchill Archives Centre, Cambridge (CACC).
Dulwich College Archives.
Imperial War Museum, London (IWM).
Liddell Hart Centre for Military Archives, King's College London (LHC).
Magdalen College Archives, Oxford.
National Archives of Australia, Canberra (NAA).
National Archives and Records Administration, Washington, DC (NARA).
National Archives and Records Administration, College Park, MD.
Naval Historical Branch, HM Naval Base Portsmouth (NHB).
Rockefeller Archive Center, Sleepy Hollow, New York.
SOAS Archives, London.
State Library of New South Wales, Sydney, Australia (SLNSW).
Surrey History Centre, Woking.
The National Archives, Kew (TNA).
University of California Berkeley Bancroft Library.
University of Colorado Boulder Archives (UCBA).
University of Sydney Archives, Australia.

Personal archives

Eileen Mary Barker (née Clark) papers: Adrian Barker, London.
David Bentliffe papers: London.
Patrick Field papers: Bishop's Stortford.

BIBLIOGRAPHY

Donald Gowing papers: Nik Gowing, London.
Ian Grimble–Wilfrid Noyce letters: Balliol College, Oxford.
Leslie Sargeant Phillips papers: SOAS.
Professor Michael Screech papers: Professor Timon Screech, London.
Robert Milne Sellar letters and photographs: Professor Robin Sellar, Edinburgh.
James Sutherland papers: Peebles.
Philip Taylor papers: Rosy Thacker, Matlock.
Oswald Tuck papers: Roger Vincent-Townend, Bromley.
Baron Twining papers: Bodleian Library, Oxford.

Interviews, letters and emails

Ballingal, Andrew (son of Neil Ballingal).
Barrow, Professor Julia Steuart (daughter of George Wallis Steuart Barrow), email of 6 January 2019.
Cook, John, email and telephone interviews, 10–12 January 2019.
Cortazzi, Sir Hugh, email of 31 March 2015 and many conversations.
De Moubray, Guy, email of 19 November 2014.
Eunson, Jim (son of David Eunson), emails, March 2020.
Gowing, Nik (son of Donald Gowing), telephone interview, 24 July 2019.
Hely-Hutchinson, Elizabeth, interview, 23 January 2019.
Jones, David le Brun, several emails in 2015.
Lefkowitz, Professor Mary (widow of Sir Hugh Lloyd-Jones), email correspondence in 2019.
Lloyd, David (son of John Lloyd), interview, 10 March 2020.
Lloyd-Jones, Ralph (son of Hugh), email correspondence in 2019.
Loewe, Michael Arthur Nathan, interview, 17 January 2019.
Marr-Johnson, His Honour Frederick James Maugham (relative of Patrick Marr-Johnson), telephone interview, 18 November 2019.
Nish, Professor Ian, interview, 6 May 2016.
Partner, David (nephew of David Eunson), telephone interview of 25 March 2020.
Pole, David, numerous emails in 2020.
Pulleyblank, David (son of Edwin Pulleyblank), email of 11 January 2019.
Russell, Professor Donald Andrew Frank Moore, letter of 12 November 2015.
Screech, Revd Professor Michael, interview 2016.
Sellar, Professor Robin (son of Robert Milne Sellar), interview, December 2018.
Sutherland, James, interviews, 5 September and 4–5 November 2019.
Tank, Andrew (son of Rowland Meyric Johnson Tank), email of 11 April 2016.

364

BIBLIOGRAPHY

Twining, Professor William (son of Edward Francis Twining, Baron Twining of Tanganyika and Godalming), interview, 11 January 2019.

Van Nieuwerburgh, Christian (son of Arthur Newington), telephone interview, 16 March 2020.

Vennis, Diana (widow of Philip Vennis), emails, January 2020.

Whitehorn, John, email and interview, February 2016.

Willison, Ian Roy, interview, 29 October 2015.

Wilson, Nigel (colleague of Hugh Lloyd-Jones), email of 29 September 2019.

Unpublished works

Aspden, George. 'Memoirs' (incomplete copy in possession of Jim Eunson).

Barker, Eileen Mary. 'Memories of Bletchley Park' (typescript of 2009 in possession of her son Adrian Barker).

Barrow, George Wallis Steuart. 'Autobiographical Memoir 1924–1946' (manuscript written in 1999–2003, in possession of Professor Dauvit Braun).

Bawden, Charles Roskelly. 'Charles Roskelly Bawden: An Academic's Life' (typescript dated 1993, in possession of his son, Richard Bawden).

Beasley, William G. 'Traveller to Japan: Incomplete and Unreliable Recollections of My Life' (typescript dated 2002, in the possession of his son, John Beasley).

Breen, Lawrence Philip. 'Autobiography' (typescript in possession of the Breen family).

Chadwick, John. 'A Relatively Peaceful War: Personal Recollections of 1939–1945' (unpublished typescript dated 1989 in the Mycenaean Epigraphy Room in the Faculty of Classics, University of Cambridge: FC1.4).

Colchester, Rozanne (née Medhurst). 'Bletchley Park 1942–1945: Italian and Japanese Air Sections' (undated typescript in the Bletchley Park Archives).

Daniels, Frank. 'War-Time Courses' (photocopied typescript in SOAS Archives; now reprinted in Peter Kornicki, 'Frank Daniels' Report on the War-Time Japanese Courses at SOAS', *Bulletin of the School of Oriental and African Studies* 81 (2018): 301–24).

De Grey, Nigel. 'India and the Far East', chapter 5 of *Allied Sigint: Policy and Organization* (typescript in TNA, HW 43/78).

Dredge, Lt./Col. A. C. L. 'History of SEATIC (South-East Asia Translation and Interrogation Centre)' (typescript in TNA, WO 203/6286).

DuBuisson, Evelyn. 'War Time Activities in Mauritius' (undated manuscript in Surrey History Centre, Woking: DuBuisson Papers, 9307/1/1/10).

General Headquarters, Far East Command, Military Intelligence Section, General Staff. *A Brief History of the G-2 Section, GHQ SWPA and Affiliated Units* (Tokyo: GHQ SWPA 1948).

BIBLIOGRAPHY

General Headquarters, Far East Command, Military Intelligence Section, General Staff. *Operations of the Allied Translator and Interpreter Section*, Intelligence Series vol. V, 2 vols. (Tokyo: GHQ SWPA 1948; according to the title page, prepared by Colonel Sidney Mashbir, edited and revised by Captain Alexander W. Grey, Australian Imperial Forces).

Grimes, Captain C. G., USN. *History of the Mission* (U.S. Technical Mission to Japan, 1946) (available online at http://www.fischer-tropsch.org/primary_ documents/gvt_reports/USNAVY/USNTMJ%20Reports/USNTMJ-200A-0022–0071%20History%20of%20Mission.pdf).

Herbert, E. S., and C. G. Des Graz, eds. *History of the Postal and Telegraph Censorship Department, 1938–1946*, 2 vols. (London: Home Office, 1952; this was a secret publication and is only available at TNA: DEFE 1/333 and 1/334).

Hindmarsh, Albert Edward. *Navy School of Oriental Languages: History, Organization, and Administration* (University of Colorado, Boulder: [1946?]) (copies in the University of Colorado Boulder archives: William J. Hudson Collection, Box 2, and Roger Pineau Collection, Box 5, and in the National Archives at College Park, Maryland, in the series 'Historical Files of Navy Training Activities, 1940–1945', Records Group 24, identifier 6293284).

Kennedy, Captain Malcolm Duncan. *The Diaries of Captain Malcolm Duncan Kennedy, 1917–1946* (transcribed by Dr Jon Pardoe; downloadable at http://librarysupport.shef.ac.uk/kennedy_diaries.pdf).

Lloyd-Jones, Sir Hugh. 'Memoir of WWII Service' (undated typescript in the possession of Professor Mary Lefkowitz).

Miles, Kieran Laurence. 'A History of the Operations of the Allied Translator and Interpreter Section' (unpublished Postgraduate Diploma of Arts thesis, University of Queensland, 1993).

Miller, Elizabeth. Untitled memoir, Betty Archdale Papers Box 5, State Library of New South Wales, Sydney.

Minto, Willie [William]. 'John MacEwan [*sic*], "Mac", R.A.F.' (copy of unpublished manuscript in author's possession).

Newlands, Juliet Norton. 'Wartime Service of Elizabeth Helen Anderson 1906–1993' (undated typescript in possession of Alice Hermione Rose Hunt, granddaughter of Elizabeth Anderson).

Norris, Hugh. *Memoirs* (undated typescript in the possession of Bletchley Park Archives).

Pardoe, Jon. 'Captain Malcolm Kennedy and Japan, 1917–1945' (unpublished PhD dissertation, University of Sheffield, 1990; available online at https://www.sheffield.ac.uk/library/special/kennpape).

Phillips, Leslie. 'Autobiography' (undated typescript).

Report of Special Intelligence Section, HQ Australian Military Forces, Melbourne [on] Japanese Diplomatic Cyphers: Cryptographic Survey (1946; NAA; released in

BIBLIOGRAPHY

Ball and Keiko Tamura (eds), *Breaking Diplomatic Codes: David Sissons and D Special Section during the Second World War* (Canberra: Australian National University Press, 2013), pp. 53–90.

Shaw, Paymaster-Captain H. L., et al. *History of Far East Combined Bureau and H.M.S. Anderson* (typescript in TNA, HW 4/25).

Stockton, David Leonard. 'Recollections' (undated typescript, Magdalen College Archives, Oxford).

Straczek, Jozef H. 'The Origins and Development of Royal Australian Naval Signals Intelligence in an Era of Imperial Defence, 1914–1945' (unpublished PhD dissertation, University of New South Wales, 2008).

Tiltman, Brigadier John H. 'Some Reminiscences' (*c*.1965–8; typescript marked 'TOP SECRET TRINE' in NARA, United States: NR4632 ZEMA37 38221 19390000; National Archives identifier 2811397; the copy in TNA in Kew is unavailable for consultation, but the US archives are happy to provide a microfilm).

Tuck, Oswald. *The Bedford Japanese School* (typescript completed in late 1945 in Churchill College Archives, Cambridge, Tuck Papers 5/5. Reprinted in Kornicki 2019).

——— 'Diaries' (official), in Churchill College Archives, Cambridge, Tuck Papers.

——— 'Diaries' (personal), in the Oswald Tuck papers, Bromley.

Ward, Joseph Haggitt. 'Notes by Joseph Haggitt Ward on Army Japanese Course at Bedford, Apr 1945–Sep 1945, and Subsequent Service' (undated typescript in possession of Joseph Ward).

Whitehorn, John Nevile. 'Memoirs' (undated typescript in possession of Mr Whitehorn).

Wilkinson, Hugh Everard. 'My Life Story' (undated typescript in possession of Mr Wilkinson).

Wyatt, Kitty. 'Kitty Wyatt's Reminiscences of Her Time at Station X: Bletchley Park' (undated typescript in possession of her daughter, Barbara Wyatt).

Published works

Adachi, Ken. *The Enemy That Never Was: A History of the Japanese Canadians*, 2nd edn, updated by Roger Daniels (Toronto: McClelland and Stewart, 1991).

Ajioka Chiaki and Maria Connie Tornatore-Loong. *Japan in Sydney: Professor Sadler and Modernism 1920–1930s* (Sydney: University of Sydney, 2011).

Allen, Louis. *Sittang: The Last Battle; The End of the Japanese in Burma, July–August 1945* (London: MacDonald, 1973).

——— *The End of the War in Asia* (London: Hart-Davis MacGibbon, 1976).

——— *Burma: The Longest War* (London: J. M. Dent & Sons, 1984).

367

BIBLIOGRAPHY

———— 'From Interrogator ... to Interpreter', interview in *Japan Digest* (October 1990), pp. 25–9.

———— 'Innocents Abroad: Investigating War Crimes in South-East Asia', in Ian Nish and Mark Allen (eds), *War, Conflict and Security in Japan and Asia Pacific, 1941–52: The Writings of Louis Allen* (Folkestone, Kent: Global Oriental, 2010), pp. xxi–xxxvi.

Andrew, Christopher. 'F. H. Hinsley and the Cambridge Moles: Two Patterns of Intelligence Recruitment', in R. T. B. Langhorne (ed.), *Diplomacy and Intelligence in the Second World War: Essays in Honour of F. H. Hinsley* (Cambridge: Cambridge University Press, 1985), pp. 22–40.

———— 'Bletchley Park in Pre-war Perspective', in Ralph Erskine and Michael Smith (eds), *Action This Day* (London: Bantam Press, 2001), pp. 1–14.

Arntson, Jessica. 'Journey to Boulder: The Japanese American Instructors at the Navy Japanese Language School, 1942–1946', in Arturo Aldama et al. (eds), *Enduring Legacies: Ethnic Histories and Cultures of Colorado* (Niwot, CO: University Press of Colorado, 2014), pp. 175–94.

Axelrod, Joseph. 'The Navy Language School Program and Foreign Languages in Schools and Colleges: Aims and Techniques', *Modern Language Journal* 29 (1945): 40–7.

Azuma Eiichiro. *Between Two Empires: Race, History, and Transnationalism in Japanese America* (New York: Oxford University Press, 2005).

Baker, Anne. *From Biplane to Spitfire: The Life of Air Chief Marshal Sir Geoffrey Salmond KCB KCMG DSO* (Barnsley: Leo Cooper, 2003).

Ball, Desmond, and Keiko Tamura (eds). *Breaking Diplomatic Codes: David Sissons and D Special Section during the Second World War* (Canberra: Australian National University Press, 2013).

Ballard, Geoffrey St Vincent. *On Ultra Active Service: The Story of Australia's Signals Intelligence Operations during World War II* (Richmond, Victoria: Spectrum Publications, 1991).

Bates, Darrell. *A Gust of Plumes: A Biography of Lord Twining of Godalming and Tanganyika* (London: Hodder & Stoughton 1972).

Bates, Peter. *Japan and the British Commonwealth Occupation Force, 1946–52* (London: Brassey's, 1993).

Batey, Mavis. 'Breaking Italian Naval Enigma', in Ralph Erskine and Michael Smith (eds), *Action This Day* (London: Bantam Press, 2001), pp. 94–109.

Bayly, C. A., and T. N. Harper. *Forgotten Armies: The Fall of British Asia 1941–1945* (London: Allen Lane. 2004).

Beckhough, Harry. *Secret Communications: The Hidden History of Code Breaking; From Early Centuries to Bletchley Park and the Cold War* (London: Minerva Press, 1995).

Best, Antony. *Britain, Japan and Pearl Harbor: Avoiding War in East Asia* (London: Routledge, 1995).

———— 'Constructing an Image: British Intelligence and Whitehall's Perception of Japan, 1931–1939', *Intelligence and National Security* 11 (1996): 403–23.

———— '"This probably over-valued military power": British Intelligence and Whitehall's Perception of Japan, 1939–1941', *Intelligence and National Security* 12 (1997): 67–91.

———— *British Intelligence and the Japanese Challenge in Asia, 1914–1941* (Basingstoke: Palgrave Macmillan, 2002).

———— 'Major-General F. S. G. Piggott (1883–1966)', in Hugh Cortazzi (ed.), *Britain and Japan: Biographical Portraits*, vol. 8 (Leiden: Global Oriental, 2013), pp. 102–16.

Binkley, Cameron. *The Defense Language Institute Foreign Language Center: A Pictorial History* (Monterey, CA: U.S. Army Presidio of Monterey, 2011).

Blacker, Carmen. 'Recollections of *Temps perdus* at Bletchley Park', in F. H. Hinsley and Alan Stripp (eds), *Codebreakers: The Inside Story of Bletchley Park* (Oxford: Oxford University Press, 1993), pp. 300–5.

———— 'Two Piggotts: Sir Francis Taylor Piggott (1952–1925) and Major General F. S. G. Piggott (1883–1966)', in Hugh Cortazzi and Gordon Daniels (eds), *Britain and Japan 1859–1991: Themes and Personalities* (London: Routledge, 1991), pp. 118–27.

Bleakley, Jack. *The Eavesdroppers* (Canberra: Australian Government Publishing Service, 1991).

Borton, Hugh. *Spanning Japan's Modern Century: The Memoirs of Hugh Borton* (Lanham, MD: Lexington Books, 2002).

Bou, Jean. *MacArthur's Secret Bureau: The Story of the Central Bureau, General MacArthur's Signals Intelligence Organisation* (Loftus, New South Wales: Australian Military History Publications, 2012).

Boyd, Carl. *Hitler's Japanese Confidant: General Ōshima Hiroshi and Magic Intelligence* (Lawrence, KS: University Press of Kansas 1993).

Bradford, Richard. 'Learning the Enemy's Language: U.S. Navy Officer Language Students in Japan, 1920–1941', *International Journal of Naval History* 1, no. 1 (2002) (online journal).

Bradley, James. *Cyril Wild: The Tall Man Who Never Slept*, 2nd edn (Bognor Regis: Woodfield Publishing, 1997).

Brett-James, Antony. *Ball of Fire: The Fifth Indian Division in the Second World War* (Aldershot: Gale and Polden, 1951).

British Commonwealth Forces. *Know Japan*, issued under the direction of the commander-in-chief, BCOF (South Yarra, Victoria: Rodney Press, 1946).

Brown, Alfred Jack. *Katakana Man: I Worked Only for Generals* (Australian Capital Territory: Air Power Development Centre, 2006).

Brown, Ian. *The School of Oriental and African Studies: Imperial Training and the Expansion of Learning* (Cambridge: Cambridge University Press, 2016).

Budiansky, Stephen. *Battle of Wits: The Complete Story of Codebreaking in World War II* (London: Viking, 2000).

Bywater, Hector C. *The Great Pacific War: A History of the American–Japanese Campaign of 1931–33* (Boston, MA: H. Mifflin Co., 1925).

Cannon, M. Hamlin. *Leyte: The Return to the Philippines* (Washington, DC: Office of the Chief of Military History, Department of the Army, 1954).

Chadwick, John. 'A Biographical Fragment: 1942–5', in Ralph Erskine and Michael Smith (eds), *Action This Day* (London: Bantam Press, 2001), pp. 110–26.

Chan, Marjorie K. M. 'In Memoriam Edwin G. Pulleyblank, 1922–2013', *Journal of Chinese Linguistics* 42 (2014): 252–66.

Chapman, Siobhan. *Paul Grice, Philosopher and Linguist* (Basingstoke: Palgrave Macmillan, 2005).

Cheah, W. L. 'An Overview of the Singapore War Crimes Trials (1946–1948): Prosecuting Lower-Level Accused', *Singapore Law Review* 34 (2017) (available at SSRN: https://ssrn.com/abstract=2861802).

Clabby, John F. *Brigadier John Tiltman: A Giant among Cryptanalysts* (Fort George G. Meade, MD: Center for Cryptologic History, National Security Agency, 2007).

Clifton, Allan S. *Time of Fallen Blossoms* (London: Cassell, 1950).

Cooper, Arthur. *The Other Greek: An Introduction to Chinese and Japanese Characters, Their History and Influence*, ed. Imre Galambos (Leiden: Brill, 2018).

Cortazzi, Sir Hugh. *Japan and Back and Places Elsewhere: A Memoir* (Folkestone: Global Oriental, 1998).

——— (ed.). *Japan Experiences: Fifty Years, One Hundred Views; Post-war Japan through British Eyes, 1945–2000* (Richmond: Curzon, 2001).

——— 'RAF Experiences', in Ian Nish (ed.), *The British Commonwealth and the Allied Occupation of Japan, 1945–1952* (Leiden: Global Oriental, 2013), pp. 135–43.

——— 'The Death of Melville James Cox (1885–1940) in Tokyo on 29 July 1940: Arrests of British Citizens in Japan in 1940 and 1941', in Hugh Cortazzi (ed.), *Britain and Japan: Biographical Portraits*, vol. 8 (Leiden: Global Oriental, 2013), pp. 491–506.

——— (ed.). *Carmen Blacker: Scholar of Japanese Religion, Myth and Folklore* (Folkestone: Renaissance Books, 2017).

Crabb, Brian James. *Passage to Destiny: The Story of the Tragic Loss of the S.S. Khedive Ismail*, rev. edn (Donington, Lincolnshire: Shaun Tyas, 2015).

Cribb, Robert. 'The Burma Trials of Japanese War Criminals, 1946–1947', in Kerstin von Lingen (ed.), *War Crimes Trials in the Wake of Decolonization and Cold War in Asia, 1945–1956* (Cham: Palgrave Macmillan, 2016), pp. 117–42.

Daniels, Frank J. *Japanese Studies in the University of London and Elsewhere* (inaugural lecture delivered on 7 November 1962) (London: School of Oriental and African Studies University of London, 1963).

Dashwood, Sir Francis. *The Dashwoods of West Wycombe* (London: Aurum Press, 1987).

Day, Geoff. 'Singapore', *Central Bureau Intelligence Corps Association Newsletter* (Australia) (March 2003), pp. 3–6.

De Moubray, Guy. *City of Human Memories* (Stanhope, County Durham: Memoir Club, 2005).

Denham, Hugh. 'Bedford—Bletchley—Kilindini—Colombo', in F. H. Hinsley and Alan Stripp (eds), *Codebreakers: The Inside Story of Bletchley Park* (Oxford: Oxford University Press, 1993), pp. 264–81.

Denniston, Alastair. 'The Government Code and Cypher School between the Wars', *Intelligence and National Security* 1 (1986): 48–70.

Dingman, Roger V. *Deciphering the Rising Sun: Navy and Marine Corps Codebreakers, Translators, and Interpreters in the Pacific War* (Annapolis, MD: Naval Institute Press, 2009).

Donovan, Peter, and John Mack. 'Sydney University, T. G. Room and Codebreaking in WW II', *Australian Mathematical Society Gazette* 29 (2002): 76–85, 141–8.

Dore, Ronald. 'Frank and Otome Daniels', in Ian Nish (ed.), *Britain and Japan: Biographical Portraits*, vol. 1 (Folkestone: Japan Library, 1994), pp. 268–78.

Dower, John W. *Embracing Defeat: Japan in the Wake of World War II* (New York: W. W. Norton, 1999).

Drea, Edward J. *MacArthur's Ultra: Codebreaking and the War against Japan, 1942–1945* (Lawrence, KS: University Press of Kansas, 1992).

Drower, William Mortimer. *Our Man on the Hill: A British Diplomat Remembers* (Berkeley, CA: Institute of Governmental Studies Press, 1993).

Dufty, David. *The Secret Code-Breakers of Central Bureau: How Australia's Signals-Intelligence Network Helped Win the Pacific War* (Brunswick: Scribe Publications, 2017).

Dunn, Peter. *Allied Translator and Interpreter Section: Translation of Japanese Documents and Interrogation of Japanese POWs in Brisbane during WWII* (n.p.: Australia @ War, 2018).

Erskine, Ralph, and Peter Freeman. 'Brigadier John Tiltman: One of Britain's Finest Cryptologists', *Cryptologia* 27 (2003): 289–318.

Evans, Lieutenant-General Sir Geoffrey, and Anthony Brett-James. *Imphal: A Flower on Lofty Heights* (London: Macmillan, 1962).

Farquharson, Robert H. *For Your Tomorrow: Canadians and the Burma Campaign, 1941–1945* (Victoria, BC: Trafford Publishing, 2004).

Feir, Gordon D. *Translating the Devil: Captain Llewellyn C. Fletcher, Canadian Army Intelligence Corps in Post-war Malaysia and Singapore* (n.p.: Lulu Publishing Services, 2014).

Fenton, Corinne. *My Friend Tertius*, illustrated by Owen Swan (Sydney: Allen & Unwin, 2017).

Ferris, John. '"Worthy of some better enemy?" The British Estimate of the Imperial Japanese Army, 1919–1941, and the Fall of Singapore', *Canadian Journal of History* 28 (1993): 223–56.

———— *Behind the Enigma: The Authorised History of GCHQ, Britain's Secret Cyber-intelligence Agency* (London: Bloomsbury, 2020).

Firth, J. R. 'Wartime Experiences in Linguistic Training', *Modern Languages: A Review of Foreign Letters, Science and the Arts* 26 (1945): 38–46.

Fletcher, Commandant Marjorie H. *The WRNS: A History of the Women's Royal Naval Service* (London: Batsford, 1989).

Footitt, Hilary, and Simona Tobia. *WarTalk: Foreign Languages and the British War Effort in Europe, 1940–47* (Basingstoke: Palgrave Macmillan, 2013).

Frei, Henry P. *Japan's Southward Advance and Australia: From the Sixteenth Century to World War II* (Melbourne: Melbourne University Press, 1991).

Fujiwara Iwaichi. *F. Kikan: Japanese Army Intelligence Operations in Southeast Asia during World War II* (London: Heinemann, 1983).

Fujiyama Naraichi. *Ichi seinen gaikōkan no taiheiyō sensō* (Tokyo: Shinchōsha, 1989).

Fukawa, Stan. 'Peter Shoji Yamauchi', *Nikkei Images* (National Nikkei Museum and Heritage Centre Newsletter, Burnaby, British Columbia) 10, no. 4 (2005): 17–18.

Funch, Colin. *Linguists in Uniform: The Japanese Experience* (Clayton, Victoria: Japanese Studies Centre, Monash University, 2003).

Gilmore, Allison B. '"We have been reborn": Japanese Prisoners and the Allied Propaganda War in the Southwest Pacific', *Pacific Historical Review* 64 (1995): 195–215.

———— 'The Allied Translator and Interpreter Section: The Critical Role of Allied Linguists in the Process of Propaganda Creation, 1943–1944', in Peter Dennis and Jeffrey Grey (eds), *The Foundations of Victory: The Pacific War 1943–1944* (Canberra: Army History Unit, 2004).

Goodman, Grant K. *America's Japan: The First Year, 1945–1946*, translated by Barry D. Steben from the Japanese edition published in 1986 (New York: Fordham University Press, 2005).

Gore-Booth, Paul. *With Great Truth and Respect* (London: Constable, 1974).

Hack, Karl, and Kevin Blackburn. *Did Singapore Have to Fall? Churchill and the Impregnable Fortress* (London: RoutledgeCurzon, 2004).

Harcourt, Cecil. 'The Military Administration of Hong Kong', *Journal of the Royal Central Asian Society* 34 (1947): 7–18.

Hastings, Max. *The Secret War: Spies, Codes and Guerrillas 1939–45* (London: William Collins, 2015).

Hinsley, Harry. *British Intelligence in the Second World War*, 2 vols. (London: HMSO, 1979 and 1981).

Hirschfeld, J. W. P., and G. E. Wall. 'Thomas Gerald Room', *Biographical Memoirs of Fellows of the Royal Society* 33 (1987): 573–601.

Honan, William H. *Bywater: The Man Who Invented the Pacific War* (London: Macdonald, 1990).

Hotta-Lister, Ayako. *The Japan–British Exhibition of 1910: Gateway to the Island Empire of the East* (Folkestone: Japan Library, 1999).

Ichinokuchi, Tad, with Daniel Aiso. *John Aiso and the M.I.S.: Japanese-American Soldiers in the Military Intelligence Service, World War II* (Los Angeles, CA: Military Intelligence Service Club of Southern California, 1988).

Iguchi Takeo. *Demystifying Pearl Harbor: A New Perspective from Japan*, trans. David Noble (Tokyo: I-House Press, 2010).

Interpreter, The. The newsletter of the Japanese Language School project, produced by the Archives, University of Boulder Colorado Libraries. Issues 1 (2000) to 246 (2018) are on the university website: https://lib-ebook.colorado.edu/sca/archives/interpreters.htm.

Ishimaru Tōta, trans. *Taiheiyō sensō to sono hihan* (Tokyo: Bunmei Kyōkai Jimusho, 1926); a translation of Hector C. Bywater's *The Great Pacific War* (1925) with comments by Ishimaru.

——— *Japan Must Fight Britain* (London: Hurst & Blackett, 1936); a translation of Guy Varley Rayment, *Nichiei hissenron* (Tokyo: Shunjūsha, 1933).

——— *The Next World War* (London: Hurst & Blackett, 1937); a translation by Matsukawa Baikin of *Tsugi no sekai taisen* (Tokyo: Shunjūsha, 1936).

Ito, Roy. *We Went to War: The Story of the Japanese Canadians Who Served in the First and Second World Wars* (Stittsville, Ontario: Canada's Wings, Inc., 1984).

Itoh, Keiko. *The Japanese Community in Pre-war Britain: From Integration to Disintegration* (London: Curzon, 2001).

Jackson, Ashley. *War and Empire in Mauritius and the Indian Ocean* (London: Palgrave, 2001).

Jansen, Marius. *Japanese Studies in the United States, Part 1: History and Present Condition* (Ann Arbor: Japan Foundation, 1988).

Jarvis, Sue. 'Captain Oswald Tuck R.N. and the Bedford Japanese School', in Hugh Cortazzi (ed.), *Britain and Japan: Biographical Portraits*, vol. 5 (Folkestone: Global Oriental, 2005), pp. 196–208.

Jenkins, David. *Battle Surface! Japan's Submarine War against Australia, 1942–44* (Milsons Point, New South Wales: Random House Australia, 1992).

BIBLIOGRAPHY

BI

Jones, Chris. 'Made in Japan', *Muse* (Sydney University Museums) 16 (2017): 16–17.

Karnad, Raghu. *Farthest Field: An Indian Story of the Second World War* (New Delhi: Fourth Estate, 2015).

Kase Toshikazu. *Journey to the Missouri* (New Haven: Yale University Press, 1950).

Keene, Donald. *Chronicles of My Life: An American in the Heart of Japan* (New York: Columbia University Press, 2008).

Kendrick, Vivienne. 'Ian Nish', *Japan Times*, 18 September 2004.

Kennedy, Captain Malcolm Duncan. *The Military Side of Japanese Life* (London: Constable and Co., 1924).

Kirby, S. Woodburn. *The Surrender of Japan*, vol. 5, *The War against Japan* (London: HMSO, 1969).

Kornicki, Peter. 'Eric Bertrand Ceadel, 1921–79: Japanese Studies at Cambridge', in Hugh Cortazzi (ed.), *Britain and Japan: Biographical Portraits*, vol. 5 (Folkestone: Global Oriental, 2005), pp. 337–43.

——— 'General Sir Ian Hamilton and the Russo-Japanese War', in Hugh Cortazzi (ed.), *Britain and Japan: Biographical Portraits*, vol. 7 (Folkestone: Global Oriental, 2010), pp. 162–78.

——— 'A Brief History of Japanese Studies in Britain from the 1860s to the 21st Century', in Hugh Cortazzi and Peter Kornicki (eds), *Japanese Studies in Britain: A Survey and History* (Folkestone: Renaissance Books, 2016), pp. 3–40.

——— 'Frank Daniels' Report on the War-Time Japanese Courses at SOAS', *Bulletin of the School of Oriental and African Studies* 81 (2018): 301–24.

——— *Captain Oswald Tuck and the Bedford Japanese School, 1942–1945* (London: Pollino Publishing, 2019).

Kornicki, Peter, Antony Best and Sir Hugh Cortazzi. *British Royal and Japanese Imperial Relations, 1868–2018: 150 Years of Association, Engagement and Celebration* (Folkestone: Renaissance Books, 2019).

Koyama, Noboru. 'William J. S. Shand (1850–1909) and Henry John Weintz (1864–1931): "Japanese self-taught"', in Hugh Cortazzi (ed.), *Britain and Japan: Biographical Portraits*, vol. 10 (Folkestone: Renaissance Books, 2016), pp. 362–70.

——— *Sensō to toshokan: Eikoku kindai Nihongo korekushon no rekishi* (Tokyo: Bensei Shuppan, 2018).

Liddell, Guy. *The Guy Liddell Diaries: MI5's Director of Counter-espionage in World War II*, ed. Nigel West, 2 vols. (London: Routledge, 2009).

Loewe, Michael. 'Japanese Naval Codes', in F. H. Hinsley and Alan Stripp (eds), *Codebreakers: The Inside Story of Bletchley Park* (Oxford: Oxford University Press, 1993), pp. 257–63.

BIBLIOGRAPHY

Loureiro, Pedro. '"Boulder Boys": Japanese Language School Graduates', in Randy Carol Balano and Craig Symonds (eds), *New Interpretations in Naval History: Selected Papers from the Fourteenth Naval History Symposium* (Annapolis, MD: Naval Institute Press, 2001), pp. 366–88.

Lyon, Cherstin M. *Prisons and Patriots: Japanese American Wartime Citizenship, Civil Disobedience, and Historical Memory* (Philadelphia: Temple University Press, 2012).

McLelland, Nicola. *German through English Eyes: A History of Language Teaching and Learning in Britain, 1500–2000* (Wiesbaden: Otto Harrassowitz, 2015).

————— *Teaching and Learning Foreign Languages: A History of Language Education, Assessment and Policy in Britain* (London: Taylor & Francis, 2017).

MacLeod, Roy. 'Margaret Mary Gowing CBE FBA', *Biographical Memoirs of Fellows of the Royal Society* 58 (2012): 67–111.

McNaughton, James C. *Nisei linguists: Japanese Americans in the Military Intelligence Service during World War II* (Washington, DC: Department of the Army, 2006).

McPhee, Ian. 'Arthur Dale Trendall 1909–1995: A Memoir', *Proceedings of the British Academy* 97 (1998): 501–17.

Macpherson, Deirdre. *The Suffragette's Daughter: Betty Archdale; Her Life of Feminism, Cricket, War and Education* (New South Wales: Rosenberg, 2002).

Maffeo, Steven E. *U.S. Navy Codebreakers, Linguists, and Intelligence Officers against Japan, 1910–1941* (Lanham, MD: Rowan & Littlefield, 2016).

Maneki, Sharon A. *The Quiet Heroes of the Southwest Pacific Theater: An Oral History of the Men and Women of CBB and FRUMEL*, United States Cryptologic History, Series IV, World War II, vol. 7 (Washington, DC: Center for Cryptologic History, National Security Agency, 2007 [1996]).

Martial, Yvan. 'Reginald Vaughan', *Royal Society of Arts and Sciences of Mauritius, Proceedings* 8 (2014): 151–68.

Mason, Richard. *The Wind Cannot Read* (London: Hodder & Stoughton, 1946).

Melinsky, Hugh. *A Code-Breaker's Tale* (Dereham, Norfolk: Larks Press, 1998).

Merrillees, Robert S. 'Professor A. D. Trendall and His Band of Classical Cryptographers', Working Paper no. 355 (Canberra: Australian National University, Strategic and Defence Studies Centre, 2001).

Mountbatten of Burma, Vice-Admiral the Earl. *Report to the Combined Chiefs of Staff by the Supreme Allied Commander South-East Asia, 1943–1945* (London: HMSO, 1951).

Nakagawa Masahiro. *Tōjō Hideki no shin'yū chūdoku taishi Ōshima Hiroshi: Yami ni hōmurareta gaikō jōhō no ekisupāto* (Tokyo: Seruba Shuppan, 2014).

Nicholls, Glenn. *Deported: A History of Forced Departures from Australia* (Sydney: University of New South Wales Press, 2007).

BIBLIOGRAPHY

Nicoll, D. R. 'Tiltman, John Hessell (1894–1982)', *Oxford Dictionary of National Biography* (Oxford: Oxford University Press, 2004).

Nish, Ian. 'Louis Allen, 1922–1991: Formidable Character and Scholar', in Ian Nish and Mark Allen (eds), *War, Conflict and Security in Japan and Asia Pacific, 1941–52: The Writings of Louis Allen* (Folkestone: Global Oriental, 2010), pp. xii–xvii.

————— *The Japanese in War and Peace, 1942–48: Selected Documents from a Translator's In-Tray* (Folkestone: Global Oriental, 2011).

O'Neill, Patrick G. *Collected Writings of P. G. O'Neill* (Richmond: Japan Library, 2001).

Ōba Sadao. *The 'Japanese' War: London University's WWII Secret Teaching Programme and the Experts Sent to Help Beat Japan*, trans. Anne Kaneko (Folkestone: Japan Library, 1995).

Ōba Sadao and Anne Kaneko. 'Yanada Senji (1906–1972): Teacher of Japanese at SOAS', in Hugh Cortazzi (ed.), *Britain and Japan: Biographical Portraits*, vol. 9 (Folkestone: Renaissance Books, 2015), pp. 413–24.

Okumura Misa. 'Aru Eikokujin futsubungakusha ga seinen jidai ni mita shūsen chokugo no Nihon', *Chūkyō Daigaku Shakai kagaku kenkyū* 33, no. 1 (2012): 1–24.

Ōkura Yūnosuke. *Kochira Rondon BBC: BBC Nihongobu no ayumi* (Tokyo: Simul Press, 1983).

Packard, George. *Edwin O. Reischauer and the American Discovery of Japan* (New York: Columbia University Press, 2010).

Packard, Wyman H. *A Century of U.S. Naval Intelligence* (Washington, DC: Office of Naval Intelligence, Naval Historical Center, 1996).

Page, Arthur. *Between Victor and Vanquished: An Australian Interrogator in the War against Japan* (Loftus, New South Wales: Australian Military History Publications, 2008).

Page, Gwendoline (ed.). *They Listened in Secret: More Memories of the Wrens* (Wymondham: Geo. R Reeve, 2003).

Paterson, Lawrence. *Hitler's Grey Wolves: U-boats in the Indian Ocean* (London: Greenhill Books, 2004).

Pfennigwerth, Ian. *A Man of Intelligence: The Life of Captain Theodore Eric Nave* ([Kenthurst], New South Wales: Rosenberg, 2006).

Phillips [sic, Philips], Sir C. H. *The School of Oriental and African Studies, University of London, 1917–1967: An Introduction* ([London: SOAS], 1967).

Phillips, Horace. *Envoy Extraordinary: A Most Unlikely Ambassador* (London: Radcliffe Press, 1995).

Piggott, Major-General F. S. G. *Broken Thread: An Autobiography* (Aldershot: Gale and Polden, 1950).

Piggott, Jan. *Dulwich College: A History, 1616–2008* (London: Dulwich College, 2008).

BIBLIOGRAPHY

Prados, John. *Combined Fleet Decoded: The Secret History of American Intelligence and the Japanese Navy in World War II* (New York: Random House, 1995).

Purvis, Phillida. 'Louis Allen (1922–91) and Japan', in Hugh Cortazzi (ed.), *Britain and Japan: Biographical Portraits*, vol. 5 (Folkestone: Global Oriental, 2005), pp. 344–57.

Reischauer, Edwin O. *My Life between Japan and America* (New York: Harper & Row, 1986).

Richmond, John. 'Classics and Intelligence', *Classics Ireland* 8 (2001): 84–101; 9 (2002): 46–61.

Robinson, Greg. *By Order of the President: FDR and the Internment of Japanese Americans* (Cambridge, MA: Harvard University Press, 2001).

———— *A Tragedy of Democracy: Japanese Confinement in North America* (New York: Columbia University Press, 2009).

Rosenthal, Eric. *Japan's Bid for Africa: Including the Story of the Madagascar Campaign* ([Johannesburg]: Central News Agency, 1944).

Roy, Reginald H. *For Most Conspicuous Bravery: A Biography of Major-General George R. Pearkes, V.C., through Two World Wars* (Vancouver: University of British Columbia Press, 1977).

Ryan, Allan A. *Yamashita's Ghost: War Crimes, MacArthur's Justice, and Command Accountability* (Lawrence, KS: University Press of Kansas, 2012).

Saint Christopher's Review, the monthly magazine of the Wireless Experimental Centre, published by St Christopher's Chapel, Delhi. The only extant copies known to me are those for August, September and October 1945 in the late James Sutherland's collection.

Seki Eiji. *Mrs Ferguson's Tea-Set, Japan and the Second World War: The Global Consequences following Germany's Sinking of the SS Automedon in 1940* (Folkestone: Global Oriental, 2006).

Shaigiya-Abdelsamad, Yahya. 'Major C. A. L. Yate VC (1872–1914): A Gallant British Officer and Admirer of Japan', in Hugh Cortazzi (ed.), *Britain and Japan: Biographical Portraits*, vol. 9 (Folkestone: Renaissance Books, 2015), pp. 524–30.

Sima, William. *China and ANU: Diplomats, Adventurers, Scholars* (Acton, Australian Capital Territory: Australian National University Press, 2015).

Singh, Rajendra. 'Post-war Occupation Forces: Japan and South-East Asia', in Bisheshwar Prasad (ed.), *Official History of the Indian Armed Forces in the Second World War 1939–45* (n.p.: Combined Inter-Services Historical Section India & Pakistan, 1958).

Sissons, D. C. S. 'The Diplomatic Special Intelligence Section: Its Origins and History', in Desmond Ball and Keiko Tamura (eds), *Breaking Diplomatic Codes: David Sissons and D Special Section during the Second World War* (Canberra: Australian National University Press, 2013), pp. 15–51.

Slesnick, Irwin Leonard and Carole Evelyn. *Kanji and Codes: Learning Japanese for World War II* (Bellingham, WA: The authors, 2006).

Smith, Michael. *The Emperor's Codes: Bletchley Park and the Breaking of Japan's Secret Ciphers* (London: Bantam Press, 2000).

———— 'An Undervalued Effort: How the British Broke Japan's Codes', in Ralph Erskine and Michael Smith (eds), *Action This Day* (London: Bantam Press, 2001), pp. 127–51.

———— *The Debs of Bletchley Park and Other Stories* (London: Aurum Press, 2015).

Smith, Simon C. 'Crime and Punishment: Local Responses to the Trial of Japanese War Criminals in Malaya and Singapore, 1946–48', *South East Asia Research* 5, no. 1 (1997): 41–56.

Snell, William. 'John Morris at Keio University, 1938–1942', *Keiō Gijuku Daigaku Hiyoshi kiyō Eigo Eibei bungaku* 51 (2007): 29–59.

SOAS: A Celebration in Many Voices (London: Third Millennium Publishing, 2007).

Stamberg, Arthur. *Footprints on a Winding Road: Recollections of an Old Jerseyman* (Jersey: La Haule Books, 1998).

Stillwell, Paul. *Battleship Missouri: An Illustrated History* (Annapolis, MD: Naval Institute Press, 1996).

Storry, Dorothie. *Second Country: The Story of Richard Storry and Japan, 1913–1982; A Biography* (Ashford, Kent: Paul Norbury, 1986).

Stripp, Alan. *Codebreaker in the Far East* (London: Frank Cass, 1989).

———— 'Japanese Army Air Force Codes at Bletchley Park and Delhi', in F. H. Hinsley and Alan Stripp (eds), *Codebreakers: The Inside Story of Bletchley Park* (Oxford: Oxford University Press, 1993), pp. 288–99.

Sugarman, Martin. 'Breaking the Codes: Jewish Personnel at Bletchley Park', *Jewish Historical Studies* 40 (2005): 197–246.

Takeda Kayoko. *Interpreting the Tokyo War Crimes Tribunal: A Socio-political Analysis* (Ottawa: University of Ottawa Press, 2010).

———— *Taiheiyō sensō Nihongo chōhōsen: Gengokan no katsuyaku to shiren* (Tokyo: Chikuma Shobō, 2018).

Taunt, Derek. 'Hut 6 from the Inside', in Ralph Erskine and Michael Smith (eds), *Action This Day* (London: Bantam Press, 2001), pp. 77–93.

Thacker, Rosy. 'Dreaming of Derbyshire—While Cracking Japanese Codes!', *Reflections* (Derbyshire) 23, no. 264 (2014): 16–20.

Thomas, Martin. 'Imperial Backwater or Strategic Outpost? The British Takeover of Vichy Madagascar, 1942', *Historical Journal* 39 (1996): 1049–74.

Turner, Leonard C. F., H. R. Gordon-Cumming and J. E. Betzler (eds). *War in the Southern Oceans: 1939–1945* (Cape Town: Oxford University Press, 1961).

BIBLIOGRAPHY

United States Far East Command Military Intelligence Section. *Operations of the Allied Translator and Interpreter Section, GHQ, SWPA* ([Tokyo?]: The Command, [1948?]).

Van der Bijl, Nicholas. *Sharing the Secret: The History of the Intelligence Corps 1940–2010* (Barnsley: Pen & Sword Military, 2013).

Von Lingen, Kerstin (ed.). *War Crimes Trials in the Wake of Decolonization and Cold War in Asia, 1945–1956* (Cham: Palgrave Macmillan, 2016).

Weighton, Robert G. P. *We Were Seven and Other Memories*, vol. 1 (Godalming: Grenville Books, 2008).

West, Nigel. *Historical Dictionary of British Intelligence* (London: Scarecrow Press, 2005).

Wiles, Maurice. 'Japanese Military Codes', in F. H. Hinsley and Alan Stripp (eds), *Codebreakers: The Inside Story of Bletchley Park* (Oxford: Oxford University Press, 1993), pp. 282–7.

Williams, Duncan Ryūken. *American Sutra: A Story of Faith and Freedom in the Second World War* (Cambridge, MA: Harvard University Press, 2019).

Wilson, Sandy. *I Could Be Happy: An Autobiography* (London: Joseph, 1975).

Wires, Richard. *The Cicero Spy Affair: German Access to British Secrets in World War II* (Westport, CT: Praeger, 1999).

Zacharias, Ellis M. *Secret Missions: The Story of an Intelligence Officer* (New York: G. P. Putnam's Sons, 1946).

INDEX

Ranks and titles are those at the end of career

INDEX

Boase, Prof. Thomas Sherrer Ross 79, 330

Bogarde, Dirk 176–177

Bormann, Martin Ludwig 93

Borton, Prof. Hugh 186

Bose, Subhas Chandra 153

Boulder, Colorado 180, 187–188, 191–196, 198–203, 230, 243, 245–246, 257–258, 267–268, 307–311

Boult, Sir Adrian 37

Bownas, Prof. Geoffrey 290, *Fig.* 38

Boyce, Wg-Cdr. Alexander Rodney 168, 247, 344

Brain, Henry Norman 81, 331

Brett-James, Antony 165

Brickley, Capt. S. 314

Brind, Rear-Adm. Patrick 243, 356

Brisbane 3, 46, 62, 66–67, 132, 181, 200, 215, 219, 221, 223–224, 228, 237, 240, 257, 288

Bristol University 59

British Admiralty Delegation, Washington DC 198, 203

British China Squadron 8

British Columbia, University of 53, 87, 169

British Commonwealth Occupation Force (BCOF) xxviii, 173–174, 251–252, 270–276, 278–280, 292, 304, 360, *Figs.* 61, 62

British Embassy, Tokyo 8, 11–12, 30, 172, 197, 203, 217, 219, 252, 268–270, 291, 311, 360

British government departments
   Admiralty 10, 15–18, 30–31, 37, 40–41, 59, 62–63, 75, 84, 87, 89, 107, 115, 128, 130, 179, 194–196, 198, 203, 256, 307, 335
   Air Ministry 16–17, 38, 49, 52, 59, 67, 86, 313

Board of Education 49–50

Ministry of Economic Warfare 106

Foreign Office 5, 10, 17–18, 29, 71–72, 81, 84, 89, 112, 117–118, 132, 136, 203, 219, 269–270, 286, 292, 318

Ministry of Information 30–31, 43, 52, 345

Postal and Telegraph Censorship Department 13, 17, 106, 108–109, 112,

Treasury 5, 16, 18, 107, 115, 118

War Office xxvii, 12, 15–18, 24–25, 28, 38, 45–46, 48–50, 59, 94, 105, 154, 160–162, 171, 260, 286

British Political Warfare Executive 203, 270, 360

Brouwer, Lt-Cdr. Leo 131

Brown, A. A. L. 314

Brown, Fg-Off. J. E. C. 314

Brown, Jack 214, 226, *Fig.* 52

Brown, Peter 303

Burma 13, 22, 39–41, 47, 55, 59–61, 92, 111, 126, 138, 141–142, 144–149, 151–153, 156–159, 163–164, 166–168, 173–174, 176, 190, 224, 230–231, 235, 246, 248, 251–253, 255, 258, 264, 266, 281, 286, 290–291, 295, 297–298, 305

Burma Campaign 69, 142, 145, 149, 154, 158, 177, 253, 283, 290–292

Burma Independence Army 152, 253

Burma-Siam Railway 162, 252, 260–262, 291

Burnett, Cdr. Malcolm Stuart Leslie 132

383

INDEX

387

INDEX

INDEX